PHP Programming in the AI Era

First Edition

Build faster PHP applications using GenAI, modern PHP features, and production-ready workflows

Doug Bierer
Rainier Sarabia

<packt>

PHP Programming in the AI Era

First Edition

Portfolio Director: Ashwin Nair
Relationship Lead: Bhavya Rao
Project Manager: Vishnu Priya R
Content Engineer: Runcil Rebello
Technical Editor: Arjun Varma
Copy Editor: Runcil Rebello
Indexer: Rekha Nair
Proofreader: Runcil Rebello
Production Designer: Salma Patel
Growth Lead: Priyadarshini Sharma

First published: July 2026

Production reference: 1140726

Published by Packt Publishing Ltd.
Grosvenor House
11 St Paul's Square
Birmingham
B3 1RB, UK.

ISBN 978-1-83588-992-3
`www.packtpub.com`

To my beloved wife, Nimol, for her never-ending patience and encouragement. To Miquéias Vinícius, for his ceaseless curiosity about new technologies.

– Doug Bierer

In memory of my beloved sister, Jenina. To Eloise, who has always supported my growth, and to my partner in life, Frezel.

– Rainier Sarabia

Contributors

About the authors

Doug Bierer has been hooked on computers since his first program, written in Dartmouth BASIC on a DEC PDP-8, in 1971. In his wide-ranging career, this author has been a professional contract programmer since 1978, having written applications in BASIC, PL/I, assembler, FORTH, C, C++, dBase/FoxBase/Clipper, Pascal, Perl, Java, and PHP. While attending and teaching at Golden Gate University in San Francisco, he took his first AI course in 1986 and has been working extensively with modern AI technology since January 2023. He speaks 4.5 languages, has traveled extensively, and has lived in the USA, France, the Netherlands, England, Sweden, Scotland, Thailand and Cambodia. He is also an accomplished musician (he has written over 60 songs) as well as a writer, under the pen name of Douglas Alan. Doug's own company is unlikelysource.com, which specializes in consulting, PHP programming, website development, and training (primarily for Zend by Perforce). His works of fiction are *The End, And Then?* and *Further Indications.*

I would like to thank my managers at GSPANN, Saurabh Madan and Rolf Kraus for leading the charge into modern AI tools. I would also like to acknowledge my friend and mentor, Andrew Caya, for his insights and encouragement. Finally, I would like to give a shout out to Matthew Weir O'Phinney and Beth Weinberger at Perforce for their roles in keeping the PHP ecosystem alive and kicking.

Rainier Sarabia is a Director of Engineering at Deel and the author of *Test-Driven Development with PHP 8* (Packt). An Australian enterprise architect based in Melbourne, he has over 20 years of experience designing scalable, distributed systems and high-quality software.

At Deel, he leads seven engineering teams while architecting AI-driven solutions and orchestration frameworks that power complex financial and operational workflows. He stays deliberately hands-on—designing and building alongside his teams to tackle large, high-stakes problems.

A language-agnostic engineer fluent in PHP, C#, TypeScript, Java, JavaScript, and SQL, Rainier has delivered platforms and cloud-native architectures built for real-world complexity.

I would like to thank Kent & Cynthia Pamintuan, Allan, Betchay & Kent Sampang, Alexis Gruet, Yaron Lavi, Stefan Nagey, Rea Bustos, Mamen, Doc Alvin Macapinlac, Doc Sese, pp Don, pp Jun, Berna n Daphne, KapJ, Jetmel, Lhane, Aris. Also to my friends who have been constantly encouraging me: Kris, Migs, Dianne, Lau, Arnell & Axzel Matic, Migoy, Murali, Mark, Eva and Andre Bellaire, Takdol, Pow, Muy, Ariz, Kervin and Debbie, Mamisu, JCabading, Jonas. To my mates at Deel: Anton, Adi, Carpes, Clarissa, Remi, Bruno, Eli, Gal, Mor, Rene, Capi & Rocky, Felix, Harel, Jon, Andre, Phil, Raunaq, Slavic, Elia, Avi, Eithan, Chloe, Abhi, Albert, David, Aviv, Aaron, Kaleigh, Alex, Nadine, and Radhika.

About the reviewers

Matthew Setter is a PHP, Go, and Rust developer, developer educator, and podcaster. He's also the author of Mezzio Essentials and Deploy with Docker Compose.

Roberto Butti is an open-source contributor, technical author, and international conference speaker. As a Senior Solutions Engineer at Storyblok, a leading headless CMS platform, he helps organizations build scalable and modern digital experiences. Passionate about sharing knowledge, Roberto maintains and contributes to open-source projects across the PHP, JavaScript, Laravel, and modern web technology ecosystems. His talks have been featured at developer conferences throughout Europe, where he shares practical insights on software architecture, developer productivity, performance, AI, and emerging technologies. Through books, articles, and community involvement, he promotes continuous learning and the collaborative spirit of open source.

Table of Contents

Preface

The AI genie is out of the bottle and there's no putting it back. AI-assisted development is rapidly becoming the de facto way of life for developers, and PHP developers are eager to embrace it. This cookbook-style book gives you invaluable advice and solid, practical, real-world code examples known as "recipes" that illustrate not only how AI can boost PHP programming, but also how AI can be used to enhance PHP-based websites. Join us and ride the wave of PHP programming in the AI era.

Who this book is for

This book targets PHP developers from beginner to advanced levels. Coverage spans environment setup, performance optimization, functional programming, OOP, database integration, web forms, REST APIs, test-driven development, algorithms, design patterns, and security—making it suitable for any PHP developer looking to modernize skills with PHP 8 and AI-assisted workflows.

What this book covers

Chapter 1, Building a Foundation, establishes a modern PHP 8 development baseline covering multiple installation methods, containerized environments using Podman, Composer autoloading, strict typing, static analysis, coding standards enforcement, and AI-assisted code generation using GenAI tools.

Chapter 2, Using PHP 8 High Performance Features, examines PHP 8 performance optimization through Generators providing memory-efficient large file iteration, easy directory traversal using the SPL's `RecursiveDirectoryIterator`, OPcache for bytecode caching, and the **Just-In-Time** (**JIT**) compiler for machine code generation and execution speed improvements.

Chapter 3, Working with PHP Functional Programming, explores PHP functional programming through AI-assisted data validation function development, improving GenAI code generation accuracy through type hinting, multi-dimensional array searches using PHP 8.5's new `array_find()` function, and match expressions that streamline decision-making logic.

Chapter 4, Working with PHP Object-Oriented Programming, presents practical OOP recipes using PHP 8, including building an AI-prompted appointment calendar system, integrating the Symfony AI Bundle, implementing PSR-11 service containers, designing class hierarchies, and using PHP 8.5 lazy objects to reduce memory consumption.

Chapter 5, Interacting with a Database, covers practical PHP database integration techniques: building a PDO connection factory via a PSR-11 service container, using AI agents to generate entity classes from SQL definitions, creating a flexible SQL query builder using the Builder pattern, and caching GenAI API responses in a PSR-16-compliant database cache.

Chapter 6, Building Scalable Forms, introduces building reusable form components in PHP: a generic element generator, separate renderers for each input type, a form factory, and chained filters and validators, with optional AI help for suggesting fields.

Chapter 7, Making AI-Assisted Web Services and WebSockets Requests, presents recipes for issuing REST requests using PHP Streams and cURL, building a middleware-based microservices REST service, tracking GenAI API token usage to help control costs, and implementing real-time asynchronous communication using WebSockets for an AI-assisted chat service.

Chapter 8, Working with Date/Time and International Aspects, covers internationalization in PHP: emoji handling, locale detection, locale-aware number, currency and date formatting, multibyte strings, and simple JSON-based translations.

Chapter 9, Implementing Test-Driven Development in a Feature, shows how to build a feature test-first: write acceptance criteria in Gherkin, use AI to generate failing PHPUnit tests, add code until they pass, then grow the suite with Behat.

Chapter 10, Looking at Advanced Algorithms, works through common algorithms and data structures in PHP 8: getters and setters, linked lists, stacks, binary search, a plugin architecture, a search engine, and displaying nested arrays with totals.

Chapter 11, Implementing Software Design Patterns, introduces creational, structural, and behavioral patterns in PHP, including the Factory, Adapter, and State patterns, and explains when each one is a good fit.

Chapter 12, Improving Web Security, includes practical security recipes for PHP: securing sessions, adding CSRF tokens, generating strong passwords, adding CAPTCHA, and building an AES-256-GCM encryption helper with help from Claude Code.

To get the most out of this book

Readers need basic PHP knowledge and command-line familiarity, with chapters progressively requiring stronger OOP skills, SQL, HTTP concepts, and testing experience. Later chapters build on earlier setups and concepts. Access to a GenAI platform and the containerized development environment established in *Chapter 1* are assumed throughout.

Software/Hardware covered in the book	OS Requirements
Podman	Windows, Mac OS X, and Linux (any)
GenAI access	Windows, Mac OS X, and Linux (any)
A code editor or IDE	Windows, Mac OS X, and Linux (any)
Google reCAPTCHA account	None
Claude (desktop, Claude.ai, or Claude Code), OpenAI API key (optional)	Windows, Mac OS X, and Linux (any)
PHP 8.5+, nginx, MariaDB, Composer, Adminer (database manager), OpenSSL extension, PHPUnit and Behat	Available in the Podman container you will build for the book

If you are using the digital version of this book, we advise you to type the code yourself or access the code via the GitHub repository (check next section). Doing so will help you avoid any potential errors related to the copying and pasting of code.

Download the example code files

This book includes a complete downloadable code bundle containing all the example projects and files used throughout the chapters. We recommend downloading the bundle so you can follow along smoothly and experiment with the examples.

Use the bundle as a practical starting point. Modify it, extend it, and apply what you learn by creating your own variations as you progress through the chapters.

Get the code bundle

If you bought the book directly from Packt:

1. Go to **packtpub.com**
2. Click your **profile picture** and select **Your Orders**
3. Find this book and click **Download Code**

If you bought this book from Amazon or any other channel partner:

1. Go to `packtpub.com/unlock` or scan the following QR code:

2. Search for this book
3. Sign up or log in to your free Packt account
4. Upload your proof of purchase and download the code bundle locally

Usage note: You're free to use and modify this code for personal learning and non-commercial projects.

Conventions used

There are a number of text conventions used throughout this book.

`Code in text`: Indicates code words in text, database table names, folder names, filenames, file extensions, pathnames, dummy URLs, user input, and Twitter handles. Here is an example: "Mount the downloaded `WebStorm-10*.dmg` disk image file as another disk in your system."

A block of code is set as follows:

```
GENAI_URL=https://api.openai.com/v1/responses
GENAI_MODEL=gpt-4.1-nano
GENAI_API_KEY=put_your_API_key_here
GENAI_BRIDGE=OpenAi
```

When we wish to draw your attention to a particular part of a code block, the relevant lines or items are set in bold:

```
GENAI_URL=https://api.openai.com/v1/responses
GENAI_MODEL=gpt-4.1-nano
GENAI_API_KEY=put_your_API_key_here
GENAI_BRIDGE=OpenAi
```

Any command-line input or output is written as follows:

```
php composer.phar require symfony/ai-scraper-tool --ignore-platform-reqs
php composer.phar require symfony/ai-agent --ignore-platform-reqs
```

Bold: Indicates a new term, an important word, or words that you see onscreen. For example, words in menus or dialog boxes appear in the text like this. Here is an example: "Select **System info** from the **Administration** panel."

> Note
>
> Tips or important notes
>
> Appear like this.

Sections

In this book, you will find several headings that appear frequently (*Getting ready*, *How to do it...*, *How it works...*, *There's more...*, and *See also*).

To give clear instructions on how to complete a recipe, use these sections as follows:

Getting ready

This section tells you what to expect in the recipe and describes how to set up any software or any preliminary settings required for the recipe.

How to do it...

This section contains the steps required to follow the recipe.

How it works...

This section usually consists of a detailed explanation of what happened in the previous section.

There's more...

This section consists of additional information about the recipe in order to make you more knowledgeable about the recipe.

See also

This section provides helpful links to other useful information for the recipe.

Get in touch

Feedback from our readers is always welcome.

General feedback: If you have questions about any aspect of this book, mention the book title in the subject of your message and email us at `customercare@packtpub.com`.

Errata: Although we have taken every care to ensure the accuracy of our content, mistakes do happen. If you have found a mistake in this book, we would be grateful if you would report this to us. Please visit www.packtpub.com/support/errata, selecting your book, clicking on the Errata Submission Form link, and entering the details.

Piracy: If you come across any illegal copies of our works in any form on the Internet, we would be grateful if you would provide us with the location address or website name. Please contact us at `copyright@packt.com` with a link to the material.

If you are interested in becoming an author: If there is a topic that you have expertise in and you are interested in either writing or contributing to a book, please visit `authors.packtpub.com`.

Reviews

Please leave a review. Once you have read and used this book, why not leave a review on the site that you purchased it from? Potential readers can then see and use your unbiased opinion to make purchase decisions, we at Packt can understand what you think about our products, and our authors can see your feedback on their book. Thank you!

For more information about Packt, please visit `packt.com`.

Free benefits with your book

This book includes free benefits designed to support your learning and help you apply what you learn effectively. Activate them now for instant access (see the *How to unlock* section for instructions).

Here's a quick overview of what you can instantly unlock with your purchase:

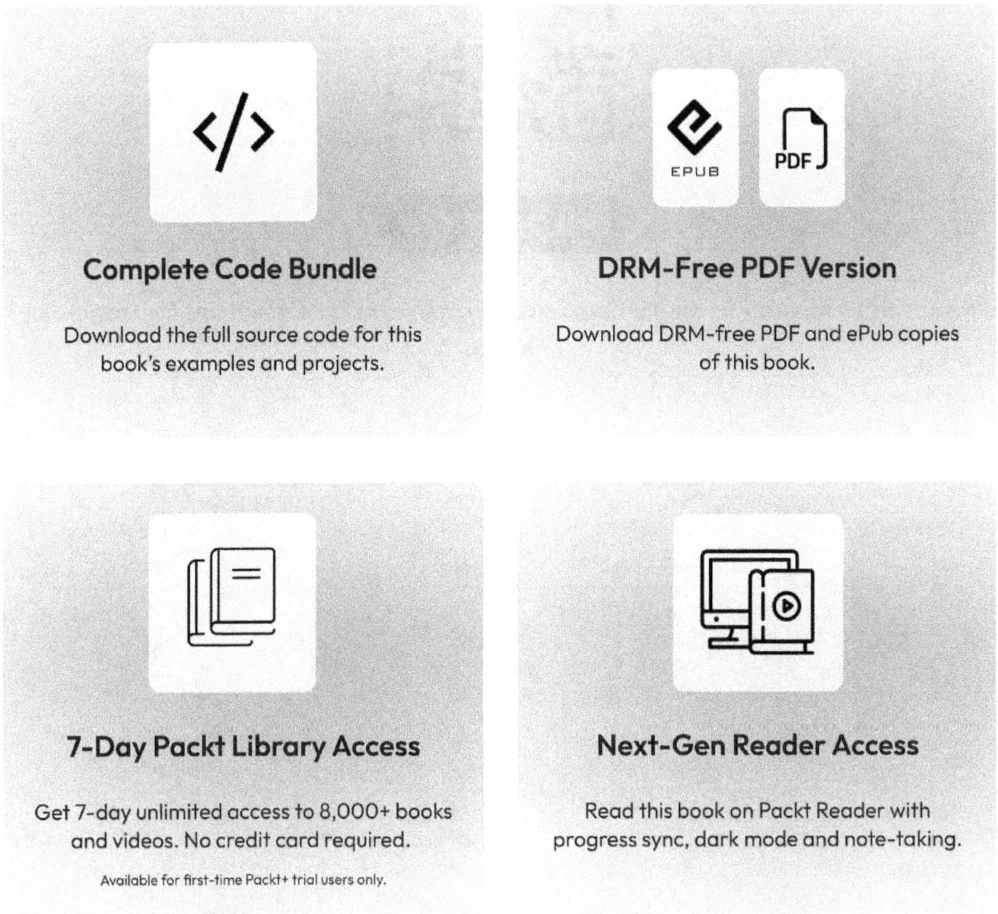

How to unlock

Scan the QR code (or go to `packtpub.com/unlock`). Search for this book by name, confirm the edition, and then follow the steps on the page.

UNLOCK NOW

Note: Have your invoice handy. Purchases made directly from the Packt website don't require an invoice.

1

Building a Foundation

This chapter establishes a modern PHP development baseline, covering PHP 8 installation, containerized environments, and Composer autoloading, while introducing strict typing, static analysis, and coding standards enforcement. Given the advanced AI coding tools available today, building a solid foundation ensures structural consistency and maintainability, supporting both human developers and AI-assisted workflows throughout every subsequent recipe in the book.

Here we have a look at a number of old and new ways that you can install PHP 8. We also have a look at the concept of containerization featuring **Podman**, a fully open-source and free tool that follows Docker syntax and shows you how to set up a complete PHP development environment in which you can experiment with the recipes covered in this book. We also have a look at how advances in **Generative AI** (**GenAI**) can be used as a tool to boost code development. The next recipe shows you how to use **Composer**, a popular PHP-based package management system, to facilitate the autoloading process. Finally, we have a look at using GenAI to create a PHP 7 to PHP 8 conversion tool.

In this chapter, we will cover the following recipes:

- PHP 8 installation considerations
- Using Podman to define a containerized development environment
- Using GenAI to build a postcode database
- Using Composer for autoloading
- Using AI to create a PHP 7 to PHP 8 code converter

Note

Download the code bundle and the PDF version of this book

Your purchase includes a DRM-free PDF copy of this book, the code bundle, and a range of exclusive benefits. To unlock everything, follow the *Free benefits with your book* section in the *Preface*.

Technical requirements

To execute the recipes in this book, you'll need a computer or laptop with a 64-bit processor, at least 4 GB of RAM, and 2 GB of free disk space. You'll also need a development environment that consists of PHP 8.4 (or above), wget, git (for version control), a web server, and a MySQL-compatible database. In the sections that follow we discuss how to set up a development environment using freely available containerization technology. For recipes that access the database, you can use the **Adminer** (`https://adminer.org/`) utility. It's similar to the well-known `phpMyAdmin` utility, but requires only a single PHP file to install. This utility is automatically installed into the PHP Docker/Podman container associated with the book, described later in this chapter.

We have created a GitHub repository containing the files and information needed to set up a containerized development environment. You can download the example project and code for this book by following the instructions in the *Download the example code files* section in the *Preface* of this book.

This chapter's code files are included in the downloadable code bundle.

PHP 8 installation considerations

There are a number of ways to install PHP 8. PHP needs to be installed on any server where you plan to run PHP-based applications. If you are a developer, it's also important to have PHP installed on your development computer.

Compiling PHP directly from source

This is the most complicated way of installing PHP, but it gives you the benefits of building a streamlined PHP installation exactly tailored to your needs. It's also ideal for situations where security is a paramount concern, as you have complete control over what gets installed and where. For the purposes of simplicity, in this recipe we'll focus on a Linux installation. Note that if you plan to install a default build, you'll also need `libxml2` and `libsqlite3`. Let's see how we can do it.

Getting ready

Read through the source installation instructions outlined at https://github.com/php/php-src. You must also have installed a C language compiler such as gcc (see https://gcc.gnu.org/).

How to do it...

1. Install the pre-requisite libraries. For Debian-based Linux systems (deb packages):

```
sudo apt install -y pkg-config build-essential autoconf bison re2c libxml2-
dev libsqlite3-dev
```

For RedHat-based Linux systems (rpm packages):

```
sudo dnf install re2c bison autoconf make libtool ccache libxml2-devel
sqlite-devel
```

2. Download the PHP source code from https://github.com/php/php-src. You can do this using git as follows:

```
git clone https://github.com/php/php-src.git
```

3. Alternatively, you can download and unzip by visiting the **Releases** page (https://github.com/php/php-src/releases) and choosing the target version of PHP. As an example, assume that the value of PHP_VER is 8.5.5:

```
ed@localhost:~/Repos/PHP-8-Programming-Cookbook
$ ./admin.sh shell
php8:/repo# export PHP_VER=8.5.5
php8:/repo# cd /tmp
php8:/tmp# wget https://github.com/php/php-src/archive/refs/tags/php-
$PHP_VER.zip
```

4. After cloning or downloading and unzipping, move into the directory created. You then create the configure script used to build and install PHP:

```
php8:/tmp# unzip php-$PHP_VER.zip
... output not shown ...
php8:/tmp# cd php-src-php-$PHP_VER/
php8:/tmp/php-src-php-8.5.5# apk add autoconf
```

```
OK: 110 MiB in 103 packages
php8:/tmp/php-src-php-8.5.5# ./buildconf --force
```

5. You can now run `configure` to create the *Makefile*. However, it's extremely important to determine which `configure` options are appropriate for your new installation. Run `./configure --help` to get a list of options.
6. When you've finished creating the *Makefile*, you can then switch to the root user, or preface your commands with `sudo`, to complete the process:

```
make
make test
make install
```

> **Note**
>
> Be sure to note where the PHP binaries are installed after running `make install`. Additionally, `make test` is optional but can provide valuable information for the PHP Community if errors are detected.

Installing PHP from community sources

In this approach, you would simply use the package manager available for your operating system to install PHP from the associated community source. In the Linux world, Debian-based systems (e.g. Ubuntu) usually prefer either `apt` or `apt-get` (`https://wiki.debian.org/AptCLI`) for package management. For RedHat-based systems (e.g. CentOS, RedHat, Fedora), either the `rpm` (`https://rpm.org/`) or the `dnf` (see: `https://docs.fedoraproject.org/en-US/quick-docs/dnf/`) package managers are used.

Getting ready

For the purposes of this recipe, we'll walk through a typical PHP installation on an Ubuntu (Debian-based) system.

How to do it...

1. Open a terminal window.
2. Update your sources list:

```
root@9b2fb55bf023:/# apt update
Get:1 http://archive.ubuntu.com/ubuntu noble InRelease [256 kB]
Get:2 http://security.ubuntu.com/ubuntu noble-security InRelease [126 kB]
```

```
Get:3 http://security.ubuntu.com/ubuntu noble-security/restricted amd64
Packages [3595 kB]
... some output omitted ...
Fetched 37.9 MB in 4s (8958 kB/s)
Reading package lists... Done
Building dependency tree... Done
Reading state information... Done
22 packages can be upgraded. Run 'apt list --upgradable' to see them.
```

3. Install PHP as a root user:

```
root@9b2fb55bf023:/# apt install php
Reading package lists... Done
Building dependency tree... Done
Reading state information... Done
The following additional packages will be installed:
  adduser apache2 apache2-bin apache2-data apache2-utils ca-certificates
krb5-locales libapache2-mod-php8.3 libapr1t64 libaprutil1-dbd-sqlite3
libaprutil1-ldap libaprutil1t64
  libargon2-1 libbrotli1 libbsd0 libcurl4t64 libedit2 libexpat1 libgdbm-
compat4t64 libgdbm6t64 libgssapi-krb5-2 libicu74 libjansson4 libk5crypto3
libkeyutils1 libkrb5-3
... some output omitted ...
Need to get 34.0 MB of archives.
After this operation, 135 MB of additional disk space will be used.
Do you want to continue? [Y/n]
```

See also

The PHP community has created an excellent download and installation instructions page that provides practical guidance on installing PHP from source or from community sources. Here is that URL: `https://www.php.net/downloads.php`.

Installing ZendPHP

ZendPHP is a set of precompiled binaries from the Zend by Perforce organization (*Disclaimer: this author (Doug Bierer) conducts PHP training for Zend by Perforce*). The advantage of this release is its easy installation. Further, if you purchase a license, you also get support. Another advantage is that a Windows MSI installer is available.

Getting ready

For Linux, download the `zendphpctl` utility, which you can then use to install and maintain the PHP installation. For Windows, download the MSI installer and follow the instructions. For the purpose of this illustration, we'll assume a CentOS installation. Complete installation documentation can be found here: `https://help.zend.com/zendphp/current/content/home.htm`.

How to do it...

1. Open a terminal window.
2. Download `zendphpctl` and signature file, and verify:

```
php8:/tmp#  curl -L https://repos.zend.com/zendphp/zendphpctl -o zendphpctl
  % Total    % Received % Xferd  Average Speed   Time    Time     Time
Current
                                 Dload  Upload   Total   Spent    Left
Speed
100  333k  100  333k    0     0   107k      0  0:00:03  0:00:03 --:--:--
107k
php8:/tmp# chmod +x ./zendphpctl
```

3. Next, you use `zendphpctl` to set up the `sources` list. The `zendphpctl` utility auto-detects your OS and uses the appropriate package manager automatically:

```
php8:/tmp# ./zendphpctl repo install
Preparing to install ZendPHP repository
Connecting to repos.zend.com (3.219.175.44:443)
saving to '/etc/apk/keys/zendphp-alpine-devel.rsa.pub'
zendphp-alpine-devel 100% |
... some output omitted ...
OK: 112 MiB in 112 packages
ZendPHP repository installed and configured!
```

4. Finally, you can install the target PHP version. In this example we install PHP 8.5:

```
php8:/tmp# ./zendphpctl php install 8.5
Installing for APK system
v3.22.4-46-g8895a0a20cd [https://dl-cdn.alpinelinux.org/alpine/v3.22/main]
v3.22.4-44-g62979ab6f4c [https://dl-cdn.alpinelinux.org/alpine/v3.22/
community]
```

```
OK: 26969 distinct packages available
(1/25) Installing php85zend-common (8.5.5-r0)
(2/25) Installing php85zend (8.5.5-r0)
(3/25) Installing php85zend-calendar (8.5.5-r0)
... some output omitted ...
(25/25) Installing php85zend-tokenizer (8.5.5-r0)
Executing busybox-1.37.0-r19.trigger
OK: 139 MiB in 137 packages
Setting default PHP version to 8.5
php8:/tmp# php -v
PHP 8.5.5 (cli) (built: Apr  8 2026 06:21:21) (NTS)
Copyright (c) The PHP Group
Built by Perforce Zend (www.zend.com)
Zend Engine v4.5.5, Copyright (c) Zend Technologies
    with Zend OPcache v8.5.5, Copyright (c), by Zend Technologies
```

See also

You can also install PHP 8 by installing an `*AMP` package. The easiest route is to install one of the excellent `*AMP` (Apache/MySQL/PHP) packages. These packages also generally include a web server and database. We will not cover `*AMP` package installation here. For information on XAMPP, look here: `https://www.apachefriends.org/`.

For more information on PHP, follow this link: `https://github.com/php/php-src/blob/master/README.md`.

Many developers prefer a more integrated approach to setting up a PHP development environment. If you plan to use the popular Laravel PHP framework for your projects, consider php.new (`https://php.new/`) or Laravel Herd (`https://herd.laravel.com/`). Another tool that's designed to get you up and running quickly is the framework-agnostic FrankenPHP (`https://frankenphp.dev/`) project.

In the next section, we will guide you through our preferred development setup, which uses **Podman**, a powerful virtualization tool that's code compatible with **Docker**. The container setup we use for the purposes of this book includes a PHP installation, an **nginx** web server, and a **MySQL**-compatible database.

Using Podman to define a containerized development environment

Containerization provides a standardized way to package and distribute software, along with its dependencies, ensuring that applications run seamlessly regardless of the environment. The containers are self-sufficient, lightweight, and can run on any system that has Podman installed, making it easier to build, ship, and run applications consistently across different environments.

The advantage of using Podman for your development work is that you can create configurations that closely match your customers' environments without interfering with the functionality of your development computer. For example, you might have one customer who uses PHP 7.4, a MySQL database, and Apache 2. Another customer might be using PHP 8.4, a PostgreSQL database, and nginx. It would be very difficult to get both these environments working on a single development computer. Podman is a good lightweight free and open-source solution for maintaining diverse environments.

> Note
>
> **Podman – a Docker Alternative**
>
> Due to recent usage and licensing restrictions imposed by Docker, in this book we use Podman, a well-regarded alternative. Podman is a Linux-native tool that operates without a daemon, facilitating the management of **Open Container Initiative** (**OCI**) containers and images for running, building, and deploying applications. It offers a **command line interface** (**CLI**) similar to Docker and can be seamlessly integrated by aliasing Docker to Podman. Moreover, it supports both root and non-privileged user modes, manages the entire container ecosystem using the `libpod` library, and provides comprehensive commands for maintaining and modifying OCI container images, making it suitable for production environments.
>
> For more information on Podman go to `https://podman.io/`.
>
> For more information on changes to the Docker license agreement, have a look here: `https://sblog.ics.uci.edu/new-docker-licensing-requirements/`.

Let's now go through what you need to do to set up Podman to run the code examples presented in this book. In order to minimize the footprint of the containerized environment on your system, and to reduce Internet bandwidth usage, we've chosen to use Alpine Linux (`https://alpinelinux.org/`). This is an extremely fast and lightweight Linux derivative that installs quickly, and gives maximum performance for the least amount of space taken.

Getting ready

You first need to install Podman and Podman Compose. You can find the installation instructions here:

- Mac installation instructions can be found at: `https://podman.io/docs/installation#macos`.
- Linux installation instructions: `https://podman.io/docs/installation#installing-on-linux`.
- For Windows, first install WSL (Windows Subsystem for Linux) using these instructions: `https://learn.microsoft.com/en-us/windows/wsl/install`.
  Following that, install a Linux client (i.e. Ubuntu 24.04). After a reboot, you can then open a Windows command prompt and use WSL to open a shell into your preferred Linux client.

You'll also need to install Podman Compose separately. For WSL, Linux or Mac, use these commands from a terminal window:

- Linux (Debian/Ubuntu): `sudo apt install podman-compose`
- Linux (RedHat/Fedora): `sudo dnf install podman-compose`
- macOS (Use Homebrew): `brew install podman-compose`

For more information see: `https://podman-desktop.io/docs/compose/setting-up-compose`.

How to do it...

Once you have Podman or Podman Desktop installed, to set up a PHP 8 development environment, begin by first copying the source code files from the GitHub repository associated with this book, and then proceed to build the image.

1. Using your computer's browser, download the source code ZIP file from the repository. Here is the path: `/archive/refs/heads/main.zip`.
2. Create a new directory (folder) named `php8cookbook` on your computer's filesystem. For the purposes of this book, we will refer to this directory as `/path/to/php8cookbook`.
3. Using your preferred ZIP archive tool, open the downloaded repository ZIP file and extract all files into `/path/to/php8cookbook`.
   Let's move on and build the image.

4. Open WSL (Windows) or a terminal window (Linux/macOS).
5. Change to the `/path/to/php8cookbook` directory.
6. Use the provided admin script to build the image by executing this command: `./admin.sh build`.
7. Here's an example of the output:

```
$ ./admin.sh build
podman-compose version: 1.0.6
['podman', '--version', '']
using podman version: 4.9.3
podman build -f ./docker/Dockerfile.NGINX -t unlikelysource/nginx_img ./
docker
STEP 1/5: FROM alpine:latest
STEP 2/5: RUN     echo "Installing basic utilities ..." &&     apk add curl
git bash nano
--> Using cache
7206111cb86b6fc87140fef6e13969670965bb3cd9198f4bfce56aa8df29c186
--> 7206111cb86b
```

8. During the build process, Podman reads a set of instructions stored in `/path/to/php8cookbook/docker/Dockerfile`. These instructions are CLI commands that install PHP, MariaDB (an open-source MySQL-compatible database), and nginx (a web server). The installation is performed on a base platform consisting of the Alpine Linux operating system.
9. Start the image running. When you run an image, it's running instance is referred to as a container. To start the image running, use this command: `./admin.sh up`.
10. To access the containerized website use your host computer's browser. You can use this URL: `http://localhost:8888/`

    Figure 1.1 shows how the opening screen might appear:

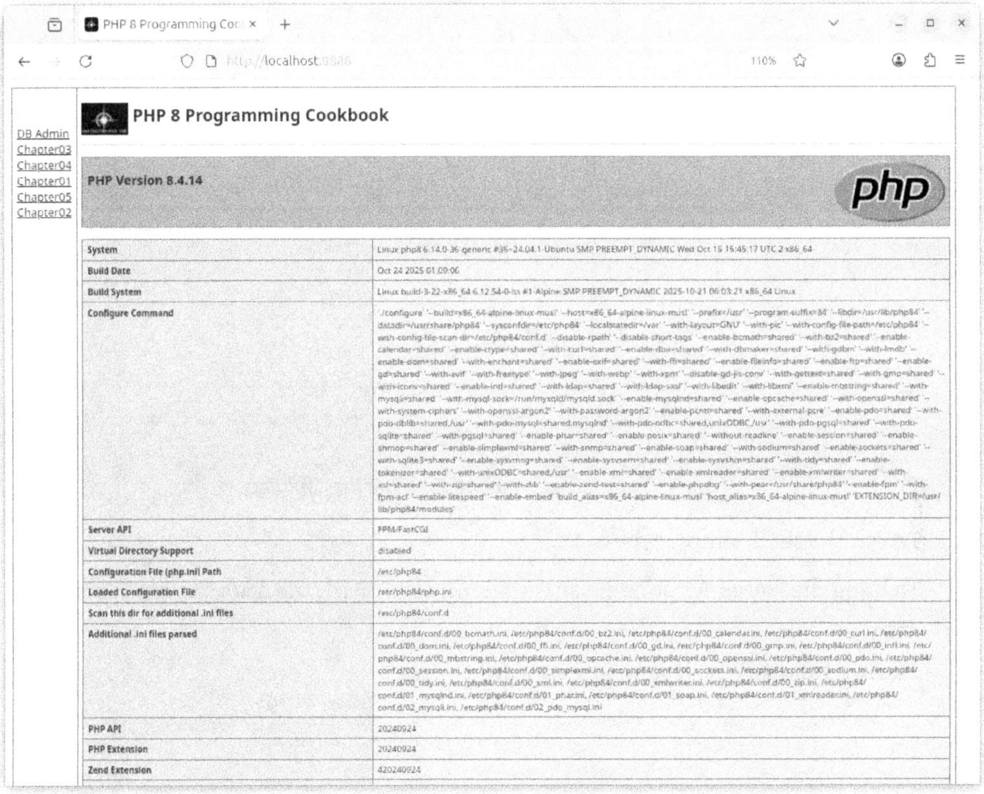

Figure 1.1 – Opening screen of the containerized website

11. To open a command shell into the container, enter this command: `./admin.sh shell`. Here's how the command shell might appear from a Linux computer:

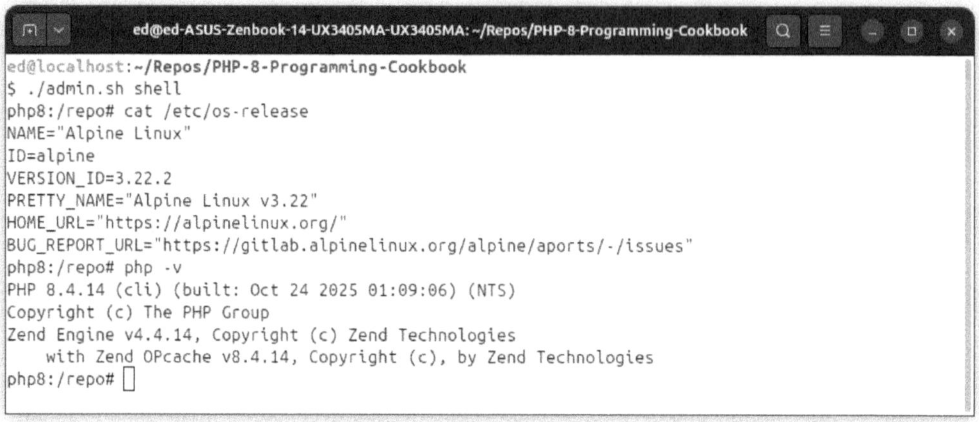

Figure 1.2 – Command shell into the container

12. To exit the shell, simply type `exit`.
13. To bring the container offline, use the admin script with the down option: `./admin.sh down`.

    Figure 1.3 shows how that might appear:

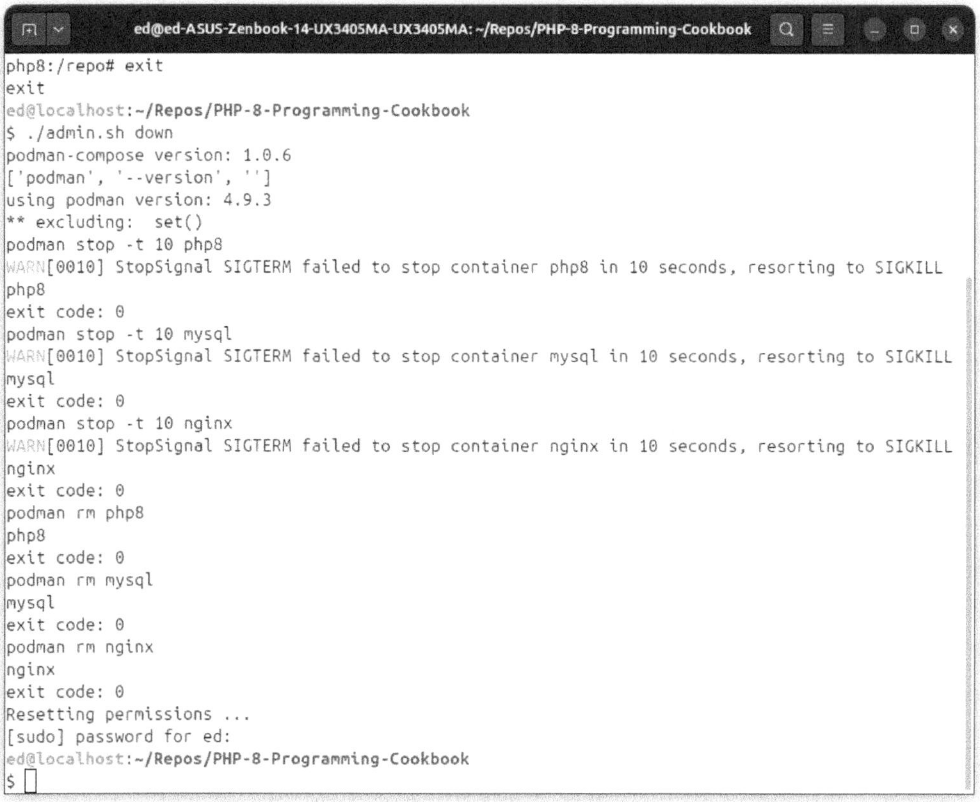

Figure 1.3 – Bringing the container down

How it works...

When you run the `admin.sh` utility, if no arguments are supplied, a usage prompt appears. The **up** option brings the container online. If the image has not yet been built, it also performs **build**. We recommend that you first run `admin.sh build` first so that the image is available for use from this point forward.

During runtime, Podman creates an isolated virtual environment that acts much like remote servers: a web server running nginx, a database server running MariaDB, and a PHP server running PHP 8. To access each of these, you must be running in a terminal window. In Windows using WSL, Linux and Mac simply open a terminal window.

To access a given server out of the three created, use the following options:

- **PHP8 Container**: `./admin.sh php8`
- **nginx Container**: `./admin.sh nginx`
- **MariaDB Container**: `./admin.sh mysql`

This concludes our discussion of building and using the containerized development environment.

See also

For more information on Podman, have a look at their main website: `https://podman.io/`. Let's now have a look at the sample database used with this book.

Using GenAI to build a postcode database

For the purposes of this book you'll find a sample raw SQL data dump named `php8cookbook.sql` located in `/path/to/php8cookbook/data/`. When you build the Docker container, the sample database is created. The admin shell script (e.g., `admin.sh` for Linux) restores the database when you bring the Docker container up. Conversely, when you take the container offline, the admin script backs up the data.

> Note
>
> **admin.sh**
>
> Once you unzip the source code file associated with this book, in the `/path/to/php8cookbook` folder you'll find one script that helps you navigate to and work with the containers: `admin.sh`. Here's the overall usage: `init.sh up|down|build|ls|init|shell [php|nginx|mysql]`

Let's understand what they do:

- `up`: brings the 3 containers up (PHP8, nginx, and mysql)
- `down`: brings the 3 containers down and resets permissions back to default
- `build`: builds the 3 containers
- `ls`: lists running containers
- `shell $2`: opens a shell into the container specified by `$2` (`php` | `nginx` | `mysql`). The default is `php`

Getting ready

For this example we'll instruct ChatGPT to create a PHP program that creates and loads up a postcode database based on data from the Geonames project (`https://www.geonames.org/`). At the bottom of the postcode downloads page (`https://download.geonames.org/export/zip/`) you'll find a description of the data structure which we'll provide to the AI. Go ahead and download and unzip one of the postcode ZIP files. For our purposes we'll use `US.zip`. We place the unzipped file (`US.txt`) into the `/path/to/php8cookbook/data` folder. You'll also need ready access to GenAI. For the purposes of this recipe we'll use a platform called monica.im (`https://monica.im/`), and choose the GPT-5.2 OpenAI model.

How to do it...

1. First, we download and unzip `US.zip`:

```
ed@localhost:~/Repos/PHP-8-Programming-Cookbook
$ ./admin.sh shell
php8:/repo# cd data
php8:/repo/data# curl -o US.zip https://download.geonames.org/export/zip/
US.zip
  % Total    % Received % Xferd  Average Speed   Time    Time     Time
Current
                                 Dload  Upload   Total   Spent    Left
Speed
100  619k  100  619k    0     0  79048      0  0:00:08  0:00:08 --:--:--
154k
php8:/repo/data# unzip US.zip
Archive:  US.zip
  inflating: readme.txt
  inflating: US.txt
php8:/repo/data# rm US.zip
php8:/repo/data# exit
exit
```

2. Before defining the ChatGPT prompt, we'll need to gather the information needed to properly instruct the AI. First, we get the exact database version. Open a shell into the `mysql` container and determine the version by entering `mariadb --version`:

```
ed@localhost:~/Repos/PHP-8-Programming-Cookbook
$ ./admin.sh shell mysql
mysql:/repo# mariadb --version
```

```
mariadb from 11.4.8-MariaDB, client 15.2 for Linux (x86_64) using readline
5.1
mysql:/repo# exit
exit
```

> **Note**
>
> Note that you can still use the `mysql` command; however, it is deprecated in favor of using the `mariadb` command. We use `mariadb` for the purposes of this book as it's free open-source software and is code compatible with MySQL.

3. We also need to get the exact version of PHP installed. Open a shell into the PHP 8 container and enter the command `php --version`:

```
ed@localhost:~/Repos/PHP-8-Programming-Cookbook
$ ./admin.sh shell php8
php8:/repo# php --version
PHP 8.4.14 (cli) (built: Oct 24 2025 01:09:06) (NTS)
Copyright (c) The PHP Group Zend Engine v4.4.14, Copyright (c) Zend
Technologies with Zend OPcache v8.4.14, Copyright (c), by Zend Technologies
php8:/repo# exit
exit
```

4. Armed with precise information, we can now define the prompt in a file `data/readme.txt`:

```
Generate a PHP 8.4 program "populate.php" that create and populate a
MariaDB version 11.4.8 database table called "postcode" with data from a
tab-delimited CSV file $fn.
The attached file "readme.txt" contains a description of the tab-delimited
CSV file.
The program needs to accept a command-line argument that contains the exact
path to $fn.
If $fn does not exist the program should exit with an appropriate error
message.
If $fn does exist the program needs to read the tab-delimited CSV data one
line at a time and insert the row into the "postcode" table.
When you produce the code use modern PHP classes and functions such as
using SplFileObject to open $fn instead of older functions such as fopen().
```

```
Provide a count of how many rows were read, and how many rows were
successfully inserted into the database upon program exit.
```

5. We then upload the `data/readme.txt` file provided in the download to our AI platform and execute the prompt. Here's the response:

GPT-5.2

Here' s a modern, CLI-friendly `populate.php` for PHP **8.4** that:

- Accepts **one command-line argument**: the **exact path** to the GeoNames tab-delimited postal code file (`$fn`)
- Exits with a clear error if the file doesn' t exist/readable
- Creates a MariaDB table named **`postcode`** (dropping nothing—safe to re-run)
- Streams the file **line-by-line** via `SplFileObject` (no loading whole file into memory)
- Inserts rows using **PDO + prepared statements**
- Prints **rows read** and **rows inserted** on exit

> Connection details are taken from environment variables (`DB_HOST` , `DB_PORT` , `DB_NAME` , `DB_USER` , `DB_PASS`) with sensible defaults.

Figure 1.4 – ChatGPT response to prompt

6. We can now examine the program the AI created. We saved it under the name `ch01_populate_first_cut.php` in the `/path/to/php8cookbook/src/Chapter01` directory.
   The AI decided to frame its response as a BASH shell script, meaning that if the execute flag is set, the file can be directly executed under Linux. In the final cut we'll remove the first line and run it as a proper PHP program:

```
#!/usr/bin/env php
<?php
declare(strict_types=1);
```

7. GPT 5.2 also provided opening comments. You'll note that the AI configured the script to use environment variables, so in the final cut we'll need to add a `__construct()` and

provide a configuration file that contains database credentials. Here is the new `__construct()` method:

```
public function __construct(private array $config) {}
```

8. The primary method is `run()`, which calls a series of private class methods to accomplish the task. However, assuming the program would be run from the command line, GPT 5.2 designed its validation methods to exit immediately. We introduced a `try {} catch {}` structure instead, and modified the validation methods to throw an exception (shown later):

```
public function run(array $argv): string {
    try {
        $fn = $this->parseArgs($argv);
        $this->assertFileRead($fn);
        $pdo = $this->connect();
        $this->ensureSchema($pdo);
        [$read, $inserted] =
            $this->importFile($pdo, $fn);
        $this->rowsRead = $read;
        $this->rowsInserted = $inserted;
        return "Rows read: {$this->rowsRead}\n" .
          "Rows inserted: {$this->rowsInserted}\n";
    } catch (Throwable $t) {
        return $t->getMessage();
    }
}
```

9. The validation methods are shown next. As mentioned earlier, instead of directly producing error messages using `fwrite(STDERR, $msg)`, we throw an exception which delivers the message:

```
private function parseArgs(array $argv): string {
    if (count($argv) !== 2) {
        $script = $argv[0] ?? 'populate.php';
        throw new Exception("Usage: php {$script}
            /exact/path/to/tab_delimited_file\n");
    }
    return (string) $argv[1];
}
```

```
private function assertFileRead(string $fn): void {
    if (!is_file($fn)) {
        throw new Exception(
            "Error: file does not exist: {$fn}\n");
    }
    if (!is_readable($fn)) {
        throw new Exception(
            "Error: file is not readable: {$fn}\n");
    }
}
```

10. Next is the `connect()` method that provides a PDO connection to the database. The AI configured this to read environment variables. Instead, we'll rewrite the code slightly to read from the configuration file provided in our new `__construct()` method:

```
private function connect(): PDO {
    $host = $this->config['db']['DB_HOST'] ?? '';
    $port = $this->config['db']['DB_PORT'] ?? '';
    $db   = $this->config['db']['DB_NAM'] ?? '';
    $user = $this->config['db']['DB_USR'] ?? '';
    $pass = $this->config['db']['DB_PWD'] ?? '';
    $dsn = sprintf('mysql:host=%s;port=%s;dbname=%s;'
    . 'charset=utf8mb4', $host, $port, $db);
    $opts = [
        PDO::ATTR_ERRMODE => PDO::ERRMODE_EXCEPTION,
        PDO::ATTR_DEFAULT_FETCH_MODE =>
            PDO::FETCH_ASSOC,
        PDO::ATTR_EMULATE_PREPARES => false];
    try {
        $pdo = new PDO($dsn, $user, $pass, $opts);
        $pdo->exec("SET NAMES utf8mb4
            COLLATE utf8mb4_unicode_ci");
        return $pdo;
    } catch (Throwable $t) {
        error_log($t->getMessage());
        throw new Exception("Database connection failed: \n");
    }
}
```

11. The `ensureSchema()` method builds the database table if it doesn't exist:

```
private function ensureSchema(PDO $pdo): void {
    $sql = <<<SQL
CREATE TABLE IF NOT EXISTS postcode (
id BIGINT UNSIGNED NOT NULL AUTO_INCREMENT,
country_code CHAR(2) NOT NULL,
postal_code VARCHAR(20) NOT NULL,
place_name VARCHAR(180) NOT NULL,
admin_name1 VARCHAR(100) NULL,
admin_code1 VARCHAR(20) NULL,
admin_name2 VARCHAR(100) NULL,
admin_code2 VARCHAR(20) NULL,
admin_name3 VARCHAR(100) NULL,
admin_code3 VARCHAR(20) NULL,
latitude DECIMAL(10,7) NULL,
longitude DECIMAL(10,7) NULL,
accuracy TINYINT UNSIGNED NULL,
PRIMARY KEY (id),
KEY idx_country_postal (country_code, postal_code),
KEY idx_place (place_name),
KEY idx_admin1 (admin_code1),
KEY idx_lat_lng (latitude, longitude)
) ENGINE=InnoDB DEFAULT CHARSET=utf8mb4 COLLATE=utf8mb4_unicode_ci
SQL;
    try {
        $pdo->exec($sql);
    } catch (Throwable $t) {
        error_log($t->getMessage());
        throw new Exception(
            "Failed to create/verify schema\n");
    }
}
```

12. The `importFile()` method is the main workhorse. We'll break it down section by section. First, we define an `SQL INSERT` prepared statement:

```
private function importFile(PDO $pdo, string $fn): array {
    $insertSql = <<<SQL
INSERT INTO postcode (
```

```
country_code, postal_code, place_name,
admin_name1, admin_code1,
admin_name2, admin_code2,
admin_name3, admin_code3,
latitude, longitude, accuracy
) VALUES (?,?,?,?,?,?,?,?,?,?,?,?)
SQL;
    $stmt = $pdo->prepare($insertSql);
```

13. Next, we open the tab-delimited Geonames postcode data file using `SplFileObject`, and set the appropriate CSV parameters. We also initialize the variables used to count rows read and inserted. In this case, the AI missed the fact that in PHP 8.4, using `SplFileObject::fputcsv()` now requires all parameters to be specified or you will receive a deprecated notice. Accordingly, we set the separator, enclosure, and escape parameters:

```
$file = new SplFileObject($fn, 'r');
$file->setFlags(
    SplFileObject::READ_CSV
    | SplFileObject::SKIP_EMPTY
    | SplFileObject::DROP_NEW_LINE);
$file->setCsvControl("\t", '"', '\\');
$rowsRead = 0;
$rowsInserted = 0;
```

14. We then set the SQL transaction batch size and loop through the file row-by-row. We also include a number of safety checks to ensure that the returned row isn't empty and has a count of 12 (to match the Geonames specifications):

```
$batchSize = 5000;
$inTx = false;
$sinceCommit = 0;
try {
  while (!$file->eof()) {
    $row = $file->fgetcsv();
    if (!is_array($row) || count($row) !== 12
        || empty($row[1]))
    { continue; }
    $rowsRead++;
```

15. We then use `array_map()` to perform additional sanitization, followed by a check to see if the first 3 critical fields are not empty:

```
// Trim fields
$row = array_map(
    static fn($v) => is_string($v) ? trim($v)
    : (is_null($v) ? '' : (string)$v), $row);
$countryCode = $row[0] ?? '';
$postalCode  = $row[1] ?? '';
$placeName   = $row[2] ?? '';
if ($countryCode === '' ||
  $postalCode === '' || $placeName === '')
{ continue; }
```

16. We then begin the transaction using `$inTx` to control the batch (set earlier to `5000`). You'll note as we build the `$params` array, we use additional sanitization methods including `nullIfEmpty()` and `nullIfNotNumeric()`:

```
if (!$inTx) {
    $pdo->beginTransaction();
    $inTx = true;
    $sinceCommit = 0;
}
$params = [
    $countryCode,
    $postalCode,
    $placeName,
    $this->nullIfEmpty($row[3]) ?? '',
    $this->nullIfEmpty($row[4]) ?? '',
    $this->nullIfEmpty($row[5]) ?? '',
    $this->nullIfEmpty($row[6]) ?? '',
    $this->nullIfEmpty($row[7]) ?? '',
    $this->nullIfEmpty($row[8]) ?? '',
    $this->nullIfNotNumeric($row[9]) ?? '',
    $this->nullIfNotNumeric($row[10]) ?? '',
    (int)($row[11] ?? 0),
];
```

17. We then wrap the execute in a nested `try {} catch {}` block. If the insert fails we simply log the error and continue in the loop. `$sinceCommit` is used as a counter. When

it reaches the batch size we execute `PDO::commit()` and set `$inTx` to false so that we can start another transaction:

```
        try {
            $stmt->execute($params);
            $rowsInserted++;
        } catch (Throwable $t) {
            error_log($t->getMessage());
        }
        $sinceCommit++;
        if ($sinceCommit >= $batchSize) {
            $pdo->commit();
            $inTx = false;
        }
    }

    if ($inTx) $pdo->commit();
```

18. We end by returning to the outer `try {} catch {}` block. If it fails, we throw a new exception. Otherwise, we return the number of rows read and rows inserted:

```
    } catch (Throwable $t) {
        if ($inTx) {
            try { $pdo->rollBack(); }
            catch (Throwable) {}
        }
        throw new Exception(
            "Import failed: {$t->getMessage()}\n");
    }
    return [$rowsRead, $rowsInserted];
}
```

19. Next, let's have a look at the additional sanitization methods used to build the query parameters:

```
private function nullIfEmpty(string $v): ?string {
    $v = trim($v);
    return $v === '' ? null : $v;
}
```

```
private function nullIfNotNumeric(string $v):?string {
    $v = trim($v);
    return ($v === '' || !is_numeric($v)) ? null : $v;
}

private function nullIfNotInt(string $v): ?int {
    $v = trim($v);
    return ($v === '' || ctype_digit($v)) ? null: (int) $v;
}}
```

20. Finally, to avoid having to create a separate calling program, we end by creating a class instance and running it, supplying the needed database configuration:

```
$app = new App(include __DIR__ .
    '/config/db_config.php');
exit($app->run($argv));
```

21. For the configuration file `db_config.php` (mentioned in the previous step), we read the `/tmp/secrets.sh` file into the `$secrets` array to obtain database credentials. As you may recall, this file is used to store important credentials used in the process of setting up the Podman containers. Next, use `array_walk()` with an arrow function to remove the leading string `'export '`:

```
<?php

$secrets = file('/tmp/secrets.sh');
array_walk($secrets, fn(&$line) => ($line = trim(str_replace('export ',
'', $line))));
```

22. We then define an anonymous function that pulls out the value from the given key:

```
$get_secret = function (string $key) use ($secrets) : string {
    $callback = function ($val) use ($key)
        { return str_contains($val, $key); };
    $line = array_find($secrets, $callback);
    if (!empty($line) && str_contains($line, '=')) {
        $val = str_replace([$key, '='], '', $line);
    } else {
        $val = '';
    }
```

```
        return $val;
    };
```

23. We then use the anonymous function to extract the needed database credentials:

```
return [
    'db' => [
        'DB_HOST' => $get_secret('DB_HOST'),
        'DB_PORT' => 3306,
        'DB_NAM'  => $get_secret('DB_NAM'),
        'DB_USR'  => $get_secret('DB_USR'),
        'DB_PWD'  => $get_secret('DB_PWD'),
    ],
];
```

24. To run the program we modified from the original AI-generated version, we open a shell into the PHP 8 container:

```
ed@localhost:~/Repos/PHP-8-Programming-Cookbook
$ ./admin.sh shell
php8:/repo#
```

25. Now we can run our newly defined program:

```
php8:/repo# php src/Chapter01/ch01_populate_refined.php /repo/data/US.txt
Rows read: 41489
Rows inserted: 41489
```

26. To access the Adminer database utility, use the information shown in *Figure 1.5*. The password, shown in the `/tmp/secrets.sh` file, is `password`. Alternatively, add `127.0.0.1 mysql.local` to your computer's `/etc/hosts` file (in Windows: `C:\Windows\System32\drivers\etc\hosts` file), after which you can enter `mysql.local` as the server entry:

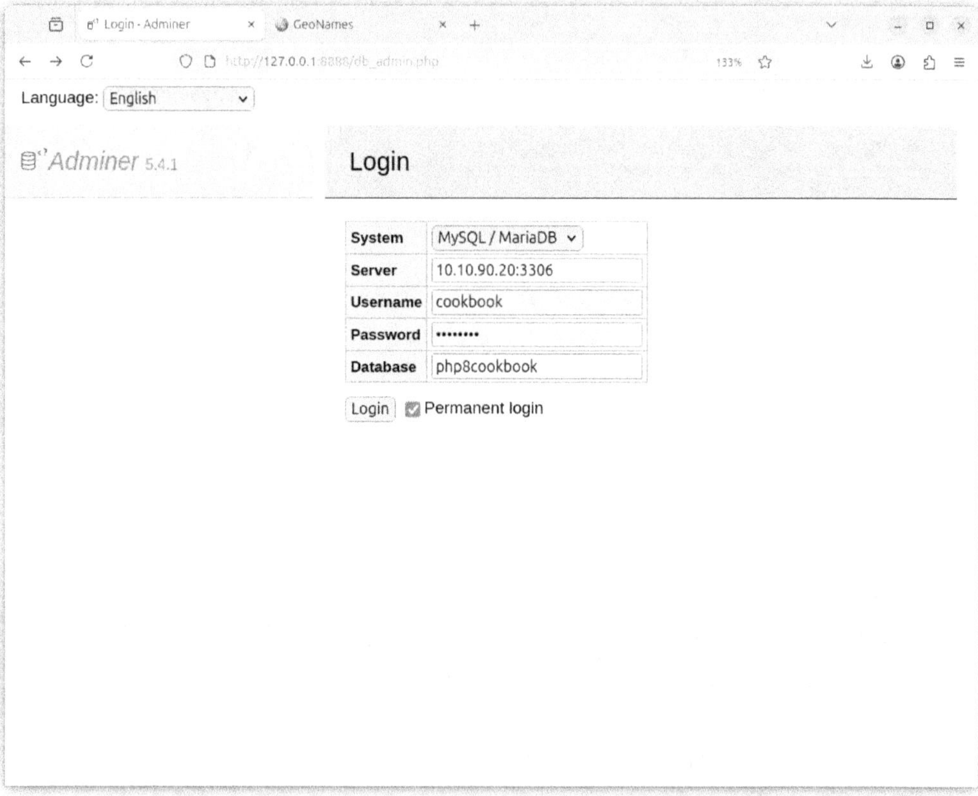

Figure 1.5 – Adminer database utility access information

27. You can now select data on the new postcode table as shown in *Figure 1.6*:

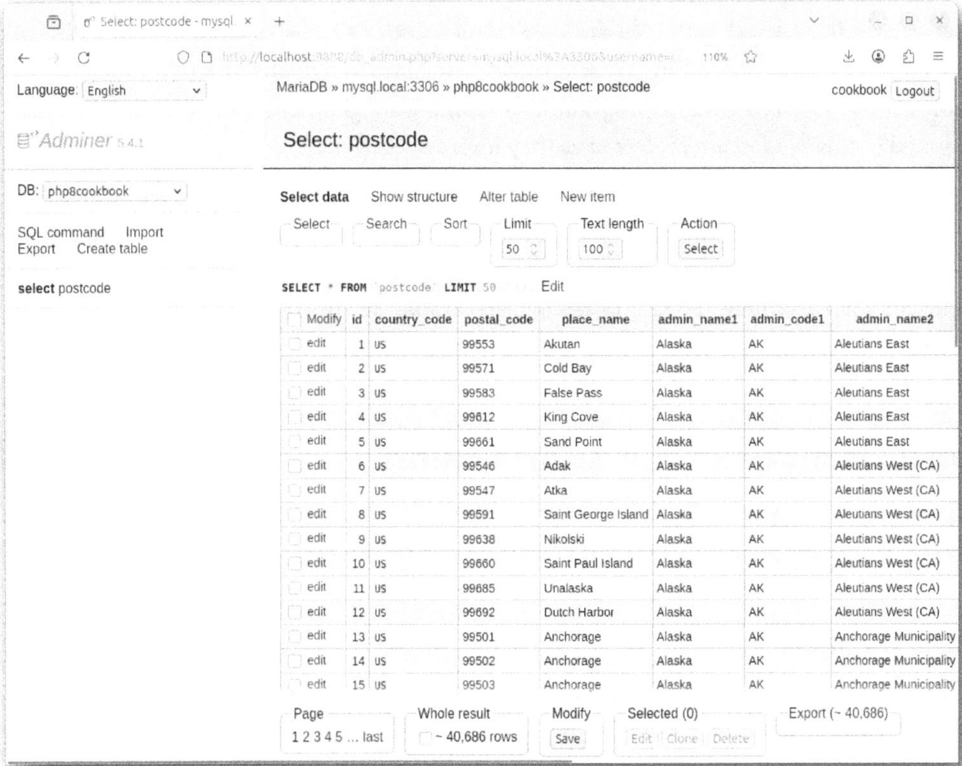

Figure 1.6 – Accessing the sample database from a browser

How it works...

Using carefully crafted AI prompts is a great way to boost code development. However, it's important to recognize that AI does not understand customer imperatives, nor does it comprehend the full context of your project. Accordingly, you need to exercise due diligence to tweak the code to fit the needs of your project, and to ensure that proper security measures are in place. You can think of AI as a Junior Developer who types at lightning speed and follows your instructions to the letter. However, just with as any code that gets written, you must have a solid review process in place. Even when using AI to generate code, there's simply no substitute for proper validation and quality control. Just because the code works does not mean it's the best fit for your particular environment.

A question many readers will have is: did the original AI-generated program work? The answer is yes! However, a few modifications were needed. As mentioned earlier, the original program created by GPT-5.2 was saved as `ch01_populate_first_cut.php` in the `/path/to/`

php8cookbook/src/Chapter01 folder. In order to remain in sync with the /tmp/secrets.sh file, on *lines 68 to 70*, we changed the database name, user, and password keys to DB_NAM, DB_USR, and DB_PWD. We then ran "./tmp/secrets.sh" first to refresh the environment variables, after which we ran the program. The results were identical; however, the changes mentioned in this section are preferred as they improve efficiency.

In an AI-assisted workflow, testing and automated validation become even more critical. If we accelerate code generation, we must also strengthen the mechanisms that validate that code. Otherwise, evaluation becomes a bottleneck—or worse, relies on hope rather than guarantees. Even in this small example, using unit testing, static analysis tools such as PHPStan, or coding standards enforcement is a critical part of the overall development process. In short, speed in code creation must be balanced by a solid quality-check ecosystem.

Using Composer for autoloading

Composer is an indispensable package management system that handles the vast majority of PHP open-source packages. It is written in PHP and is used to install third-party software, handle updates, and ensure that package dependencies are met.

Getting ready

Download the composer.phar file from the Composer website using your browser. Alternatively, from a terminal window you can use this curl command:

```
php8:/repo# curl -o composer.phar \
    -L https://getcomposer.org/composer.phar
  % Total    % Received % Xferd  Average Speed   Time    Time     Time  Current
Dload  Upload   Total   Spent    Left  Speed
100 3200k  100 3200k    0     0   612k      0  0:00:05  0:00:05 --:--:--  692k
```

How to do it...

1. The composer.phar file is a shell script that's directly executable once you've assigned the execute file permission. Just entering the name of the file activates the script, revealing a basic help screen, as seen in *Figure 1.7*:

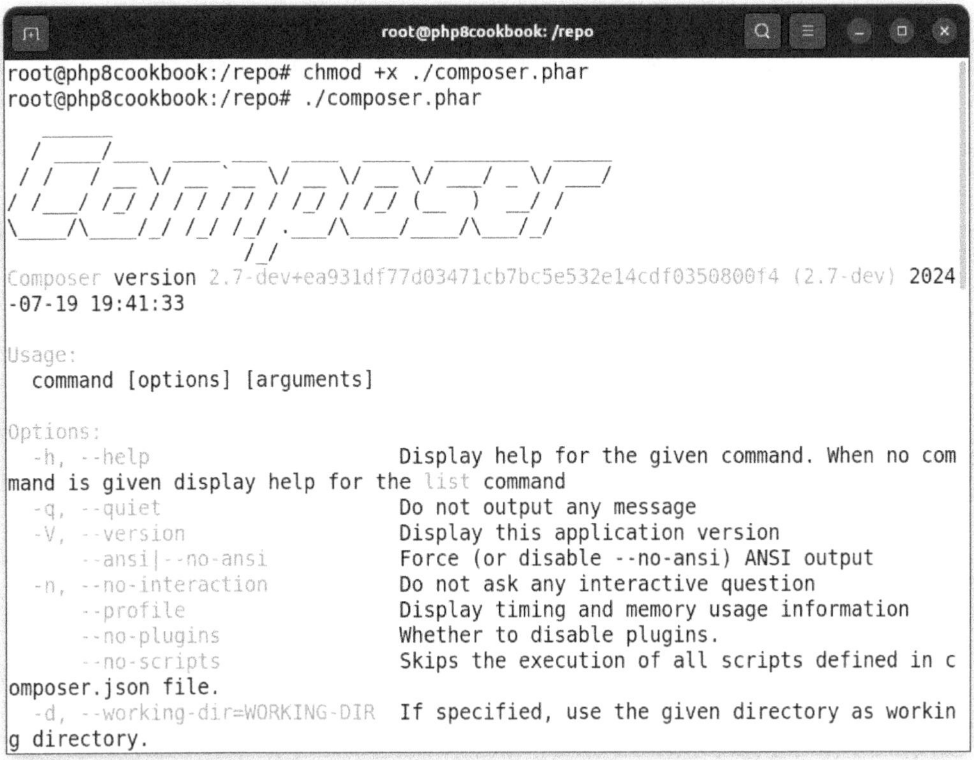

Figure 1.7 – Executing composer.phar

2. Alternatively, you can preface the filename with the command to invoke PHP, achieving the same result:

```
php composer.phar
```

> **Note**
>
> If you want to install Composer as a command available globally on your computer, move it to a directory in your path and make it executable.

One of the most popular uses for Composer, aside from installing and maintaining packages, is for the purposes of **autoloading**. Autoloading is a mechanism built into the PHP language whereby requested class definitions not already in use are automatically located and loaded. The command `spl_autoload_register()` is used to register an **autoloader**. An autoloader is a PHP function that uses either the `include`, `include_once`, `require`, or `require_once` command to load the appropriate class file. Composer includes a world-class autoloader to autoload the classes within the packages it maintains. It's super easy for you to hitch a ride and have Composer autoload your own classes as well!

3. Shown next is the `composer.json` file used for this book. The top level of the namespace used for the book is `Cookbook`, which is mapped to the `src` directory relative to the location of the `composer.json` file. Here is the `composer.json` file:

```
{
    "require" : {
        "php" : ">= 8.4",
        "phpmailer/phpmailer": "^6.9",
        "phpunit/phpunit": "10.1"
    },
    "autoload" : {
        "psr-4" : {
            "Cookbook\\" : "src/"
        }
    }
}
```

4. In order to activate autoloading for the `Cookbook` namespace, you can use either of the following Composer subcommands:
   - `composer update`
   - `composer dump-autoload`
5. Note that the `composer update` command not only refreshes the autoloading class-to-file mapping, but also updates any installed Composer packages. Also note that there are two backslashes (\\). This is because the backslash is also an **escape character**. By adding two backslashes, you are telling Composer that you have deliberately *escaped* the second backslash:

```
php8:/repo# php composer.phar dump-autoload
Generating autoload files
Generated autoload files
```

> **Note**
>
> **PSR 4**
>
> **PHP Standards Recommendations** (**PSR**) are a set of definitions, guidelines, and best practices which have been adopted by the **PHP Framework Interop Group** (**PHP-FIG**). PSR-4 supersedes PSR-0, both of which pertain to autoloading. For more information on PSR-4 have a look here: `https://www.php-fig.org/psr/psr-4/`.

6. Here is a simple class that displays `"Hello World"`:

```
namespace Cookbook\Chapter01\Hello;

class HelloWorld {
    public static function hello() {
        return __METHOD__ . PHP_EOL;
    }
}
```

7. The file `HelloWorld.php` is located in the `src/Chapter01/Hello` directory. The best practice is as follows:

    - The namespace should match the directory structure.
    - The filename should match the classname.

    Figure 1.8 shows the tree structure of this simple example:

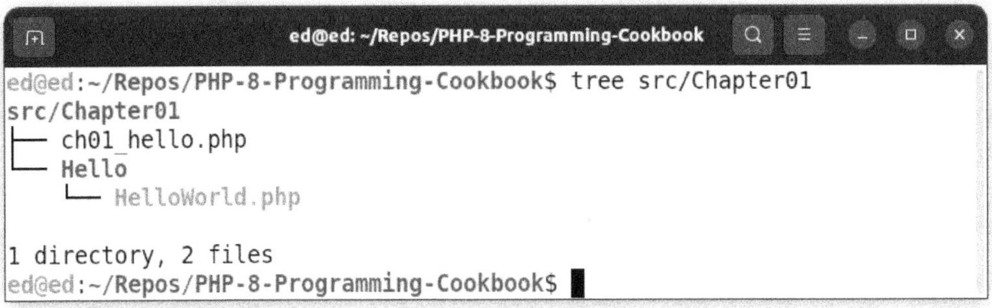

Figure 1.8 – Tree structure of the HelloWorld example

8. The calling program needs to include the Composer autoloader and *import* the class. You can invoke the autoloader by including a file `/path/to/php8cookbook/vendor/autoload.php`. This file calls an auto-generated class loader produced when you use either the `update` or `dump-autoload` Composer options. Here is the simple calling program:

```
include __DIR__ . '/../../vendor/autoload.php';
use Cookbook\Chapter01\Hello\HelloWorld;
echo HelloWorld::hello();
```

9. PHP will throw a fatal error if any of the following conditions are true:
    - Autoloading is improperly configured in the `composer.json` file.
    - Composer autoloading has not been activated.
    - The directory path does not match the namespace.
    - The filename does not match the class's name.
10. *Figure 1.9* shows the results after autoloading has been properly configured and activated:

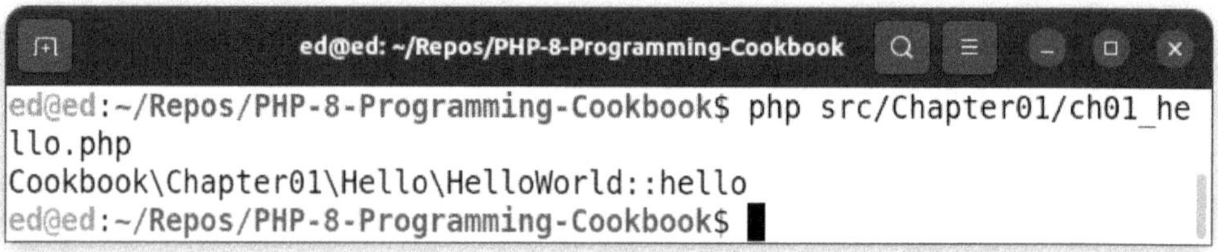

Figure 1.9 – Output from the simple "hello" program

How it works...

Composer is an essential tool to master as it's used by the vast majority of PHP developers and corporate software development teams that use PHP. We've just scratched the surface when it comes to Composer sub-commands. If you have a look at the documentation, you'll see a wide variety of additional commands that can help you manage a project with lots of dependencies.

It might be a good idea to bone up on the PSR-4 standard. As we showed in this section, you can leverage Composer's autoloader to shoehorn in your own project's code. This will save you an endless series of `include` or `require` statements.

One last consideration is where and how to use Composer. We recommend using `composer.phar` locally in projects where you may need to have a specific version of Composer. Otherwise, especially when you use your own computer for development, moving `composer.phar` into a directory in your system path might be more helpful for overall development.

See also

Composer can use PHP package repositories other than packagist.org. The most famous of these is `https://wpackagist.org/`, which hosts WordPress plugins and themes that can be installed using Composer.

For more information on JSON and JSON syntax have a look here: `https://www.json.org/json-en.html`.

For a complete list of all `composer.json` properties, have a look here: `https://getcomposer.org/doc/04-schema.md`.

Using AI to create a PHP 7 to PHP 8 code converter

Upgrading from one major PHP release to another is a nightmare for developers. In this section, we show you how to use GenAI to create a simple code converter class able to convert PHP 7 code to PHP 8.

The core of a converter class could use the incredibly under-utilized function `preg_replace_callback_array()`. This function takes an array argument consisting of key/value pairs as an argument along with a string that represents the document to be processed. In the array argument, the key is the regular expression, and the value is a callback that performs the appropriate substitution.

Here is the generic signature for `preg_replace_callback_array()`:

```
preg_replace_callback_array(
    array $pattern,
    string|array $subject,
    int $limit = -1,
    int &$count = null,
    int $flags = 0
): string|array|null
```

Note

For more information on `preg_replace_callback_array()`, have a look at this documentation page: `https://www.php.net/preg_replace_callback_array`.

However, it's important to note that although a simple replacement strategy leveraging this function will help, there exist a number of excellent tools available via Composer that are expressly designed to facilitate code base migration, such as Rector and PHP-Parser. Accordingly, it's important for you to recognize that the role of AI in code development should be as a complementary tool for higher-level improvements such as identifying outdated patterns, suggesting architectural refinements, detecting redundant code, or proposing the introduction of DTOs instead of loosely structured arrays.

Getting ready

Before getting started on developing the `Converter` class, you must first gather a list of PHP 8 changes that are of concern. A good place to look is in the migration guide appendices included in the main PHP documentation page located here: `https://www.php.net/manual/en/appendices.php`. Note that this recipe features GPT-5.5 rather than 5.2.

In the migration guides, you should look for sections titled *Backward Incompatible Changes*. These sections describe changes that will cause your code to malfunction. You might also consider adding regular expressions that search for deprecated functionality.

How to do it...

1. Your first thought might be to start defining the array of regular expressions and callbacks either in a separate configuration file or in the main `Converter` class itself.
2. Following this line of reasoning, we instruct ChatGPT to scan the appropriate list of dependencies and produce an array of regular expressions and callbacks that spot deprecated and backward-incompatible changes. Here is a sample prompt:

```
Based upon the provided URLs, give me a PHP array that consists of the
following:
1. The array element key will be a regular expression that detects
deprecated or backward incompatible syntax in the provided PHP 7 script.
2. The array element value will be an anonymous function that replaces the
deprecated or backward incompatible syntax.
Here are the provided URLs:
https://www.php.net/manual/en/migration80.php
https://www.php.net/manual/en/migration81.php
```

```
https://www.php.net/manual/en/migration82.php
https://www.php.net/manual/en/migration83.php
https://www.php.net/manual/en/migration84.php
https://www.php.net/manual/en/migration85.php
```

3. Here's the result from GPT 5.5:

```
$rules = [

    /*
     * PHP 8.0
     * Curly brace array/string offsets were removed.
     *
     */
    '~(\$[A-Za-z_\x80-\xff][A-Za-z0-9_\x80-\xff]*(?:->\w+|\[[^\]]+\])*)\s*\
{\s*([^{}\r\n]+?)\s*\}~' =>
        function (array $m): string {
            return $m[1] . '[' . trim($m[2]) . ']';
        },

    /*
     * PHP 8.0
     * create_function() was removed.
     *
     */
    '~\bcreate_function\s*\(\s*([\'"])(.*?)\1\s*,\s*([\'"])(.*?)\3\s*\)~s'
=>
        function (array $m): string {
            $args = stripcslashes($m[2]);
            $body = stripcslashes($m[4]);

            return 'function (' . $args . ') { ' . $body . ' }';
        },
    // remaining output is omitted
```

4. What is perhaps more interesting than the actual code generated is that GPT 5.5 also pointed this out:

```
Important: regex-based PHP migration is useful for simple mechanical
replacements, but it is not a complete substitute for an AST-based tool
```

```
like Rector or PHP-Parser. Some PHP 8.x changes require semantic
understanding of classes, parameters, types, and runtime behavior.
```

5. This illustrates another potential use for AI-assisted development: the process of discovery. While developing code assisted by AI, it's entirely possible that you'll discover new tools and design patterns that will lead you to better and more efficient ways of developing code.
6. Accordingly we can change direction and ask the AI to help us develop a PHP 7 to PHP 8 code converter using Rector. The result is a set of steps starting with Rector installation, and followed by an example of a PHP script that invokes the Rector-based converter. Here is the first step suggested by GPT 5.5:

```
composer require rector/rector --dev
```

7. GPT 5.5 then produced a sample program that can perform the migration. In the / `path/to/php8cookbook/src/Chapter01/` folder we created a calling program `ch01_php_7_to_8_code_converter.php` that defines the paths containing code to be converted, and leverages Rector to perform the migration:

```
<?php
use Rector\Config\RectorConfig;
use Rector\Set\ValueObject\LevelSetList;
use Rector\Set\ValueObject\SetList;

return RectorConfig::configure()
    ->withPaths([
        __DIR__ . '/app', __DIR__ . '/src', __DIR__ . '/public', // etc.
    ])

    /*
     * Tell Rector what PHP version you want to upgrade to.
     *    LevelSetList::UP_TO_PHP_80
     *    LevelSetList::UP_TO_PHP_81
     *    LevelSetList::UP_TO_PHP_82
     *    LevelSetList::UP_TO_PHP_83
     */
    ->withSets([ LevelSetList::UP_TO_PHP_84 ])
    ->withSets([
        SetList::CODE_QUALITY, SetList::DEAD_CODE,
```

```
SetList::TYPE_DECLARATION])
    ->withSkip([
        __DIR__ . '/vendor', __DIR__ . '/cache', // etc.
    ]);
```

8. In this particular case, GPT 5.5 went even one step further by recommending we leverage PHPStan, an excellent standards-enforcement package, in order to address typing and compatibility problems. First we install the package using Composer:

```
composer require phpstan/phpstan --dev
```

9. We then create a `phpstan.neon` YAML file that identifies the paths we wish to include in our migration:

```
parameters:
    level: 5
    paths:
        - app
        - src
        - public
        - etc.
```

10. We would follow our migration by running PHPStan:

```
vendor/bin/phpstan analyse
```

How it works...

In the `/path/to/php8cookbook/src/Chapter01/file_test` folder, we created PHP 7 files loaded with backward compatibilities and deprecations. We don't show the entire contents of both files here, but from this snippet from `Seven.php` you can already see some issues:

```
<?php
namespace Test;
class Seven {
    public $config = [];
    public function seven(array $config) {
            $this->config = $config;
     }
      public function add(real $a, real $b) {
              return (real) $a + $b;
```

```
    }
    // other code not shown
```

Here are the results after running the conversion program. Not all results are shown to conserve space:

```
$ ./admin.sh shell
php8:/repo# php src/Chapter01/ch01_php_7_to_8_code_converter.php
php8:/repo/src/Chapter01# php ch01_php_7_to_8_code_converter.php
```

```
Converting: /repo/src/Chapter01/test_file/test_seven.php
***************************************
<?php
// ******* DETECTED: The 3rd argument to "define()" is now ignored.
define('BASE_DIR', __DIR__);
// ******* DETECTED: "__autoload()" is longer supported for autoloading. Use
"spl_autoload_register()".
spl_autoload_register('autoload');
function autoload($class)
{
    $fn = __DIR__ . str_replace('\\', '/', $class) . '.php';
    require ($fn);
}
use Test\Seven;
$test = new Seven(['A' => 111, 'B' => 222, 'C' => 333]);
echo $test->getConf('A');
echo PHP_EOL;
echo $test->add(5.55, 6.66);
var_dump((unset) $test);

Converting: /repo/src/Chapter01/test_file/Test/Seven.php
***************************************
<?php
namespace Test;
// ******* DETECTED:
/*
A method with the same name as the class
is no longer used as a default construct method.
This method was converted to __construct.
*/
```

```
#[\AllowDynamicProperties]
class Seven
{
    public $config = [];
    public function __construct(array $config)
    {
      $this->config = $config;
    }
    public function add(float $a, float $b)
    {
         return (float) $a + $b;
    }
   // ******* DETECTED: "match" is now a keyword and cannot be used to define a
function
    public function match(string $str, float $f)
    {
          return str_contains($str, $f);
    }
  // ******* DETECTED: "mixed" is now a keyword and cannot be used to define a
function
   public function mixed(string $str, int $factor = 1)
    {
          $new   = '';
          for ($x = 0; $x < strlen($str); $x++) {
               $new .= chr(ord($str[$x]) + $factor);
          }
           return $new;
     }
     public function getConf(string $key)
     {
         return $this->config[$key] ?? NULL;
    }
}
```

As you can see, our new PHP 7 to 8 code converter performed the conversions where no intervention was required. Where Rector was unable to make a determination, it added a `DETECTED` comment along with change advice.

We then ran PHPStan, with the following results:

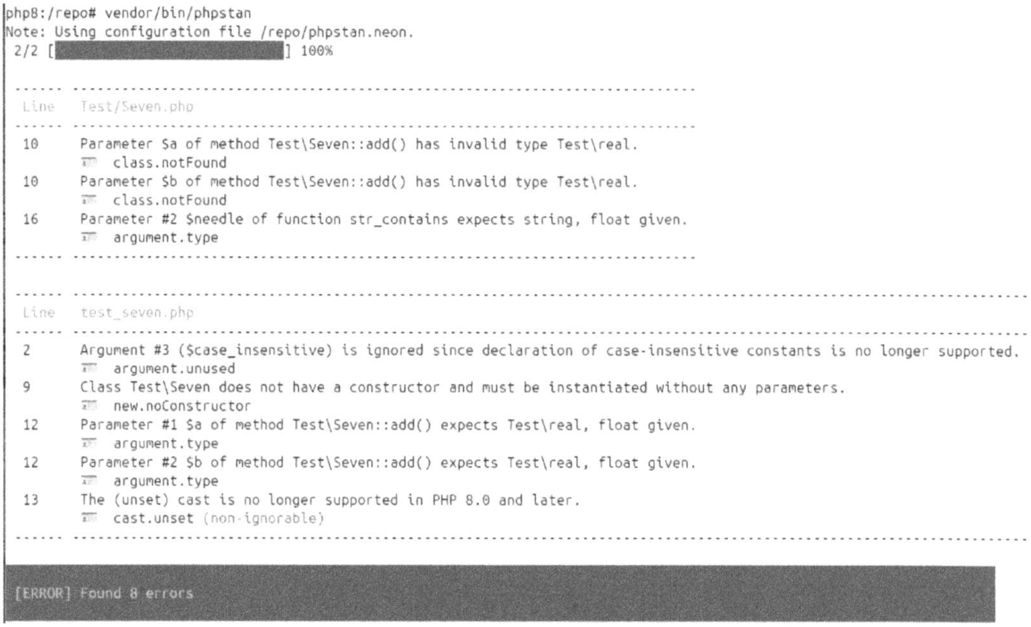

Figure 1.10 – PHPStan results post-conversion

We could then follow up by addressing the issues raised by PHPStan.

The key takeaway from this recipe is that AI is an excellent coding assistant that can also help you discover new ways to develop your code. AI should not be used to replace deterministic upgrade tools. Instead, consider using AI to support architectural decisions and best-practice alignment especially when guided by clear context about the existing codebase and coding standards.

2

Using PHP 8 High Performance Features

In this chapter, we'll show you how to leverage PHP 8's high-performance features through practical recipes. You'll learn how to effectively use Generators to vastly reduce memory usage when processing large data sets, such as multi-gigabyte files. Another recipe demonstrates how to use the SPL's `RecursiveDirectoryIterator` and related classes to traverse directory trees. In the last two recipes you'll discover how to implement OPcache to bypass script interpretation overhead by caching byte code, and use PHP 8's **Just-In-Time** (**JIT**) compiler to generate and cache machine code. Using code that generates a Mandelbrot set, you'll see how OPcache and JIT can produce up to a 70% reduction in execution time.

This chapter features the following recipes:

- Using a generator to speed up large file iteration
- Using the recursive directory iterator
- Using OPcache to boost performance
- Taking the next step with JIT

Using a generator to speed up large file iteration

Functions such as `file_get_contents()` and `file()` are quick and easy to use; however, owing to memory limitations, they quickly cause problems when dealing with massive files. The default setting for the `php.ini::memory_limit` setting is 128 megabytes. Accordingly, any file larger than this will not be loaded. You could override this limit using `ini_set()`; however, at some point you are going to need to process a file that vastly exceeds any reasonable PHP memory limit.

Another consideration when parsing through massive files is how quickly your function or class method produces output. When producing user output, for example, the traditional approach is to accumulate output in an array which is then returned as output. Unfortunately, this approach might have an adverse impact on memory and resource usage. It might be better to create a **generator**, and use the `yield` keyword to produce immediate results.

Getting ready

As mentioned before, the `file*` functions (that is, `file_get_contents()`), are not suitable for large files. The simple reason is that these functions, at one point, have the entire contents of the file represented in memory. Your first inclination might be to switch to the `f*` functions (that is, `fopen()`). In a slight twist, however, instead of using the `f*` functions directly, we will use the `SplFileObject` class, which is included in the **SPL** (**Standard PHP Library**).

To test this recipe we'll also need to download *War and Peace* from the Project Gutenberg website. From a terminal window, change to the `/path/to/php8cookbook` directory, open a shell into the PHP 8 container using: `./admin.sh shell php8`. In the container shell, change to the `/repo/data` directory and download the text for *War and Peace* with this command:

```
curl -o war_and_peace.txt https://gutenberg.org/cache/epub/2600/pg2600.txt
```

How to do it...

1. First, we define a `Cookbook\Iterator\LargeFile` class with the appropriate properties and constants, which you can see in the code block ahead. As you may recall from previous chapters, source code is in various directories that branch off the `/path/to/php8cookbook/src` folder. Thus, the `LargeFile.php` file is located in the `Iterator` directory which is directly off the `src` folder.
   You'll note that we implement `IteratorAggregate`, which mandates a method `getIterator()` that returns a `Traversable` instance. We do this to make class usage more flexible. For example, this practice allows this class to be used as the primary target of a `foreach()` loop.

```
<?php
namespace Cookbook\Iterator;
use Exception;
use InvalidArgumentException;
use SplFileObject;
use ArrayObject;
use Generator;
```

```
use Traversable;
use IteratorAggregate;
class LargeFile implements IteratorAggregate {
  const ERROR_UNABLE = 'ERROR: Unable to open file';
  const ERROR_TYPE   = 'ERROR: Type must be "ByLength", "ByLine" or
"ByArrayObj"';
  protected $file;
  protected $allowedTypes = ['ByLine', 'ByLength', 'ByArrayObj'];
```

2. We then define a `__construct()` method that accepts a filename as an argument and populates the `$file` property with an `SplFileObject` instance. This is also a good place to throw an exception if the file does not exist. This technique is referred to as *failing early*:

```
public function __construct(string $filename, string $mode = 'r',
    // the last two parameters use PHP 8 constructor argument promotion
    public string $delim = ',', public bool $hasHeaders = TRUE) {
    if (!file_exists($filename)) {
        $message = __METHOD__ . ' : ' . self::ERROR_UNABLE . PHP_EOL;
        $message .= strip_tags($filename) . PHP_EOL;
        throw new Exception($message); }
    $this->file = new SplFileObject($filename, $mode);
}
```

> **Note**
>
> The concept of *Failing early* boils down to validating assumptions as soon as possible and stopping execution right away if something goes wrong. Otherwise, you run the risk of letting invalid data continue through the code. In a PHP class method, this might mean checking required arguments, object state, permissions, or configuration at the start of the method and throwing an Exception if they are invalid. This makes bugs easier to find, prevents hidden side effects, and keeps later code simpler because it can assume inputs are valid. For example, a method might throw an `InvalidArgumentException` if an ID is empty before attempting a database lookup.

3. We then define a method `fileIteratorByArrayObj()` that uses a traditional approach where we append lines to an `ArrayObject` instance, and simply return the instance:

```
protected function fileIteratorByArrayObj() : Traversable {
    $lines = new ArrayObject();
    while (!$this->file->eof()) {
        $line = trim($this->file->fgets() ?? '');
        if (!empty($line)) $lines[] = $line;
    }
    return $lines;
}
```

4. Next, we define a method `fileIteratorByLine()` which uses `SplFileObject::fgets()` to read one line of the file at a time and does not count empty lines. It's not a bad idea to create a `fileIteratorByLength()` method that does the same thing but uses `SplFileObject::fread()` instead. The method that uses `SplFileObject::fgets()` would be suitable for text files that include linefeeds. The other method could be used if parsing a large binary file:

> **Note**
>
> Note that the return data type of this method is `Generator`. That is because instead of building and returning an array, which consumes memory and resources, we `yield` each line, one at a time. Effectively, this method is a form of iteration. Although this method returns a value, that value is only available after all iteration has completed.

```
protected function fileIteratorByLine(): Generator {
    $count = 0;
    while (!$this->file->eof()) {
        $line = trim($this->file->fgets() ?? '');
        if (!empty($line)) {
            yield $line . PHP_EOL;
            $count++;
        }
    }
    return $count; // only available post-iteration
}
```

```
protected function fileIteratorByLength(
      $numBytes = 1024) : Generator {
  $count = 0;
  while (!$this->file->eof()) {
    yield $this->file->fread($numBytes);
    $count++;
  }
  return $count;
}
```

5. Finally, we define a `getIterator()` method that allows us to choose which iterator to use (i.e. ByLine or ByArrayObj). Defining this method also satisfies the requirements of `IteratorAggregate`. This method accepts as arguments either `ByLine`, `ByArrayObj`, or `ByLength`, defined in the previous steps. This method also needs to accept `$numBytes` in case `ByLength` is called:

```
public function getIterator($type = 'ByLine', $numBytes = NULL) : iterable
{
    if(!in_array($type, $this->allowedTypes)) {
        $message = __METHOD__ . ' : '  . self::ERROR_TYPE . PHP_EOL;
        throw new InvalidArgumentException($message);
    }
    $method = 'fileIterator' . $type;
    if (!empty($numBytes)) {
        return $this->$method($numBytes);
    } else {
        return $this->$method();
    }
}
```

6. In the `/path/to/php8cookbook/Chapter02` directory, we create two calling program scripts. The first script, `ch02_iterating_file_normal.php`, invokes the traditional approach. The second script, `ch02_iterating_file_generator.php`, produces a `Generator` instance. Let's look at the first calling program. We invoke the Composer autoloader, and define the location of the target file. We then get a `LargeFile` instance, and grab an iterator instance based upon `ArrayObject`. We then run through the file

line by line, collecting the lines into an array, and calculating word count. At the end we display elapsed time and memory usage:

```
<?php
require __DIR__ . '/../../vendor/autoload.php';
$fn = __DIR__ . '/../../data/war_and_peace.txt';
try {
    $start = microtime(TRUE);
    $largeFile = new Cookbook\Iterator\LargeFile($fn);
    $iterator = $largeFile->getIterator('ByArrayObj');
    $words = 0;
    foreach ($iterator as $line) {
        echo $line; $words += str_word_count($line); }
        echo str_repeat('-', 52) . PHP_EOL;
        printf("%-40s : %8d\n", 'Total Words', $words);
        printf("%-40s : %8.2f\n", 'Average Words Per Line',
             ($words / $iterator->count()));
        printf("%-40s : %2.6f\n", 'Elapsed Time', (
            microtime(TRUE) - $start));
        printf("%-40s : %8d\n", 'Peak Memory Usage',
            memory_get_peak_usage());
        echo str_repeat('-', 52) . PHP_EOL;
} catch (Throwable $e) {
    echo $e->getMessage();
}
```

The other calling program, `ch02_iterating_file_generator.php`, does exactly the same as the first, with the difference that it invokes the `fileIteratorByLine()` method. The result is that instead of carrying the file information in an `ArrayObject`, it returns a `Generator`. Here's the second calling program:

```
<?php
require __DIR__ . '/../../vendor/autoload.php';
$fn = __DIR__ . '/../../data/war_and_peace.txt';
try {
    $start = microtime(TRUE);
    $largeFile = new Cookbook\Iterator\LargeFile($fn);
    $iterator = $largeFile->getIterator('ByLine');
    $words = 0;
    foreach ($iterator as $line) {
```

```
            echo $line;
            $words += str_word_count($line);
        }
        echo str_repeat('-', 52) . PHP_EOL;
        printf("%-40s : %8d\n", 'Total Words', $words);
        printf("%-40s : %8.2f\n", 'Average Words Per Line',
            ($words / $iterator->getReturn()));
        printf("%-40s : %2.6f\n", 'Elapsed Time', (
            microtime(TRUE) - $start));
        printf("%-40s : %8d\n", 'Peak Memory Usage',
            memory_get_peak_usage());
        echo str_repeat('-', 52) . PHP_EOL;
    } catch (Throwable $e) {
        echo $e->getMessage();
    }
```

How it works...

Our program code opens a file handle using `SplFileObject`. Benchmarks have shown that using this class gives you a marginal performance boost of around 3% compared with the standard `fopen()`/`fgets()` file handling process. The main advantage of using `SplFileObject` compared to `fopen()`/`fgets()` is that all the needed methods are embedded in the class, and it fits neatly into the overall OOP paradigm. However, unlike `file_get_contents()`, using `SplFileObject` allows you to read files of any size one line at a time.

The expected output for the Project Gutenberg version of *War and Peace* is too large to show in its entirety. Here are the last few lines of output from the calling program that uses ArrayObject, `ch02_iterating_file_normal.php`:

```
php8:/repo# php src/Chapter02/ch02_iterating_file_normal.php
... previous output omitted
Most people start at our website which has the main PG searchfacility:
www.gutenberg.org. This website includes information about Project
Gutenberg,including how to make donations to the Project Gutenberg LiteraryArchive
Foundation, how to help produce our new eBooks, and how tosubscribe to our email
newsletter to hear about new eBooks.
----------------------------------------------------
Total Words                                :     584705
Average Words Per Line                     :     11
Elapsed Time                               :     0.211378
```

```
Peak Memory Usage                          :     7,191,680
---------------------------------------------------
```

Here is the output from `ch02_iterating_file_generator.php`:

```
php8:/repo# php src/Chapter02/ch02_iterating_file_generator.php
... previous output omitted
Most people start at our website which has the main PG searchfacility:
www.gutenberg.org. This website includes information about Project
Gutenberg,including how to make donations to the Project Gutenberg LiteraryArchive
Foundation, how to help produce our new eBooks, and how tosubscribe to our email
newsletter to hear about new eBooks.
---------------------------------------------------
Total Words                              :     584705
Average Words Per Line                   :     11
Elapsed Time                             :     0.173467
Peak Memory Usage                        :     1,966,272
```

The first two data points, the Total Words, and Average Words Per Line figures are the same. However you'll notice a significant difference in time and a massive difference in memory usage. The more traditional approach required 0.211378 seconds compared with the Generator approach, which took 0.173467 seconds. Thus, in terms of time, using a Generator took approximately 20% less time. Given that this is a relatively trivial example, imagine the performance gain you could achieve using this approach.

When we turn our attention to memory usage, the difference is substantive. The more traditional approach used a whopping 7,191,680 bytes of memory whereas using a Generator only used 1,966,272 bytes. Put in other terms, the Generator approach used 75% less memory than the traditional approach. When you consider that the average PHP session is only allocated 128 M of memory, using more than 7 M can really eat into available memory resources and can easily result in an out-of-memory error condition.

There's more...

For more information on the concept of *failing early*, have a look at an excellent article titled *Fail Fast*, written by Jim Shore, on Martin Fowler's website. Here's the link: `https://martinfowler.com/ieeeSoftware/failFast.pdf`.

Using the recursive directory iterator

Getting a list of files in a directory is extremely easy. Traditionally, developers have used the `glob()` function for this purpose. To recursively get a list of all files and directories from a specific point in a directory tree is more problematic. This recipe takes advantage of an **SPL (Standard PHP Library)** class `RecursiveDirectoryIterator`, which will serve this purpose admirably.

What this class does is to parse the directory tree finding the first child, then it follows the branches until there are no more children, and then it stops! Unfortunately, this is not what we want. Somehow, we need to get the `RecursiveDirectoryIterator` to continue parsing every tree and branch, from a given starting point, until there are no more files or directories. It so happens there is a marvelous class, `RecursiveIteratorIterator`, that does exactly that. By wrapping `RecursiveDirectoryIterator` inside `RecursiveIteratorIterator`, we accomplish a complete traversal of any directory tree.

Note

Warning!

Be very careful where you start the filesystem traversal. If you start at the root directory, you could end up crashing your server as the recursion process will not stop until all files and directories have been located!

Getting ready

As we'll be using classes from the SPL in this recipe, there are no specific tasks to be performed prior to diving into the recipe.

How to do it...

1. First, in the `/path/to/php8cookbook/src/Iterator` folder, we create a file `Directory.php` that represents the `Cookbook\Iterator\Directory` class. First we define the appropriate properties and constants and use external classes:

```
<?php
namespace Cookbook\Iterator;

use Iterator;
use InvalidArgumentException;
use RegexIterator;
use Generator;
use RecursiveIteratorIterator;
use RecursiveDirectoryIterator;
class Directory {
    const ERROR_UNABLE =
```

```
        'ERROR: Unable to read directory';
    protected Iterator $rdi;
```

2. The constructor creates a `RecursiveDirectoryIterator` instance inside `RecursiveIteratorIterator` based on a directory path:

```
// set up recursive directory iterator
public function __construct(public string $path) {
    if (!file_exists($path)) {
        throw new InvalidArgumentException(
            static::ERROR_UNABLE);
    }
    $this->rdi = new RecursiveIteratorIterator(
        new RecursiveDirectoryIterator($path),
        RecursiveIteratorIterator::SELF_FIRST
    );
}
```

3. Next, we decide what to do with the iteration. One possibility is to mimic the output of the Linux `ls -l -R` command. Notice that we use the `yield` keyword, effectively making this method into a **Generator**, which can then be called from the outside. Each object produced by the directory iteration is an SPL `FileInfo` object, which can give us useful information on the file. Here is how this method might look:

```
// mimics Linux "ls -l"
public function ls(string $pattern='') : Generator {
    $outerIterator = (!empty($pattern))
    ? $this->regex($this->rdi, $pattern)
    : $this->rdi;
    foreach($outerIterator as $obj){
        if ($obj->isDir()) {
            if ($obj->getFileName() == '..') continue;
            $line = $obj->getPath() . PHP_EOL;
        } else {
            $line = sprintf(
                '%4s %1d %4s %4s %10d %12s %-40s',
                substr(sprintf('%o',
                    $obj->getPerms()), -4),
                ($obj->getType() == 'file') ? 1 : 2,
                $obj->getOwner(),
```

```
                    $obj->getGroup(),
                    $obj->getSize(),
                    date('M d Y H:i', $obj->getATime()),
                    $obj->getFileName()
                );
            }
            yield $line;
        }
    }
```

4. You may have noticed that the method call includes a file pattern. We need a way of filtering the recursion to only include files that match. There is another iterator available from the SPL that perfectly suits this need: the `RegexIterator` class:

```
// applies a regex (regular expression) to filter the iteration
protected function regex($iterator, $pattern) {
    $pattern = '!^.' .
        str_replace('.', '\\.', $pattern) . '$!';
    return new RegexIterator($iterator, $pattern);
}
```

5. Finally, here is another method, but this time we will mimic the DOS `dir /s` command:

```
// mimics DOS "dir /s"
public function dir(string $pattern='') : Generator {
    $outerIterator = (!empty($pattern))
        ? $this->regex($this->rdi, $pattern)
        : $this->rdi;
    foreach($outerIterator as $name => $obj){
        yield $name;
    }
}
} // closing bracket for this class
```

6. Next, in the `/path/to/php8cookbook/src/Chapter02` directory, we define a calling program, `ch02_recursive_directory_iterator.php`. We use `$argv[]` to capture command-line parameters for starting path and type of output:

```
<?php
require __DIR__ . '/../../vendor/autoload.php';
$path = $argv[1] ?? realpath(__DIR__ . '/../');
$action = $argv[2] ?? 'ls';
$dirObj = new Cookbook\Iterator\Directory($path);
```

7. Then, in a `try {...} catch () {...}` block, we make a call to our two methods, using an example directory path:

```
try {
    if ($action === 'dir') {
        $label = 'Mimics "dir /s" ';
        $result = $dirObj->dir('*.php');
    } else {
        $label = 'Mimics "ls -l -R" ';
        $result = $dirObj->ls('*.php');
    }
    echo $label . PHP_EOL;
    foreach ($result as $info) echo $info . PHP_EOL;
} catch (Throwable $e) {
    echo $e->getMessage();
}
```

How it works...

Our `Cookbook\Iterator\Directory` class creates a `RecursiveDirectoryIterator` instance nested inside a `RecursiveIteratorIterator` instance. This provides the full recursion needed to traverse the directory tree. We then rely upon the `ls()` and `dir()` methods to format the output as appropriate, making this class useful for both Linux and Windows users.

The output for `ls()` might look something like this:

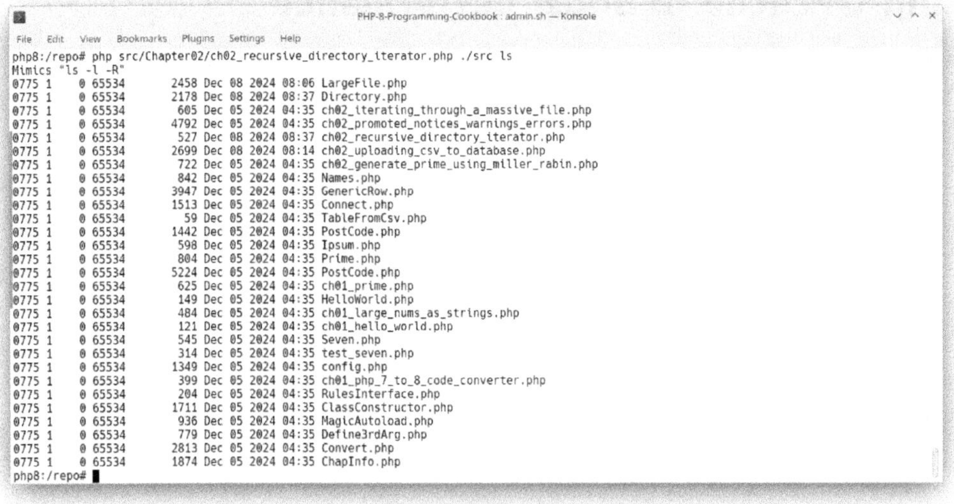

Figure 2.1 – Directory Iterator ls

The output for `dir()` might appear as follows:

Figure 2.2 – Directory Iterator dir

Using OPcache to boost performance

One of the disadvantages of scripted languages such as Perl, Python, and PHP, is that for every individual application request, the script must go through the stages shown in *Figure 2.3*:

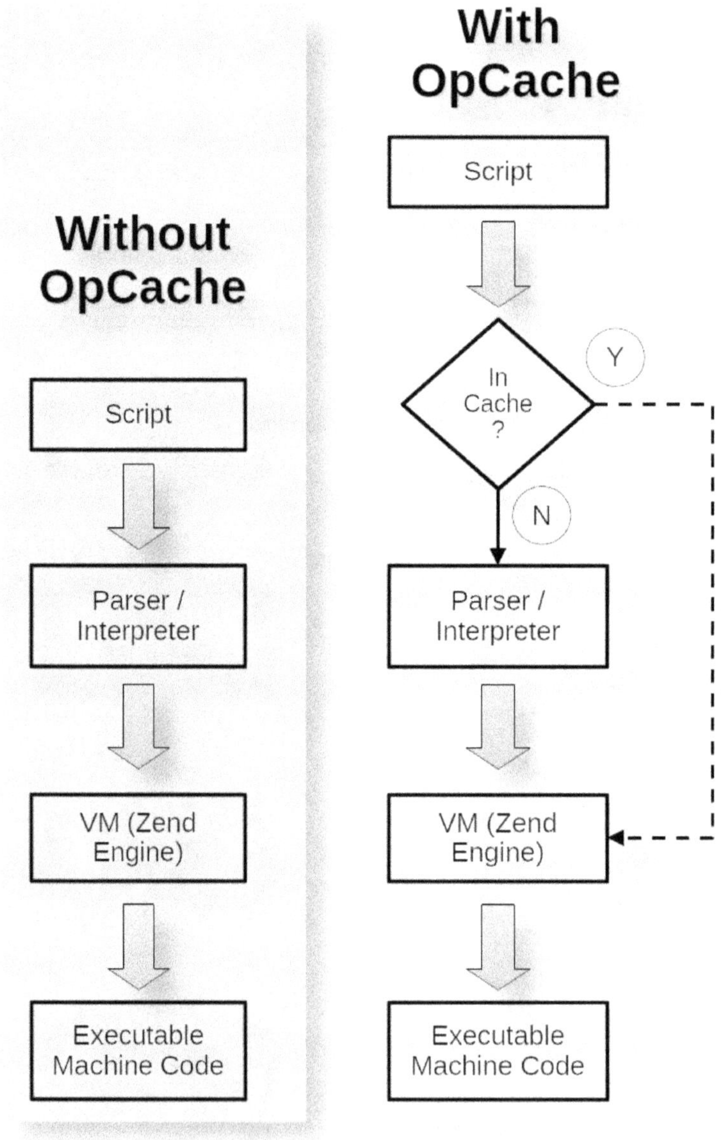

Figure 2.3 – Execution flow with and without OPcache

The Interpreter, also called the Parser, scans the script and produces a compressed binary pseudo-code equivalent of the script known as **byte code** or **opcode**. If you do a dump of the byte code you can see that it somewhat resembles assembler language, which is the next step before conversion to machine language.

The byte code cannot be executed directly, however. Just as you can't expect a computer to execute a flowchart, the byte code is almost a universal language, which must then be translated into a language the CPU can understand. This is the job of the **virtual machine**, the **Zend Engine**, which is installed as part of installing PHP. For those readers who are familiar with Java programming, when you compile a Java application, the resulting byte code must then be converted to machine code by the **Java Virtual Machine** (**JVM**), which is directly analogous to the PHP Zend Engine.

Getting ready

The default execution flow shown on the left side of *Figure 2.3* is not a highly performing arrangement. Historically, most server administrators enabled the original **APC** (**Alternative PHP Cache**) (`https://pecl.php.net/package/APC`) extension, which was later replaced as the default byte code cache solution by OPcache starting with PHP 5.5.

Looking at the right side of *Figure 2.3*, you can see that when OPcache is enabled, PHP first checks to see if this web application has been cached. If so, it retrieves the byte code from cache and turns control immediately over to the Zend Engine. This saves quite a bit of time for program execution as the interpretation stage is bypassed.

Another important consideration is that any extension that affects the actual operation of the Zend Engine, such as OPcache, needs to be loaded with the `zend_extension` INI directive.

To test the effectiveness of OPcache, we can create a simple class `Services\Mandelbrot` in the `/path/to/php8cookbook/src/Services` folder. This class generates a **Mandelbrot set**, a famous fractal pattern created by repeatedly applying a simple mathematical formula to complex numbers and coloring points based on whether they stay bounded or fly off to infinity. Here is the opening portion of the class:

```
<?php
namespace Cookbook\Services;
class Mandelbrot {
    public static int $bailout = 16;
    public static int $maxIterations = 50_000;
```

The `generate()` method performs the overall set generation:

```
public function generate() {
    $txt = '';
    $d1  = microtime(1);
    for ($y = -39; $y < 39; $y++) {
        for ($x = -39; $x < 39; $x++) {
            if ($this->iterate($x/40.0, $y/40.0)
                === 0) {
                $txt .= '*';
            } else {
                $txt .= ' ';
            }
        }
        $txt .= PHP_EOL;
    }
    $d2 = microtime(1);
    $diff = $d2 - $d1;
    return $txt . 'Elapsed Time: ' . $diff;
}
```

The `iterate()` method does the actual work:

```
public function iterate($x,$y)
{
    $cr = $y-0.5;
    $ci = $x;
    $zr = 0.0;
    $zi = 0.0;
    $i = 0;
    while (true) {
        $i++;
        $temp = $zr * $zi;
        $zr2 = $zr * $zr;
        $zi2 = $zi * $zi;
        $zr = $zr2 - $zi2 + $cr;
        $zi = $temp + $temp + $ci;
        if ($zi2 + $zr2 > self::$bailout)
            return $i;
        if ($i > self::$maxIterations)
            return 0;
```

```
    }
}
```

We then create a calling program `ch02_mandelbrot_test.php` located in the `/path/to/cookbook/src/Chapter02` folder that produces the Mandelbrot set:

```
<?php
include __DIR__ . '/../../vendor/autoload.php';
use Cookbook\Services\Mandelbrot;

$output = (new Mandelbrot())->generate();
if (empty($_SERVER['HTTP_HOST'])) {
    echo $output;
} else {
    echo '<pre>' . $output . '</pre>';
}
```

How to do it...

1. The first thing you need to do is to install and enable the OPcache extension. If you are compiling PHP from source, you can add the `--enable-opcache` flag when you run `configure`. If you're using ZendPHP, you can use these two commands to install and enable OPcache:

```
# zendphpctl ext install opcache
# zendphpctl ext enable opcache
```

2. Otherwise, the extension can be installed using your normal package management system. For example, in the Docker/Podman container associated with this book, we use `apk add php ${PHP_VERSION}-opcache`.
3. Once you have the OPcache extension installed, you can enable it in the `php.ini` file. At a minimum, you must also allocate memory for the extension to be effective. This can be accomplished in the `php.ini` file using the `opcache.memory_consumption` setting. The number you assign is in megabytes. Bear in mind that the memory is taken from your server, so please be sure you have enough RAM.
4. In the container provided with the book, you can find the primary `php.ini` file here: `/usr/local/php8/etc/php.ini`.

5. Here's a snippet of the php.ini file showing the recommended settings:

```
zend_extension=opcache.so
opcache.enable=1
opcache.enable_cli=1
opcache.memory_consumption=128
opcache.interned_strings_buffer=8
opcache.max_accelerated_files=4000
opcache.revalidate_freq=60
```

6. A full list of settings is found here: https://www.php.net/manual/en/opcache.configuration.php.

> Note
>
> **PHP INI Files**
>
> In most PHP installations, individual extensions are not loaded in the primary php.ini file. Instead, you will typically find a directory titled mods-available, found under the /etc/php/PHP_VERSION/* directory structure, containing a series of individual *.ini files. Each individual ini file loads only that extension.
>
> When you want to enable an extension, you create a symbolic link between the mods-available directory and a conf.d directory used when PHP runs. If, for example, you're using PHP-FPM and PHP 8.4, the directory with symbolic links might be located in /etc/php/8.4/fpm/conf.d/*.

7. On the test computer we ran the calling program three times with OPcache disabled using the browser. For a run of 50,000 iterations, the average time over three executions was 3.723 seconds.
8. We then enabled OPcache by adding the typical settings shown above to the file /usr/local/php8/etc/php.ini in the Podman container:

```
nano /usr/local/php8/etc/php.ini
# Here are the new settings:
zend_extension=opcache.so
opcache.enable=1
opcache.enable_cli=1
opcache.memory_consumption=256
```

```
opcache.interned_strings_buffer=8
opcache.max_accelerated_files=4000
opcache.revalidate_freq=60
opcache.fast_shutdown=1
```

9. We then had to restart PHP-FPM to force PHP to reload the `php.ini` file settings. If you're running this experiment from the command line, the `php.ini` file is read as part of each run, but when running through a web server using the PHP-FPM process, the `php.ini` file settings are loaded only during PHP-FPM startup.

10. For most Linux servers you can use `systemctl` to restart the PHP-FPM process. Because our demo environment is using Alpine Linux, however, all you need to do is to locate the **process ID** (**PID**) using the `ps` (process status) command, kill the process, and then reload it:

```
php8:/repo# ps
PID   USER     TIME  COMMAND
    1 root      0:00 {startup.sh} /bin/bash /tmp/startup.sh
    9 root      0:00 /bin/bash
   27 root      0:00 php-fpm: master process (/usr/local/php8/etc/php-
fpm.conf)
   28 nobody    0:00 php-fpm: pool www
   29 nobody    0:00 php-fpm: pool www
   79 root      0:00 sleep 60
   81 root      0:00 ps
php8:/repo# kill 27
php8:/repo# /usr/local/php8/sbin/php-fpm
php8:/repo# ps
PID   USER     TIME  COMMAND
    1 root      0:00 {startup.sh} /bin/bash /tmp/startup.sh
    9 root      0:00 /bin/bash
   79 root      0:00 sleep 60
   83 root      0:00 php-fpm: master process (/usr/local/php8/etc/php-
fpm.conf)
   84 nobody    0:00 php-fpm: pool www
   85 nobody    0:00 php-fpm: pool www
```

11. After launching the Podman/Docker containers associated with this book, we had a look at the home page (http://localhost:8888). From the `phpinfo()` output, we confirmed that OPcache was up and running (as shown in *Figure 2.4*):

Zend OPcache	
Opcode Caching	Up and Running
Optimization	Enabled
SHM Cache	Enabled
File Cache	Disabled
JIT	Disabled

Figure 2.4 – Using phpinfo() to confirm OPcache status

12. The time for the first run was 3.524. The next three runs averaged 3.348, which means we boosted performance by around 5%. This is a nice improvement, but let's see if we can improve the time even more by implementing JIT.

How it works...

When we run the calling program to generate the Mandelbrot set, OPcache parses the script and compiles the code into byte code which is immediately cached. Subsequent runs then draw from this cache, bypassing the parsing process. However, the second stage that involves converting the byte code into machine code is still required on each program run.

You'll note that although OPcache gives us a nice performance boost, the performance gain is far from impressive. To get even better performance requires work at the machine code level. This aspect is covered by the PHP 8 **Just-In-Time** (**JIT**) compiler discussed in the next recipe.

Taking the next step with JIT

The limitation of OPcache by itself is that you'll only see a performance boost in terms of the initial interpretation phase. In the case of applications like generating a Mandelbrot set, it's possible that further gains can be made by activating the JIT.

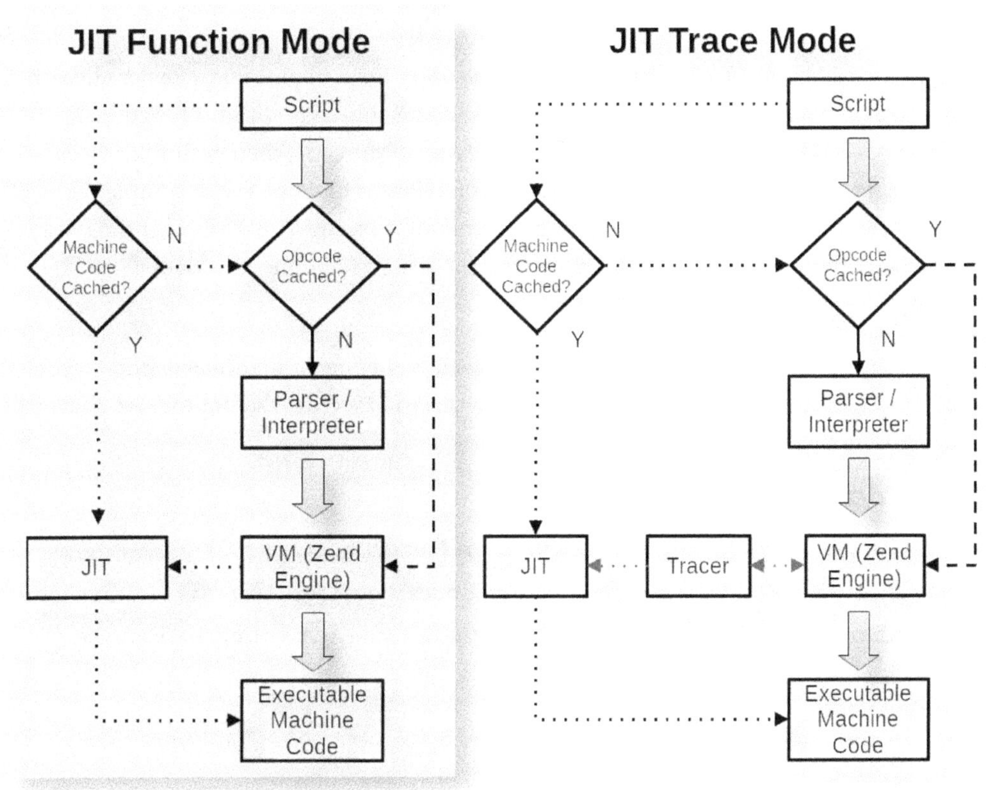

Figure 2.5 – JIT execution flow

As you can see from *Figure 2.5*, the PHP 8 just-in-time compiler is able to generate and cache machine code in memory. This feature alone is enough to give you a nice performance boost as PHP bypasses the interpretation and the compile phases. If the machine code has been cached, PHP retrieves the machine code and jumps to execution immediately. Effectively, this means that your PHP applications can run at compiled C language speed!

PHP 8's JIT compiler provides two operating modes that map to different types of code patterns:

- **JIT Function Mode**: The PHP 8 JIT compiler Function mode uses an older algorithm that compiles entire functions at once. When a function is called frequently enough to meet the JIT threshold, the compiler generates machine code for the entire function. This mode is generally faster for code with fewer branches and loops, as it optimizes the function as a whole, potentially reducing function call overhead and improving performance for straightforward, frequently called functions.

- **JIT Trace Mode**: The JIT Trace mode, on the other hand, represents a newer algorithm that compiles only the most frequently executed C sub-calls within a function. It records and analyzes the actual execution traces of the code, then optimizes these specific *hot* paths. This mode can be more effective for functions with complex control flow, as it focuses on optimizing the most common execution paths, potentially leading to better performance for code with many conditional statements or loops.

Getting ready

Before running the code in this recipe, in order to get a proper performance benchmark, you should first disable JIT in the php.ini file. In the *How to do it...* section that follows we show you how to enable or disable JIT.

How to do it...

1. To test the impact of JIT we can use the same Mandelbrot class as before.
2. We then enable JIT by assigning 64 M to the `opcache.jit_buffer_size` setting in the `php.ini` file. We also set a value of "on" to the `opcache.jit` setting. Here are the settings we added:

```
opcache.jit=on
opcache.jit_buffer_size=64M
```

3. Next, we restarted PHP-FPM using the command shown in the earlier section.
4. Using `phpinfo()` we confirm that OPcache is running and that JIT is enabled (as seen in *Figure 2.6*):

Zend OPcache

Opcode Caching	Up and Running
Optimization	Enabled
SHM Cache	Enabled
File Cache	Disabled
JIT	On

Figure 2.6 – Using phpinfo() to confirm JIT operation

5. Now, we can run the calling program `ch02_mandelbrot_test.php` again three times to get the new average time. Using the tracing mode, the average run time dropped to an astounding 1.140 seconds! This means that the JIT execution time is approximately three times faster.

How it works...

JIT operates as a part of OPcache, which means that OPcache must be enabled for JIT to work. JIT memory is taken out of the memory allocated for OPcache. Use the `opcache.jit_buffer_size` php.ini setting to assign memory to the JIT process. The value you specify here must be smaller than the `opcache.memory_consumption` setting. The value is in bytes, and you can use the K, M, or G suffixes (e.g., 64M for 64 megabytes). Setting this to `0` effectively disables JIT compilation.

Arguably the most important JIT setting is `opcache.jit`. *Table 2.1* summarizes the possible options:

opcache.*Setting	**Explanation**
`disable`	Deactivates JIT completely.
`off`	Turns off JIT, but allows you to turn it on selectively using `ini_set()` at runtime.
`on / tracing`	These two settings are the same and are used to activate JIT and set it to use the tracing algorithm.
`function`	Turns on JIT and sets it to the older function algorithm.
4 digits that represent **CRTO**	• **C** provides granular CPU optimization flags • **R** sets register allocation • **T** tells JIT when it should be triggered • **O** represents the optimization level See: the JIT settings in the PHP documentation: `https://www.php.net/manual/en/opcache.configuration.php#ini.opcache.jit`

Table 2.1 – Possible opcache.jit settings

As an example, have a look at *Table 2.2*, which shows how a number of important options might be set in the development and production environments:

Setting	Development	Production
`validate_timestamps`	1	0
`revalidate_freq`	2	0
`memory_consumption`	64	128+
`max_accelerated_files`	4000	10,000+
JIT	off	on
Preloading	off	on

Table 2.2 – Typical JIT settings: development vs. production

OPcache periodically checks (every `opcache.revalidate_freq` seconds) whether your PHP files have been modified on disk and automatically refreshes the cache. This is preferred for development environments or frequently-updated codebases, since changes appear without manual intervention. The trade-off is a small but real performance cost due to recurring filesystem stat calls on every request (or every N seconds).

When disabled, OPcache skips those checks entirely. This is the best choice for stable production deployments. The downside is that any code change requires a manual cache reset using `opcache_reset()`, `opcache_invalidate()`, or a web server restart. It also affects related directives. For example, `opcache.revalidate_freq` is ignored when disabled, and features like `opcache.enable_file_override` risk returning outdated results.

There's more...

For more information on how OPcache and the JIT operate, have a look at an excellent article by Matthew Weir O'Phinney titled *Exploring the New PHP JIT Compiler*, which you can find here: `https://www.zend.com/blog/exploring-new-php-jit-compiler`.

OPcache functions are shown here: `https://www.php.net/opcache`.

You can review the complete list of OPcache and JIT settings here: `https://www.php.net/manual/en/opcache.configuration.php`.

3

Working with PHP Functional Programming

This chapter explores essential PHP functional programming techniques enhanced by Generative AI capabilities. Readers will discover how to leverage AI prompts to develop robust data validation functions, implement type hinting for improved code accuracy, and utilize PHP 8.4's new `array_find()` function for efficient multi-dimensional array searches, as well as modern match expressions for decision-making logic.

In this chapter we'll cover the following recipes:

- Using GenAI prompts to develop PHP data validation functions
- Hinting at data types to improve AI code generation accuracy
- Searching multi-dimensional arrays using `array_find()`
- Making decisions using `match` expressions

> Note
>
> **Download the code bundle and the PDF version of this book**
>
> Your purchase includes a DRM-free PDF copy of this book, the code bundle, and a range of exclusive benefits. To unlock everything, follow the *Free benefits with your book* section in the *Preface*.

Using GenAI prompts to develop PHP data validation functions

To take the most advantage of GenAI's ability to generate program code, break down complex tasks into functions. In this chapter, we focus strictly on small, focused functions. In the next chapter, we delve into classes and methods used for larger scale applications. In some cases, you can simply describe what you want to accomplish to your preferred AI platform. However, to reduce the amount of refining you'll need to do and to retain control over the overall result, it's best to instruct the AI to write code one function at a time.

Getting ready

The end result of this recipe is a PHP script that produces an HTML form that accepts username and address information. We will use GenAI to create a series of functions that generate the HTML and sanitize and validate the submitted information.

How to do it...

1. The first prompt we'll define, requests our preferred GenAI platform (in this case Claude 4.7 Sonnet) to define a PHP function that generates the HTML for a name and address form:

```
Create a PHP function that generates the HTML code needed for a name and
address form.
The form should accept UTF8 encoded input, and address an English speaking
audience.
Here is a list of form elements:
1. "first_name" is the user's first name, limited to 20 characters.
2. "last_name" is the user's last name, limited to 40 characters.
3. "address1" is the first line of address for the user's house or building
number.
4. "address2" is the optional 2nd line of address that can be used for
apartment number, floor number, etc.
5. "city" is the city or town where the user lives.
6. "state_province" is the user's state or province.
7. "post_code" is the user's postal code.
8. "country" is a 2 digit ISO2(ISO 3166-1 alpha-2) country code. Ideally
this should be an HTML SELECT field where the option value is the ISO2
code, and the option label is the full country name (in English).
```

2. The resulting code works OK; however it was rather inflexible in that Claude Sonnet produced the form HTML in its entirety, leaving little room for change. Accordingly, we added this refinement to the above prompt:

```
In the function, represent the form elements in a PHP array where the
element name is the key, and the element label is the value.
In the function, loop through the array, and produce a block of HTML for
each element.
```

3. The final result was quite satisfactory. The AI went a little overboard in that it also provided the opening `<head>` tag and styling, which we removed and placed into the main calling program `index.php`. Here is the function as it stands (minus the opening and closing HTML):

```
function generateNameAddressForm(
    $formAction = '', $formMethod = 'POST') {
    // Define form elements with their labels
    $formElements = [
        'first_name' => 'First Name',
        'last_name' => 'Last Name',
        'address1' => 'Address Line 1',
        // some code omitted
    ];

    // Define field attributes
    $fieldAttributes = [
        'first_name' => ['type' => 'text', 'maxlength' => 20,
'required' => true, 'placeholder' => ''],
        'last_name' => ['type' => 'text', 'maxlength' => 40, 'required' =>
true, 'placeholder' => ''],
        'address1' => ['type' => 'text', 'required' => true, 'placeholder'
=> 'House or building number and street name'],
        // some code omitted
    ];
```

4. Having two separate arrays is not very efficient, so we had to modify the code to combine the two. Here's the result:

```
    $fieldAttrs= [
        'first_name' => ['label' => 'First Name', 'type' => 'text',
```

```
'maxlength' => 20, 'required' => true, 'placeholder' => ''],
        'last_name' => ['label' => 'Last Name', 'type' => 'text',
'maxlength' => 40, 'required' => true, 'placeholder' => ''],
        'address1' => ['label' => 'Address Line 1', 'type' => 'text',
'required' => true, 'placeholder' => 'House or building number and street
name'],
        // some code omitted
    ];
```

5. Next, Sonnet produced an array of key/value pairs where the key is the **ISO2** code (**International Standards Organization** two-letter country codes). It also performed a sort, which ensures a consistent list:

```
    $countries = [
        'AU' => 'Australia',
        // some code omitted
        'VN' => 'Vietnam',
        'YE' => 'Yemen',
        'ZM' => 'Zambia',
        'ZW' => 'Zimbabwe'
    ];
    asort($countries);  // retains the keys!
```

6. The code then starts building the HTML, stored in `$html`: You'll note that the AI added `htmlspecialchars()` without being asked. This change does not affect the program logic and enhances security, so we decided to retain the change:

```
    $html = '<form action="'
        . htmlspecialchars($formAction)
        . '" method="' . $formMethod
        . '" accept-charset="UTF-8">';
```

7. We also had to alter the primary `foreach()` loop, as it was expecting two separate arrays. Here's the code originally produced:

```
    foreach ($formElements as $fieldName => $fieldLabel) {
        $attrs = $fieldAttributes[$fieldName];
        $isRequired = $attrs['required'];
```

8. Here are the alterations we made to account for only one array of form fields:

```
foreach ($fieldAttrs as $fieldName => $fieldInfo){
    $fieldLabel = $fieldInfo['label'];
    $attrs = $fieldInfo;
    unset($attrs['label']);
    $isRequired = $attrs['required']??false;
```

9. Here's the logic that produces the input element label. We cleaned up the code to make it more readable by replacing the `if () {}` clauses generated by the AI with ternary expressions. We also replaced `"\n"` with `PHP_EOL` to make the code more portable:

```
$html .= '<div class="form-group">' . PHP_EOL;
$html .= '<label for="' . $fieldName . '"';
$html .= ($isRequired) ? ' class="required"' : '';
$html .= '>' . $fieldLabel;
$html .= (!$isRequired)
  ? ' <span class="optional">(Optional)</span>'
  : '';
$html .= '</label>' . PHP_EOL;
```

10. Finally, the AI created an `if` statement to check to see if the field was an HTML SELECT or not, processing the output accordingly. To improve readability, we replaced the `if () {}` statements with ternary expressions and used `PHP_EOL`:

```
if ($attrs['type'] === 'select') {
    // Generate select dropdown for country
    $html .= '<select id="' . $fieldName
        . '" name="' . $fieldName . '"';
    $html .= ($isRequired) ? ' required': '';
    $html .= '>' . PHP_EOL;
    $html .= '<option value="">' .
    '-- Select a country --</option>' . PHP_EOL;
    foreach ($countries as $code => $name) {
        $html .= '<option value="' . $code
        . '">' . $name . '</option>' . PHP_EOL;
    }
    $html .= '</select>' . PHP_EOL;
} else {
    // Generate text input
```

```
        $html .= '<input type="' . $attrs['type']
              . '" ';
        $html .= 'id="' . $fieldName . '" ';
        $html .= 'name="' . $fieldName . '"';
        $html .= (isset($attrs['maxlength']))
        ? ' maxlength="' . $attrs['maxlength'] . '"'
        : '';
        $html .= (!empty($attrs['placeholder']))
        ? ' placeholder="' . $attrs['placeholder']
        . '"' : '';
        $html .= ($isRequired) ? ' required' : '';
        $html .= '>' . PHP_EOL . PHP_EOL;
    }
    $html .= '</div>'  . PHP_EOL . PHP_EOL;
```

11. The last part of the new function adds the submit button and closes the form, and returns the HTML:

```
    // Add submit button
    $html .= '<div class="form-group">'
           . '<button type="submit">Submit</button>'
           . '</div>'
           . '</form>';

    return $html;
}
```

12. We then saved the resulting code block into a temporary PHP file.
13. In order to get our AI platform to generate a validation function, we uploaded the temporary file to the AI and requested it add a function to perform validation on submitted form data using this prompt:

```
Add a PHP function to the attached code file that performs validation on
each form field as follows:
1. first_name should have a maximum length of 20 characters and only
contain A-Z, a-z, spaces, commas and periods.
2. last_name should have a maximum length of 40 characters and only contain
A-Z, a-z, spaces, dashes, commas and periods.
3. address1 and address2 should have a maximum length of 64 characters.
4. country should be an ISO2 code that is a key in the $countries array.
```

```
For all input fields, perform trim() and strip_tags().
For all output fields that contain suspect data, use htmlspecialchars() to
prevent potential XSS attacks.
```

14. The result was a virtually unreadable and inefficient series of nested if/then statements. Here's an example from the code produced:

```
if (isset($data['last_name'])) {
    $cleanData['last_name'] = trim(strip_tags($data['last_name']));

    if (empty($cleanData['last_name'])) {
        $errors['last_name'] = 'Last name is required.';
    } elseif (strlen($cleanData['last_name']) > 40) {
        $errors['last_name'] = 'Last name must not exceed 40 characters.';
    } elseif (!preg_match('/^[A-Za-z \-,.]+$/', $cleanData['last_name'])) {
        $errors['last_name'] =
'Last name can only contain letters, spaces, dashes, commas, and periods.';
    }
} else {
    $errors['last_name'] = 'Last name is required.';
}
```

15. Accordingly, we need to be more specific in our prompt. Here's a revised prompt:

```
Modify the attached code file as follows:
1. Move the $fieldAttrs and $countries arrays out of the
generateNameAddressForm() function, and make them input arguments to the
generateNameAddressForm() function.
2. Modify $fieldAttrs array by adding a new key "validator" to the form
element sub-array.
3. The "validator" key should return an anonymous function that performs
validation for that field.
4. Here is the criteria for form field validation:
4A. first_name should have a maximum length of 20 characters and only
contain A-Z, a-z, spaces, commas and periods.
4B. last_name should have a maximum length of 40 characters and only
contain A-Z, a-z, spaces, dashes, commas and periods.
4C. address1, address2, state_province, and city should have a maximum
length of 64 characters.
4D. country should be an ISO2 code that is a key in the $countries array.
5. For all fields, perform trim() and strip_tags().
```

```
6. Create a new function that performs validation on each form field
defined in $fieldAttrs by running the callbacks in the "validator" key
against the submitted form data.
7. The new function will have $fieldAttrs, $countries, and the submitted
form data ($_POST) as input arguments.
```

16. The revised result is much better. The advantage of keeping the `$fieldAttrs` array outside the functions is that we could move it into a separate config file, providing even more flexibility. Here's the first part of the modified `$fieldAttrs` array:

```
$fieldAttrs = [
    'first_name' => [
        'label' => 'First Name',
        'type' => 'text',
        'maxlength' => 20,
        'required' => true,
        'placeholder' => '',
        'validator' => function($value,
                                 $countries = null) {
            $value = trim(strip_tags($value));
            $errors = [];
            if (empty($value)) {
                $errors[] = 'First name is required.';
            } elseif (strlen($value) > 20) {
                $errors[] = 'First name must not exceed 20 characters.';
            } elseif (!preg_match('/^[A-Za-z ,.]+$/', $value)) {
                $errors[] = 'First name can only contain letters, spaces,
punctuation.';
            }
            return ['value' => $value, 'errors' => $errors];
        }
    ],
    // other code omitted
```

17. You'll note that the generated code does not take into account the possibility that this is an international website. Thus it would be advised to add the `u` modifier. This modifier instructs `preg_match()` to treat the string being examined as UTF-8 encoded. Likewise, it might be advisable to use `mb_strlen()` in place of `strlen()` to account for multi-byte encoding.

18. Our regenerated function to create the form has been modified as shown here. We also had to add a statement to remove the `validator` key when the HTML form input elements are created:

```
function generateNameAddressForm($fieldAttrs, $countries, $formAction =
'', $formMethod = 'POST') {
    // code omitted
    foreach ($fieldAttrs as $fieldName => $fieldInfo) {
        $fieldLabel = $fieldInfo['label'];
        $attrs = $fieldInfo;
        unset($attrs['label']);
        unset($attrs['validator']);
        // code omitted
```

19. The validation function was created pretty much as described in the prompt:

```
function validateFormData($fieldAttrs,
                          $countries, $formData) {
    $allErrors = [];
    $cleanData = [];

    foreach ($fieldAttrs as $fieldName => $fieldInfo){
        $value = isset($formData[$fieldName])
               ? $formData[$fieldName] : '';
        if (isset($fieldInfo['validator']) &&
is_callable($fieldInfo['validator'])) {
            $result = $fieldInfo['validator']
                      ($value, $countries);
            $cleanData[$fieldName] = $result['value'];
            if (!empty($result['errors'])) {
                $allErrors[$fieldName] =
                    $result['errors'];
            }
        }
    }
    return [
        'valid' => empty($allErrors),
        'errors' => $allErrors,
        'data' => $cleanData
```

```
    ];
}
```

20. The AI also created the logic to intercept and validate posted form data. We had to modify it to produce a string rather than directly echoing from inside the PHP code block:

```
if ($_SERVER['REQUEST_METHOD'] === 'POST') {
    $html = '';
    $validation = validateFormData($fieldAttrs, $countries, $_POST);
    if ($validation['valid']) {
        $html .= '<h3>Successful Submission</h3>';
        // code omitted
    } else {
        $html .= '<h3>Please correct errors:</h3>';
      // code omitted
    }
} else {
    $html = generateNameAddressForm(
        $fieldAttrs, $countries,
        basename(__FILE__), 'POST');
}
```

21. And in the body portion of the generated HTML code, all we need to do is to echo the value of `$html`:

```
<body>
<h1>Name and Address Form</h1>
<?= $html ?>
</body>
</html>
```

22. In the `/path/to/php8cookbook/src/Chapter03` directory, we save the final generated output into a file `ch03_gen_ai_prompts_address_form.php`

How it works...

The key takeaway from this recipe is that developing code via GenAI prompts is an iterative process. There's a high probability that you won't get exactly what you need the first time around. After a series of incremental refinements, you'll end up with the desired results. The other key point regarding interacting with GenAI is that providing more detail returns better results.

Once the code is completed, we can access it via PHP-FPM/nginx running in the Podman container (described in *Chapter 1, Building a Foundation*). From a browser on our host computer we use this URL:

`http://localhost:8888/src/Chapter03/ch03_gen_ai_prompts_address_form.php`. *Figure 3.1* shows the result:

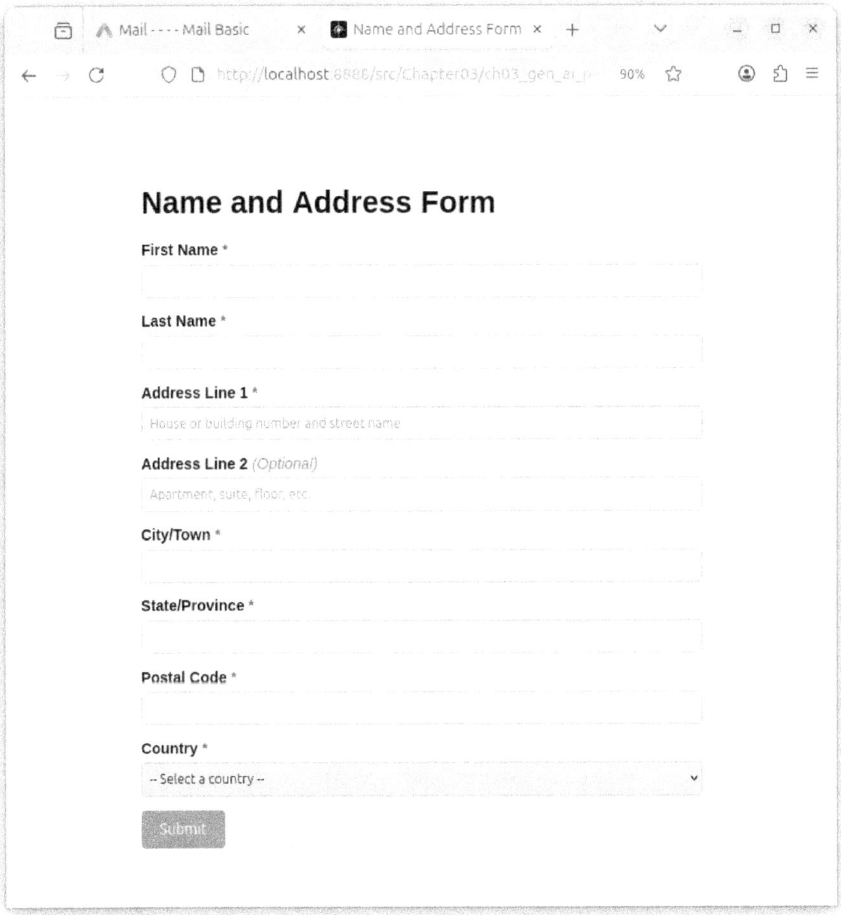

Figure 3.1 – Final name and address form

When we run the script, the `generateNameAddressForm()` function is called. We pass the `$fieldAttrs` and `$countries` arrays, filename, and form method (in this case `POST`). The `generateNameAddressForm()` function loops through the array of field attributes and builds the appropriate HTML <input> and <select> elements. This function progressively builds a string `$html`, which is then displayed.

When the user provides data and hits the submit button, the code checks the `$_SERVER['REQUEST_METHOD']` key. If set to "POST", the `validateFormData()` function is called. In a loop, the code runs the `validator` callback for each form field, producing an array that contains the sanitized value and an array of messages for any validation failure. If the validation process detects any failures, an error screen appears, as shown in *Figure 3.2*, with detailed error messages for each field:

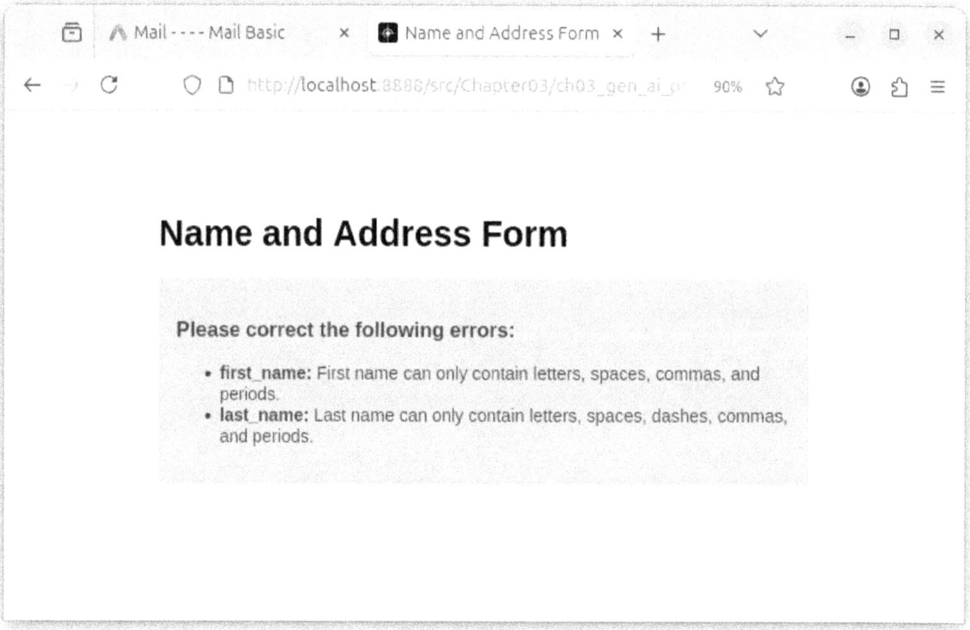

Figure 3.2 – Detailed validation error messages

Hinting at data types to improve AI code generation accuracy

In many cases when developing functions, you might reuse the same library of functions in other projects. Also, if you work with a team, your code might be used by other developers. In order to control the use of your code, it might be appropriate to make use of a **type hint**. This involves specifying the data type your function expects for that particular parameter. The benefits of using type hints include tightening up the use of your code and reducing maintenance down the road. In addition, adding type hints makes function use quite clear and has the side effect of improving the code generated by GenAI.

How to do it...

1. With type hints in place, if a call to the function is made, and the wrong parameter type is passed, a `TypeError` is thrown. The following example requires an array, an instance of `DateTime`, and an anonymous function:

```
function someTypeHint(
  array $a, DateTime $t, callable $c)
{
  $message = '';
  $message .= 'Array Count: ' . count($a) . PHP_EOL;
  $message .= 'Date: ' . $t->format('Y-m-d') . PHP_EOL;
  $message .= 'Callable Return: ' . $c() . PHP_EOL;
  return $message;
}
```

> Note
>
> **Best practice**
>
> It's considered a best practice to provide a type hint for every parameter. Aside from causing you to write tighter code, it saves time down the road when you need to review your code. Adding a type hint to each function signature parameter helps to make the intention of this function crystal clear to you and any developers who inherit your code in the future.

2. In PHP 7 and 8, presuming the appropriate `declare()` directive is made, **scalar** (that is, integer, float, boolean, and string) type hints are enforced. Without the `declare(strict_types=1)` directive, type hints have the effect of coercing the related type. Adding this directive disables the automatic internal type coercion process. Another function demonstrates how this is accomplished. At the top of the code library file which contains the function in which you wish to use scalar type hinting, add this `declare()` directive just after the opening PHP tag:

```
declare(strict_types=1);
```

3. Now you can define a function that includes scalar type hints:

```
function someScalarHint(bool $b, int $i, float $f, string $s)
{
  return sprintf("\n%20s : %5s\n%20s : %5d\n%20s " .
                 ": %5.2f\n%20s : %20s\n\n",
                 'Boolean', ($b ? 'true' : 'false'),
                 'Integer', $i,
                 'Float',   $f,
                 'String',  $s);
}
```

> Note
>
> **Strict type declarations**
>
> Do not overuse the `declare(strict_types=1)` directive. It causes the interpreter to produce extra code which causes the compiled program size to marginally increase. The extra code needed for low-level strict type checking also bogs down performance slightly. Only use this directive in code files where a major program malfunction would occur if the wrong type is passed.

4. In PHP 7 and 8, assuming strict type hinting has not been declared, boolean type hinting works a bit differently from the other three scalar types (that is, integer, float, and string). You can supply any scalar as an argument and no `TypeError` will be thrown! However, the incoming value will automatically be converted to the boolean data type once passed into the function. If you pass any data type other than scalar (that is, array or object) a `TypeError` will be thrown. Here is an example of a function that defines a `boolean` data type. Note that the return value will be automatically converted to a `boolean`:

```
function someBoolHint(bool $b):bool
{
  return $b;
}
```

5. PHP also provides a number of special built-in types that allow you to pass arguments that satisfy a number of criteria. The pseudo-types include:
   - **iterable**: A compound type that includes classes that implement the `Iterator` interface and `array` (`Iterator|array`). (PHP 7.1+)
   - **callable**: Any PHP built-in function, user-defined function, or class that defines `__invoke()`. Any method that can be called statically, and an array tuple that consists of an object and a method name, are also considered callable.
   - **object**: This data type can be any object. (PHP 7.2+)
   - **void**: This data type tells users that this function deliberately does not return anything. (PHP 7.1+)
   - **mixed**: Use this data type to indicate a parameter that allows any data type. This has the same effect as leaving out the data type entirely. However, for code clarity, it's best to use this type as it makes your intent for the function clear. (PHP 8.0+)
   - **never**: This indicates that the function never returns anything. An example would be a monitoring function that checks something in a continuous loop. (PHP 8.1+)
   - **true**, **false,** and **null**: These three are reserved key words, but as of PHP 8.2 they can also be used as direct type hints.
6. First of all, you can place the three functions, `someTypeHint()`, `someScalarHint()`, and `someBoolHint()`, into a separate file to be included. For this example, we will name the file `ch03_developing_func_type_hints_library.php`. Don't forget to add `declare(strict_types=1)` at the top!
7. In our calling code (`ch03_dev_func_type_hints_lib_runner.php`), you would then include the file:

```
include (__DIR__ . DIRECTORY_SEPARATOR .
'ch03_developing_func_type_hints_library.php');
```

8. To test `someTypeHint()`, call the function twice, once with the correct data types, and the second time with incorrect types. This will throw a `TypeError`, however, so you will need to wrap the function calls in a `try { ... } catch () { ...}` block:

```
try {
    $callable = function () { return 'Callback Return'; };
```

```
    echo someTypeHint([1,2,3], new DateTime(), $callable);
    echo someTypeHint('A', 'B', 'C');
} catch (TypeError $e) {
    echo $e->getMessage();
    echo PHP_EOL;
}
```

9. As you can see from the output shown here, when passing the correct data types there is no problem. When passing the incorrect types, a `TypeError` is thrown. Here's the output so far:

```
ed@localhost:~/Repos/PHP-8-Programming-Cookbook $ ./admin.sh shell php8:/
repo# php src/Chapter03/ch03_dev_func_type_hints_lib_runner.php Array
Count: 3 Date: 2026-05-24 Callable Return: Callback Return
Library\someTypeHint(): Argument #1 ($a) must be of type array, string
given, called in /repo/src/Chapter03/
ch03_dev_func_type_hints_lib_runner.php on line 10)
         Boolean :  TRUE
         Integer :    11
           Float : 22.22
          String :     This is a string
Library\someScalarHint(): Argument #2 ($i) must be of type int, string
given, called in /repo/src/Chapter03/
ch03_dev_func_type_hints_lib_runner.php on line 19bool(true)
```

Note

As of PHP 7, most errors are now thrown as an `Error` class instance, which is processed in a similar manner to an `Exception`. This means you can catch an `Error`. `TypeError` is a descendant of `Error` that is thrown when incorrect data types are passed to functions.

All PHP 7 and 8 `Error` classes implement the `Throwable` interface, as does the `Exception` class. If you are not sure if you need to catch an `Error` or an `Exception`, you can add a block which catches `Throwable`.

10. Next you can test `someScalarHint()`, calling it twice with correct and incorrect values, wrapping the calls in a `try { ... } catch () { ...}` block:

```
try {
    echo someScalarHint(true, 11, 22.22,
        'This is a string');
    echo someScalarHint('A', 'B', 'C', 'D');
} catch (TypeError $e) {
    echo $e->getMessage();
}
```

11. As expected, the first call to the function works, and the second throws a `TypeError`:

```
Boolean :  true
Integer :    11
Float : 22.22
String :     This is a string

Library\someScalarHint(): Argument #2 ($i) must be of type int, string
given, called in /repo/src/Chapter03/
ch03_dev_func_type_hints_lib_runner.php on line 21
```

12. When type hinting for boolean values, any scalar value passed will *not* cause a `TypeError` to be thrown! Instead, the value will be interpreted into its boolean equivalent. If you subsequently return this value, the data type will be changed to boolean.

13. To test this, call the `someBoolHint()` function defined previously, and pass any scalar value in as an argument. The `var_dump()` function reveals that the data type is consistently boolean:

```
try {
    // positive results
    $b = someBoolHint(true);
    $i = someBoolHint(11);
    $f = someBoolHint(22.22);
    $s = someBoolHint('X');
    var_dump($b, $i, $f, $s);
    // negative results
    $b = someBoolHint(false);
```

```
        $i = someBoolHint(0);
        $f = someBoolHint(0.0);
        $s = someBoolHint('');
        var_dump($b, $i, $f, $s);
    } catch (TypeError $e) {
        echo $e->getMessage();
    }
```

14. If you now try the same function call, but pass in a non-scalar data type, a `TypeError` is thrown:

```
    try {
        $a = someBoolHint([1,2,3]);
        var_dump($a);
    } catch (TypeError $e) {
        echo $e->getMessage();
    }
    try {
        $o = someBoolHint(new stdClass());
        var_dump($o);
    } catch (TypeError $e) {
        echo $e->getMessage();
    }
```

Let's look at the effect of type hints on GenAI prompts.

15. The effect of type hints on AI prompts can produce good results with fewer iterations. As an example, let's ask GenAI to produce a function that iterates through a list of numeric values and applies a factor of 8% to each value:

```
Generate a PHP function that goes through a list of numeric values and
returns the list with a given percentage factor applied to each element in
the list.
```

16. Claude 4.5 Opus returns a function that's completely within character, taking the simplest possible path to reach the objective. You'll note that Claude Opus naturally assumed that we'll supply an array to the function:

```
function applyPercentage(array $numbers, float $percentage): array {
    return array_map(fn($n) =>
```

```
        $n * ($percentage / 100), $numbers);
}
```

17. However, what if we plan to use an `ArrayObject` instance instead? In the `/path/to/php8cookbook/src/Chapter03` directory, we paste in the generated code to a file `ch03_gen_ai_prompts_type_hint.php`, and add the following two lines:

```
$arr = new ArrayObject(range(1,10));
var_dump(applyPercentage($arr, 8));
```

18. Here is the result:

```
php8:/repo# php src/Chapter03/ch03_gen_ai_prompts_type_hint.php
PHP Fatal error:  Uncaught TypeError: applyPercentage(): Argument #1
($numbers) must be of type array, ArrayObject given, called in /repo/src/
Chapter03/ch03_gen_ai_prompts_type_hint.php on line 8
```

19. Let's now improve the prompt using type hints:

```
Generate a PHP function "applyPercentage(iterable $arr, int $percent) :
iterable" that goes through a list of numeric values and returns the list
with a given percentage factor applied to each element in the list.
```

20. The resulting code is much more flexible and efficient:

```
function applyPercentage(iterable $arr, int $percent): iterable {
    foreach ($arr as $key => $value) {
        yield $key => $value * ($percent / 100);
    }
}
```

21. We then apply `iterator_to_array()` to the output:

```
$arr = new ArrayObject(range(1,10));
var_dump(iterator_to_array(applyPercentage($arr, 8)));
```

22. Here's the final output:

```
php8:/repo#
php src/Chapter03/ch03_gen_ai_prompts_type_hint.php
```

```
array(10) {
  [0]=>   float(0.08)
  [1]=>  float(0.16)
  [2]=>  float(0.24)
  [3]=>  float(0.32)
  [4]=>  float(0.4)
  [5]=>  float(0.48)
  [6]=>  float(0.56)
  [7]=>  float(0.64)
  [8]=>  float(0.72)
  [9]=>  float(0.8)
}
```

How it works...

The primary focus of this recipe is on the benefits accrued by providing proper type hints. This best practice cannot be stressed enough. Proper type hinting produces tighter code, helps identify potential errors when passing incorrect values, and serves to make the intention of the function or method crystal clear.

A side benefit is that when you are building code with GenAI assistance, providing detailed type hints in your prompts or skeleton code, clarifies your intention, which in turn causes the AI to produce code that is much more closely aligned with your overall intention.

See also

For a background discussion on the rationale behind the implementation of scalar type hinting, have a look at this article: `https://wiki.php.net/rfc/scalar_type_hints_v5`.

For a list of types, have a look here: `https://php.net/manual/en/language.types.declarations.php`.

Searching multi-dimensional arrays using array_find

A lot of your program development will be spent searching through arrays. Historically, PHP has included a number of excellent functions that serve this purpose, starting with PHP 4. As the years went by, however, it became clear that the existing set of array search functions worked well for simple searches, but often failed to meet the demands placed on the language by modern application needs. In order to fill the gap, PHP 8.4 introduces two new members of this set: `array_find()` and `array_find_key()`. These functions are a great way to search multi-dimensional arrays as they utilize a callback as one of the arguments. This gives you a great deal of flexibility in search. (Note that in this recipe array_find_key() is not used.)

How to do it...

1. For the purposes of demonstration, in the /path/to/php8cookbook/src/Chapter03 directory, we create a file ch03_array_search_func_lib.php. In this file, we define a function that leverages the Cookbook\Iterator\LargeFile class discussed in *Chapter 2, Using PHP 8 High Performance Features*:

```
<?php
namespace Library;
require __DIR__ . '/../../vendor/autoload.php';
```

2. Our demo function buildArrays() pulls every 10th line out of the GeoNames tab-delimited file for the United States. You'll note that even though the GeoNames file format is tab-delimited, we can still use CSV-related methods to access data:

```
function buildArrays() : array
{
    $fn = __DIR__ . '/../../data/US.txt';
    $largeFile =
        new \Cookbook\Iterator\LargeFile($fn);
    $iterator = $largeFile->getIterator('ByLine');
    $gap = 10;  // every 10th line
    $pos = $gap;
    $multi  = [];
    foreach ($iterator as $line) {
        if (--$pos > 0) {
            continue;   // skip $gap # lines
        } else {
            $pos = $gap;
        }
        $line = trim($line);
        if (!empty($line)) {
            $row = str_getcsv($line, "\t");
           if (isset($row[1])) $multi[$row[1]] = $row;
        }
    }
    return $multi;
}
```

3. Next, we define a function `fetch()` that is able to search both single and multi-dimensional arrays. Further, this function is able to return the first element that matches our search criteria, or all elements that match. You'll also note that we define a return type of `mixed` as the return value could be a single matching element, an array of matches, or null:

```
function fetch(array $arr,
               string|float $needle, // float type hint also allows int
arguments
               bool $case = true,
               bool $first = true) : mixed
{
```

4. The first thing we do in our `fetch()` function is to check to see if we need to return the first match or all matches. We then call either the `array_find()` or `array_filter()` built-in functions. The former returns the first match or null. The latter returns all matches and preserves the keys. Note that both built-in functions accept the *haystack* array as the first argument and a callback as the second argument.
The second argument we define using an anonymous function that accepts an argument `$value`, automatically passed by PHP as it parses the haystack array. Note that we need to use the `$needle` and `$case` in order to have these available inside the anonymous function. It's also worth noting that PHP passes the key as an optional second argument:

```
    $func = ($first) ? 'array_find' : 'array_filter';
    return $func($arr,
        function ($value) use ($needle, $case) {
```

5. Inside the anonymous function we're using as a callback, we use `is_array()` to check to see if `$value` is an array. If so, we use `implode()` to convert the array to a string to facilitate the search. It's important to note that `implode()` expects a single dimension array. In our example, each row extracted from the GeoNames data will take this form:

```
            // is $value an array?
            $haystack = (is_array($value))
                      ? implode(' ', $value)
                      : (string) $value;
```

6. Next, we convert `$needle` to a string and check to see if we're asked to perform a case-insensitive search. If the latter is true, we convert both `$needle` and `$haystack` to lowercase. It's worth pointing out that when operating an international website, you might consider using `mb_strtolower()`, which can handle multi-byte strings:

```
            $needle = (string) $needle;
            if (!$case) {
                $haystack = strtolower($haystack);
                $needle   = strtolower($needle);
            }
```

7. Finally, we use `str_contains()`, a fast function introduced in PHP 8, to return `true` or `false` depending on the results of the search:

```
            return str_contains($haystack, $needle);
        }
    );
}
```

> **Note**
>
> **Needle and haystack**
>
> PHP search functions generally use the terms needle and haystack. *Needle* refers to what you are looking for. *Haystack* is where you are searching for the needle. You might also note that this is an inside joke fostered by the early PHP language developers, as it's a play on the old saying "*looking for a needle in a haystack.*"

8. To test the `fetch()` function, we create a runner program `ch03_array_search_runner.php` located in the `/path/to/php8cookbook/src/Chapter03` directory. `$multi` is a multi-dimensional array consisting of every 10th entry from the US GeoNames post code data:

```
<?php
require __DIR__ . '/ch03_array_search_func_lib.php';
$multi = \Library\buildArrays();
```

9. We then define two search items, one near the start of the array and one near the end. The reason why we do this is to test how long it takes to search, and to see if the position of the element has an effect on search speed:

```
$srch1 = 'Anch'; // near the start
$srch2 = 'Lyma'; // near the end
```

10. We then define a set of eight different calls to the `fetch()` function. Four calls are made using `$srch1`, and four using `$srch2`. We also vary the `$case` and `$first` arguments to get single or multiple results. Here is an example of this usage. Note that we use the `microtime()` function to record the time as a float value:

```
$start  = microtime(true);
$label  = 'Search array near start, '
            . 'case sensitive, return first match';
$result = \Library\fetch($multi, $srch1, true, true);
printf('Label: %80s | Time: %.8f' . PHP_EOL,
       $label, (microtime(true) - $start));
echo implode("\t", $result) . PHP_EOL;
```

11. *Figure 3.3* shows the results of our tests. You'll note that the position of the element in the haystack array has a major impact on search performance:

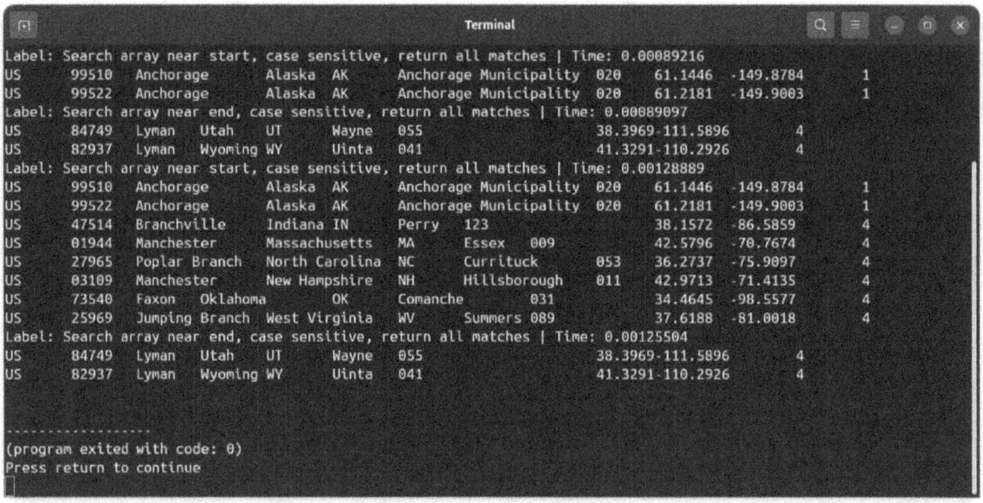

Figure 3.3 – Searching Arrays Results

> **Note**
>
> Any array search function using a callback will impact performance. Using the earlier functions such as `array_search()` offers improved performance, at the cost of not being able to search multi-dimensional arrays. The other problem with the existing array search functions is that they only match the entire entry and don't support substring searches within nested structures. You can use `preg_grep()` to search an array using a regular expression; however, you suffer a similar performance drop, and it's not designed to search a multi-dimensional array.

How it works...

Prior to the introduction of `array_find()` and `array_find_key()`, the only way to find a substring of an array element key or value was to use a `foreach()` loop or `preg_grep()`. However, the latter introduces additional overhead because it has to first analyze the pattern before performing the search.

The `array_filter()` function allows you to provide a callback; however, it was designed to search the *entire array* and to provide all possible results. If your objective is to find the first array element that meets the criteria of your callback, `array_find()` is the better choice.

See also

For more information on array functions, have a look here:`https://www.php.net/manual/en/ref.array.php`.

Making decisions using match expressions

The venerable `switch {}` statement, inherited from the C language, has been available since the inception of PHP. However, over the years, developers have been clamoring for a more concise syntax. PHP 8 introduced the `match {}` expression, a lean alternative to `switch {}`.

The two primary differences between `match {}` and `switch {}` are:

- `match` performs a *strict* comparison, meaning that a string will not match a number even if the numeric value of the string is the same. Further, unless you provide a default, an `UnhandledMatchError` is thrown if no match is found. In contrast, `switch` performs a *non-strict* comparison. Data types are *juggled* before the comparison, often producing unexpected results and false positives.

- `match` only allows for a single expression in each branch whereas with `switch` you can have as many lines of code as desired. However, you can easily get around this limitation by defining a function where multiple lines of code are needed.

All this having been said, `match` does not require a `break` statement, and its concise syntax can vastly improve readability.

How to do it...

1. For the purposes of demonstration, we'll create a recipe that produces different types of output depending on the value of either the HTTP `Accept` header, or a POST argument named `accept`.
2. In the `/path/to/php8cookbook/src/Chapter03` folder, we define a file `ch03_match_func_lib.php` that contains `MIME type` definitions for the data formats we'll accept, along with a set of callbacks that produce array output matching the target MIME type.
3. First, we create constants that define our target MIME types:

```
<?php
// define supported MIME types
define('ACCEPT_X', 'application/xml');
define('ACCEPT_J', 'application/json');
define('ACCEPT_H', 'text/html');
define('ACCEPT_T', 'text/plain');
```

4. Next, we define a set of callbacks in the form of anonymous functions that set the appropriate output headers and produce output in the desired format:

```
// XML
$x = function ($data) {
    header('Content-Type: ' . ACCEPT_X);
    $xml = xmlwriter_open_memory();
    $xml->startDocument( '1.0', 'UTF-8');
    $xml->startElement('Item');
    foreach ($data as $key => $value) {
        $xml->startElement('Key');
        $xml->text((string) $key);
        $xml->endElement();
```

```
        $xml->startElement('Value');
        $xml->text((string) $value);
        $xml->endElement();
    }
    $xml->endElement();
    return $xml->outputMemory();
};
// JSON
$j = function ($data) {
    header('Content-Type: ' . ACCEPT_J);
    return json_encode($data, JSON_PRETTY_PRINT |
       JSON_THROW_ON_ERROR);
};
// HTML
$h = function ($data) {
    header('Content-Type: ' . ACCEPT_H);
    $output = '<table border=1>' . PHP_EOL;
    foreach ($data as $key => $value) {
        $output .= sprintf(
            "<tr><th>%s</th><td>%s</td></tr>\n",
            htmlspecialchars((string) $key, ENT_QUOTES, 'UTF-8'),
            htmlspecialchars((string) $value, ENT_QUOTES, 'UTF-8'));
    }
    $output .= '</table>' . PHP_EOL;
    return $output;
};

// Text
$t = function ($data) {
    header('Content-Type: ' . ACCEPT_T);
    $output = '';
    foreach ($data as $key => $value) {
        $output .= $key . ":\t" . $value . PHP_EOL;
    }
    return $output;
};
```

5. Next, in a file `ch03_match_runner.php`, we load the library, determine the acceptable output format, and sanitize the data using `array_map()`:

```
<?php
include __DIR__ . '/ch03_match_func_lib.php';

if (!empty($_POST)) {
    $accept = strtolower(trim(
        $_POST['accept'] ?? $_SERVER['HTTP_ACCEPT']
            ?? ACCEPT_T));
    $data = array_map(function ($val) { return trim(strip_tags($val)); },
($_POST ?? [])); // NOTE: assumes $_POST does not contain any arrays
```

6. The heart of this script is the `match () {}` construct. We build a *decision tree* using match and return the appropriate output. Using true as an argument allows us to specify an expression as the key for each branch of the `match () {}` construct:

```
    echo match (true) {
        str_contains($accept, ACCEPT_X) => $x($data),
        str_contains($accept, ACCEPT_J) => $j($data),
        str_contains($accept, ACCEPT_H) => $h($data),
        str_contains($accept, ACCEPT_T) => $t($data),
        default => $t($data)
    };
    exit;
}
```

> **Note**
>
> Note that we used `strtolower()` to force the `accept` format to lowercase. The reason why this is important is because we later use `str_contains()`, which by default performs a case-sensitive search. By forcing the `accept` input to lowercase, and by ensuring that the formats defined in our constants are lowercase, we avoid any false positives coming from `str_contains()`.

7. We can then make a series of `curl` requests from the command line to view the results. Here's an example of the JSON output:

```
ed@localhost:~/Repos/PHP-8-Programming-Cookbook
$ curl -X POST -H 'Accept:application/json' \
  -d "first=Fred&last=Flintstone&email=fred@slate.com" \
  http://localhost:8888/src/Chapter03/ch03_match_runner.php
{
    "first": "Fred",
    "last": "Flintstone",
    "email": "fred@slate.com"
}
```

8. Here's the same request using `application/xml` for the `Accept` header:

```
$ curl -X POST -H 'Accept:application/xml' \
  -d "first=Fred&last=Flintstone&email=fred@slate.com" \
  http://localhost:8888/src/Chapter03/ch03_match_runner.php
<?xml version="1.0"?>
<Item>
<Key>first</Key><Value>Fred</Value>
<Key>last</Key><Value>Flintstone</Value>
<Key>email</Key><Value>fred@slate.com</Value>
</Item>
```

How it works...

Our example *runner* program first checks to see if the request is an HTTP POST. If so, it checks to see if an `accept` POST argument or HTTP `Accept` header is provided. From these two sources, we determine what format the client is willing to accept. If no format is provided, the default is plain text. Armed with this information, we use the `match() {}` expression to run the callback appropriate to the acceptable format.

The bigger picture is that *callback trees*, based upon the `match() {}` expression, are an extremely valuable tool that can be used in a variety of situations. An example would be to provide a callback tree of filters and validators to be used in conjunction with form processing.

See also

For more information on MIME types, have a look here: `https://developer.mozilla.org/en-US/docs/Web/HTTP/MIME_types/Common_types`.

4

Working with PHP Object-Oriented Programming

In this chapter, we present several practical recipes that leverage the **object-oriented programming** (**OOP**) capabilities of PHP 8. We cover a range of OOP-oriented topics, including using GenAI prompts to build an OOP appointment calendar system and integrating the Symfony AI Bundle to build an AI-powered service. The chapter also addresses important OOP concepts, including designing practical class hierarchies, implementing **PSR-11**-compliant service containers, and utilizing PHP 8.4's lazy object features that optimize performance and reduce memory consumption.

In this chapter we cover:

- Using focused GenAI prompts to build a simple OOP appointment calendar
- Using the Symfony AI Bundle to build a GenAI-based service
- Developing a practical class hierarchy
- Creating a service container
- Using lazy objects to improve performance

Using focused GenAI prompts to build a simple OOP appointment calendar

A simple Google search will show that most experts agree that GenAI isn't good at generating entire production-ready projects. For one thing, GenAI cannot understand the full business context and requirements of a given project. Another factor is that due to the technical limitations of GenAI platforms in terms of how much data they can handle at one time, a limitation known as the **context window**. Accordingly, to make yourself a highly valuable developer, it's important to keep a clear picture of project architecture as you start to develop narrowly focused prompts that coach GenAI to produce the most suitable code.

Getting ready

For the purposes of this recipe, you'll need to have access to a GenAI platform and a code editor. In the `/path/to/php8cookbook/src/` directory, create a subdirectory `Appointment` in which we'll place the generated class files. For this recipe, we'll use Anthropic Claude Code, which has a large context window and is optimized for generating code. Bear in mind that you can achieve similar results by pasting the prompts we provide into your preferred GenAI web interface.

> Tip
>
> **Watch your token count!**
>
> When you start Claude Code in a given directory, it first asks for permission to access files in the directory structure. This allows it to read files to gain a proper context. Fortunately, it only reads files directly referenced. It's extremely important to recognize that for large projects with a lot of `use` statements, your token usage will shoot up, and you might end up with a massive bill at the end of the month!

When considering prompt-based code development, it's always best to have your final goal clearly in mind. This allows you to mentally break down the final result into precisely defined stages. Ideally, each prompt will produce one or more classes to progressively build the needed functionality.

In this recipe, our goal is to build an appointment calendar system. This will include an `appointment` database table and a corresponding entity class that represents rows in this table. We'll also need a class that provides a calendar view of appointments.

How to do it...

1. Now that we have a clear picture of the final goal of the project, let's start with the first prompt. In the prompt we'll instruct GenAI to create an SQL definition for the `appointment` table and corresponding entity class. You'll note that for simplicity we request properties to be marked with `public` visibility. However, many production teams prefer encapsulation or immutable entities:

```
1. Create a MySQL database definition of a table named "appointment" with
the following columns:
* id (unsigned int)
```

```
* title (char 16)
* location (varchar 255)
* contact_info (varchar 255)
* start_date_and_time (datetime)
* end_date_and_time (datetime)
2. Create a PHP entity class "Cookbook\Appointment\Appointment" that
represents a row in the "appointment" table described above.
* Use PHP 8 constructor argument promotion so that property values can be
defined upon object instantiation.
* Make all properties public with the appropriate data type.
* Do not create "getter" or "setter" methods.
* The start and end date and time properties should have a data type of
string.
* The default value for all properties should be an empty value that
matches the data type (i.e. use '' for string, 0, for integers, etc.).
* The "id" column needs to be auto-increment.
```

We presented this prompt to Claude Code, and this is the SQL that it produced:

```
CREATE TABLE appointment (
    id INT UNSIGNED NOT NULL AUTO_INCREMENT,
    title  CHAR(16) NOT NULL DEFAULT '',
    location VARCHAR(255) NOT NULL DEFAULT '',
    contact_info VARCHAR(255)  NOT NULL DEFAULT '',
    start_date_and_time DATETIME NOT NULL,
    end_date_and_time DATETIME NOT NULL,
    PRIMARY KEY (id)
) ENGINE=InnoDB DEFAULT CHARSET=utf8mb4;
```

2. And here is the new `Appointment` class. The only significant change was to add a method named `extract()` with a parameter `$insert`. If set `true`, the first element (`id`) is removed. This is needed because when we insert an appointment, the `id` column is automatically incremented and there's no need to supply our own value:

```
<?php
namespace Cookbook\Appointment;
class Appointment {
    public function __construct( public int    $id = 0,
    public string $title  = '',
    public string $location  = '',
```

```
        public string $contact_info  = '',
        public string $start_date_and_time = '',
        public string $end_date_and_time  = '', )
        {}
        // manually added
        public function extract(bool $insert = false) : array {
            $arr = get_object_vars($this);
            if ($insert) unset($arr['id']);
            return $arr;
        }
    }
```

3. The next step, perhaps the most important, is to define an `ApptRepository` class that provides functionality to add, remove and update entries in the appointment table. We also need an `ApptService` class that produces appointment query results. To better guide the AI, we created skeleton code files, filling in the methods where the code is obvious, and providing comments where we want the AI to complete the code. Here's the skeleton code for the `ApptRepository` class:

```
<?php
namespace Cookbook\Appointment;
use PDO;
use PDOStatement;
use Cookbook\Appointment\ApptAdapter;
use Cookbook\Appointment\Appointment;
class ApptRepository {
    public ?PDO $pdo = null;
    // fill in this array with the columns for the "appointment" table
    public array $cols = [];
    public function __construct(array $config)  {
        $this->pdo = ApptAdapter::getInstance($config);
    }
    public function buildCols() : string {
        $cols = '';
        foreach ($this->cols as $name)
            $cols .= $this->pdo->quote($name) . ',';
        return substr($cols, 0, -1);     // last arg removes trailing comma
    }
    public function add(Appointment $appt) : bool {
     // build SQL INSERT prepared statement using $this->buildCols()
```

```
            // run PDO::prepare() and PDO::execute($appointment)
            // return true on success, false otherwise
        }
        public function edit(Appointment $appt) : bool {
         // build SQL UPDATE prepared statement using $this->buildCols()
            // run PDO::prepare() and PDO::execute($appointment)
            // return true on success, false otherwise
        }
        public function delete(Appointment $appt) : bool {
            // build SQL DELETE prepared statement
            // do not hard-code the colums: use $cols for future flexibility
            // run PDO::prepare() and PDO::execute($appointment)
            // return true on success, false otherwise
        }
    }
```

4. Here is the skeleton code for the `ApptService` class:

```
<?php
namespace Cookbook\Appointment;
use PDOStatement;
use InvalidArgumentException;
use Cookbook\Appointment\ApptRepository;
class ApptService {
    public function __construct(public PDO $pdo) {}
    public function list(string $start_date, string $end_date) : ?
PDOStatement {
        // build SQL SELECT statement using $repo->buildCols()
          /* add a WHERE clause that returns "appointment" table entries
          including and between start and end dates */
        // return a PDOStatement instance or null
    }
}
```

5. The prompt we used to get Claude Code to fill in the blanks is shown here:

```
2. Review the listed code files and fill in the code as indicated by the
comments. Ask me if you have any questions or doubts. Here are the files:
ApptRepository.php
ApptService.php
```

6. Here is the result produced by Claude for the `ApptRepository` class. The changes we made post-generation were relatively minor and are indicated in the comments:

```
<?php
namespace Cookbook\Appointment;
use PDO;
// use PDOStatement;    // no longer needed
use Cookbook\Appointment\Appointment;
class ApptRepository {
    public const string TABLE = 'appointment';
    public array $cols = ['title', 'location', 'contact_info',
'start_date_and_time',
        'end_date_and_time'];
    // modified to accept PDO instance directly
    public function __construct(public PDO $pdo)  {}
    public function add(Appointment $appt) : bool {
        // replaced hard-coded column list with an implode()
        $cols = '`' . implode('`,`', $this->cols) . '`';
        $placeholders = ':' . implode(', :', $this->cols);
        // replaced with sprintf() to improve readability
        $sql = sprintf('INSERT INTO `%s` (%s) VALUES (%s)',
            static::TABLE, $cols, $placeholders);
        $stmt = $this->pdo->prepare($sql);
        return (bool) $stmt->execute($appt->extract(true));
    }
    public function edit(Appointment $appt) : bool {
        $set = implode(', ', array_map(fn($col) => "`{$col}` = :{$col}",
$this->cols));
        $sql = sprintf('UPDATE `%s` SET %s WHERE `id` = :id',
static::TABLE, $set);
        $stmt = $this->pdo->prepare($sql);
        return (bool) $stmt->execute($appt->extract());
    }
    public function delete(Appointment $appt) : bool {
        // replaced with sprintf() to improve readability
        $sql = sprintf('DELETE FROM `%s` WHERE `id` = :id', static::TABLE);
        $stmt = $this->pdo->prepare($sql);
        return (bool) $stmt->execute(['id' => $appt->id]);
    }
}
```

7. Here's what the AI generated for our `ApptService` class. Again, the slight changes made are noted in the comments:

```
<?php
namespace Cookbook\Appointment;
// use PDOStatement;    // no longer needed
use InvalidArgumentException;
use Cookbook\Appointment\ApptRepository;
class ApptService {
    public function __construct(public ApptRepository $repo) {}
    //  replaced PDO with ApptRepository as constructor argument
    public function list(string $start_date, string $end_date) : ?
PDOStatement {
        // replaced hard-coded column list with an implode()
        $sql = 'SELECT `id`, ' . '`' . implode('`,`', $this->repo->cols) .
'` '

            . 'FROM `appointment` WHERE `start_date_and_time`  '
            . 'BETWEEN :start_date AND :end_date';
        $stmt = $this->repo->pdo->prepare($sql);
        $result = $stmt->execute(['start_date' => $start_date,
            'end_date' => $end_date]);
        return $result ? $stmt : null;
    }
}
```

8. Finally we defined a prompt that instructs Claude to create a PHP-based website that allows us to manage appointments. Pay particular attention to the last portion of our prompt: "`Let me know if you have any questions before you start`". We'll get more into that later. For now, here's the full text of the final prompt:

```
3. Create a nicely styled PHP-based website as follows {
  3A. PHP/HTML page that allows the user to add or edit an appointment with
an option to delete it.
  3B. PHP/HTML page that allows the user to list appointments by start and
end dates {
    3B.1 If no start or end dates are provided, display a paginated list of
all appointments.
    3B.2 If only the start date is provided, display a paginated list of
all appointments from and including the start date all the way to the end.
    3B.3 If only the end date is provided, display a paginated list of all
```

```
appointments from the beginning up to and including the end date.
    3B.4 In the list of appointments displayed, for each row, add a button
to edit or delete the appointment.
    3B.5 At the bottom of the page provide a button to add a new
appointment.
    3B.6 You'll need to modify the ApptService class to provide the methods
to satisfy the different combinations of start or end dates described here.
  }
  3C. Let me know if you have any questions before you start.
}
```

9. As a result of these instructions, Claude made additions to the `ApptRepository` and `ApptService` classes. We will not show the entire class again, just the additions. As above, we indicate changes made via single-line comments. First we'll show methods added to `ApptRepository`:

```
private function buildWhere(?string $start, ?string $end): array {
    if ($start !== null && $end !== null) {
        return [
            ' WHERE `start_date_and_time` BETWEEN :start AND :end',
            [':start' => $start, ':end' => $end],
        ];
    }
    if ($start !== null)
        return [' WHERE `start_date_and_time` >= :start', [':start' =>
$start]];
    if ($end !== null)
        return [' WHERE `start_date_and_time` <= :end', [':end' => $end]];
    return ['', []];
}
public function fetchList(?string $start, ?string $end, int $limit, int
$offset): array
{
    [$where, $params] = $this->buildWhere($start, $end);
    // replaced hard-coded column list with an implode() using $this->cols
    $sql  = 'SELECT ' . '`id`,`' . implode('`,`', $this->cols) . '` '
          . 'FROM `appointment` '
          . $where . ' '
          . 'ORDER BY `start_date_and_time` ASC LIMIT :limit
OFFSET :offset';
```

```
        $stmt = $this->pdo->prepare($sql);
        foreach ($params as $key => $val)
            $stmt->bindValue($key, $val);
        $stmt->bindValue(':limit',  $limit,  PDO::PARAM_INT);
        $stmt->bindValue(':offset', $offset, PDO::PARAM_INT);
        $stmt->execute();
        return $stmt->fetchAll(PDO::FETCH_ASSOC);
    }
    public function countList(?string $start, ?string $end): int {
        [$where, $params] = $this->buildWhere($start, $end);
        $sql  = 'SELECT COUNT(*) FROM `appointment` ' . $where;
        $stmt = $this->pdo->prepare($sql);
        $stmt->execute($params);
        return (int) $stmt->fetchColumn();
    }
    public function fetchById(int $id): ?Appointment {
        // replaced hard-coded column list with an implode() using $this->cols
        $sql  = 'SELECT ' . '`id`,`' . implode('`,`', $this->cols) . '`'
              . ' FROM `appointment` WHERE `id` = :id';
        $stmt = $this->pdo->prepare($sql);
        $stmt->execute([':id' => $id]);
        $row  = $stmt->fetch(PDO::FETCH_ASSOC);
        return (!empty($row)) ? new Appointment(...$row) : null;
    }
```

10. Now we'll show changes made to `ApptService`:

```
    public function list(
        string $start_date = '',
        string $end_date   = '',
        int    $page       = 1,
        int    $per_page   = 20
    ): array {
        // replace *date == '' with !empty(*date)
        $start = (!empty($start_date)) ? $start_date . ' 00:00:00' : null;
        $end   = (!empty($end_date))   ? $end_date   . ' 23:59:59' : null;
        $total = $this->repo->countList($start, $end);
        $pages = max(1, (int) ceil($total / $per_page));
        $page  = max(1, min($page, $pages));
        $rows  = $this->repo->fetchList($start, $end, $per_page,
            ($page - 1) * $per_page);
```

```
        return ['rows' => $rows, 'total' => $total, 'pages' => $pages, 'page'
    => $page];
    public function getById(int $id): ?Appointment {
        return $this->repo->fetchById($id);
    }
```

11. Before getting into the `index.php` file created by Claude, it's important to revisit our last instruction to Claude. The AI did indeed ask a few questions. *Figure 4.1* shows the initial output from our session with Claude:

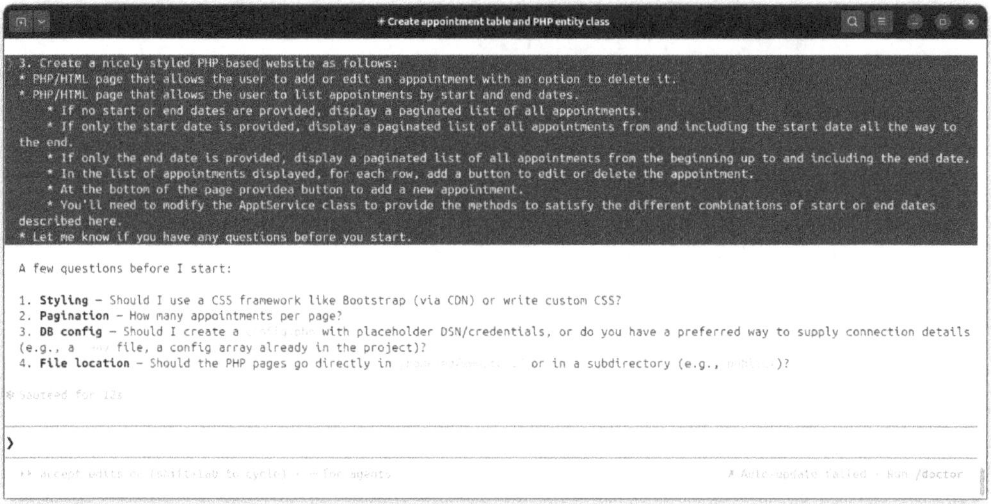

Figure 4.1 – Claude questions from last prompt

12. Once we answered the questions shown in *Figure 4.1*, Claude created two primary point-of-entry files: `index.php` and `edit.php`. We moved these into the `/path/to/php8cookbook/src/Chapter04` folder, and renamed them to `ch04_appointment.php` and `ch04_appointment_edit.php`, respectively.

13. In the `/path/to/php8cookbook/config` folder, we moved the `config.php` file created by Claude and renamed it `ch04_appt_get_pdo.php`. In this file we entered the database credentials used throughout recipes in this book:

```
<?php
$config = [
    'dsn'  => 'mysql:host=mysql.local:3306;dbname=php8cookbook',
    'db_usr'     => 'cookbook',
```

```
    'db_pwd'      => 'password',
    'db_host'     => 'mysql.local',
    'db_opts'     => [PDO::ATTR_ERRMODE => PDO::ERRMODE_EXCEPTION]
];
return new PDO($config['dsn'], $config['db_usr'],
    $config['db_pwd'], ($config['db_opts'] ?? null));
```

14. Claude also created an identical set of `helper` functions to be used to safely render the view. We moved these into a separate class `ApptViewHelpers` (named after the class, placed in the same folder as the other appointment classes). In the HTML portions of the `ch04_appointment.php` and `ch04_appointment_edit.php` scripts we call these helpers using static method calls. Here's the new class:

```
<?php
namespace Cookbook\Appointment;
class ApptViewHelpers {
    public const DATE_FMT = 'j M Y H:i:s';
    public static function h(string $s): string {
        return htmlspecialchars($s, ENT_QUOTES | ENT_SUBSTITUTE, 'UTF-8');
    }
    public static function fmtDt(string $dt): string {
        return $dt !== '' ? date(static::DATE_FMT, strtotime($dt)) : '—';
    }
    public static function pageUrl(array $base, int $p): string {
        return 'ch04_appointment.php?' .
http_build_query(array_merge($base, ['page' => $p]));
    }
    public static function dtToInput(string $dt): string
    {
        return $dt !== '' ? substr(str_replace(' ', 'T', $dt), 0, 16) : '';
    }
}
```

15. Next we show you the PHP code portion of `ch04_appointment.php`. As with the results shown in previous steps in this recipe, we added comments to indicate changes made. One obvious change was to use the Composer autoloader, alleviating the need for the `require_once()` statements created by Claude. To be fair, we developed the code in a

directory independent of the /path/to/php8cookbook folder. Accordingly, Claude was unable to take in the autoloading environment. Here is the code:

```
<?php
// Removed declare()
// declare(strict_types=1);
// Replaced "require_once" statements with composer autoloader
require __DIR__ . '/../../vendor/autoload.php';
use Cookbook\Appointment\ApptService;
use Cookbook\Appointment\ApptRepository;
use Cookbook\Appointment\ApptViewHelpers as Helper;
$pdo     = require __DIR__ . '/../../config/ch04_appt_get_pdo.php';
$repo    = new ApptRepository($pdo);
$svc     = new ApptService($repo);
```

16. Claude nicely added a block of code that effectively produces a **PRG** (**Post-Redirect-Get**) effect:

```
if ($_SERVER['REQUEST_METHOD'] === 'POST' && ($_POST['action'] ?? '') ===
'delete') {
    $id = (int) ($_POST['id'] ?? 0);
    if ($id > 0 && ($appt = $svc->getById($id))) $repo->delete($appt);
    // Replaced "index.php" with new filename
    header('Location: ch04_appointment.php?'
        . http_build_query([
            'start_date' => $_POST['start_date'] ?? '',
            'end_date'   => $_POST['end_date']   ?? '',
            'page'       => max(1, (int) ($_POST['page'] ?? 1)),
            'msg'        => 'deleted'])
    );
    exit;
}
```

17. We added `strip_tags()` to sanitize inputs. For any suspect output, Claude wrapped such data in `htmlspecialchars()` in the helper functions described when we introduced `ApptHelper`. This helps to avoid XSS attacks in the HTML portion of the script (not shown):

```
// Added strip_tags()
$start_date = trim(strip_tags($_GET['start_date'] ?? ''));
```

```
$end_date    = trim(strip_tags($_GET['end_date']   ?? ''));
$page        = max(1, (int) ($_GET['page'] ?? 1));
$result = $svc->list($start_date, $end_date, $page);
['rows' => $rows, 'total' => $total, 'pages' => $pages, 'page' => $page] =
$result;
$flashMap = [ 'deleted' => ['success',
    '<i class="bi bi-check-circle-fill me-2"></i>Appointment deleted.'],
    'added'   => ['success',
        '<i class="bi bi-check-circle-fill me-2"></i>Appointment added.'],
    'edited'  => ['success',
        '<i class="bi bi-check-circle-fill me-2"></i>Appointment
updated.'],
];
[$flashType, $flashHtml] = $flashMap[$_GET['msg'] ?? ''] ?? ['', ''];
$filterParams = array_filter(['start_date' => $start_date,
    'end_date' => $end_date]);
// remaining code (not shown) produces HTML
```

18. Here's the PHP code portion of `ch04_appointment_edit.php`. The opening lines are pretty much as seen in `ch04_appointment.php`:

```
<?php
// Removed declare()
// declare(strict_types=1);
// Replaced "require_once" statements with composer autoloader
require __DIR__ . '/../../vendor/autoload.php';
use Cookbook\Appointment\Appointment;
use Cookbook\Appointment\ApptService;
use Cookbook\Appointment\ApptRepository;
use Cookbook\Appointment\ApptViewHelpers as Helper;
$pdo     = require __DIR__ . '/../../config/ch04_appt_get_pdo.php';
$repo    = new ApptRepository($pdo);
$svc     = new ApptService($repo);
$id      = (int) ($_REQUEST['id'] ?? 0);
$isEdit = $id > 0;
$errors = [];
$appt    = new Appointment();
```

19. Claude added an option to reload `ch04_appointment.php` if the requested appointment is not available for editing:

```
if ($isEdit && $_SERVER['REQUEST_METHOD'] !== 'POST') {
    $loaded = $svc->getById($id);
    if (!$loaded) {
        header('Location: ch04_appointment.php');
        exit;
    }
    $appt = $loaded;
}
```

20. The next section deals with form submission:

```
if ($_SERVER['REQUEST_METHOD'] === 'POST') {
    $action = $_POST['action'] ?? 'save';
    if ($action === 'delete' && $isEdit) {
        $target = $svc->getById($id);
        if ($target) $repo->delete($target);
        header('Location: ch04_appointment.php?msg=deleted');
        exit;
    }
    // added strip_tags()
$title    = trim(strip_tags($_POST['title']                ?? ''));
$loc      = trim(strip_tags($_POST['location']             ?? ''));
$contact  = trim(strip_tags($_POST['contact_info']         ?? ''));
$startRaw = trim(strip_tags($_POST['start_date_and_time'] ?? ''));
$endRaw   = trim(strip_tags($_POST['end_date_and_time']   ?? ''));
$startDt = $startRaw !== '' ? str_replace('T', ' ', $startRaw) . ':00' :
'';
$endDt   = $endRaw   !== '' ? str_replace('T', ' ', $endRaw)   . ':00' :
'';
```

21. Claude next provided a validation section. This would have to be further managed manually as the AI has no idea of the overall business context:

```
    if ($title === '') {
        $errors[] = 'Title is required.';
    } elseif (mb_strlen($title) > 16) {
        $errors[] = 'Title cannot exceed 16 characters.';
    }
```

```
    if ($startRaw === '') {
        $errors[] = 'Start date and time is required.';
    }
    if ($endRaw === '') {
        $errors[] = 'End date and time is required.';
    }
    if ($startRaw !== '' && $endRaw !== '' && $endRaw <= $startRaw) {
        $errors[] = 'End date/time must be after start date/time.';
    }
```

22. After error handling, code to populate the instance is defined, followed by a call to the `ApptRepository::add()` or `edit()` methods:

```
    if (empty($errors)) {
        $appt = new Appointment(
            id:                  $id,
            title:               $title,
            location:            $loc,
            contact_info:        $contact,
            start_date_and_time: $startDt,
            end_date_and_time:   $endDt,
        );
        $ok = $isEdit ? $repo->edit($appt) : $repo->add($appt);
        if ($ok) {
            header('Location: ch04_appointment.php?msg=' .
                ($isEdit ? 'edited' : 'added'));
            exit;
        }
        $errors[] = 'A database error occurred. Please try again.';
    }
    // Repopulate form values on validation failure
    $appt = new Appointment(
        id:                  $id,
        title:               $title,
        location:            $loc,
        contact_info:        $contact,
        start_date_and_time: $startDt,
        end_date_and_time:   $endDt,
    );
```

```
}
$pageTitle = $isEdit ? 'Edit Appointment' : 'New Appointment';
```

23. Again, the HTML portion is not shown; however, you can view the last two code files just described, in their entirety, in the `/path/to/php8cookbook/src/Chapter04` folder.
24. Assuming our virtual environment is up and running, we had to first create the `appointment` database table using our database administration utility and the SQL file shown earlier in this recipe. From our host computer's browser, we accessed the URL `http://localhost:8888/db_admin.php` and pasted in the SQL statement to create the appointments table:

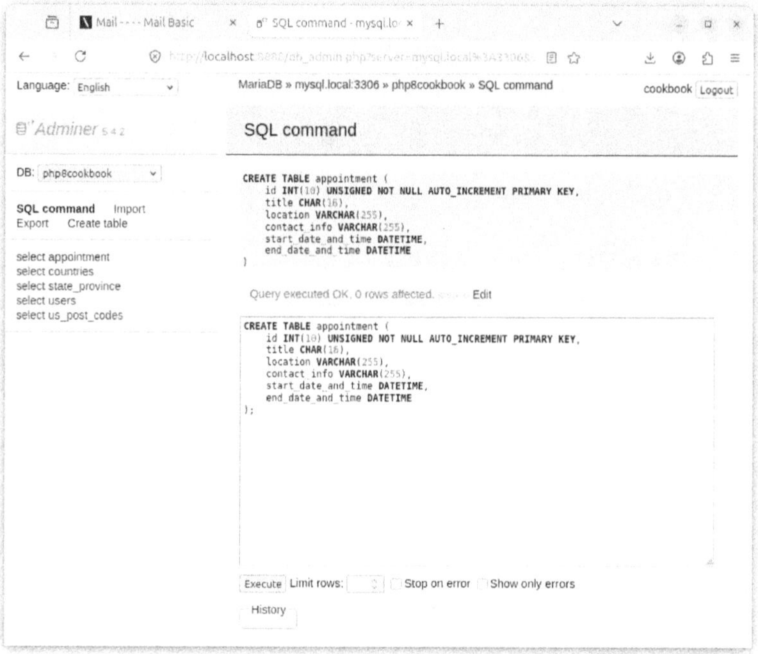

Figure 4.2 – Creating the appointments table

25. Next we sent Claude another prompt requesting the creation of realistic test data. We took the SQL file Claude generated, and ran it through the SQL Command prompt in the Adminer database administration tool:

```
Using ./appointment.sql as a reference, create an SQL import file
consisting of 40 rows of realistic test data.
```

> **Note**
>
> **Privacy and security considerations**
>
> When using AI prompts to generate code, it's extremely important to be cautious about including sensitive or proprietary information in your prompt. Anything you send to your preferred AI platform is the same as publicly posting on the Internet! Different AI platforms will have varying privacy and security policies that you need to carefully review. At the very least you are adding to the AI's knowledge base, and it's unclear how the AI might decide to deploy that information (despite its creator's safeguards and guardrails).

How it works...

To view the GenAI initiated results, open your browser to this URL: `http://localhost:8888/src/Chapter04/ch04_appointment.php`

Here's an example of what you might see:

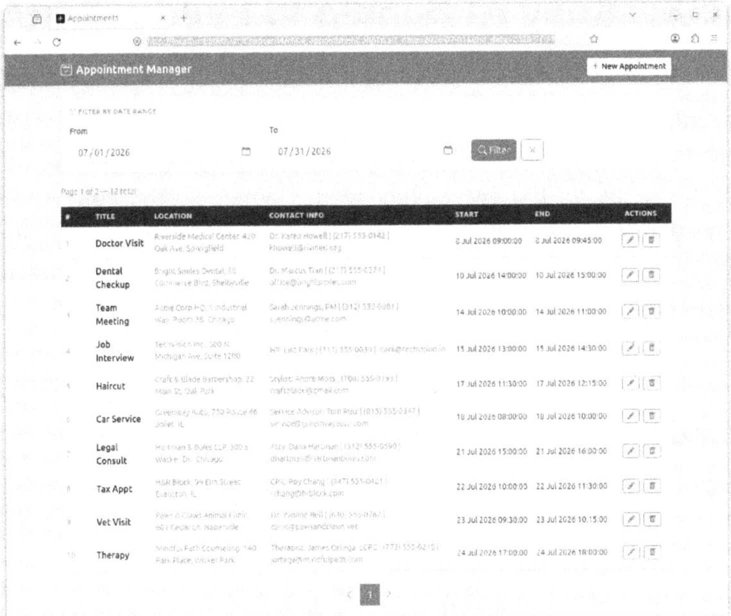

Figure 4.3 – Results of GenAI-assisted OOP calendar program

The key takeaway you should get from this recipe is the approach to use when using GenAI to assist in coding. If your application involves a database, a great way to start is to provide the AI with the database structure. Most GenAI platforms, and most locally-installed coding tools, such as Cursor or Claude Code, retain previous information in a single session. This means that the AI is able to refer back to the database structure as needed as long as you continue in the same session.

The most important thing is to have a clear goal in mind. Developing skeleton classes, as well as using abstract classes and interfaces, helps for larger and more complex projects. We spent a considerable amount of time defining precise instructions to provide to the AI. This is of interest as it alters your programming workflow. From just writing lines of code you instead focus on what is the final objective for each method.

The amount of time spent defining the instructions is estimated to be around 40% less than the time it would have taken to just write the code. Also, the instructions remain, providing useful documentation for later maintenance. However, we did have to spend another 20% of the overall time taken to get the AI-generated pieces to fit together, and to integrate it into our existing infrastructure.

Using the Symfony AI Bundle to build a GenAI-based service

Most of the major PHP frameworks have launched AI initiatives. In Laravel, for example, there are dozens of new projects, one of the best known being `openai-php/laravel`. However, for the purposes of this recipe, we'll show you how to incorporate the **Symfony** AI-Bundle into a Symfony website. **Symfony** is one of the most widely used PHP frameworks, along with Laravel, and this bundle is well integrated into the framework itself. For demonstration purposes, we'll define a website that displays headlines and summaries, with links, to news articles from different pre-selected categories. Bear in mind that because we're making backend calls to a GenAI service, the website can literally do anything we can imagine.

Getting ready

In order to follow this recipe, you'll need to retrieve an API token from your preferred GenAI platform. For the purposes of illustration, in this recipe, we'll use an API token acquired from OpenAI.

You'll also need to refresh the packages in the basic demo Symfony website we've created for this purpose. The project root for this basic website is in the `/path/to/php8cookbook/src/Chapter04/symfony.test`. From the `/path/to/php8cookbook` folder, open a command shell into the PHP 8 container by running `./admin.sh shell php8` (Linux/Mac) or `.\admin.ps1 shell php8` (Windows Powershell).

Once you're in the container, run these commands to refresh the Symfony website code. Please note that because these AI packages evolve rapidly, their declared platform requirements may temporarily lag behind experimental environments. The `--ignore-platform-reqs` flag should only be used in controlled development environments:

```
ed@localhost:~/Repos/PHP-8-Programming-Cookbook
$ ./admin.sh shell php8
php8:/repo# cd symfony.test/
php8:/repo/symfony.test# php composer.phar self-update
You are already using the latest available Composer version 2.9.5 (stable
channel).
php8:/repo/symfony.test# php composer.phar update --ignore-platform-reqs
Loading composer repositories with package information
Restricting packages listed in "symfony/symfony" to "8.0.*"
... lines omitted
Bumping dependencies
./composer.json has been updated (1 changes).
```

Note

OpenAI API Keys

To get an API key from OpenAI, you need to first create an account. Once done, you can go to `https://platform.openai.com/` to create a new API key. It's important to know that when you first create an OpenAI API key, the key itself will be fully displayed only once. You *must* copy and store this key in a secure location. It's also important to take steps to prevent this key from appearing in your source code repository.

How to do it...

1. The first step is to install the desired Symfony AI components. It's important to note that these components are in a constant state of flux. Accordingly, there's a good chance that the component requirements do not match our virtual environment. Therefore, when using Composer to install these cutting-edge components, be sure to add the `--ignore-platform-reqs` flag:

```
php8:/repo/symfony.test#
php composer.phar require symfony/ai-platform --ignore-platform-reqs
php8:/repo/symfony.test#
php composer.phar require symfony/ai-agent --ignore-platform-reqs
php8:/repo/symfony.test#
php composer.phar require symfony/ai-store --ignore-platform-reqs
php8:/repo/symfony.test#
php composer.phar require symfony/ai-chat --ignore-platform-reqs
php8:/repo/symfony.test#
php composer.phar require symfony/ai-bundle --ignore-platform-reqs
```

2. We must also install the driver package for our chosen AI provider. Symfony refers to these as *bridge* packages. You can find a list of Symfony AI bridge classes on the Packagist website by running this query:

```
https://packagist.org/search/?query=symfony%20ai%20bridge
```

3. For the purposes of this recipe, we'll add the OpenAI bridge platform component:

```
php8:/repo/symfony.test# php composer.phar require symfony/ai-open-ai-
platform  --ignore-platform-reqs
```

4. Store your API key in the `.env.local` file at the root of the Symfony project. You might also add information on the model and bridge component you plan to use. Here's an example of how that might appear:

```
GENAI_MODEL=gpt-4.1-nano
GENAI_API_KEY=put_your_API_key_here
GENAI_BRIDGE=OpenAi
```

Tip

Very important!

When using version control, make sure that you prevent your version control system from committing your API key. When you install a Symfony skeleton website, it automatically adds a `.gitignore` file that excludes the `.env.local` file.

5. **Twig** is a powerful templating language often used in Symfony applications. In order to use Twig in our Symfony project, we'll also need to add the Symfony Twig bundle:

```
php8:/repo/symfony.test# php composer.phar require symfony/twig-bundle --
ignore-platform-reqs
```

Tip

For more information on Twig, have a look at this web page: `https://twig.symfony.com/`

6. This recipe builds a news summary application, which means it needs to browse the web. For this purpose, we'll also create a *scraper* tool, and will instruct Symfony AI to invoke this tool when making the GenAI call. Here's our custom scraper tool, defined in the file `CustomScraper.php`, located in the `/path/to/php8cookbook/symfony.test/src/Service` directory:

```
<?php
namespace App\Service;
use Symfony\AI\Agent\Toolbox\Attribute\AsTool;
use Symfony\Component\DomCrawler\Crawler as DomCrawler;
use Symfony\Contracts\HttpClient\HttpClientInterface;
#[AsTool('scraper', 'Loads the visible text and title of a website by
URL.')]
class CustomScraper {
    private const MAX_CHARS = 40000;
    public function __construct(private readonly HttpClientInterface
$httpClient)
    {}
    public function __invoke(string $url): array {
```

```
        $response = $this->httpClient->request('GET', $url);
        $crawler  = new DomCrawler($response->getContent());
        $title    = $crawler->filter('title')->text('');
        $content  = substr($crawler->filter('body')->text(''), 0,
self::MAX_CHARS);
        return ['title' => $title, 'content' => $content];
    }
}
```

Tip

Symfony produces a scraper tool that can be used with its AI Agent. However, in our experience, this tool feeds the *entire contents* of all the scraped web pages, radically upping the token count, and eventually triggering a rate limit exceeded error. To get around this problem, we created our own scraper tool, modeled after the one provided by Symfony.

If you are interested in the Symfony AI Scraper tool, you can install it using Composer as follows:

```
php composer.phar require symfony/ai-scraper-tool  --ignore-
platform-reqs
php composer.phar require symfony/ai-agent --ignore-platform-
reqs
```

7. Next, we create a `GenAiService` class to be made available to our controller. First, we add `use` statements to identify needed external Symfony AI components:

```
<?php
namespace App\Service;
use InvalidArgumentException;
use App\Service\CustomScraper as Scraper;
use Symfony\AI\Agent\Agent;
use Symfony\AI\Agent\Toolbox\Toolbox;
use Symfony\AI\Agent\Toolbox\AgentProcessor;
use Symfony\AI\Platform\Message\Message;
use Symfony\AI\Platform\Message\MessageBag;
use Symfony\AI\Platform\PlatformInterface;
use Symfony\AI\Platform\Result\ResultInterface;
```

```
use Symfony\Component\HttpClient\HttpClient;
class GenAiService {
```

8. Next, we define a class constructor that accepts arguments ultimately supplied from the environment variables in `.env.local`. We'll later create a Symfony service definition that reads these variables:

```
public const LOG_FN = __DIR__ . '/../../var/api.log';
public ?PlatformInterface $platform = null;
public function __construct(
    public string $apiKey, public string $apiBridge, public string
$apiModel) {
    $factory = '\\Symfony\\AI\\Platform\\Bridge\\' .
        $apiBridge . '\\PlatformFactory';
    if (!class_exists($factory))
        throw new InvalidArgumentException('ERROR: provider unavailable');
    $this->platform = $factory::create($this->apiKey,
HttpClient::create());
}
```

9. The `chat()` method conveys the prompt provided in `$text` to the chosen AI platform and model. We first create a scraper tool instance, place it in a Toolbox instance, and then add it to the Agent via an `AgentProcessor` (whew!). You'll note that the `MessageBag` instance can include system instructions using `Message::forSystem()` as well as the user prompt. System messages are general prompts to provide the AI with added information such as the identity it's to assume, assumptions, and other contextual information:

```
public function chat(string $text_sys, string $text_usr): ResultInterface {
    $scraper = new Scraper(HttpClient::create());
    $toolbox = new Toolbox([$scraper]);
    $agentProcessor = new AgentProcessor($toolbox);
    $agent = new Agent($this->platform, $this->apiModel,
        [$agentProcessor], [$agentProcessor]);
    $messages       = new MessageBag(
        Message::forSystem($text_sys),
        Message::ofUser($text_usr)
    );
    $result = $agent->call($messages);
    // remove after testing
```

```
    file_put_contents(self::LOG_FN, __METHOD__ . ':' . var_export($result,
true));
    return $result;
}}
```

10. We can now create a definition for the new service that reads information from the environment file. The definition is added at the end of the `services.yaml` file located in the `/path/to/php8cookbook/symfony.test/config/` directory. As this is a YAML file, it's important to respect the indentation. When the service is invoked, the defined PHP variables are automatically provided by the `__construct()` method of our new `GenAiService` class:

```
    App\Service\GenAiService:
        arguments:
            $apiKey: '%env(GENAI_API_KEY)%'
            $apiBridge: '%env(GENAI_BRIDGE)%'
            $apiModel: '%env(GENAI_MODEL)%'
```

11. We're now in a position to create the controller. As there's only one controller in this project, we'll call it `IndexController`. We start with a series of `use` statements to identify needed classes:

```
<?php
namespace App\Controller;
use Throwable;
use App\Service\GenAiService;
use Symfony\Component\Routing\Attribute\Route;
use Symfony\Component\HttpFoundation\Request;
use Symfony\Component\HttpFoundation\Response;
use Symfony\Component\HttpFoundation\JsonResponse;
use Symfony\Bundle\FrameworkBundle\Controller\AbstractController;
class IndexController extends AbstractController {
```

12. Next, we define a set of useful class constants, one of which is our prompt:

```
public const NO_NEWS = 'No News [%d]';
public const ERR_API = 'Unable to make API call';
public const CATEGORIES = ['World','North America','South
America','Europe','Middle East','Asia','South Pacific'];
public const DEFAULT_CATEGORY = 'World';
```

```
public const DEFAULT_NEWS_SRC = 'https://www.yahoo.com/news/';
public const INFO_MISSING = 'Info Missing';
public const PROMPT_SYS = 'Use %s as the news source. '
    . 'Do not provide any other explanations or reasoning -- just give
'
    . ' me the JSON string with "headline", "summary", and "link" '
    . 'for each news item. For each item only give me these 3 things: '
    . 'headline: The news item headline with a link to the news story. '
    . 'summary: A concise 50 word summary of the news story. '
    . 'link: A URL link to the news story. ';
public const PROMPT_USR = 'In JSON format, give me headlines and '
    . 'summaries of the top 10 news stories in this category: %s.';
```

13. There are three public methods. The first method generates content for the main page. The second method is designed to react to AJAX requests and avoid having to do a full-page refresh for subsequent queries. Let's have a look at the first method. This method directly invokes our Twig template (shown later in this recipe). You'll note that our `GenAiService` is provided as an argument to this method. The default category (`World`) and the service are then passed to the protected `getChat()` method that makes the actual GenAI call:

```
#[Route('/', name: 'app_news', methods: ['GET'])]
public function index(Request $request, GenAiService $service): Response {
    return $this->render(
        'index.html.twig', [
            'categories' => self::CATEGORIES,
            'news_src' => self::DEFAULT_NEWS_SRC,
            'news' => $this->getChat(self::DEFAULT_CATEGORY,
                self::DEFAULT_NEWS_SRC, $service)]);
}
```

14. The second public method updates the news source (which defaults to Yahoo news),and stores it in the session (NOTE: direct $_SESSION usage is discouraged!):

```
#[Route('/source', name: 'app_source', methods: ['GET'])]
public function updateSrc(Request $request): Response {
    $data = $request->getContent('news_src') ?? self::DEFAULT_NEWS_SRC;
    $_SESSION['news_src'] = strip_tags($data);
    return $this->json(['success' => true]);
}
```

15. The third public method is designed to intercept POST AJAX calls. You'll note that this method also calls the protected `getChat()` method:

````
#[Route('/api/news', name: 'app_news_api', methods: ['POST'])]
public function newsAjax(Request $request, GenAiService $service):
    JsonResponse {
    $data = json_decode($request->getContent(), true);
    $category = strip_tags($data['category'] ?? self::DEFAULT_CATEGORY);
    $news_src = $_SESSION['news_src'] ?? self::DEFAULT_NEWS_SRC;
    if (empty($category) || !in_array($category, self::CATEGORIES)) {
        return $this->json(['success' => false,
            'error' => 'Missing required fields'], 400);
    } elseif (empty($news_src)) {
        return $this->json(['success' => false,
             'error' => 'Missing news source'], 400);
    } else {
        return $this->json(['success' => true,
            'html' => $this->getChat($category, $news_src, $service)]);
    }
}
````

16. The remaining method, `getChat()`, uses the `GenAiService` to make the API call and processes the results appropriately. You'll see that even though we instructed the AI to only return a JSON string, it wraps the string in markup language (` ```json ... ``` `), which needs to be removed:

````
protected function getChat(string $category, string $news_src,
    GenAiService $service) : string {
    $prompt_sys = sprintf(self::PROMPT_SYS, $news_src);
    $prompt_usr = sprintf(self::PROMPT_USR, $category);
    $response = $service->chat($prompt_sys, $prompt_usr);
    $json     = trim($response->getContent() ?? '');
    $json     = str_replace(['```json','```'], '', $json);
    $arr      = json_decode($json, true);
    $html     = sprintf(self::NO_NEWS, __LINE__);
````

17. It's critical to understand that the output from your AI platform originates from an outside source, and must therefore be treated with due diligence. Accordingly, we use

`strip_tags()` to sanitize the included information before adding to the final HTML output:

```
            if (!empty($arr)) {
                $html = '<table>';
                $html .= '<tr><th>Headline</th><th>Summary</th></tr>';
                foreach ($arr as $item) {
                    $link = strip_tags($item['link'] ?? '#');
                    $head = strip_tags($item['headline'] ?? 'No Headline');
                    $summ = strip_tags($item['summary'] ?? 'No Summary');
                    $html .= '<tr>';
                    $html .= '<td><a href="' . htmlspecialchars($link) . '">';
                    $html .= htmlspecialchars($head) . '</a></td>';
                    $html .= '<td>' . htmlspecialchars($summ) . '</td>';
                    $html .= '</tr>';
                }
                $html .= '</table>';
            }
            return $html;
        }
    }
```

18. The only remaining task is to define the Twig templates. In the `/path/to/php8cookbook/symfony.test/templates` folder we create `base.html.twig`. In this, we place the outer HTML and leave open blocks for styling and JavaScript code:

```
<!DOCTYPE html>
<html lang="en">
<head>
    <meta charset="UTF-8">
    <meta name="viewport" content="width=device-width, initial-scale=1.0">
    <title>{% block title %}Symfony App{% endblock %}</title>
    {% block stylesheets %}{% endblock %}
</head>
<body>
    {% block body %}{% endblock %}
    {% block javascripts %}{% endblock %}
</body>
</html>
```

19. We then create a Twig template tied to our new controller. It then loads the base template and displays the header:

```
{% extends 'base.html.twig' %}
{% block title %}News Roundup{% endblock %}
{% block body %}
<h1>News Roundup</h1>
```

20. As you will recall, when the `IndexController::index()` method invokes the template, it passes the news source and an array of categories. In this template, we set up a Twig `for` loop that displays the category buttons:

```
<div id="categories">
    {% for category in categories %}
        <button class="category-btn" data-category="{{ category }}">
        {{ category }}</button>
    {% endfor %}
</div>
```

21. The next DIV tag provides an input element for the news source and houses the AI-generated news article summaries:

```
<div id="news-table">
    <p>News Source: <form action="/source" method="get"><input type="text"
name="news_src" value="{{ news_src }}" /><input type="submit" /></form></p>
    {{ news|raw }}
</div>
```

22. The last bit of code in the index template is the jQuery JavaScript logic needed to intercept button clicks:

```
<script src="https://code.jquery.com/jquery-4.0.0.min.js" ></script>
<script>
$(document).ready(function() {
    $('.category-btn').click(function() {
        var category = $(this).data('category');
        $.ajax({
            url: '/api/news',
            method: 'POST',
            data: JSON.stringify({ category: category }),
```

```
            contentType: 'application/json',
            success: function(response) {
                if (response.success) {
                    $('#news-table').html(response.html);
                } else {
                    $('#news-table').html('<p>Error: ' + response.error +
'</p>');
                }
            },
            error: function() {
                $('#news-table').html('<p>An error occurred while fetching
news.</p>');
            }
}); }); });
</script>
{% endblock %}
```

23. To see the effect of this recipe, add the following entry to your local `/etc/hosts` file (`C:\Windows\System32\drivers\etc\hosts` for Windows computers):

```
127.0.0.1       symfony.test
```

24. You can then enter this URL in your host computer browser:

```
http://symfony.test:8888
```

25. The initial page load makes a backend request to OpenAI and returns the top 10 world news stories. Here's an example of what you might see:

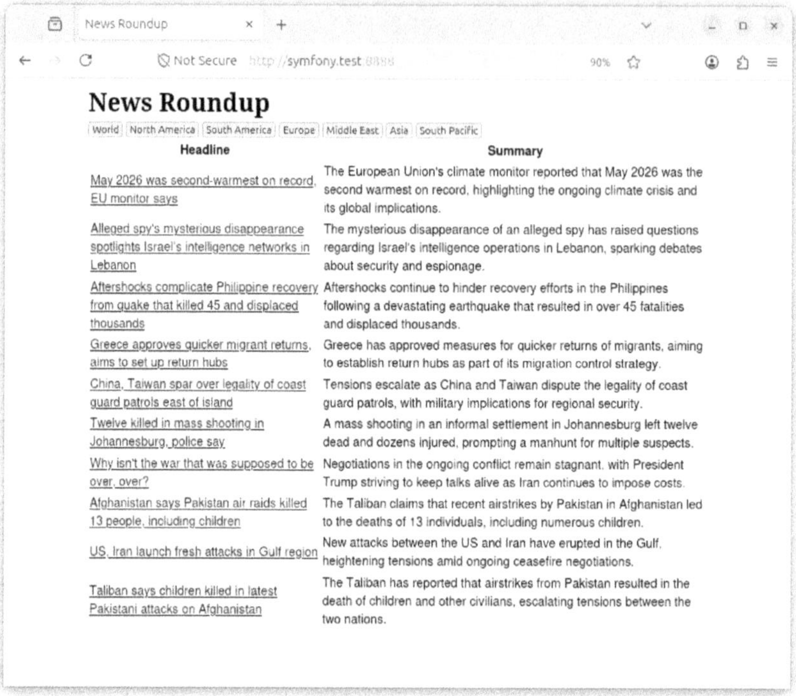

Figure 4.4 – AI-generated summary of news headlines and excerpts

If you press any of the category buttons, summaries of the top 10 news items for that category appear.

Note

AI platform cost control

Making an API call to your AI platform will cost you money! The information you send in the prompt, and the information the AI returns, are usually counted in **tokens**. Although not an exact estimate, a token equates to approximately 4 characters. It's important for testing purposes to select an AI model that gives you a reasonable approximation of the information you expect at the least cost. In general, better models will yield higher quality results, but will cost more. It's also important to understand that the format of the output between models may vary. This might necessitate revising your prompt and also tweaking the code you use to clean up the results.

How it works...

The most important aspect of this recipe is that we are using an AI component from a major PHP framework, in this case Symfony. The advantage to this approach is that if the GenAI provider changes its API request/response format, the framework maintainers will keep up with the changes, saving you hours of work as you try to keep up with the changes. Both the Symfony and Laravel frameworks have a substantial commitment to incorporating GenAI technology. Taking advantage of these components can save you time and help you keep your focus on the end result rather than the nitty-gritty mechanics of making a GenAI API call.

Like many frameworks, Symfony provides a clear path toward full separation of concerns. In the case of Symfony, output is handled through Twig templates. Use the Symfony services architecture to develop GenAI-specific services, which you can then inject into controllers. The controllers provide a point-of-entry and can also provide specific routes. The Symfony `config/services.yaml` file is used to tie services to controllers. You can also define routes in the `config/routes.yaml` file; however, we have found it more convenient to define the route as a PHP 8 Attribute just above each controller method.

Developing a practical class hierarchy

Defining a class in PHP is easy. What is more difficult is developing a *hierarchy* of classes that serves a distinct practical purpose. In this recipe we return to our old friend the Geonames project and define a hierarchy of classes to hold city and post code data.

To jog your memory, the Geonames project has two main branches. One branch is devoted to collecting data on cities and localities within given countries. The data collected includes city names, latitude, longitude, population, and elevation, among other bits of information. The other branch collects postcode data for given countries.

Getting ready

To start building a practical class hierarchy, we can start from the top and move down, or we can start from the lowest level and work our way up. The approach you choose depends on the complexity of the project and accessibility of the data that needs to be modeled as a class. In this case, the two data sets have clearly defined data structures, so we'll work from the lowest levels and move upwards.

To test the code in this recipe, download the Geonames city data as follows:

```
ed@localhost:~/Repos/Packt/PHP-Programming-in-the-AI-Era $ ./admin.sh shell php8
php8:/repo# cd data php8:/repo/data# wget https://download.geonames.org/export/
dump/cities15000.zip
```

```
php8:/repo/data# unzip cities15000.zip
php8:/repo/data# rm cities15000.zip
```

How to do it...

1. The first class to build is the `City` class. This will house data from the primary Geonames project data set. This information is visible at the bottom of this web page: `https://download.geonames.org/export/dump/`. The project has kindly laid out the data structure of its CSV files in a README file that shows the following. Please note that some lines were omitted:

```
The main 'geoname' table has the following fields :
---------------------------------------------------
geonameid : integer id in geonames database
name      : varchar(200) geographical name (utf8)
asciiname : varchar(200) name in ascii characters
...
timezone  : the IANA timezone id
modification date : date in yyyy-MM-dd format
```

2. We now have enough information to create our `City` class. In the `/path/to/php8cookbook/src/Geonames` directory, we create a file `City.php`. We name the file after the class to facilitate autoloading. For simplicity, we mark all properties as public with the appropriate data types to model dataset rows directly. In addition, we use an `Attribute` called `#[City]` to identify the main purpose of the class. You'll note that we assign a default value that matches the data type. This helps avoid undefined property warnings:

```
<?php
namespace Cookbook\Geonames;
/* This class holds Geonames city data. Source:
     https://download.geonames.org/export/dump/   */
class City {
    public int    $geonameid = 0;  // integer id
    public string $name = '';    // city name
    public string $asciiname = ''; // ascii chars
    public string $alternatenames = '';
    public float  $latitude = 0.0; //degrees (wgs84)
    public float  $longitude = 0.0; //degrees (wgs84)
    public string $feature_class = ''; // char(1)
```

```
    public string $feature_code = ''; // varchar(10)
    public string $country = ''; // ISO 2 code
    public string $cc2      = ''; // other codes
    public string $admin1  = ''; // FIPScode
    public string $admin2  = ''; // varchar(80)
    public string $admin3  = ''; // varchar(20)
    public string $admin4  = ''; // varchar(20)
    public int  $population = 0; // bigint
    public int    $elevation = 0;   // in meters
    public string $dem      = ''; // elevation model
    public string $timezone = '';  // iana timezone
    public string $modification = ''; // date
    // methods (shown next)
}
```

3. We're now ready to do the same thing for the post code Geonames data set. Here is how that might appear for a class we'll call `PostCode`:

```
<?php
namespace Cookbook\Geonames;
/* This class holds Geonames post code data:
    https://download.geonames.org/export/zip/   */
class PostCode {
    public string $country      = '';  // iso2 code
    public string $postal_code = '';  // varchar(20)
    public string $place_name  = '';  // varchar(180)
    public string $admin_name1 = '';  // varchar(100)
    public string $admin_code1 = '';  // varchar(20)
    public string $admin_name2 = '';  // varchar(100)
    public string $admin_code2 = '';  // varchar(20)
    public string $admin_name3 = '';  // varchar(100)
    public string $admin_code3 = '';  // varchar(20)
    public float $latitude      = 0.0; // latitude
    public float $longitude     = 0.0; // longitude
    public int $accuracy        = 0;   // accuracy
    // methods go here
}
```

4. Now the easy part is done! If you're creating classes that are designed to model data sets, all you need to do is examine the data set schema and create a class that mimics it.

You can do the same for any data that needs to be stored. Create a class that models the schema of the storage target and you're done. The more complicated part of designing a practical class hierarchy is deciding what to define at the upper levels. In this example, we'll stick with two levels, but the same principles we lay out here can help you design more complicated structures.

5. The next task is to define a **super class** (also called **parent class**) that serves to tie the lower-level classes together. In this super class, you would place methods common to all of the descendant classes. Because the data source for both data sets is a tab-delimited CSV file, we need a way to instantly build an instance of either class from a row of CSV data. As you might have guessed, we can create a common `__construct()` method for this purpose. We can leverage the `Cookbook\Iterator\LargeFile` class developed in *Chapter 2, Using PHP 8 High Performance Features* to iterate through the Geonames files, producing data one row at a time. We can feed the row into the new class constructor and use this to populate properties.

6. In the `/path/to/php8cookbook/src/Geonames` directory, we create a file `GeoBase.php` that houses our new super class. Here is how the class, complete with the new `__construct()` method, might appear:

```
<?php
namespace Cookbook\Geonames;
use InvalidArgumentException;
abstract class GeoBase implements NameInterface {
    public const ERR_COUNT = 'ERROR: column count mismatch';
    public function __construct(array $data) {
        $vars = get_object_vars($this);
        if (count($data) !== count($vars)) {
            throw new InvalidArgumentException(self::ERR_COUNT);
        }
        // IMPORTANT: property order must match the order in the Geonames
files
        foreach (array_keys($vars) as $idx => $name) {
            $this->$name = match (gettype($this->$name)) {
                'integer' => (int) ($data[$idx] ?? 0),
                'float', 'double'   => (float) ($data[$idx] ?? 0.0),
                default   => trim(strip_tags($data[$idx] ?? ''))
            };
        }
    }
```

```
    // other methods covered in subsequent steps in this recipe
}
```

7. Because the data in the Geonames files will be captured as a string, we needed to add a `foreach()` loop combined with a `match {}` expression to assign the correct data type. Without this extra logic, we would encounter a `TypeError` when assigning values to typed properties.
8. We wish to have methods that reveal the city name, state or province, and country code. Examining the actual data, we discover that all property names differ except for the `$country` property. Accordingly, we can define a common method in the base class to retrieve the country code. As for the city and state/province names, we'll need to handle them separately. Here's how the new `getCountry()` method might appear in the `GeoBase` class:

```
abstract class GeoBase {
    // other code not shown
    public function getCountry() : string {
        return $this->country ?? '';
    }
}
```

9. Next, we have each of the subclasses extend the new `GeoBase` class. This ensures they inherit the common `__construct()` and `getCountry()` methods, allowing unique instances to be created from Geonames data:

```
class PostCode extends GeoBase {
    // other code not shown
}
class City extends GeoBase {
    // other code not shown
}
```

10. Next, we turn our attention to functionality. To promote flexibility, we can incorporate one or more **interfaces** to ensure that certain mandatory methods are present. In this case, both of our subclasses house city data, including the name. However, the property that contains the city name is different. In the `PostCode` class, the `$place_name` property is either the name of a city or the name of a significant landmark. In contrast, in the `City` class, the property with the city name is simply called `$name`. Due to this

difference, if we define a `getCityName()` method in `GeoBase`, we would have to modify the data structure in one of the subclasses. This could cause confusion as the Geonames documentation calls the property one name and we would be calling it another.

11. We could define a `getCityName()` method in `GeoBase`, and mark it as `abstract`. However, a better option would be to create an interface that mandates this functionality. Here is how such an interface might appear. Note that we also define a method `getStateProvCode()` as the actual code body needs to occur at the subclass level:

```
namespace Cookbook\Geonames;
interface NameInterface {
    public function getCityName() : string;
    public function getStateProvCode() : string;
}
```

12. At this point we have the option of implementing the interface in each class where the method is required, or, in our situation, we can have `GeoBase` implement the interface, which passes the mandate down the inheritance tree:

```
abstract class GeoBase implements NameInterface {
    // other code not shown
}
```

Note

Interfaces and abstract classes

It's important to note that if a class implements an interface, but does not define the method(s) mandated by the interface, that class must be marked as abstract.

13. We are now free to implement the `getCityName()` method as per the requirements of each subclass. Here is the implementation in our `City` class:

```
class City extends GeoBase {
    // other code not shown
    public function getCityName() : string {
        return $this->name ?? '';
```

```
    }
}
```

14. And here is the same method defined in the `PostCode` class:

```
class PostCode extends GeoBase {
    // other code not shown
    public function getCityName() : string {
        return $this->place_name ?? '';
    }
}
```

15. We then define methods to extract the value of the state or province in each of the two subclasses:

```
class City extends GeoBase {
    // other code not shown
    public function getStateProvCode() : string {
        return $this->admin1 ?? '';
    }
}
```

16. Here's the same method defined in the `PostCode` class:

```
class PostCode extends GeoBase {
    // other code not shown
    public function getStateProvCode() : string {
        return $this->admin_code1 ?? '';
    }
}
```

17. Now our small but functional hierarchy is ready to be put to use.

> **Tip**
>
> It is considered best practice to name the file after the class. Although class names in PHP are case-insensitive, it is further considered best practice to use an uppercase letter for the first letter of a class name. You should not put executable code in a class definition file either before or after the actual class definition. The only exception would be using the keyword `namespace` (shown

> in this example) and also using the `declare()` function to impose file-based restrictions such as enforcing strict type checking.

> **Note**
>
> It's possible to define more than one class per file; however, this would negatively affect your application's ability to autoload classes and is therefore highly discouraged.

18. To test our new hierarchy, in the `/path/to/php8cookbook/src/Chapter04` directory we create a file `ch04_basic_oop_hierarchy.php` that leverages `Cookbook\Iterator\LargeFile`. Later we create the `LargeFile` instance using the Geonames file `cities15000.txt` containing city data or `US.txt` for post code data.

```
// Usage: php __FILE__ city|postcode item[,item,item]
include __DIR__ . '/../../vendor/autoload.php';
use Cookbook\Geonames\{City,PostCode};
use Cookbook\Iterator\LargeFile;
$city_fn    = __DIR__ . '/../../data/cities15000.txt';
$post_fn    = __DIR__ . '/../../data/US.txt';
```

19. We then capture output from the URL using `$_GET`, or alternatively from the command line using `$argv`. The variable `$action` can be either *city* or *postcode*. The variable `$item` can be a list of search criteria, which we turn into an array using the `explode()` function:

```
$action = trim(strip_tags(
    $_GET['action'] ?? $argv[1] ?? 'city'));
$item = trim(strip_tags(
    $_GET['search'] ?? $argv[2] ?? 'Rochester'));
$item = explode(',', $item);
$largeFile = new LargeFile(($action === 'city') ? $city_fn : $post_fn);
$iterator  = $largeFile->getIterator();
```

20. We then define an anonymous class that extends the **SPL** (**Standard PHP Library**) class `FilterIterator`. In our new class we define the `accept()` method which is called for each element during iteration. If this method returns `true`, that element is added to

the output. In this manner, we can filter out iteration elements that do not meet our search criteria. After defining the anonymous class, we set the public property `$item` to match the user-provided search criteria:

```
$filter = new class ($iterator) extends FilterIterator {
    public array $item = [];
    public function accept() : bool
    {
        $count = count($this->item);
        $found = 0;
        $row   = parent::current();
        foreach ($this->item as $search)
            $found += (int) str_contains($row, $search);
        return ($found === $count);
    }
};
$filter->item = $item;
```

21. Finally, we define which class to use based on the value of `$action` after which we loop through the filtered iteration and produce results:

```
$class = match($action) {
    'city' => City::class,
    default => PostCode::class
};
printf("%30s | %10s | %4s\n",
    'City', 'State/Prov', 'ISO2');
printf("%30s | %10s | %4s\n",
    '------------------------------', '----------', '----');
foreach ($filter as $row) {
    $item = new $class(str_getcsv($row, "\t"));
    printf( "%20s | %10s | %4s\n",
            $item->getCityName(),
            $item->getStateProvCode(),
```

```
        $item->getCountry());
}
```

22. Here is how the output might appear(any line that contains the search term is included):

```
php8:/repo# php src/Chapter04/ch04_basic_oop_hierarchy.php
                        City | State/Prov | ISO2
---------------------------- | ---------- | ----
                   Rochester |        ENG |   GB
             Rochester Hills |         MI |   US
                   Rochester |         MN |   US
                   Rochester |         NH |   US
                   Rochester |         NY |   US
              North Kingstown |         RI |   US
```

How it works...

The City and PostCode classes mirror the original Geonames file structures. Typed properties help prevent misuse of the code and also facilitate maintenance. The data type associated with each property helps maintainers recognize the purpose of the property. Default values ensure that new objects begin in a valid state and help prevent undefined property warnings. Since Geonames rows are read as strings, values must be converted before assignment to typed properties.

The GeoBase class is marked abstract because it isn't meant to represent a complete Geonames record on its own. Instead, it provides shared functionality, such as constructing an object from a data row and retrieving the country code.

The GeoBase class constructor accepts one row of tab-delimited Geonames data as an array. Calling get_object_vars($this) allows the same constructor to populate either a City or a PostCode object, depending on which class was instantiated.

We use count() to ensure that the incoming row has the expected number of fields. If the data does not match the class structure, an exception is thrown to prevent a partially populated object.

The foreach() loop assigns each field to the matching property by position. A match expression checks each property's default type and casts the incoming value accordingly. Integers become int, decimals become float, and strings are cleaned with trim() and strip_tags().

The `getCountry()` method belongs in `GeoBase` because both data sets use the same `$country` property. However, city and state/province values use different property names in each subclass, so those methods are implemented separately.

An interface, which we call `NameInterface`, defines this shared requirement. It ensures that each subclass provides methods for retrieving the city name and state or province code, even though each class gets those values from different properties. Because `GeoBase` implements this interface, it passes this requirement down the hierarchy.

There's more...

For more information on the two Geonames data sets, have a look at these two download pages:

- Post code data: `https://download.geonames.org/export/zip/`
- Geoname data: `https://download.geonames.org/export/dump/`

Creating a service container

A **service container** is a PHP component that centralizes how application services are instantiated and managed. As defined by **PSR-11** (**PHP Standards Recommendations 11**), it provides a standardized interface with methods for retrieving services by their identifier and checking service availability. Containers resolve dependencies automatically, eliminating manual instantiation throughout the codebase. They promote loose coupling by allowing developers to request services by interface rather than concrete implementation, facilitating testability, and maintainability. Service containers support autowiring, lazy-loading, and service configuration, becoming an essential architectural pattern in modern PHP frameworks like Symfony, Laravel, and Laminas for managing complex dependency graphs.

In this recipe we demonstrate how to register and retrieve services. In other recipes in other chapters in this book we get into how to incorporate factory classes that can auto-wire object production.

Getting ready

In order to remain standards-based, we use Composer to download and install `psr/container`, the **PHP Standards Recommendation** (**PSR**) package that includes the appropriate interface to define a service container. From a command shell into our virtual environment, you can use this command:

```
php8:/repo# php composer.phar require psr/container
```

Here is the output from command execution:

```
./composer.json has been updated
Running composer update psr/container
Loading composer repositories with package information
Updating dependencies
... lines omitted ...
Using version ^2.0 for psr/container
```

How to do it...

1. To begin, we need to define a class that we'll simply call `Container` that implements `Psr\Container\ContainerInterface`. In the `/path/to/php8cookbook/src/Services` directory, we create a file `Container.php`. Here is how the class might appear:

```
<?php
namespace Cookbook\Services;
use ArrayObject;
use Psr\Container\ContainerInterface;
class Container implements ContainerInterface
{
    public ArrayObject $storage;
    protected static $instance = null;
```

2. Because we need to ensure there is only one service container active at any given moment, we mark the `__construct()` method private to prevent its direct instantiation. We then define a static method `getInstance()` that allows us to retrieve an instance, ensuring that the internal property `$instance` has been created. This effectively makes the service container a singleton; however, in production environments that use modern frameworks, the service container is often produced externally and injected where needed. Note that we use the return data type of `static` to indicate that what is returned is an instance of exactly this class:

```
private function __construct() {
    $this->storage = new ArrayObject();
}
public static function getInstance() : static {
    if (empty(static::$instance)) {
        static::$instance = new static();
    }
```

```
        return static::$instance;
    }
```

3. From the description of PSR-11 from this web page, `https://www.php-fig.org/psr/psr-11/`, you'll note that in order to be standards-compliant, our service container must implement two methods: `get()` and `has()`:

```
    public function get(string $key) : mixed {
        return static::$instance->storage[$key] ?? NULL;
    }
    public function has(string $key) : bool {
            return !empty(static::$instance?->storage[$key]);
    }
```

4. There is no specific provision in PSR-11 for how to add a service to the container, so we will also arbitrarily define two additional methods `add()` and `remove()`. Because we want to have the ability to immediately invoke the service as if it were a function, in the second parameter in the `add()` method, we use the data type `mixed` for the service to be added. This allows us to add services of all types:

```
    public function add(string $key, mixed $service) : bool {
        static::$instance->storage[$key] = $service;
        return static::$instance->has($key);
    }
    public function remove(string $key) : bool {
        $ok = false;
        if ($this->has($key)) {
            unset(static::$instance->storage[$key]);
            $ok = true;
        }
        return $ok;
    } }
```

5. For the purposes of illustration, in the `/path/to/php8cookbook/src/Chapter04` directory we create a file `ch04_using_service_container.php`. We load the Composer

autoloader, add a `use` statement to identify the full namespace class name, and grab an instance of the service container:

```
include __DIR__ . '/../../vendor/autoload.php';
use Cookbook\Services\Container;
$container = Container::getInstance();
```

6. Next, we add a set of simple services that add, subtract, multiply, and divide two integers. For the purposes of illustration, we define these services as anonymous functions:

```
$container->add('add',
    function ($a, $b) { return $a + $b; });
$container->add('sub',
    function ($a, $b) { return $a - $b; });
$container->add('mul',
    function ($a, $b) { return $a * $b; });
$container->add('div',
    function ($a, $b) {
        return ($b === 0) ? 0 : $a / $b; });
```

7. We then define values for `$a` and `$b`, and call each of the services in turn:

```
$a = 222;
$b = 111;
echo 'Add: ' . $container->get('add')($a, $b) . PHP_EOL;
echo 'Sub: ' . $container->get('sub')($a, $b) . PHP_EOL;
echo 'Mul: ' . $container->get('mul')($a, $b) . PHP_EOL;
echo 'Div: ' . $container->get('div')($a, $b) . PHP_EOL;
```

8. Here is the output from our simple set of services:

```
php8:/repo# php src/Chapter04/ch04_using_service_container.php
Add: 333
Sub: 111
Mul: 24642
Div: 2
```

How it works...

This recipe is loosely based on Martin Fowler's notion of Inversion of Control Containers and the Dependency Injection pattern. A service container in PHP OOP gives you a central place to define how objects are built, configured, and connected. Dependency injection separates configuration from use, so your classes depend on interfaces rather than concrete implementations. This lowers coupling, makes dependencies explicit, and allows different services to be swapped without major code rewrites. As your applications evolve, the services stored in the container can be developed independently, allowing different teams to work on the same project without fear of interference.

Bear in mind that we could just as easily add services in the form of classes that implement `__invoke()`, which would make the class callable.

There's more...

For information on Inversion of Control Containers and the Dependency Injection pattern, have a look at an excellent article on Martin Fowler's website found here: `https://martinfowler.com/articles/injection.html`.

For more information on PSR-11, have a look here: `https://www.php-fig.org/psr/psr-11/`.

Using lazy objects to improve performance

A much sought-after feature, treasured by the PHP community, is the ability to partially create objects and to delay full instantiation until such time as the object is actually put to use. The ability to create **lazy objects** is of special interest when using service containers. Although the idea of having a central service container is a brilliant concept, loading the container with services that are not used for every request consumes valuable resources and drags down performance. This is especially evident for *heavy* objects that might take a noticeable amount of time to construct.

Getting ready

In order to properly demonstrate the concept of lazy objects, we will create a class that emulates a *lorem ipsum* generator. The idea is to create a class that can extract random paragraphs from classical literature. For this purpose, we turn to **Project Gutenberg** (`https://gutenberg.org/`), and download ASCII text files of selected classic works. For our demonstration, we download the text file for Leo Tolstoy's *War and Peace*, and also *The Complete Works of William Shakespeare*. The text files are then placed in the `/path/to/php8cookbook/data` directory.

How to do it...

1. In the `/path/to/php8cookbook/src/Services` directory, we create a file `Ipsum.php`. In this file, we define a number of constants and properties. This is a general-purpose class, and we can create any number of instances, each being tied to a specific text file. Initially, we set the default text file to *War and Peace*:

```
<?php
namespace Cookbook\Services;
use SplFileObject;
class Ipsum {
    public string $fn = '';
    public array $paragraphs = [];
    public ?SplFileObject $obj = null;
    public const FN   =  __DIR__ . '/../../data/war_and_peace.txt';
    public const SIZE = 40; // line length
```

2. The `__construct()` method assigns values and runs the `analyze()` method (shown next):

```
public function __construct(string $fn = '') {
    $this->fn = (empty($fn)) ? static::FN : $fn;
    $this->obj =
        new SplFileObject($this->fn, 'r');
    $this->paragraphs = $this->analyze();
}
```

3. The `analyze()` method is extremely time-consuming, but vital to the primary purpose of the Ipsum class. It needs to build an array of starting and ending offsets representing paragraphs within the text. When random blocks of text are requested, all the class needs to do is to retrieve random offsets. Thus, the most time-consuming tasks occur when the class is first instantiated:

```
public function analyze(int $size = 0) : array {
    $size = $size ?: static::SIZE;
    $paragraphs = [];
    $this->obj->rewind();
    do {
        $line = $this->obj->fgets() ?? '';
        $len = mb_strlen($line);
```

```
            $line = trim($line);
        } while (!$this->obj->eof() && mb_strlen($line) < $size);
        $paragraphs[] = $this->obj->ftell() - $len;
        while (!$this->obj->eof()) {
            // 1: look for next non-blank line
            do {
                $line = trim($this->obj->fgets() ?? '');
            } while (!$this->obj->eof() &&!empty($line));
            // look for line length >= $size
            while (!$this->obj->eof()
                && strlen($line) < $size) {
                $line = $this->obj->fgets() ?? '';
                $len = strlen($line);
                $line = trim($line);
            }
            // get current offset
            $paragraphs[] =
                $this->obj->ftell() - $len;
            // 2: loop until you get a blank line
            if ($this->obj->eof()) break;
            do {
                $line = trim($this->obj->fgets() ?? '');
            } while (!$this->obj->eof()&&!empty($line));
        }
        return $paragraphs;
    }
```

4. The `getParagraph()` method seeks the given offset within the associated text file and returns the text between offsets:

```
    public function getParagraph(int $offset) {
        $text = '';
        $this->obj->rewind();
        $this->obj->fseek($offset);
        $line = trim($this->obj->fgets() ?? '');
        while (!$this->obj->eof() && !empty($line)) {
            $text .= $line . PHP_EOL;
            $line = trim($this->obj->fgets() ?? '');
        }
```

```
        return $text . PHP_EOL;
    }
```

5. We also define the magic `__invoke()` method so that we can use this class in the service container described in the previous section. As you can see, extracting a random paragraph is trivial once the `analyze()` method has identified suitable blocks of text:

```
public function __invoke(int $num = 1) {
    $text = '';
    for ($x = 0; $x < $num; $x++) {
        $offset = $this→paragraphs[array_rand($this->paragraphs)];
        $text .= $this->getParagraph($offset);
    }
    return $text;
}
```

6. Of most importance is the `LazyIpsum` class. This class returns a **lazy ghost** instance, which can then be stored in the service container. You'll note that we use `ReflectionClass` for this purpose. You'll also note that the class constructor is called using deferred logic, which in this case takes the form of an anonymous function:

```
namespace Cookbook\Services;
use ReflectionClass;
class LazyIpsum {
    public static function getLazy(string $fn) {
        $reflect = new ReflectionClass(Ipsum::class);
        return $reflect->newLazyGhost(
            function (Ipsum $obj) use ($fn) {
             $obj->__construct($fn); });
    }
}
```

> Note
>
> **ReflectionClass lazy methods**
>
> The `ReflectionClass` methods `newLazyGhost()`, `newLazyProxy()`, `resetAsLazyGhost()`, and `resetAsLazyProxy()` are lazy loading mechanisms introduced in PHP 8.4 that create or reset objects as lazy instances, allowing for deferred initialization until the object is actually accessed. For more information, see: `https://www.php.net/ReflectionClass`.

7. In the `/path/to/php8cookbook/src/Chapter04` directory, we create a calling program `ch04_using_non_lazy_objects.php` that loads our service container with `Ipsum` instances. We record the start and stop times as well as the peak memory usage:

```
<?php
require __DIR__ . '/../../vendor/autoload.php';
use Cookbook\Services\Container;
use Cookbook\Services\Ipsum;
$container = Container::getInstance();
$start = microtime(true);
$source = [
    'war_peace' => __DIR__ . '/../../data/war_and_peace.txt',
    'shakespeare' =>__DIR__ . '/../../data/shakespeare.txt'
];
foreach ($source as $key => $fn)
    $container->add($key, new Ipsum($fn));
echo $container->get('shakespeare')(5);
echo 'Elapsed Time: ' . (microtime(true) - $start);
echo 'Peak Memory Usage: ' . memory_get_peak_usage();
```

8. We then define another similar program `ch04_using_lazy_objects.php` that loads the service container with lazy objects rather than actual instances. Everything about this program is the same as the one mentioned above, except that we use the `LazyIpsum` class to load lazy instances into the service container:

```
<?php
include __DIR__ . '/../../vendor/autoload.php';
use Cookbook\Services\Container;
use Cookbook\Services\LazyIpsum;
```

```
$container = Container::getInstance();
// lines omitted
foreach ($source as $key => $fn) {
    $container->add($key, LazyIpsum::getLazy($fn));
}
// lines omitted
```

9. Here's a sample output from `ch04_using_non_lazy_objects.php`, where the service container is loaded with fully initialized Ipsum instances:

```
php8:/repo# php src/Chapter04/ch04_using_non_lazy_objects.php
Look what thou want'st shall be sent after thee.
... lines omitted ...
Are then most humble; I have no ambition
To see a goodlier man.
Elapsed Time      : 0.037732839584351
Peak Memory Usage: 1890232
```

10. When we run `ch04_using_lazy_objects.php`, it loads lazy instances instead of fully initialized instances:

```
php8:/repo# php src/Chapter04/ch04_using_lazy_objects.php
What should he say, but as the cardinal?
... lines omitted ...
Now, Nurse, what news? What hast thou there?
The cords that Romeo bid thee fetch?

Canst thou so daff me? Thou hast kill'd my child;
If thou kill'st me, boy, thou shalt kill a man.
Elapsed Time      : 0.028305053710938
Peak Memory Usage: 1610952
```

How it works...

You'll note that there's a noticeable difference in both performance and memory usage. Without using lazy objects, on the host system used for this demonstration, the elapsed time was approximately 0.0377 seconds whereas when using lazy objects, the time elapsed fell to approximately 0.0283 seconds. In this sample run we observed reduced initialization time and lower peak memory usage. Further, you'll note that when not using lazy objects, the peak memory usage was around 1.89 M bytes compared to 1.61 M bytes when using lazy objects, representing a 15% reduction.

The reason for the difference is that when we don't use lazy objects, service objects need to be initialized as they're stored in the service container, expending time and memory. When using lazy objects, services are stored in a partially initialized state. The initialization only occurs for services that are actually used. In this example, the `war_peace` service was not used, so only the service associated with the `shakespeare` service was initialized.

5

Interacting with a Database

In this chapter, we explore practical techniques for integrating PHP applications with relational databases using classic design patterns. The first recipe shows you how to build a PDO-based database connection factory leveraging a central services container. Next, we demonstrate how **AI agents** can accelerate development by generating database entity classes from SQL definitions. We then walk through how you might build a flexible SQL query builder using the Builder design pattern. Finally, we address performance and cost efficiency by providing a recipe that defines a PSR-16 compliant caching class that stores and retrieves GenAI API responses directly from a database.

In this chapter we cover the following main topics:

- Defining a factory class to produce a PDO database connection
- Using AI Agents to define database entity classes
- Creating an SQL query builder
- Using a database to cache GenAI queries

Technical requirements

To test the code presented in this chapter, you'll need a functional MySQL-equivalent database, along with PHP 8.4 and a web server. Follow the instructions in *Chapter 1, Building a Foundation,* to build the virtualized environment based upon Podman, a Docker-compatible virtualization package. Once completed, the virtual environment will have a functional database and other requirements you need to test the recipes presented in this chapter.

Defining a factory class to produce a PDO database connection

Building on the concept of a central services container, in this recipe we show you how to define a flexible database connection service that's based upon a separate configuration file. In this recipe, we'll define a **factory class** that uses a configuration array to produce a database connection. Further, we'll set up our connection class as a service leveraging the central services container discussed in *Chapter 4, Working with PHP Object-Oriented Programming*.

> Note
>
> **What is PDO?**
>
> **PDO** stands for **PHP Data Objects**. It's a lightweight database access abstraction extension that follows the Adapter software design pattern. Using PDO allows you to write non-database-specific code. Through configuration, you can later switch the underlying database technology without having to change your source code.

Getting ready

For the purposes of this recipe, we will leverage the services container discussed in *Chapter 4* which we called `Cookbook\Services\Container`. We also need a configuration array with the appropriate database credentials. In the case of the virtual environment used with this book, the database credentials are stored in a configuration file `/path/to/php8cookbook/config/db.config.php`. Here are the contents of this file:

```
<?php
return [
    'db_driver'  => 'mysql',
    'db_name'    => 'php8cookbook',
    'db_usr'     => 'cookbook',
    'db_pwd'     => 'password',
    'db_host'    => 'mysql.local',
    'options'    => [\PDO::ATTR_ERRMODE => \PDO::ERRMODE_EXCEPTION]
];
```

How to do it...

1. To start, we create a configuration service and add it to our `Cookbook\Services\Container` services container. Some developers prefer to create a

formal configuration class. However, seeing as the configuration needed for this recipe is a simple array returned by the above-mentioned `db.config.php` script, we can simply wrap the configuration array in an anonymous function and add it to the services container using `db_config` as the service name:

```
define('DB_CONFIG_FN', __DIR__
    . '/../../config/db.config.php');
$container->add('db_config',
    function () { return require DB_CONFIG_FN; });
```

2. Next, we define a connection class `Cookbook\Database\Connect` designed to produce a database connection based upon the supplied array. The `__construct()` method does most of the work by building the PDO connection or throwing an exception. We add `__invoke()` to make the instance callable (to fit the needs of the services container) and simply have it return the `PDO` instance. In the `catch` block, we record the original error or exception class and the actual error message in the error log. We then throw a `RuntimeException` error with a benign message that does not reveal the actual situation as a security precaution:

```
<?php
namespace Cookbook\Database;
use PDO;
use Throwable;
use RuntimeException;
class Connect {
    public const ERR_PDO = 'ERROR: unable to create PDO instance';
    public ?PDO $pdo = null;
    public function __construct(array $config) {
        $options  = $config['options']
            ??  [PDO::ATTR_ERRMODE => PDO::ERRMODE_EXCEPTION];
        $username = $config['db_usr']  ?? '';
        $password = $config['db_pwd']  ?? '';
        try {
            $dsn = sprintf('%s:host=%s;dbname=%s',
                $config['db_driver'],
                $config['db_host'],
                $config['db_name']);
            $this->pdo = new PDO(
                $dsn, $username, $password, $options);
```

```
        } catch(Throwable $t) {
            error_log(__METHOD__ . ':'
                . get_class($t) . ':'
                . $t->getMessage());
            throw new RuntimeException(
                static::ERR_PDO);
        }
    }
    public function __invoke() : PDO|null {
        return $this->pdo;
    }
}
```

It's important to note that we will not directly store this class as a service. The reason why not is because our connection class has a hard dependency on the configuration array. Accordingly, we'll use a factory that injects the configuration array and builds an instance of this class.

3. Here's our `Cookbook\Services\ConnectionFactory` class that pulls in the configuration array to produce a `Connect` instance. What's notable about this class is that all it requires as a constructor argument is an instance of the services container:

```
namespace Cookbook\Services;
use PDO;
use Throwable;
use Cookbook\Database\Connect;
use Psr\Container\ContainerInterface;

class ConnectionFactory {
    public function __construct(
        public ContainerInterface $container) {}
```

4. The `__invoke()` method makes the factory callable. You'll note that the factory uses the previously defined `db_config` service to retrieve the database configuration array. Although this arrangement might initially seem overly complicated, it greatly simplifies how developers obtain database connections. Developers that need a database connection just need to make a call to the service container, and don't have to worry about where or what's in the database configuration array. Note that an extra set of empty parentheses `()` are needed on return. The reason is because the `Connect` class

is invokable, and we want its product, a `PDO` instance, not an instance of the `Connect` class itself:

```
    public function __invoke() : PDO|null {
        return (new Connect($this->container->get('db_config')))();
    }
}
```

> Note
>
> **Factory Classes**
>
> A **factory class** is a design pattern that creates objects without exposing instantiation logic, enabling flexible object creation. Factory classes are deeply intertwined with the notions of inversion of control containers and dependency injection. For a great discussion on these concepts, have a look at this article on Martin Fowler's website: `https://martinfowler.com/articles/injection.html`.

5. In the `/path/to/php8cookbook/src/Chapter05` directory, we define a test script `ch05_creating_a_connection_service.php` that defines the location of the database config file and creates a services container instance:

```
define('DB_CONFIG_FN',  __DIR__ . '/../../config/db.config.php');
include __DIR__ . '/../../vendor/autoload.php';
use Cookbook\Services\Container;
use Cookbook\Services\ConnectionFactory;
$container = Container::getInstance();
```

6. Next, we add the `db_config` service, and use `var_dump()` to display the contents of this service:

```
$container->add('db_config', function () { return require DB_CONFIG_FN; });
var_dump($container->get('db_config'));
```

7. Finally, we add the `db_connect` service, and then invoke it to produce a `$pdo` instance. We also run `var_dump()` to confirm that we now have a valid `PDO` connection:

```
$container->add('db_connect' , new ConnectionFactory($container));
$pdo = $container->get('db_connect');
var_dump($pdo);
```

How it works...

The importance of the services container workflow illustrated here cannot be overstated. The problem all developers face is how to provide services without exposing the mechanisms required to bring the service into play. In this recipe we create a services container, and define two distinct services. The first service may hardly qualify as such as it's just a configuration array. However, by adding the database configuration service to the central services container, we no longer need to worry about providing database configuration. As long as the container is available, the database configuration is also now universally available.

The second service we provide is a factory class that pulls the database configuration from the services container and uses it to create a database connection class instance. You'll note that all we need to provide to the factory is a services container instance. The factory class can then find in the services container all the information it needs to construct the database connection class instance.

Here is how the output from the test script might appear:

```
ed@localhost:~/Repos/PHP-8-Programming-Cookbook
$ ./admin.sh shell
php8:/repo# php src/Chapter05/ch05_creating_a_connection_service.php
array(6) {
  ["db_driver"]=> string(5) "mysql"
  ["db_name"]=>  string(12) "php8cookbook"
  ["db_usr"]=>  string(8) "cookbook"
  ["db_pwd"]=>  string(8) "password"
  ["db_host"]=>  string(11) "mysql.local"
  ["options"]=>  array(1) {    [3]=>    int(2)  }
```

```
}
object(PDO)#8 (0) {}
```

Note

Design patterns

There is often confusion between **dependency injection** and the **service locator** and **factory patterns**. Dependency injection passes required dependencies into an object from the outside, usually through a constructor, method, or property, making dependencies explicit and easier to test. The service locator pattern lets an object request dependencies from a central registry or container, which can simplify access but hides what the object actually needs. The factory pattern focuses on object creation. In the factory pattern, instead of directly instantiating classes, your code asks a factory to create the appropriate object, often based on configuration or runtime conditions. In short, dependency injection supplies dependencies, service locator retrieves dependencies, and factory pattern creates objects while encapsulating construction logic.

Using AI agents to define database entity classes

In this recipe, we'll create a simple AI agent that accepts an SQL definition and creates an entity class that matches our specifications. AI agents can be thought of as loosely analogous to stored procedures in a database. In the case of a stored procedure, you define a function that encompasses one or more SQL statements, and the function can be recalled at any time going forward. In a similar manner, an AI agent is created from one or more prompts, and is often fed with pertinent information. You can then directly call the agent which is designed to work autonomously until the task completes.

Getting ready

In this recipe, we'll create an AI agent using the interface provided by monica.im. Bear in mind that the agent creation procedure will vary depending on the AI provider that you use. Although we don't specifically endorse the Monica platform, it does offer a free tier, making it a good choice for those developers just diving into the AI world. You can just as easily replicate this recipe using Google Gemini, OpenAI ChatGPT or Anthropic Claude.

How to do it...

1. We start by defining an entity class template that we'll add to the agent's *knowledge*: We use an arbitrary constant in curly braces to help the GenAI system determine which are the variable aspects of the template:

```
<?php
use Traversable;
use ArrayIterator;
use IteratorAggregate;
/**
 * {ENTITY_CLASS_NAME} :
* Entity class that represents a single row in a table
 */
class {ENTITY_CLASS_NAME} implements IteratorAggregate {
    protected array $properties = [];
    public const FIELDS = [];
    public function __construct(array $data = []) {
        foreach (static::FIELDS as $key)
            $this->properties[$key] =
                ($data[$key] ?? null);
    }
    public function getIterator() : Traversable {
        return new ArrayIterator($this->properties);
    }
    public function __get(string $key) : mixed {
        return $this->properties[$key] ?? null;
    }
    public function __set(string $key, mixed $value)
        : void {
        if (in_array($key, static::FIELDS))
            $this->properties[$key] = $value;
    }
}
```

2. We can then craft a prompt that we'll use to program our new agent. It's a good idea to first test the prompt directly to ensure you get the desired results:

```
The name of the agent will be EntityClassAgent. As part of your knowledge,
I have attached a PHP entity class template. The user will provide you with
an SQL statement that creates a table in a relational database. From this
```

```
SQL statement, do the following: 1. Replace "{ENTITY_CLASS_NAME}" with the
name of the database table. The class name should follow PHP standards
recommendations as defined in PSR-1 (https://www.php-fig.org/psr/psr-1/).
2. Populate the "FIELDS" constant as an array of column names drawn from
the SQL statement.
```

3. After the AI platform responds, we can upload an SQL statement and test the results:

```
CREATE TABLE `state_province` (
  `id` int NOT NULL AUTO_INCREMENT,
  `state_province_name` varchar(128) NOT NULL,
  `state_province_code` char(2) NOT NULL,
  PRIMARY KEY (`id`),
  KEY `state_province_code` (`state_province_code`)
) ENGINE=InnoDB AUTO_INCREMENT=375 DEFAULT CHARSET=utf8mb4;
```

4. Here is the class produced by the new AI agent. The only real change needed is to add a namespace declaration at the top; however, you'll also likely want to add any project-specific conventions:

```
<?php
use Traversable;
use ArrayIterator;
use IteratorAggregate;
/**
 * StateProvince: Entity class that represents a single row in a table
*/
class StateProvince implements IteratorAggregate {
    protected array $properties = [];
    public const FIELDS = ['id',
        'state_province_name', 'state_province_code'];
    public function __construct(array $data = []) {
        foreach (static::FIELDS as $key)
            $this->properties[$key] =
                ($data[$key] ?? null);
    }
    public function getIterator() : Traversable {
        return new ArrayIterator($this->properties);
    }
    public function __get(string $key) : mixed {
        return $this->properties[$key] ?? null;
```

```
        }
        public function __set(string $key, mixed $value)
            : void {
            if (in_array($key, static::FIELDS))
                $this->properties[$key] = $value;
        }
    }
```

How it works...

Our first prompt creates the agent. Bear in mind that the agent creation process varies depending on the platform used. In our case, we simply switched to the Monica +Agent prompt, which both creates and runs the agent.

Here's the output from the platform following agent creation:

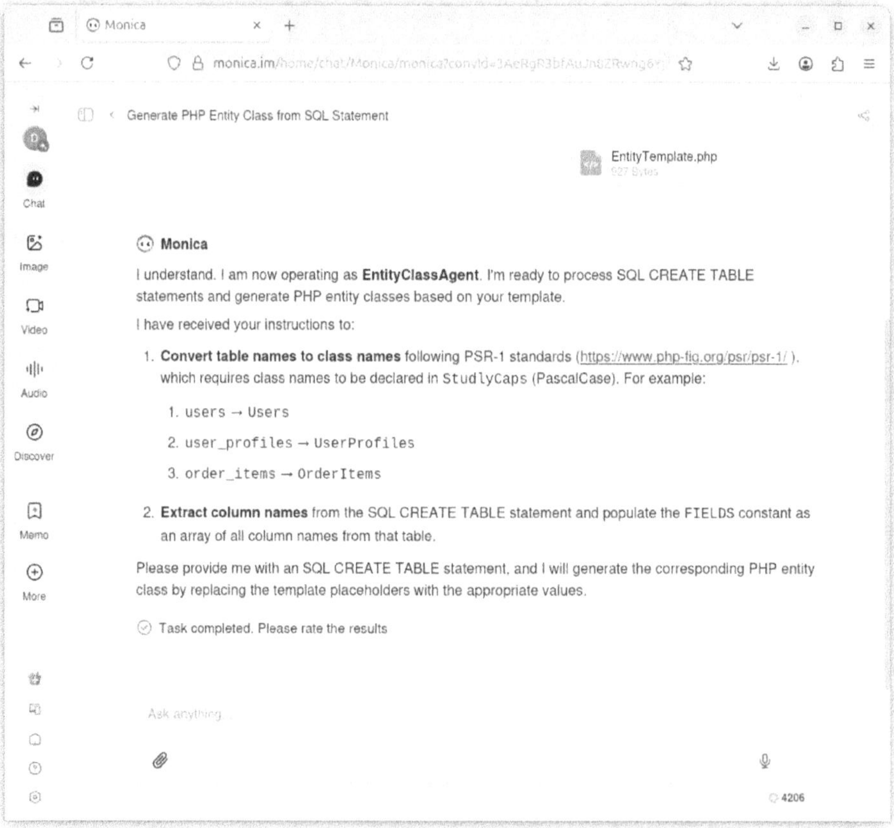

Figure 5.1 – Results from initial AI agent creation

We then supply the SQL statement creating a table, and the agent responds by filling out the template class according to our instructions. Most platforms will also provide you with a specially crafted URL allowing you to directly invoke the agent going forward.

Creating an SQL query builder

Creating an SQL query string is extremely problematic in that you need to be acutely aware of the exact placement of the various components of the statement, not to mention which characters are needed to quote column names and values. Accordingly, we now present a recipe for an SQL query builder with two variations. The first variation produces directly quoted SQL statements. The second produces an SQL statement suitable for prepared statements. You'll note that in this recipe, we use the Builder software design pattern. This design pattern is uniquely suited for query building due to its progressive and additive nature.

> Note
>
> **Builder pattern**
>
> The Builder pattern separates complex object construction from its representation, allowing the same construction process to create different representations through a step-by-step building approach.

Getting ready

The primary pieces of information you'll need to create an SQL query builder are to find out the character needed for quoting the table name and columns. In addition, you'll need to know which character is used for quoting values within the SQL statement.

For demonstration purposes we'll leverage the `GeoNames` postcode data covered in *Chapter 1, Building a Foundation*, in the *Using GenAI to build a postcode database* recipe. However, we'll need to add two constants. `TABLE` identifies the table name, and `COLS` lists column names. Here's the code we add to the `PostCodeTable` class:

```
<?php
namespace Cookbook\Database;
use PDO;
use Generator;
class PostCodeTable {
    public const TABLE = 'us_post_codes';
    public const COLS = [ 'id', 'country_code', 'postal_code', 'place_name',
        'admin_name1', 'admin_code1', 'admin_name2', 'admin_code2',
        'admin_name3', 'admin_code3', 'latitude', 'longitude', 'accuracy'];
```

```
public function __construct(private PDO $pdo) {}
// remaining code not shown
```

How to do it...

1. The plan is to create a base class with two subclasses. The base class holds properties and methods needed by both subclasses. The first subclass is designed to produce straight SQL query strings. The second subclass produces an SQL statement suitable for a prepared statement.
2. In the `/path/to/php8cookbook/src/Database` directory, we define a file `QueryBuilderBase.php` that will house the shared methods. In the first few lines, we define class properties that will hold the query prefix, an array that will hold `WHERE` clause conditions, and a property that will manage additional options such as `LIMIT` and `OFFSET`. This class is marked abstract because it mandates an abstract method quoteExp(). This method varies between the two subclasses, and cannot be implemented at this high level. Here is how the starting code might appear:

```
<?php
namespace Cookbook\Database;
abstract class QueryBuilderBase {
    public string $sql    = '';
    public string $prefix = '';
    public array $where   = [];
    public array $control = [];
    protected abstract function quoteExp(string $a) : string;
```

3. The class constructor accepts arguments that define the column names, table name, and the characters used to quote identifiers (i.e. table and column names), as well as the one used to quote values:

```
    public function __construct(
        public array $cols,
        public string $table,
        public string $quoteColChar = '`',
        public string $quoteValChar = '\'')  {}
```

4. We then define two useful methods, one to surround identifiers with the pertinent quote character and another to surround values with the associated quotes:

```
    protected function quoteCol(string $a) : string {
return ($a==) ? '' : $this->quoteColChar . $a . $this->quoteColChar;
    }
    protected function quoteVal(string $a) : string {
return ($a==) ? '' : $this->quoteValChar . $a . $this->quoteValChar;
    }
```

5. We then add a method that creates a core SQL `SELECT` statement. The reason why we can include this in the base class is because the `SELECT` prefix doesn't include any values. Thus, whether or not we're creating an SQL statement with quoted literal values or one that uses placeholders, the column quoting done in this method applies to both situations. You might note that a `substr()` call is needed to remove any trailing commas. You'll also note that, following the Builder software design pattern, this method returns the current instance, in its current state, to be used as input to any chained method. This allows us to progressively *build* the final SQL statement:

```
    public function select() : static {
        $this->sql = '';
        $this->where = [];
        $this->control = [];
        $this->prefix = 'SELECT ';
        foreach ($this->cols as $col)
            $this->prefix .= $this->quoteCol($col) . ',';
        $this->prefix = substr($this->prefix, 0, -1);
        $this->prefix .= ' FROM ' . $this->quoteCol($this->table) . ' ';
        return $this;
}}
```

6. Another core method is `where()`, which can take an expression directly and build a simple SQL `WHERE` clause. If there's no expression, the builder simply adds `WHERE` to the final string. We store `WHERE` clauses as elements in the `$this->where` array property:

```
public function where(string $a = '') : static {
    $this->where[0] = 'WHERE ' . ((empty($a)) ? '' : $this->quoteExp($a))
. ' ';
```

```
        return $this;
    }
```

7. We follow with a series of methods that represent `AND`, `OR`, and `NOT`. You'll note that they all call the `exp()` method, which returns the SQL operator and a properly quoted expression:

```
    public function and(string $a = '') : static {
        $this->where[] = $this->exp($a, 'AND');
        return $this;
    }
    public function or(string $a = '') : static {
        $this->where[] = $this->exp($a, 'OR');
        return $this;
    }
    public function not(string $a = '') {
        $this->where[] = $this->exp($a, 'NOT');
        return $this;
    }
    public function exp(
        string $a = '', string $exp = 'AND') {
        return ' ' . $exp . ' ' . (((empty($a)) ? '' : $this->quoteExp($a))) .
    ' ';
    }
```

8. The methods that represent `LIKE` and `IN` are slightly more complicated. For the `LIKE` expression, we need to bracket the value with `%`, and for `IN` we need to produce a quoted list of values:

```
    public function like(string $a, string $b) : static {
        $this->where[] = $this->quoteCol($a) . ' LIKE '
            . $this->quoteVal('%' . $b . '%') . ' ';
        return $this;
    }
    public function in(string $col, array $arr) : static {
        $vals = '';
        foreach ($arr as $item)
            $vals .= $this->quoteVal($item) . ',';
        $this->where[] = $this->quoteCol($col) . ' IN ( ' . substr($vals, 0,
    -1) . ' )';
```

```
        return $this;
    }
```

9. The methods that correspond to `LIMIT` and `OFFSET` go at the end of the final statement and therefore cannot be added to `$where`. Accordingly, we add these values to the `$control` property. The argument provided is a simple integer, which means no need for quoting:

```
public function limit(int $num) : static {
    $this->control[0] = ' LIMIT ' . $num;
    return $this;
}
public function offset(int $num) : static {
    $this->control[1] = ' OFFSET ' . $num;
    return $this;
}
```

10. The last method we define builds and returns the final SQL string. You'll note that we make a simple call to `str_replace()` to get rid of double spaces within the composed string:

```
public function getSql()  : string {
    $this->sql = $this->prefix . implode(' ', $this->where) . ' '
               . ($this->control[0] ?? '') . ' ' . ($this->control[1] ?? '');
    $this->sql = preg_replace('/\s+/', ' ',  $this->sql);
    return trim($this->sql);
} }
```

11. In the `/path/to/php8cookbook/src/Database` directory, we define a file `QueryBuilder.php` that will house the methods needed to produce a pre-quoted SQL string. In the first few lines, we define class properties that will hold the query prefix, `WHERE` clause conditions, and a property that will manage additional options such as `LIMIT` and `OFFSET`. Here is how the starting code might appear:

```
<?php
namespace Cookbook\Database;
use InvalidArgumentException;
class QueryBuilder extends QueryBuilderBase {
```

```
    public const ERR_EXP =
        'Expressions need to take this form: COL OPERATOR VALUE';
```

12. Next, we provide an implementation of the quoteExp() method to properly quote an SQL expression. For this to work, we remove any double spaces, and use explode() to break up the expression into three parts: column, operator, and value. The count() function in an if () construct ensures we have at least three elements. Finally, to accommodate situations where multiple values might be needed, we glue the remaining array elements using implode():

```
protected function quoteExp(string $a) : string {
        $a = preg_replace('/  /', ' ', $a);
        $list = explode(' ', $a);
        if (empty($list) || count($list) < 3)
            throw new InvalidArgumentException(static::ERR_EXP);
        $col  = trim(array_shift($list));
        $op   = trim(array_shift($list));
        $val  = trim(implode(' ', $list ?? []));
        return $this->quoteCol($col) . ' ' . $op . ' ' . $this-
>quoteVal($val);
}
```

13. We then define a demo file ch05_sql_query_builder.php in the /path/to/php8cookbook/src/Chapter05 directory that tests our new query builder. First, we use the PostCodeTable class constants to get the appropriate arguments to pass to our QueryBuilder instance:

```
<?php
include __DIR__ . '/../../vendor/autoload.php';
use Cookbook\Database\QueryBuilder;
use Cookbook\Database\PostCodeTable;
$query = new QueryBuilder(PostCodeTable::COLS, PostCodeTable::TABLE);
```

14. We're then ready to formulate a query. In this case, a simple query that checks for any entries where the admin_name1 field is New York and the postal code is 13676:

```
echo $query->select()->where('admin_name1 = New York')
    ->and('postal_code = 13676')->getSql();
```

15. Here is the output from this query:

```
php8:/repo# php src/Chapter05/ch05_sql_query_builder.php
SELECT
id,country_code,postal_code,place_name,admin_name1,admin_code1,admin_name2,
admin_code2,admin_name3,admin_code3,latitude,longitude,accuracy FROM
us_post_codes WHERE admin_name1 = 'New York' AND postal_code = '13676'
```

16. We now try a more complex query where we combine `AND`, `OR`, `IN`, `NOT`, `LIMIT` and `OFFSET` clauses:

```
$query->sql = '';
echo $query->select()->where('country_code = US')
    ->and()
    ->like('admin_name1', 'New York')
    ->or()->in('postal_code', ['10606', '10607', '10610'])
    ->and()->not('accuracy < 3')
    ->limit(10)
    ->offset(20)
    ->getSql();
```

17. Here is the output for this simple example that works like *(A AND B) OR (C AND D)*:

```
php8:/repo# php src/Chapter05/ch05_sql_query_builder.php
SELECT
`id`,`country_code`,`postal_code`,`place_name`,`admin_name1`,`admin_code1`,
`admin_name2`,`admin_code2`,`admin_name3`,`admin_code3`,`latitude`,`longitu
de`,`accuracy` FROM `us_post_codes` WHERE `admin_name1` = 'New York' AND
`postal_code` = '13676'
SELECT
`id`,`country_code`,`postal_code`,`place_name`,`admin_name1`,`admin_code1`,
`admin_name2`,`admin_code2`,`admin_name3`,`admin_code3`,`latitude`,`longitu
de`,`accuracy` FROM `us_post_codes` WHERE `country_code` = 'US' AND
`admin_name1` LIKE '%New York%' OR `postal_code` IN
( '10606','10607','10610' ) AND NOT `accuracy` < '3' LIMIT 10 OFFSET 20
```

18. The last class we develop, in the `/path/to/php8cookbook/src/Database` directory, is defined in a file `QueryBuilderWithPrep.php`. This class creates SQL with placeholders, to be used in conjunction with prepared statements. In the initial class code you'll see

we defined an array that is used to hold the values to be supplied in either *bind* methods or in the execute phase:

```
<?php
namespace Cookbook\Database;
use InvalidArgumentException;
class QueryBuilderWithPrep extends QueryBuilderBase {
    public array $values = [];
```

19. This class inherits all the core methods. The only method that needs customization is `quoteExp()`, which defines how an expression is crafted. You'll note that it follows the same logic as shown in the `QueryBuilder` class. The main difference is that instead of quoting the value, a placeholder is added, and the actual value is placed into a separate holding array `$values`, used by the calling program in conjunction with a prepared statement. A further enhancement (not shown) would be to incorporate placeholders in the IN and LIKE clauses:

```
    protected function quoteExp(string $a) : string {

    $a = preg_replace('/  /', ' ', $a);
        $list = explode(' ', $a);
        if (empty($list) || count($list) < 3)
            throw new InvalidArgumentException(static::ERR_EXP);
        $col  = trim(array_shift($list));
        $op   = trim(array_shift($list));
        $this->values[$col] = trim(implode(' ', $list ?? []));
        return $this->quoteCol($col) . ' ' . $op . ' :' . $col;
    }
```

20. In the `/path/to/php8cookbook/src/Chapter05` folder we create a calling program that performs the same function as the previous calling program mentioned in this recipe. The main difference is that we invoke `QueryBuilderWithPrep` , reset `$values` between queries, and add a `print_r()` statement to display the contents of the `$values` property, which can be used in `bind*()` or `execute()` statements.

21. Here is the output from the second calling program, using identical SQL statements:

```
php8:/repo# php src/Chapter05/ch05_sql_query_builder_with_prep.php
SELECT
`id`,`country_code`,`postal_code`,`place_name`,`admin_name1`,`admin_code1`,
```

```
`admin_name2`,`admin_code2`,`admin_name3`,`admin_code3`,`latitude`,`longitu
de`,`accuracy` FROM `us_post_codes` WHERE `admin_name1` = :admin_name1 AND
`postal_code` = :postal_code
Values to use when executing prepared statement:
Array
(
    [admin_name1] => New York
    [postal_code] => 13676
)
SELECT
`id`,`country_code`,`postal_code`,`place_name`,`admin_name1`,`admin_code1`,
`admin_name2`,`admin_code2`,`admin_name3`,`admin_code3`,`latitude`,`longitu
de`,`accuracy` FROM `us_post_codes` WHERE `country_code` = :country_code
AND `admin_name1` LIKE '%New York%' OR `postal_code` IN
( '10606','10607','10610' ) AND NOT `accuracy` < :accuracy LIMIT 10 OFFSET
20
Values to use when executing prepared statement:
Array
(
    [country_code] => US
    [accuracy] => 3
)
```

How it works...

The first thing to note is the use of the Builder software design pattern. One way to implement this pattern in PHP is to have each method return the current object instance. In this manner, the output of each method becomes the input to the next. The result is that the code reads very much like the actual SQL query finally generated.

Another thing to note is that using a query-builder approach frees the developer from having to remember the order and exact SQL syntax. Further, although we didn't go this route in this recipe, this approach opens the door to creating a database-agnostic SQL query builder where you can enable *platform* support that provides syntax specific to any given database. This approach can be extended to support multiple database platforms, although significant SQL dialect differences must still be addressed, such as:

- `LIMIT` vs `TOP`
- `OFFSET` syntax
- `UPSERT` syntax

- Date functions
- JSON support

> **Tip**
>
> This recipe demonstrates the Builder design pattern. For production applications, parameterized queries and prepared statements should be used instead of directly embedding values into generated SQL.

Using a database to cache GenAI queries

The back-end costs associated with making API calls to a GenAI platform can quickly add up. This is especially true for complex queries and the more sophisticated models. Accordingly, it makes sense to set up a cache class that caches GenAI query results when the query matches one already made.

Getting ready

In order to make our caching class universally usable, we'll need to use Composer to install the PSR-16 `Simple Cache` interface:

```
ed@localhost:~/Repos/PHP-8-Programming-Cookbook
$ ./admin.sh shell
php8:/repo# curl -o composer.phar -L https://getcomposer.org/composer.phar
  % Total    % Received % Xferd  Average Speed   Time    Time     Time  Current
Dload  Upload   Total   Spent    Left  Speed
100 3266k  100 3266k    0     0   339k      0  0:00:09  0:00:09 --:--:--  615k
php8:/repo# php composer.phar require psr/simple-cache
./composer.json has been updated
Running composer update psr/simple-cache
... some lines omitted
Using version ^3.0 for psr/simple-cache
```

How to do it...

1. We'll need a database table to fulfill our purpose of caching GenAI queries. We'll create a hash of the request that, along with other arbitrary information, will serve as a cache key. We'll also store the response received from our GenAI platform. Because the request hash is unique we'll use it as our primary key. Here's how the database table might appear:

```
CREATE TABLE gen_ai_cache (
  `cache_key` char(128) NOT NULL,
  `response` text NOT NULL,
  `ttl_exp` int DEFAULT 0,
  PRIMARY KEY (`cache_key`)
) ENGINE=InnoDB DEFAULT CHARSET=utf8mb4 COLLATE=utf8mb4_general_ci;
```

2. Next, in the `/path/to/php8cookbook/src/Database` folder we create a file `GenAiCache.php` that implements `Psr\SimpleCache\CacheInterface`. We begin with a set of `use` statements and a constant that defines the database table name. We also define constants representing the SQL statements needed to verify, retrieve, add, or remove entries from cache. Here's the starting code:

```
<?php
namespace Cookbook\Database;
use PDO;
use DateTime;
use DateInterval;
use Psr\SimpleCache\CacheInterface;
use Psr\Container\ContainerInterface;
class GenAiCache implements CacheInterface {
    public ?PDO $pdo = null;
    public const string TABLE   = 'gen_ai_cache';
    public const int DEFAULT_TTL = 604800;  // 1 week in seconds
    public const string FIND_SQL  =
        'SELECT response,ttl_exp FROM %s WHERE cache_key = ?';
    public const string HAS_SQL   =
        'SELECT count(cache_key) FROM %s WHERE cache_key = ?';
    public const string SAVE_SQL  =
        'INSERT INTO %s (cache_key, response, ttl_exp) VALUES (?,?, ?)';
    public const string DEL_SQL   = 'DELETE FROM %s WHERE cache_key = ?';
    public const string CLEAR_SQL = 'DELETE FROM %s';
```

3. In the `__construct()` method, we accept a `Psr\Container\ContainerInterface` instance, leveraging the service container and database service described in the first recipe in this chapter:

```
public function __construct(
    ContainerInterface $container) {
    // use the database service to get a PDO instance
    $this->pdo = $container->get('db_connect');
}
```

4. The `set()` method is where we add an entry to the cache. You'll note that according to PSR-16, this method accepts a third argument representing when this cache entry expires. The method signature in the formal PSR-16 definition for this method defines the default TTL value as null. The rationale, according to PSR-16, is that if the driver supports TTL, the library may set the default value or let the driver take care of it.
5. In our implementation we first check to see if the `ttl` argument is a `DateInterval` instance. If so, we add it to a `DateTime` instance and retrieve the timestamp. Otherwise, assuming the `ttl` value is non-zero, we add it to the current timestamp to produce the future expiration date. You'll note that we leverage the `INSERT SQL` defined in our `SAVE_SQL` constant. Here is the code:

```
public function set(string $key, mixed $value, DateInterval|int|null
$ttl = null) :
    bool {
    if (is_object($ttl) && $ttl instanceof DateInterval) {
        $ttl = (new DateTime())->add($ttl)->getTimestamp();
    } else {
        $ttl = (int) $ttl;
        if ($ttl > 0) $ttl = time() +  $ttl;
    }
    $stmt = $this->pdo->prepare(sprintf(static::SAVE_SQL, static::TABLE));
    return (bool) $stmt->execute([$key, $value, $ttl]);
}
```

> **Tip**
>
> Additional logic may be needed to scan the response. Otherwise it's important to note that you may end up caching hallucinations, temporary API failures, or malformed output.

6. The `get()` method is used to retrieve the cached response. The second argument is mandated by PSR-16, but we are not using it. We use array element 0 of the `PDOStatement::fetchAll()` output to retrieve the final result. Note that the actual structure of the returned array will vary depending on which GenAI platform you're using.
7. In our implementation, we check to see if the result is not empty, and, if not, if the value of our `ttl_exp` column is greater than 0. If it's zero we assume the item should remain in cache indefinitely. Otherwise, we compare the `ttl_exp` value with the current timestamp. If the cached TTL value is less than the current timestamp, we invoke `delete()`. This forces the calling code to regenerate the AI call, and to cache the new value. We return the cached response if it's not expired:

```
    public function get(string $key, mixed $default = null) : mixed {
        $value  = '';
        $stmt   = $this->pdo->prepare(sprintf(static::FIND_SQL,
static::TABLE));
        $stmt->execute([$key]);
        $result = $stmt->fetch(PDO::FETCH_ASSOC) ?? [];
        if (!empty($result)) {
            if ((int) $result['ttl_exp'] === 0) {
                $value = $result['response'] ?? '';
            } elseif ($result['ttl_exp'] < time()) {
                $this->delete($key);
            } else {
                $value = $result['response'] ?? '';
            }
        }
        return $value;
    }
```

8. The `has()` method is also mandated by PSR-16:

```
public function has(string $key) : bool {
        $stmt = $this->pdo->prepare(sprintf(static::HAS_SQL,
static::TABLE));
        $stmt->execute([$key]);
        return (bool) $stmt->fetchColumn();
}
```

9. The `delete()` method removes a single entry, whereas the `clear()` method wipes out all cached entries. For both methods, a boolean value is returned based upon the value returned by `PDO::exec()`. This method returns an integer representing the number of rows affected. A boolean `false` value is returned if `exec()` returns 0. Here are those two methods:

```
    public function delete(string $key) : bool {
        $stmt = $this->pdo->prepare(sprintf(static::DEL_SQL,
static::TABLE));
        return (bool) $stmt->execute([$key]);
    }
    public function clear() : bool {
        return (bool) $this->pdo->exec(sprintf(static::CLEAR_SQL,
static::TABLE));
    }
```

10. Three additional `*Multiple()` methods are mandated by PSR-16, but since they're not needed for this purpose, we define them but will do nothing in the method body. These methods are not shown here. Note that if you wish your cache class to be fully PSR-16 compliant, you should define the code for these methods.
11. Now that we have the cache class defined, let's turn our attention to a class `MonicaRequest` that handles the call to our GenAI platform. First, we define a series of `use` statements to identify needed classes that reside outside the current namespace. We also define a set of useful class constants containing informative messages. In addition, we define properties to hold our GenAI configuration and the services container:

```
<?php
namespace Cookbook\Database;
use DateInterval;
```

```
use Psr\SimpleCache\CacheInterface;
use Psr\Container\ContainerInterface;
#[MonicaRequest("Processes GenAI request")]
class MonicaRequest {
    public const NO_RESPONSE = 'No response from your AI platform';
    public const FROM_CACHE  = 'Returned from cache: ' . PHP_EOL;
    public const FROM_ORIG   = 'Returned from GenAI: ' . PHP_EOL;
    public array $ai_config  = [];
    public ?CacheInterface $cache = null;
```

12. The `__construct()` method accepts our service container as an argument. We then use the container to pull GenAI configuration and create an instance of the `GenAiCache` class:

```
public function __construct( ContainerInterface $container) {
    $this->ai_config = $container->get('ai_config');
    $this->cache     = new GenAiCache($container);
}
```

13. We then define `__invoke()` to create a hash key from the request. We then check to see if this key is available in cache. If so, we simply return the cached response. Otherwise, we make the call to our GenAI platform (Monica in this example) and cache the response. You might consider exerting additional control over the request text in order to avoid a prompt injection attack. We do not cover that subject in this chapter. You'll also note that we accept the default TTL of 0 when adding to cache:

```
public function __invoke(string $request, int $ttl = 0
) : string {
    $request = trim(strip_tags($request));
    $key = $this->createKey($request);
    $text = $this->cache->get($key);
    $prefix = self::FROM_CACHE;
    if (empty($text)) {
        $text = $this->makeCall($request);
        $this->cache->set(
            $key, $text, $ttl);
        $prefix = self::FROM_ORIG;
    }
    return $prefix . $text;
}
```

14. We generate our cache key using the `createKey()` method. The reason for making this a separate method is to give us flexibility to choose another hashing algorithm should `sha1()` prove insufficient for our needs. The reason we chose `sha1()` for this example is because it quickly produces a hash, helping us avoid performance drag. In this usage, we only need a deterministic cache key, and not a cryptographically secure hash.
15. Something else to note is how many factors you should include to form a proper key. Factors such as the GenAI model, system prompt, temperature, API version, among other factors, can affect output. For this example we include the GenAI model name in the cache key:

```
protected function createKey(string $text) {
    return $this->ai_config['AI_MODEL'] . ':' . sha1($text);
}
```

16. Finally, we define the `makeCall()` method, which makes the actual GenAI query using the PHP cURL extension. It's rather long, so let's break it down section by section. First, we grab the GenAI API key from a separate file as indicated in our `$ai_config`. We then create a PHP array with arguments to be sent to the AI that's subsequently JSON encoded:

```
protected function makeCall(string $request):string {
    $apiKey = trim(file_get_contents(
        $this->ai_config['AI_KEY_FN']));
    $data = [
        'model' => $this->ai_config['AI_MODEL'],
        'messages' => [[ 'role' => 'user',
            'content' => [['type'=>'text', 'text'=>
                $this->ai_config['AI_SYS_TEXT']
                . ' ' . $request]],
    ]]];
    $json = json_encode($data);
```

17. We then set up the cURL connection in accordance with the guidelines provided by our GenAI platform. Please note that the API setup will vary depending on the requirements of your platform. Please note that in this example we disable SSL peer

verification. These should be enabled in production. We then make the call by running the `curl_exec()` and gather any potential transmission errors:

```
$ch = curl_init($this->ai_config['AI_API_URL']);
curl_setopt($ch, CURLOPT_RETURNTRANSFER, true);
curl_setopt($ch, CURLOPT_POST, true);
curl_setopt($ch, CURLOPT_POSTFIELDS, $json);
curl_setopt($ch, CURLOPT_HTTPHEADER, [
    'Content-Type: application/json',
    'Authorization: Bearer ' . $apiKey
]);
curl_setopt($ch, CURLOPT_SSL_VERIFYPEER,false);
curl_setopt($ch, CURLOPT_SSL_VERIFYHOST,false);
$response = curl_exec($ch);
$httpCode = curl_getinfo($ch, CURLINFO_HTTP_CODE);
$error = curl_error($ch);
curl_close($ch);
```

> **Tip**
>
> **Warning**: disabling SSL verification exposes requests to man-in-the-middle attacks and should never be used in production.

18. Next, we provide some error handling. We check for a cURL error, and an HTTP response code other than `200`. We then capture the response message content and throw an exception if the response is empty. Here again, it's important to stress that there are currently no standards regarding the format of the GenAI response. Accordingly, for your own GenAI platform you'll need to review the response format and make the appropriate adjustments as to the array key that's assigned to `$text`:

```
if (!empty($error))
    throw new Exception('ERROR ' . __LINE__
        . ' [' . $error . ']');
if ($httpCode !== 200)
    throw new Exception('ERROR ' . __LINE__
        . ' [HTTP:' . $httpCode . '] ');
$text = json_decode($response, TRUE)
    ['choices'][0]['message']['content'] ?? '';
if (empty($text)) {
    throw new Exception(static::NO_RESPONSE);
```

```
        }
        return $text;
    }}
```

19. Finally, to test our new system, in the `/path/to/php8cookbook/src/Chapter05` folder, we create a file `ch05_caching_gen_ai_query.php` that allows us to make a GenAI query from the command line.
20. We start by invoking the autoloader, and add a set of `use` statements that identify the needed classes:

```
<?php
define('DB_CONFIG_FN', __DIR__ . '/../../config/db.config.php');
include __DIR__ . '/../../vendor/autoload.php';
use Cookbook\Services\Container;
use Cookbook\Services\ConnectionFactory;
use Cookbook\Database\GenAiCache;
use Cookbook\Database\MonicaRequest;
```

21. We then configure our services container as described in the first recipe in this chapter. You'll note that we do not put the key directly in the code; rather, we define the file name containing the key. In the GenAI configuration, we also specify the API endpoint and the model we wish to use. In this example, we use `gpt-4.1-nano`, which is cheap, fast, and provides a response of reasonable quality. The `AI_SYS_TEXT` key is provided to give the GenAI an overall context. By limiting the response to 256 words, we save time and backend costs:

```
$container = Container::getInstance();
$container->add('db_config', function () { return require DB_CONFIG_FN; });
$container->add('db_connect', new ConnectionFactory($container));
$container->add('ai_config', function () { return [
        'AI_KEY_FN'   => __DIR__ . '/../../secure/monica_api_key.txt',
        'AI_MODEL'    => 'gpt-4.1-nano', // old but cheap -- good for
testing
        'AI_API_URL'  => 'https://openapi.monica.im/v1/chat/completions',
        'AI_SYS_TEXT' => 'Keep your responses concise. Limit to 256 words
```

```
or less.'];
});
```

22. Finally, we make the request, and receive either an original response, or one that's drawn from the cache. We also provide timing information in order to establish performance benchmarks:

```
$request = new MonicaRequest($container);
$start = microtime(TRUE);
$prompt = $argv[1] ?? '';
if (empty($prompt))
    exit('Usage:  php ' . basename(__FILE__) . ' "PROMPT"' . PHP_EOL);
$ttl = $argv[2] ?? 5;
echo $request($prompt, $ttl) . PHP_EOL;
echo 'TTL set to   : ' . $ttl . ' seconds' . PHP_EOL;
echo 'Elapsed Time: ' . (microtime(TRUE) - $start) . PHP_EOL;
```

How it works...

The calling program accepts query text as an argument, which is passed to the `__invoke()` method of the `MonicaRequest` class. If the query has already been cached, we receive the cached response. Otherwise, the request class makes the GenAI API call and returns the response after caching it.

Here's the output from a sample run of our program:

```
php8:/repo# php src/Chapter05/ch05_caching_gen_ai_query.php "What is the time
difference between New York City and Bangkok?"
Returned from GenAI:
The time difference between New York City (Eastern Daylight Time, EDT) and Bangkok
(Indochina Time, ICT) is typically 11 hours.
Always check current local times as daylight saving schedules may vary slightly.
TTL set to   : 5 seconds
Elapsed Time: 2.2814230918884
php8:/repo# php src/Chapter05/ch05_caching_gen_ai_query.php "What is the time
difference between New York City and Bangkok?"
Returned from cache:
The time difference between New York City (Eastern Daylight Time, EDT) and Bangkok
(Indochina Time, ICT) is typically 11 hours.
Always check current local times as daylight saving schedules may vary slightly.
```

```
TTL set to  : 5 seconds
Elapsed Time: 0.00052881240844727
```

As you can see, caching the response results in a massive performance boost! In this example, retrieving a cached response was dramatically faster than making a new API request because it avoided network latency and model inference time.

Of course, as time goes by and more and more queries are cached, the performance will drop slightly. This is expected as your cache database grows in size, increasing the storage engine workload. However, it's clear that caching responses not only vastly improves performance but also results in lower costs due to reduced calls to your GenAI platform.

6

Building Scalable Forms

The design and implementation of HTML forms are the responsibility of front-end developers, while the logic — such as validation, data storage, and integration with services (email, databases, queues) — falls under the responsibility of PHP developers. In this chapter, we will explore how to structure and design form logic (including validation, error handling, and selectable data) to separate concerns across the various micro-functionalities of a form, making the system more scalable, dynamic, and adaptable to different scenarios.

As web applications increase in complexity, the demand for dynamic form generation and management becomes more critical. Automating these processes not only accelerates development but also ensures that forms remain adaptable to evolving project requirements. This flexibility is particularly valuable in large-scale systems, where form fields may need to change based on user roles, preferences, or workflow variations. Utilizing automation tools and frameworks to manage forms boosts maintainability and scalability, allowing developers to concentrate on enhancing functionality and user experience. Ultimately, this approach supports the development of robust, efficient, and future-ready web applications.

In this chapter, we'll cover the following topics:

- Creating a generic form element generator
- Enhancing form generation using AI suggestions
- Creating an HTML radio element generator
- Creating an HTML select element generator
- Implementing a form factory
- Chaining filters
- Chaining validators
- AI-driven dynamic form systems

Technical requirements

In this chapter, ensure that your local development environment is set up and running with PHP 8. If you haven't already done so, follow the setup instructions provided in *Chapter 1, Building a Foundation*. For an efficient development experience, it is recommended to use an **Integrated Development Environment** (**IDE**) for editing and writing PHP code. Additionally, this chapter assumes the reader has a basic understanding of HTML forms and how they are used for user input in web applications. It is also assumed that the reader has a basic understanding of **Object-Oriented Programming** (**OOP**).

Creating a generic form element generator

PHP, as a server-side scripting language, can generate and manipulate dynamic HTML content for web applications. One of its key strengths is the ability to programmatically create HTML forms based on specific conditions or logic. This allows developers to customize forms for different user needs while reducing manual coding. As a result, PHP enhances development efficiency and scalability by supporting more flexible and adaptable form structures.

Getting ready

We will be creating a reusable and configurable HTML input form generator through PHP, which renders both the form elements, as well as the structure elements to wrap the form into one. In this example, we will be working on the following:

- `GenericFormGenerator` class that will abstract the form generation process
- Enumerable class to contain all types of supported inputs
- Renderer classes for the input types
- Factory class to dynamically create an instance of the renderer needed
- Configurable Form element that wraps the entire array of input items
- A submit button to trigger submission
- A consumer file to demonstrate the usage

In the following steps, we will create the required classes and configuration needed to implement this functionality. Each file will be introduced with its purpose before the code is presented.

How to do it...

1. First, we will create the consumer PHP file to make it easier for the reader to understand the end goal. Create a new PHP file at the following path within your

project directory. This file will act as the consumer or implementation script demonstrating how the components are used:

`src/Chapter06/ch06_generic_form_gen.php`

```
<?php

use Cookbook\Chapter06\GenericInputForm\GenericFormGenerator;
use \Cookbook\Chapter06\GenericInputForm\InputType;

include __DIR__ . '/../../vendor/autoload.php';

// Instantiate generator, and add input fields.
$generator = new GenericFormGenerator();
$generator->addInput(InputType::Text, ['label' => 'Username', 'name' =>
'username']);
$generator->addInput(InputType::Password, ['label' => 'Password',
'name' => 'password']);

// Echo the entire form.
echo $generator->generate('my-form', '');

// Add styling
echo "<style>input { width: 200px; } label {float:left; width:100px; }</
style>";

// Output Array.
print_r($_POST);
```

2. Next, we'll create an `Enumerable` class called `InputType`. This will contain an enumerable list of valid input types that we will use as a method signature in the next step:

```
<?php

namespace Cookbook\Chapter06\GenericInputForm;

enum InputType
{
    case Text;
    case Email;
```

```
    case Password;
    case Radio;
    case Select;
}
```

3. Next, we'll create the `GenericFormGenerator` class. This class will contain the code to easily generate an entire HTML form that can support multiple input types. Create a new PHP file at the following path within your project directory. This file will act as the consumer or implementation script demonstrating how the components are used: `src/Chapter06/GenericFormGenerator.php`

```
<?php

namespace Cookbook\Chapter06\GenericInputForm;

use Cookbook\Chapter06\GenericInputForm\Renderer\InputRendererFactory;
```

4. Next, we define an interface that standardizes how different input renderers will generate their HTML output:

```
use Cookbook\Chapter06\GenericInputForm\Renderer\InputRendererInterface;
use Exception;

class GenericFormGenerator implements FormGeneratorInterface
{
    private array $inputForms = [];

    private InputRendererInterface $renderer;

    public function generate(string $formName, string $submitUrl, array
$options = []): string
    {
        if (empty($this->inputForms)) {
            throw new Exception('No input forms have been added.');
        }

        $form = "<form name='$formName' action='$submitUrl'
method='POST'>";

        foreach ($this->inputForms as $input) {
```

```
            $form .= $input;
        }

        $form .= "<div>
                    <button type='submit' name='submit'>Submit</button>
                  </div>
                </form>";

        return $form;
    }

    /**
     * @throws Exception
     */
    public function addInput(InputType $inputType, array $options = []):
void
    {
        $this->inputForms[] = $this->renderInputForm($inputType, $options);
    }

    /**
     * @throws Exception
     */
    private function renderInputForm(InputType $inputType, array
$options): string
    {
        $renderer = InputRendererFactory::createRenderer($inputType);
        return $renderer->render($inputType, $options);
    }
}
```

5. Create a new PHP file at the following path within your project directory. This file will act as the consumer or implementation script demonstrating how the components are used:
   `src/Chapter06/FormGeneratorInterface.php`

```
<?php

namespace Cookbook\Chapter06\GenericInputForm;

interface FormGeneratorInterface
```

```
{
    public function generate(string $formName, string $submitUrl, array
$options = []);
    public function addInput(InputType $inputType, array $options = []);
}
```

6. You'll notice that the `renderInputForm` method uses a factory class that creates an instance of an input renderer. We'll need to create the Factory class as well as the renderers.
   Create a new PHP file at the following path within your project directory. This file will act as the consumer or implementation script demonstrating how the components are used:

`src/Chapter06/GenericInputForm/Renderer/InputRendererFactory.php`

```
<?php

namespace Cookbook\Chapter06\GenericInputForm\Renderer;

use Cookbook\Chapter06\GenericInputForm\InputType;

class InputRendererFactory
{
    public static function createRenderer(InputType $inputType):
InputRendererInterface
    {
```

The following snippet shows the relevant section of the factory configuration used to register the new renderer implementation:

```
        // Map input types to specific renderer classes
        $renderers = [
            InputType::Text->name => TextInputRenderer::class,
            InputType::Password->name => TextInputRenderer::class,
            InputType::Email->name => TextInputRenderer::class,
        ];

        if (!isset($renderers[$inputType->name])) {
            throw new \Exception("Unsupported input type");
        }
```

```
            // Dynamically instantiate the appropriate renderer
            return new $renderers[$inputType->name]();
        }
    }
```

7. Create a new PHP file at the following path within your project directory. This file will act as the consumer or implementation script demonstrating how the components are used:

   `src/Chapter06/GenericInputForm/Renderer/InputRendererInterface.php`

```
<?php

namespace Cookbook\Chapter06\GenericInputForm\Renderer;

use Cookbook\Chapter06\GenericInputForm\InputType;

interface InputRendererInterface
{
    public function render(InputType $inputType, array $options): string;
}
```

8. Create a new PHP file at the following path within your project directory. This file will act as the consumer or implementation script demonstrating how the components are used:

   `src/Chapter06/GenericInputForm/Renderer/TextInputRenderer.php`

```
<?php

namespace Cookbook\Chapter06\GenericInputForm\Renderer;

use Cookbook\Chapter06\GenericInputForm\InputType;

class TextInputRenderer implements InputRendererInterface
{
    public function render(InputType $inputType, array $options): string
    {
        $label  = $options['label'];
        $name   = $options['name'];
        $input  = "<div>
                    <label>$label</label>
```

```
                    <input type='$inputType->name' name='$name'>
                </div>";

        return $input;
    }
}
```

How it works...

In the `GenericFormGenerator` class, we have two public methods: the `generate` method, which handles the generation of the entire form, and the `addInput` method, which handles the addition of input forms to generate.

The `addInput` method will call the generation of the HTML input through a renderer class generated by a factory class, and then add it to the array of input fields. The main `generate` method will generate the main wrapper form and will loop through the array of input fields and add them inside the form itself.

Here is the output from a web browser:

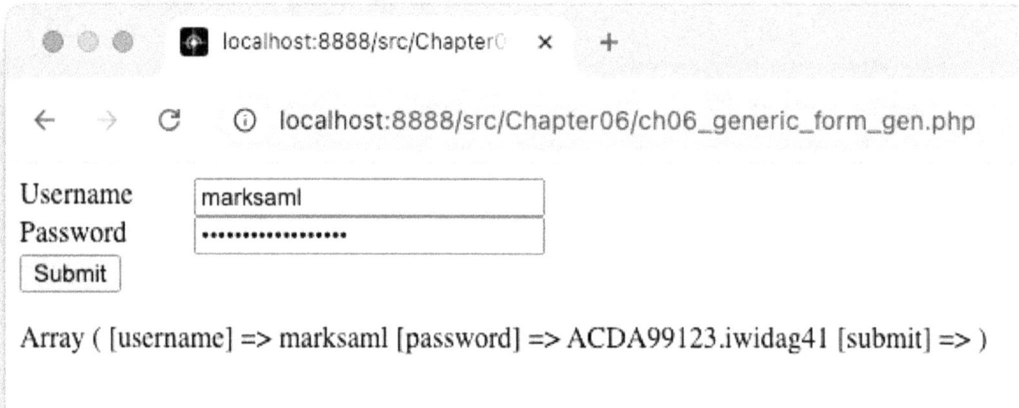

Figure 6.1 – Generic form generator

You can modify the consumer file `ch06_generic_form_gen` to demonstrate the usage of the same exact generator but with more fields:

```
<?php

use Cookbook\Chapter06\GenericInputForm\GenericFormGenerator;
use \Cookbook\Chapter06\GenericInputForm\InputType;
```

```
include __DIR__ . '/../../vendor/autoload.php';

// Instantiate generator, and add input fields.
$generator = new GenericFormGenerator();
$generator->addInput(InputType::Email, ['label' => 'Email', 'name' => 'email']);
$generator->addInput(InputType::Text, ['label' => 'Street Address', 'name' =>
'street1']);
$generator->addInput(InputType::Text, ['label' => 'Suburb', 'name' => 'suburb']);
$generator->addInput(InputType::Text, ['label' => 'State', 'name' => 'state']);
$generator->addInput(InputType::Text, ['label' => 'Postal Code', 'name' =>
'postal_code']);

// Echo the entire form.
echo $generator->generate('my-form', '');// Add styling

// Add styling
echo "<style>input { width: 200px; } label {float:left; width:150px; }</style>";

// Output Array.
print_r($_POST);
```

As you can see, we can easily change the entire form and add more input forms to it. Here's the output after the modifications on the consumer side:

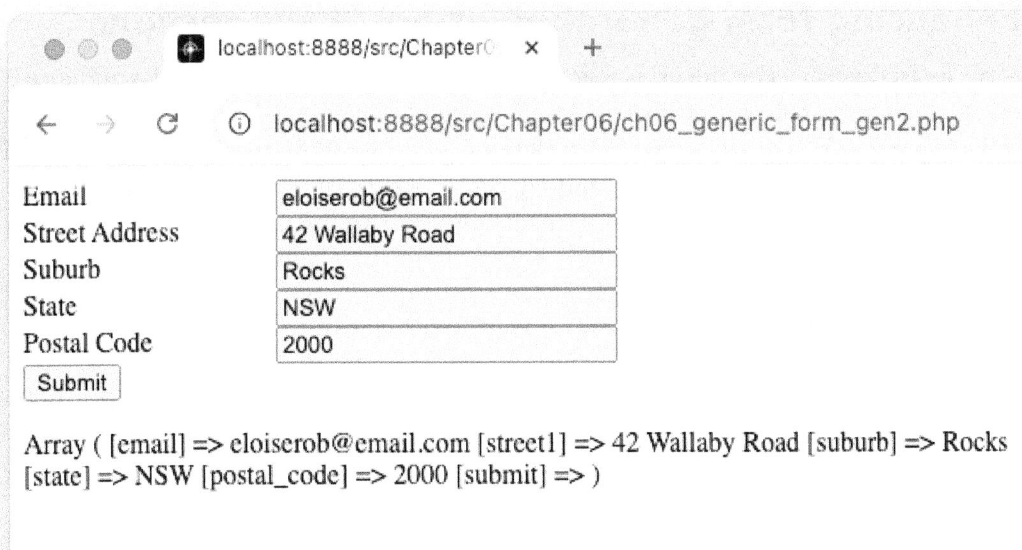

Figure 6.2 – Generic form generator, additional fields

There are several alternative ways to implement a form factory, including fluent builders, configuration-driven factories, or framework-based solutions such as Symfony Forms or Laravel Form Requests, depending on project complexity.

Since we've already created a generator class that can handle text input types, we can easily modify this to be able to handle additional types of inputs.

There's more...

In production, you would typically separate two concerns this recipe deliberately combines for clarity:

- **Rendering vs. generation**: The form-generation logic and the HTML output are tightly coupled in the example above, which keeps the recipe to a single file. In production, you would typically render via a templating engine such as Twig (`https://twig.symfony.com`) or Blade (Laravel), keeping the PHP side focused on defining the form structure and data while delegating presentation to the template. The same generator pattern fits unchanged — it just emits field metadata rather than HTML strings.
- **Submission handling**: The recipe focuses on form generation; it doesn't cover what happens when the form posts back. Any production form needs CSRF protection on the submission path — see *Chapter 12, Improving Web Security,* recipe *Securing forms with a token*, for the synchronizer token pattern applied to PHP forms.

Enhancing form generation using AI suggestions

AI can assist developers by proposing relevant form fields based on a high-level description of the form's purpose, reducing manual design effort. By integrating AI-generated suggestions with the existing form generator, we can quickly produce a usable first draft that can be refined and validated through standard application logic. This approach improves development speed while still maintaining full control over the final form structure.

Getting ready

In some projects, the set of fields required for a form is not known up front. For example, a product team might describe a form in plain language (*a registration form for an event*), and the development team needs a reasonable first draft of field labels and names. In this recipe, we'll use a small AI client class to request a suggested list of fields, then feed those suggestions into the existing `GenericFormGenerator` workflow.

How to do it...

1. Create a simple AI client class that can send a prompt to an LLM endpoint and return the generated text:

   src/Chapter06/AI/AiClient.php

```
<?php

namespace Cookbook\Chapter06\AI;

class AiClient
{
    private string $endpoint = 'https://api.openai.com/v1/chat/
completions';

    public function __construct(private string $apiKey)
    {
    }

    public function generateText(string $prompt, string $model = 'gpt-4.1-
mini'): string
    {
        $payload = [
            'model' => $model,
            'messages' => [
                ['role' => 'user', 'content' => $prompt],
            ],
        ];

        $ch = curl_init($this->endpoint);
        curl_setopt_array($ch, [
            CURLOPT_RETURNTRANSFER => true,
            CURLOPT_POST => true,
            CURLOPT_HTTPHEADER => [
                'Authorization: Bearer ' . $this->apiKey,
                'Content-Type: application/json',
            ],
            CURLOPT_POSTFIELDS => json_encode($payload),
        ]);

        $response = curl_exec($ch);
```

```
        if ($response === false) {
            return '';
        }

        $data = json_decode($response, true);
        return $data['choices'][0]['message']['content'] ?? '';
    }
}
```

2. Request AI-suggested fields and feed them into the generator.
   For demonstration, the AI will return a JSON array of field definitions with label/name pairs:

   `src/Chapter06/ch06_generic_form_gen.php (AI-assisted variant)`

```
<?php

use Cookbook\Chapter06\AI\AiClient;
use Cookbook\Chapter06\GenericInputForm\GenericFormGenerator;
use Cookbook\Chapter06\GenericInputForm\InputType;

include __DIR__ . '/../../vendor/autoload.php';

$generator = new GenericFormGenerator();
$ai = new AiClient($_ENV['OPENAI_API_KEY'] ?? '');

$prompt =
'Return JSON array of fields (label,name) for a user registration form. '
    . 'Example: [{"label":"Email","name":"email"}]';
$json = $ai->generateText($prompt);
$fields = json_decode($json, true) ?: [];

foreach ($fields as $field) {
    $label = $field['label'] ?? null;
    $name  = $field['name'] ?? null;
    if (!$label || !$name) {
        continue;
    }
    $generator->addInput(InputType::Text, ['label' => $label, 'name' =>
$name]);
}
```

```
echo $generator->generate('ai-form', '');
```

How it works...

The `AiClient` class is a small wrapper around an LLM endpoint. The consumer script sends a prompt requesting a JSON array of fields, then decodes the JSON and passes each suggestion into the existing `addInput()` workflow. This keeps the form generation logic unchanged—AI is only used to propose a first draft of labels and field names that you can refine.

There's more...

The preceding recipe uses AI to generate the form itself — you describe the form's purpose, and the model proposes the fields, validation rules, and input types. A complementary direction worth knowing about is AI-assisted data collection, where instead of presenting a static set of fields, the system holds a structured conversation with the user and gathers the information one step at a time.

This approach can be useful when:

- The required inputs vary per user and aren't known up front
- User experience benefits from a guided dialog rather than a long form
- The system needs to ask clarifying follow-up questions based on prior answers

It does not replace static forms — accessibility, audit trails, and straightforward submission semantics are easier with a traditional form — but it can complement them in onboarding flows, intake questionnaires, and search-style data gathering. Open-source projects such as neuron-core/ai-form (`https://github.com/neuron-core/ai-form`) demonstrate this conversational pattern in PHP and JavaScript stacks.

Creating an HTML radio element generator

In some cases, it's important to clearly indicate that only one option can be selected for a particular question. This is common for yes/no questions or multiple-choice questions where only a single response is allowed. By setting this expectation, you ensure that the user understands the restriction and selects only one answer.

For example, if you ask a user which meal—breakfast, lunch, or dinner—they would prefer for a free coffee, only one option should be selected. This ensures clarity and avoids confusion, particularly when multiple options are presented but only one is intended to be chosen.

Getting ready

This recipe will heavily depend on the previous section, so it is very important that you've gone through it and created all the classes specified.

In the following steps, we will create the required classes and configuration needed to implement this functionality. Each file will be introduced with its purpose before the code is presented.

How to do it...

1. Create a new class to render a radio group using a multidimensional array for the options.
   Create a new PHP file at the following path within your project directory. This file will act as the consumer or implementation script demonstrating how the components are used:

   `src/Chapter06/GenericInputForm/Renderer/RadioInputRenderer.php`

```
<?php

namespace Cookbook\Chapter06\GenericInputForm\Renderer;

use Cookbook\Chapter06\GenericInputForm\InputType;
```

2. Next, we define an interface that standardizes how different input renderers will generate their HTML output:

```
class RadioInputRenderer implements InputRendererInterface
{
    public function render(InputType $inputType, array $options): string
    {
        $groupOptions   = $options['radio_group_options'];
        $elementOptions = $options['radio_element_options'];

        return $this->generate($groupOptions, $elementOptions);
    }

    private function generate(array $groupOptions, array $elementOptions):
string
    {
        $html = "";
```

```
        $fieldSetTitle = $groupOptions['fieldSetTitle'];
        $html .= "<fieldset><legend>$fieldSetTitle</legend>";

        foreach ($elementOptions as $elementOption) {
            $html .= $this->generateRadioElement($elementOption);
        }

        $html .= "</fieldset>";

        return $html;
    }

    private function generateRadioElement(array $elementOptions): string
    {
        $name = $elementOptions['radio']['radioElementName'];
        $id = $elementOptions['radio']['radioElementId'];
        $value = $elementOptions['radio']['radioElementValue'];
        $labelFor = $elementOptions['label']['labelFor'];
        $labelText = $elementOptions['label']['labelText'];
        return "<input type='radio' name='$name' id='$id' value='$value' /
> <label for='$labelFor'>$labelText</label><br />";
    }
}
```

3. Next, create the consumer PHP file to demonstrate the usage.
   Create a new PHP file at the following path within your project directory. This file will act as the consumer or implementation script demonstrating how the components are used:

`src/Chapter06/ch06_radio_form.php`

```
<?php

use Cookbook\Chapter06\GenericInputForm\GenericFormGenerator;
use \Cookbook\Chapter06\GenericInputForm\InputType;

include __DIR__ . '/../../vendor/autoload.php';

// Radio Options:
$freeCoffeeGroupOptions = [
    'fieldSetTitle' => 'Do you want a free cup of coffee?',
```

```
];

$freeCoffeeRadioElementsOptions = [
    [
        'radio' => [
            'radioElementName' => 'free-coffee',
            'radioElementId' => 'coffee-yes',
            'radioElementValue' => 'yes',
        ],
        'label' => [
            'labelFor' => 'coffee-yes',
            'labelText' => 'Yes',
        ],
    ],

    [
        'radio' => [
            'radioElementName' => 'free-coffee',
            'radioElementId' => 'coffee-no',
            'radioElementValue' => 'no',
        ],
        'label' => [
            'labelFor' => 'coffee-no',
            'labelText' => 'No',
        ],
    ],
];

// Instantiate generator, and add input fields.
$generator = new GenericFormGenerator();
$generator->addInput(InputType::Radio,
    ['radio_group_options' => $freeCoffeeGroupOptions,
'radio_element_options' => $freeCoffeeRadioElementsOptions]);

// Echo the entire form.
echo $generator->generate('my-radio-form', '');
```

4. Register this new renderer class to the `InputRendererFactory` class:

The following snippet shows the relevant section of the factory configuration used to register the new renderer implementation:

```
// Map input types to specific renderer classes
$renderers = [
    InputType::Text->name => TextInputRenderer::class,
    InputType::Password->name => TextInputRenderer::class,
    InputType::Email->name => TextInputRenderer::class,
    InputType::Radio->name => RadioInputRenderer::class,
];
```

How it works...

The new `RadioInputRenderer` class we created implements the same `InputRendererInterface` that the `TextInputRenderer` class we created in the previous section. Meaning, they will have the same exact public method signature. That allows us to interchange the renderer that the generator will use depending on the input type, if we want to use Text, Email, Password or Radio:

```
private function renderInputForm(InputType $inputType, array $options): string
{
    $renderer = InputRendererFactory::createRenderer($inputType);
    return $renderer->render($inputType, $options);
}
```

The preceding snippet from the `factory` class will create an instance of the `RadioInputRenderer` because in the `consumer` class, we have specified that we want to add an input type of radio, along with the array options required by the renderer in this line:

```
$generator->addInput(InputType::Radio,
    ['radio_group_options' => $freeCoffeeGroupOptions, 'radio_element_options' =>
$freeCoffeeRadioElementsOptions]);
```

The following output will be:

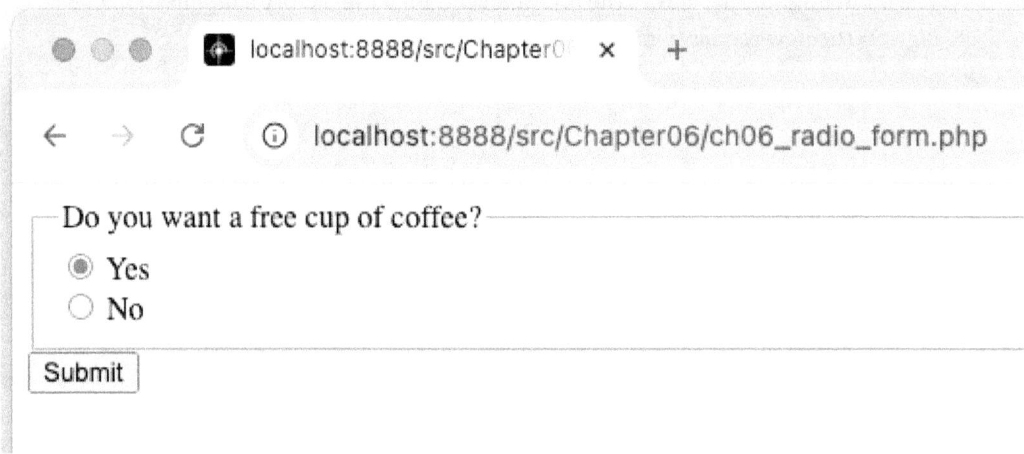

Figure 6.3 – Radio input renderer

The code will generate a radio group as seen in the preceding screenshot. The generator used the array of radio options and converted them into an HTML radio form.

Creating an HTML select element generator

Similar to radio elements, HTML Select elements allow users to choose a single option from a list of options. But unlike a group of radio buttons, Select elements are much more efficient in terms of webpage real estate.

Select options can easily scale for larger datasets without using up an entire block section of a web page. Similar to the previous example, we have displayed 24 line items to represent each hour in a day in *Figure 6.4*. As you've noticed, this radio button group has taken a lot of space. And imagine now if you have to display all available countries in the world; using HTML select elements will become even more practical in that scenario.

Getting ready

We will need the classes we created in the earlier section, *Creating a generic form element generator* and will continue building on top of it.

In the following steps, we will create the required classes and configuration needed to implement this functionality. Each file will be introduced with its purpose before the code is presented.

How to do it...

1. Akin to what we did in the previous section, *Creating an HTML radio element generator*, we will also create a new renderer class to support the select element.

Create a new PHP file at the following path within your project directory. This file will act as the consumer or implementation script demonstrating how the components are used:

`src/Chapter06/GenericInputForm/Renderer/SelectInputRenderer.php`

```
<?php

namespace Cookbook\Chapter06\GenericInputForm\Renderer;

use Cookbook\Chapter06\GenericInputForm\InputType;
```

2. Next, we define an interface that standardizes how different input renderers will generate their HTML output:

```
class SelectInputRenderer implements InputRendererInterface
{
    public function render(InputType $inputType, array $options): string
    {
        $selectOptions   = $options['select_options'];
        $elementOptions = $options['select_element_options'];

        return $this->generate($selectOptions, $elementOptions);
    }

    public function generate(array $selectOptions, array $elementOptions):
string
    {
        $html = "";
        $selectName = $selectOptions['selectName'];
        $selectId = $selectOptions['selectId'];

        // Start the select element
        $html .= "<select name='$selectName' id='$selectId'>";

        // Generate options
        foreach ($elementOptions as $elementOption) {
            $html .= $this->generateOptionElement($elementOption);
        }

        // Close the select element
```

```
        $html .= "</select>";

        return $html;
    }

    private function generateOptionElement(array $elementOptions): string
    {
        $value = $elementOptions['option']['optionValue'];
        $text = $elementOptions['option']['optionText'];

        return "<option value='$value'>$text</option>";
    }
}
```

3. Next, we will have to create a new consumer PHP file for the demo.
   Create a new PHP file at the following path within your project directory. This file will act as the consumer or implementation script demonstrating how the components are used:

   `src/Chapter06/ch06_select_form.php`

```
<?php

use Cookbook\Chapter06\GenericInputForm\GenericFormGenerator;
use \Cookbook\Chapter06\GenericInputForm\InputType;

include __DIR__ . '/../../vendor/autoload.php';

$selectOptions = [
    'selectName' => 'select-when-free-coffee',
    'selectId' => 'select-when-free-coffee'
];

$elementOptions = [];
for ($i = 0; $i < 24; $i++) {
    $hour = str_pad($i, 2, "0", STR_PAD_LEFT) . ":00";
    $elementOptions[] = ['option' => ['optionValue' => (string)$i,
'optionText' => $hour]];
}

// Instantiate generator, and add input fields.
```

```
$generator = new GenericFormGenerator();
$generator->addInput(InputType::Select,
    ['select_options' => $selectOptions, 'select_element_options' =>
$elementOptions]);

// Echo the entire form.
echo $generator->generate('my-select-form', '');
```

4. Then, we have to update and register the new `SelectInputRenderer` inside the `InputRendererFactory` class.
   Create a new PHP file at the following path within your project directory. This file will act as the consumer or implementation script demonstrating how the components are used:

   `src/Chapter06/GenericInputForm/Renderer/InputRendererFactory.php`

```
// Map input types to specific renderer classes
$renderers = [
    InputType::Text->name => TextInputRenderer::class,
    InputType::Password->name => TextInputRenderer::class,
    InputType::Email->name => TextInputRenderer::class,
    InputType::Radio->name => RadioInputRenderer::class,
    InputType::Select->name => SelectInputRenderer::class,
];
```

How it works...

Very much like what we did in the *Creating an HTML radio element generator* recipe, we have simply created a new concrete instance of the `InputRendererInterface` called `SelectInputRenderer`. We then registered this in our `InputRendererFactory` class, and we've let the main generator class create this select renderer object as we have specified in consumer code that we want to add a `Select` input, along with the required array options in this line `$generator->addInput(InputType::Select, ['select_options' => $selectOptions, 'select_element_options' => $elementOptions]);`.

The consumer file will output the following:

Figure 6.4 – Select generator

Implementing a form factory

We developers build and use tools to help us work faster in solving business problems. One good way to help us make our lives easier is to use design patterns. One design pattern that we can use to help us generate forms easier and quicker is by using the Factory Design Pattern, which is discussed more in *Chapter 11, Implementing Software Design Patterns.*

One big advantage of creating a form factory is its ability to generate different form types dynamically, which are very customizable. It also abstracts the details of the actual HTML syntax itself, which can help us developers focus more on the logic rather than the tedious task of writing raw HTML code.

As you might have noticed, we were already using this pattern in the previous sections. We can take it even further by making our generation process even easier through the use of array options and a new factory object to generate an entire form with different types of inputs.

Getting ready

As with the previous two sections before, we will need the classes we created in the earlier section, *Creating a generic form element generator.*

In the following steps, we will create the required classes and configuration needed to implement this functionality. Each file will be introduced with its purpose before the code is presented.

How to do it...

1. First, create an interface that all form builder classes will implement. This will make it easy and consistent when adding different types of forms to build:
   `src/Chapter06/FormBuilderInterface.php`

```
<?php

namespace Cookbook\Chapter06\GenericInputForm\Factory;

use Cookbook\Chapter06\GenericInputForm\FormGeneratorInterface;

interface FormBuilderInterface
{
    public function build(FormGeneratorInterface $formGenerator): void;
}
```

2. Next, create the concrete implementations for the `FormBuilderInterface`. We'll create a simple login and a registration form:

   `src/Chapter06/LoginFormBuilder.php`

```
<?php

namespace Cookbook\Chapter06\GenericInputForm\Factory;

use Cookbook\Chapter06\GenericInputForm\FormGeneratorInterface;
use Cookbook\Chapter06\GenericInputForm\InputType;

class LoginFormBuilder implements FormBuilderInterface
{
    public function build(FormGeneratorInterface $formGenerator): void
    {
        $formGenerator->addInput(InputType::Text, ['label' => 'Username',
'name' => 'username']);
        $formGenerator->addInput(InputType::Password, ['label' =>
'Password', 'name' => 'password']);
    }
}
```

3. Create the `RegisterFormBuilder` class:

   `src/Chapter06/RegisterFormBuilder.php`

```
<?php

namespace Cookbook\Chapter06\GenericInputForm\Factory;

use Cookbook\Chapter06\GenericInputForm\FormGeneratorInterface;
use Cookbook\Chapter06\GenericInputForm\InputType;

class RegisterFormBuilder implements FormBuilderInterface
{
    public function build(FormGeneratorInterface $formGenerator): void
    {
        $formGenerator->addInput(InputType::Text, ['label' => 'Username',
'name' => 'username']);
        $formGenerator->addInput(InputType::Password, ['label' =>
'Password', 'name' => 'password']);
```

```
        $formGenerator->addInput(InputType::Email, ['label' => 'Email',
'name' => 'email']);
    }
}
```

4. Create an enumerable to contain the types of forms that will be available to be used by the consumer. This is better than using strings or arrays that can return empty values or cause unimplemented issues:
   `src/Chapter06/FormType.php`

```
<?php

namespace Cookbook\Chapter06\GenericInputForm\Factory;

enum FormType: string
{
    case LOGIN = 'login';
    case REGISTER = 'register';
}
```

5. Create the `FormFactory` class itself. The most important method in the factory is the `create()` method which will contain the logic of automatically creating the entire form we want:
   `src/Chapter06/FormFactory.php`

```
<?php

namespace Cookbook\Chapter06\GenericInputForm\Factory;

use Cookbook\Chapter06\GenericInputForm\FormGeneratorInterface;
use Cookbook\Chapter06\GenericInputForm\GenericFormGenerator;

class FormFactory
{
    private FormGeneratorInterface $formGenerator;

    private array $formBuilders = [
        FormType::LOGIN->name => LoginFormBuilder::class,
        FormType::REGISTER->name => RegisterFormBuilder::class,
    ];
```

```
    public function __construct(FormGeneratorInterface $formGenerator =
null)
    {
        $this->setFormGenerator($formGenerator);
    }

    public static function createInstance(): FormFactory
    {
        return new static();
    }

    public function create(FormType $type): GenericFormGenerator
    {
        if (!isset($this->formBuilders[$type->name])) {
            throw new \Exception('Form builder not found: ' . $type->name);
        }

        $builder = new $this->formBuilders[$type->name]();
        $builder->build($this->formGenerator);

        return $this->formGenerator;
    }

    public function getFormGenerator(): FormGeneratorInterface
    {
        return $this->formGenerator;
    }

    public function setFormGenerator(FormGeneratorInterface $formGenerator
= null): FormFactory
    {
        if (!$formGenerator) {
            $this->formGenerator = new GenericFormGenerator();
        }
        return $this;
    }
}
```

6. Lastly, create the consumer PHP file to demonstrate the usage:

src/Chapter06/ch06_form_builder.php

```
<?php

use \Cookbook\Chapter06\GenericInputForm\Factory\FormFactory;
use \Cookbook\Chapter06\GenericInputForm\Factory\FormType;

include __DIR__ . '/../../vendor/autoload.php';

echo "<h1>Login</h1>\n";
echo FormFactory::createInstance()->create(FormType::LOGIN)-
>generate('login-form', '/login');

echo "<h1>Register</h1>\n";
echo FormFactory::createInstance()->create(FormType::REGISTER)-
>generate('registration-form', '/register');

// Add styling
echo "<style>body {font-family: arial,serif; } input { width: 200px; }
label {float:left; width:100px; }</style>";
```

How it works...

The `GenericFormGenerator` class we built in one of the previous sections is already very flexible and easy to use. We can also extend this functionality by wrapping pre-configured sets of input forms and use a factory class to automatically generate them for us.

By just writing a single line in the consumer file, we can automatically generate an entire login form. This is the convenience provided by factories:

```
echo FormFactory::createInstance()->create(FormType::LOGIN)->generate('login-
form', '/login');
```

In the `FormFactory` class, we have a static `createInstance` method that returns an object instance of the class itself. This helps in making the class and actual creation methods themselves non-static. This is beneficial when building unit-testable classes.

The factory class itself contains a form builder map in the private `$formBuilders` array.

In the factory's `create` method, we pass the enumerable form type. In this example, the user can only ever choose `FormType::LOGIN` and `FormType::REGISTER`. As you can see, it will not allow the user to enter any random, unregistered form type or string, not even an array. This will help reduce the mistakes the consumer can make when using the factory.

In the following two lines, we create an instance of the concrete form builder we need, pass the `GenericFormGenerator` we created earlier in the previous sections, and then simply use the generator's `addInput` method to add the inputs we want for this specific builder class.

This approach does not rely heavily on array configurations, that can easily be misspelled or misconfigured.

Running the consumer file should output the following example:

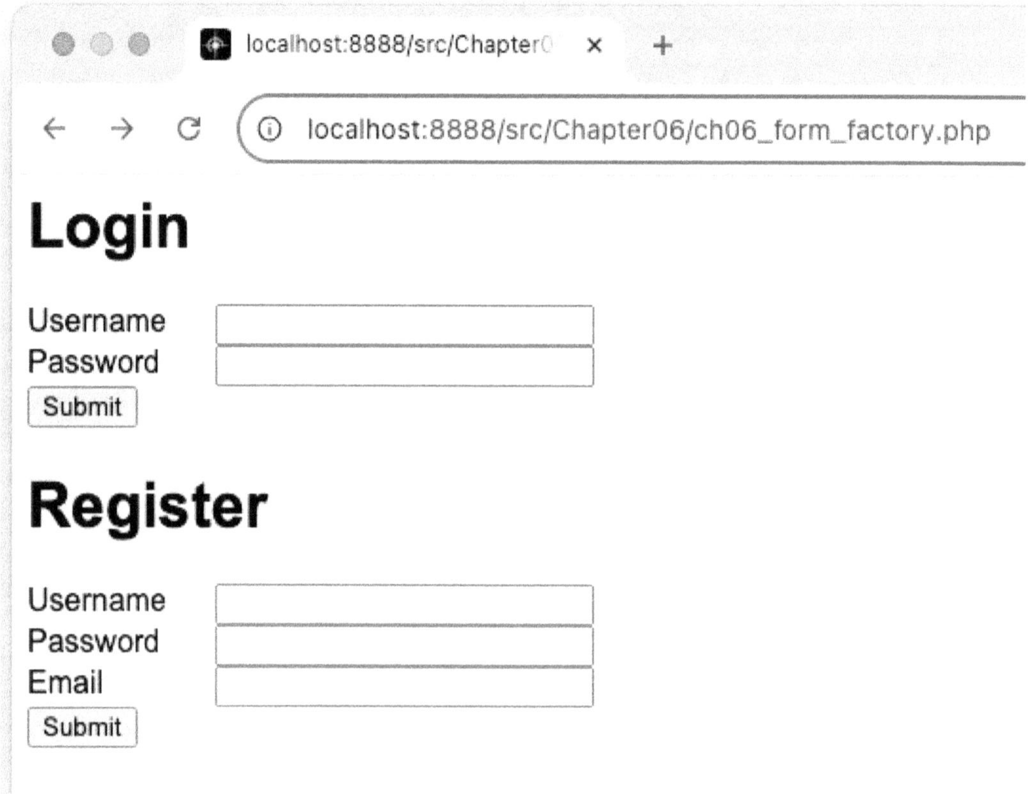

Figure 6.5 – Factory class usage

There's more...

There are several alternative ways to implement a form factory, including fluent builders, configuration-driven factories, or framework-based solutions such as Symfony Forms or Laravel Form Requests, depending on project complexity.

There are a lot of other ways to implement the factory design pattern for form factory usage, and this is just one of them. You can check `https://refactoring.guru/design-patterns/factory-method` for more information about this pattern.

Chaining filters

When handling input from websites or web applications, it's crucial to ensure that the data provided by users conforms to the structure and format expected by the application. This helps maintain data consistency and supports the integrity of the overall application design. One effective way to achieve this is by using filters to sanitize, validate, and transform the input.

Filters can help strip out unwanted characters, enforce specific formats (like email addresses or integers), and ensure that the data is safe to work with. Even better, by chaining multiple filters together, we can create a flexible and reusable data-processing pipeline that handles complex input scenarios in a clean and systematic way.

Getting ready

We will create an extensible and scalable filter chaining solution by using the Decorator Design pattern, along with the Factory Design pattern. Here, we will be able to implement multiple filters, while being able to segregate the actual filter logic from the model containing the data that we need to work on.

In the following steps, we will create the required classes and configuration needed to implement this functionality. Each file will be introduced with its purpose before the code is presented.

How to do it...

1. First, let's create the base and interface classes we need that will be implemented and extended by the actual concrete filters.
   Create a new PHP file at the following path within your project directory. This file will act as the consumer or implementation script demonstrating how the components are used.

   We begin by defining a common interface to standardize how filters are applied across different implementations:

   `src/Chapter06/InputHandler/Filter/FilterInterface.php`

   ```
   <?php

   namespace Cookbook\Chapter06\InputHandler\Filter;
   ```

```
interface FilterInterface
{
    public function apply(object $entity): void;
}
```

2. Create a new PHP file at the following path within your project directory. This file will act as the consumer or implementation script demonstrating how the components are used:

   `src/Chapter06/InputHandler/Filter/BaseFilter.php`

```
<?php

namespace Cookbook\Chapter06\InputHandler\Filter;

class BaseFilter implements FilterInterface
{
    public function apply(object $entity): void
    {
        // TODO: Implement apply() method.
    }
}
```

3. Next, let's create the concrete implementation of the filters. These are also called Decorators in the Decorator Design Pattern. These classes will contain the actual logic to implement the filter logic we want.
   Create a new PHP file at the following path within your project directory. This file will act as the consumer or implementation script demonstrating how the components are used:

   `src/Chapter06/InputHandler/Filter/TrimFilter.php`

```
<?php

namespace Cookbook\Chapter06\InputHandler\Filter;

class TrimFilter implements FilterInterface
{
    public function __construct(private FilterInterface $next)
    {
    }
```

```
    public function apply(object $entity): void
    {
        $rules = method_exists($entity, 'getFilterRules') ? $entity-
>getFilterRules() : [];
        foreach ($rules as $field => $meta) {
            if (!($meta['trim'] ?? false)) {
                continue;
            }

            $getter = $meta['getter'] ?? null;
            $setter = $meta['setter'] ?? null;

            if ($getter && $setter && method_exists($entity, $getter) &&
method_exists($entity, $setter)) {
                $value = $entity->{$getter}();
                $entity->{$setter}(trim($value));
            }
        }

        $this->next->apply($entity);
    }
}
```

4. Create a new PHP file at the following path within your project directory. This file will act as the consumer or implementation script demonstrating how the components are used:
   `src/Chapter06/InputHandler/Filter/UpperCaseFilter.php`

```
<?php

namespace Cookbook\Chapter06\InputHandler\Filter;

class UpperCaseFilter implements FilterInterface
{
    public function __construct(private FilterInterface $next)
    {
    }

    public function apply(object $entity): void
    {
        $rules = method_exists($entity, 'getFilterRules') ? $entity-
```

```
>getFilterRules() : [];

        foreach ($rules as $field => $meta) {
            if (!($meta['uppercase'] ?? false)) {
                continue;
            }

            $getter = $meta['getter'] ?? null;
            $setter = $meta['setter'] ?? null;

            if ($getter && $setter && method_exists($entity, $getter) &&
method_exists($entity, $setter)) {
                $value = $entity->{$getter}();
                $entity->{$setter}(mb_strtoupper($value));
            }
        }

        $this->next->apply($entity);
    }
}
```

5. And to easily instantiate these decorators, let's just use a Factory class to do the work for us.
   Create a new PHP file at the following path within your project directory. This file will act as the consumer or implementation script demonstrating how the components are used:

   `src/Chapter06/InputHandler/Filter/FilterFactory.php`

```
<?php

namespace Cookbook\Chapter06\InputHandler\Filter;

class FilterFactory
{
    public static function create(array $stack): FilterInterface
    {
        $filter = new BaseFilter();
        foreach ($stack as $className) {
            if (class_exists($className)) {
                $filter = new $className($filter);
```

```
            }
        }
        return $filter;
    }
}
```

6. Finally, let's create the consumer PHP file that will contain our demo usage. Create a new PHP file at the following path within your project directory. This file will act as the consumer or implementation script demonstrating how the components are used:

   `src/Chapter06/ch06_chain_filter.php`

```
<?php

use Cookbook\Chapter06\InputHandler\User;
use Cookbook\Chapter06\InputHandler\Filter\FilterFactory;

include __DIR__ . '/../../vendor/autoload.php';

$firstName = "   Nirali   ";
$lastName = "  Zave  ";
$email = '  niralizave@email.com  ';
$password = 'abc123123';

$user = new User($firstName, $lastName, $email, $password);
$filter = FilterFactory::create($user->getFilterStack());
$filter->apply($user);

echo "========= \n";
echo "Before Filters: ";
echo 'First Name: ' . $firstName . "\n";
echo 'Last Name: ' . $lastName . "\n";
echo 'Email: ' . $email . "\n";
echo "First Name Length: " . strlen($firstName) . "\n";
echo "Last Name Length: " . strlen($lastName) . "\n";
echo "Email Length: " . strlen($email) . "\n";

echo "\n";
echo "After Filters:\n";
echo 'First Name: ' . $user->getFirstName() . "\n";
```

```
echo 'Last Name: ' . $user->getLastName() . "\n";
echo 'Email: ' . $user->getEmail() . "\n";
echo "First Name Length: " . strlen($user->getFirstName()) . "\n";
echo "Last Name Length: " . strlen($user->getLastName()) . "\n";
echo "Email Length: " . strlen($user->getEmail()) . "\n";
echo "========= \n";
```

How it works...

As you can see, we have intentionally added white spaces before and after the first name, last name, and email variables. We should not accept these as valid characters for these specific fields. And what if we want to uppercase both the first and last names? Well, we can create filters and chain them and apply them to these input fields.

First, we created a `User.php` model class that contains the properties we would want to apply the filter to. In the `User` class, we have added a method `getFilterRules()` that returns an array of filter configurations:

```
public function getFilterRules(): array
    {
        return [
            'first_name' => [
                'getter' => 'getFirstName',
                'setter' => 'setFirstName',
                'trim' => true,
                'uppercase' => true,
            ],
            'last_name' => [
                'getter' => 'getLastName',
                'setter' => 'setLastName',
                'trim' => true,
                'uppercase' => true,
            ],
            'email' => [
                'getter' => 'getEmail',
                'setter' => 'setEmail',
                'trim' => true,
            ]
        ];
    }
```

For the `first_name`, we want to both trim and uppercase this specific field, so we set the values to `true` for both. We also have added a `getFilterStack()` method to return the filter classes we want to use for this User model.

Next, we have created a `FilterInterface` interface that has a single apply() method which will contain the logic we want to implement for a concrete filter. We have two concrete filters, the `TrimFilter` and `UpperCaseFilter`. Take note of the constructor method. This is how we achieve the filter chaining, through the decorator pattern. Both concrete filters have the public `function __construct(private FilterInterface $next)`, meaning we can set the next filter class we want to use after we execute the logic in the current filter. As you can see in the apply method of both concrete implementations, we call the `$this->next->apply($entity);` line to execute the next class's apply method. This is how we achieved chaining.

We then used the `FilterFactory` class to automatically create the filter instances we need, and apply them to our `User` model:

```
$user = new User($firstName, $lastName, $email, $password);
$filter = FilterFactory::create($user->getFilterStack());
$filter->apply($user);
```

Run the following command from your terminal:

```
$ php src/Chapter06/ch06_chain_filter.php
```

Here is the resulting program output:

```
=========
Before Filters: First Name:    Nirali
Last Name:   Zave
Email:   niralizave@email.com
First Name Length: 12
Last Name Length: 8
Email Length: 24

After Filters:
First Name: NIRALI
Last Name: ZAVE
Last Name: niralizave@email.com
First Name Length: 6
Last Name Length: 4
```

```
Email Length: 20
=========
```

As you can see, we have intentionally added white spaces before and after the first name, last name, and email variables. We want to remove the trailing white spaces and also uppercase both the first and last names.

Chaining validators

It is essential to consistently validate user input to ensure that the data being submitted is accurate, safe, and aligns with the expectations of the application. Input validation helps prevent a range of issues, from data inconsistencies to security vulnerabilities. For instance, you might enforce a maximum character limit on a text field to prevent overflow or abuse, or ensure that required fields are not left empty to maintain the integrity of the data model. By applying validation rules—such as type checks, length constraints, format verification, and presence requirements—you can safeguard your application against malformed or malicious input while also providing a better user experience through clear and immediate feedback.

Getting ready

We will be reusing the structure we've already implemented in the previous section, *Chaining Filters*. We will follow the same exact approach, creating multiple filters and chaining them through the use of the Decorator design pattern.

In the following steps, we will create the required classes and configuration needed to implement this functionality. Each file will be introduced with its purpose before the code is presented.

How to do it...

1. First, let's create the base and interface classes we need that will be implemented and extended by the actual concrete filters.
   Create a new PHP file at the following path within your project directory. This file will act as the consumer or implementation script demonstrating how the components are used.

   We now define validator components that verify whether processed input satisfies business rules such as required fields, length constraints, and format validation:

   `src/Chapter06/InputHandler/Validator/ValidatorInterface.php`

   ```php
   <?php

   namespace Cookbook\Chapter06\InputHandler\Validator;
   ```

```
interface ValidatorInterface
{
    public function validate(object $entity): array;
}
```

2. Create a new PHP file at the following path within your project directory. This file will act as the consumer or implementation script demonstrating how the components are used:
   `src/Chapter06/InputHandler/Filter/BaseValidator.php`

```
<?php

namespace Cookbook\Chapter06\InputHandler\Validator;

class BaseValidator implements ValidatorInterface
{
    public function validate(object $entity): array
    {
        return [];
    }
}
```

3. Next, let's create the concrete implementation of the validators. These classes will contain the actual logic to implement the validation.
   Create a new PHP file at the following path within your project directory. This file will act as the consumer or implementation script demonstrating how the components are used:

   `src/Chapter06/InputHandler/Filter/RequiredFieldValidator.php`

```
<?php

namespace Cookbook\Chapter06\InputHandler\Validator;

class RequiredFieldValidator implements ValidatorInterface
{
    public function __construct(private ValidatorInterface $next)
    {
    }
```

```
    public function validate(object $entity): array
    {
        $errors = $this->next->validate($entity);
        $rules = $entity->getValidationRules();

        foreach ($rules as $field => $meta) {
            if (!($meta['required'] ?? false)) {
                continue;
            }
            $getter = $meta['getter'];
            $value = trim((string)$entity->{$getter}());
            if ($value === '') {
                $errors[$field][] = ucfirst(str_replace('_', ' ',
$field)) . ' is required.';
            }
        }

        return $errors;
    }
}
```

4. Create a new PHP file at the following path within your project directory. This file will act as the consumer or implementation script demonstrating how the components are used:

   `src/Chapter06/InputHandler/Filter/LengthValidator.php`

```
<?php

namespace Cookbook\Chapter06\InputHandler\Validator;

class LengthValidator implements ValidatorInterface
{
    public function __construct(private ValidatorInterface $next)
    {
    }

    public function validate(object $entity): array
    {
        $errors = $this->next->validate($entity);
        $rules = $entity->getValidationRules();
```

```
        foreach ($rules as $field => $meta) {
            if (!isset($meta['max_length'])) {
                continue;
            }
            $getter = $meta['getter'];
            $value = (string)$entity->{$getter}();
            if (strlen($value) > $meta['max_length']) {
                $errors[$field][] = ucfirst(str_replace('_', ' ',
$field)) .
                    " must not exceed {$meta['max_length']} characters.";
            }
        }

        return $errors;
    }
}
```

5. Create a new PHP file at the following path within your project directory. This file will act as the consumer or implementation script demonstrating how the components are used:

   `src/Chapter06/InputHandler/Filter/NoNumericValidator.php`

```
<?php

namespace Cookbook\Chapter06\InputHandler\Validator;

class NoNumericValidator implements ValidatorInterface
{
    public function __construct(private ValidatorInterface $next)
    {
    }

    public function validate(object $entity): array
    {
        $errors = $this->next->validate($entity);
        $rules = $entity->getValidationRules();

        foreach ($rules as $field => $meta) {
            if (!($meta['no_numeric'] ?? false)) {
                continue;
            }
```

```
                $getter = $meta['getter'];
                $value = (string)$entity->{$getter}();
                if (preg_match('/\\d/', $value)) {
                    $errors[$field][] = ucfirst(str_replace('_', ' ',
$field)) . ' must not contain numbers.';
                }
            }

            return $errors;
        }
}
```

6. And like what we did for the filters in the previous section, to easily instantiate these decorators, let's create a factory class.
   Create a new PHP file at the following path within your project directory. This file will act as the consumer or implementation script demonstrating how the components are used:

   `src/Chapter06/InputHandler/Filter/ValidationFactory.php`

```
<?php

namespace Cookbook\Chapter06\InputHandler\Validator;

class ValidationFactory
{
    public static function create(array $stack): ValidatorInterface
    {
        $validator = new BaseValidator();
        foreach ($stack as $className) {
            if (class_exists($className)) {
                $validator = new $className($validator);
            }
        }
        return $validator;
```

```
    }
}
```

7. Finally, in the consumer PHP file, we will combine both the filter and validator usage in one go:

```
<?php

use Cookbook\Chapter06\InputHandler\User;
use Cookbook\Chapter06\InputHandler\Filter\FilterFactory;
use Cookbook\Chapter06\InputHandler\Validator\ValidationFactory;

include __DIR__ . '/../../vendor/autoload.php';

$firstName = "   Alexi5    ";
$lastName = "  Surfer5322 Very Long String Name Not Allowed   ";
$email = '  gru37@email.com   ';
$password = 'bac-123-182-WDj-sd';

$user = new User($firstName, $lastName, $email, $password);
$filter = FilterFactory::create($user->getFilterStack());
$filter->apply($user);

$validator = ValidationFactory::create($user->getValidationStack());
$errors = $validator->validate($user);

echo "========= \n";
echo "Before Filters: ";
echo 'First Name: ' . $firstName . "\n";
echo 'Last Name: ' . $lastName . "\n";
echo 'Email: ' . $email . "\n";
echo "First Name Length: " . strlen($firstName) . "\n";
echo "Last Name Length: " . strlen($lastName) . "\n";
echo "Email Length: " . strlen($email) . "\n";

echo "\n";
echo "After Filters:\n";
echo 'First Name: ' . $user->getFirstName() . "\n";
echo 'Last Name: ' . $user->getLastName() . "\n";
echo 'Last Name: ' . $user->getEmail() . "\n";
echo "First Name Length: " . strlen($user->getFirstName()) . "\n";
```

```
echo "Last Name Length: " . strlen($user->getLastName()) . "\n";
echo "Email Length: " . strlen($user->getEmail()) . "\n";
echo "========= \n";

echo "\nValidation Errors: \n";
print_r($errors);
```

How it works...

Very similar to how it works with the previous section, *Chaining Filters*, we simply utilized OOP concepts and utilized the Decorator design pattern. We created three different validator classes, chained them using the array of validation classes, and then set it into the constructor in the following line: `$validator = ValidationFactory::create($user->getValidationStack());` and literally just executed the chained validators through `$validator->validate($user);`

In your terminal, run the following command:

```
% php src/Chapter06/ch06_chain_validator.php
```

You should get the following result:

```
=========
Before Filters: First Name:    Alexi5
Last Name:    Surfer5322 Very Long String Name Not Allowed
Email:    gru37@email.com
First Name Length: 12
Last Name Length: 48
Email Length: 19

After Filters:
First Name: ALEXI5
Last Name: SURFER5322 VERY LONG STRING NAME NOT ALLOWED
Last Name: gru37@email.com
First Name Length: 6
Last Name Length: 44
Email Length: 15
=========

Validation Errors:
Array
```

```
(
    [first_name] => Array
        (
            [0] => First name must not contain numbers.
        )

    [last_name] => Array
        (
            [0] => Last name must not contain numbers.
            [1] => Last name must not exceed 30 characters.
        )

)
```

We now define validator components that verify whether the processed input satisfies business rules such as required fields, length constraints, and format validation.

From the output, you can see how we were able to combine multiple filters and multiple validators. Now you have the mini-framework that allows you to keep adding validators and filters depending on your needs. We've created the `NoNumericValidator`, `RequiredFieldValidator`, and `LengthValidator` decorators; you can easily just implement the same `ValidatorInterface` and keep building more validators.

AI-driven dynamic form systems

AI-driven dynamic form systems allow applications to generate entire form structures from natural language requirements or business descriptions. Instead of manually defining each field, developers can request a structured schema from an AI service and translate it into standardized form elements using the generator patterns introduced earlier. This approach enables rapid prototyping, easier adaptation to changing requirements, and more scalable form management.

Getting ready

As applications scale, it's common for business stakeholders to describe a form in natural language (*job application form*, *customer support intake form*, and so on). Instead of manually translating those requirements into HTML inputs, we can ask an LLM to generate a lightweight JSON form schema and then render it using the same generator patterns you built earlier in this chapter.

How to do it...

1. Ask the AI to generate a compact JSON schema describing the fields you want.
2. Convert the schema into generator calls (`InputType` plus options).

   The following example asks for a form schema and renders it using `GenericFormGenerator`:

   `src/Chapter06/ch06_ai_schema_form.php`

```
<?php

use Cookbook\Chapter06\AI\AiClient;
use Cookbook\Chapter06\GenericInputForm\GenericFormGenerator;
use Cookbook\Chapter06\GenericInputForm\InputType;

include __DIR__ . '/../../vendor/autoload.php';

$ai = new AiClient($_ENV['OPENAI_API_KEY'] ?? '');
$generator = new GenericFormGenerator();

$prompt = 'Generate a JSON schema for a job application form. '
    . 'Return: {"fields":[{"type":"text","label":"Full
Name","name":"full_name"}] }';
$schemaJson = $ai->generateText($prompt);
$schema = json_decode($schemaJson, true) ?: [];

foreach (($schema['fields'] ?? []) as $field) {
    $type  = strtolower((string)($field['type'] ?? 'text'));
    $label = (string)($field['label'] ?? '');
    $name  = (string)($field['name'] ?? '');

    if ($label === '' || $name === '') {
        continue;
    }

    $inputType = match ($type) {
        'email' => InputType::Email,
        'password' => InputType::Password,
        default => InputType::Text,
    };
```

```
    $generator->addInput($inputType, ['label' => $label, 'name' => $name]);
}

echo $generator->generate('job-app', '');
```

How it works...

The AI produces a minimal JSON description of a form rather than raw HTML. Your code remains responsible for rendering HTML, while the schema acts as a structured contract that can be validated, logged, and reviewed. The mapping step converts the schema's field types into your `InputType` enum, preserving the consistency and safety of your existing generator design.

7

Making AI-Assisted Web Services and WebSockets Requests

In this chapter, we present recipes that show you how to communicate effectively with external APIs and AI platforms. The ability to issue **Representational State Transfer** (**REST**) requests using both Streams and **Client URL** (**cURL**) (`https://www.php.net/curl`) gives you tremendous flexibility across different hosting environments. Designing **middleware**-based **microservices** forms the basis of a clean and maintainable architecture that scales gracefully as business requirements expand.

As GenAI integration becomes increasingly common, our token usage tracking recipe is essential for helping your organization and customers control costs and optimize performance. In the last recipe, we present a fundamental shift away from traditional request-response patterns via real-time **asynchronous WebSockets** communications.

The main topics in this chapter include:

- Using standard I/O and PHP cURL to issue REST requests
- Creating a middleware-based microservices REST service
- Tracking GenAI token usage
- Building an AI-assisted real-time chat service using asynchronous PHP WebSockets

Technical requirements

In order to follow the recipes in this chapter, you'll need to set up an account on your preferred GenAI platform. You'll also need to provide funds for the account sufficient for the volume of queries you plan to perform. For the purposes of this recipe, we'll focus on OpenAI and platforms that give us access to its models. However, you can easily adapt the recipes in this chapter to fit your preferred GenAI platform. GenAI models tend to be specialized (e.g. models trained for image recognition and generation, text-to-speech models), and will often produce different results. Also of note is that as GenAI technology progresses, the output quality is expected to improve as well as its ability to interpret prompts.

> Note
>
> **GenAI pricing**
>
> Pricing will vary depending on the chosen model. As a general rule, the more expensive models will produce higher quality output. Pricing is calculated in millions of *tokens* (approximately 4 characters of text). The total price for a given query is calculated based upon how much text is provided for the query (including uploaded documents), and how much text is produced as output. However, experience has shown that if you choose a less expensive model, costs for most GenAI platforms will fall well within a budget of $10 USD.

Using standard I/O and PHP cURL to issue REST requests

A REST service is a web API that uses standard HTTP methods (`GET`, `POST`, `PUT`, `PATCH`, and `DELETE`) to perform operations on resources identified by URLs. It is stateless, meaning each request contains all necessary information, and typically exchanges data in JSON or XML format. Both Streams (the standard PHP I/O functions) and the cURL extension can be used to make REST requests to external web services. In this recipe we show you how to make requests to a remote REST service using both techniques.

Note

Standards-based requests

It's important to note that the PHP Framework Interop Group (PHP-FIG) has defined a number of standards you can use when developing components making REST requests. The pertinent standards include:

- PSR-7: HTTP message interfaces [`https://www.php-fig.org/psr/psr-7/`]
- PSR-17: HTTP Factories [`https://www.php-fig.org/psr/psr-17/`]
- PSR-18: HTTP Client [`https://www.php-fig.org/psr/psr-18/`]

Getting ready

For the purposes of this recipe, we'll make a request to a publicly available service hosted on `api.unlikelysource.com`. The first service supports `HTTP GET` requests and provides post code information based on Geonames data. The second service performs a simple echo that returns data sent via an `HTTP POST` request. As we'll be using standard PHP capabilities, no special setup is required.

How to do it...

1. In the `/path/to/php8cookbook/src/REST` folder, we create two files `EnumMethod.php` and `EnumExt.php` that house **enumerations** that determine acceptable choices for HTTP methods and PHP extensions. The nice thing about PHP enumerations (also called **enums**) is that they serve as natural type hints. If you pass an argument that's not included in the **enum**, a `TypeError` is thrown:

```
<?php
namespace Cookbook\REST;
enum EnumExt {
    case STREAMS;    // standard I/O
    case CURL;       // cURL extension
}
```

2. Here's the second enumeration:

```
<?php
namespace Cookbook\REST;
```

```
enum EnumMethod {
    case GET;   // HTTP GET
    case POST;  // HTTP POST
}
```

> **Tip**
>
> PHP files can represent different components in an application such as classes, interfaces, traits, and enumerations. However, when looking through a directory listing of your source code, it's difficult for you to tell which file contains which component. Accordingly, we've adopted the convention of including the type of component in the class and filename. Accordingly, the filenames for the enumerations would be `EnumExt.php` and `EnumMethod.php` respectively. This allows for easier maintenance down the road.

3. Next, we create a file `SimpleAPICall.php`. In this class, we identify test API endpoints for `HTTP GET` and `POST` requests, an error message, and the number of bytes to read:

```
<?php
namespace Cookbook\REST;
use Exception;
use SplFileObject;
use Throwable;
class SimpleAPICall {
    const API_GET_URL =
        'https://api.unlikelysource.com/api';
    const API_POST_URL =
        'https://api.unlikelysource.com/post';
    const API_ERROR = 'ERROR: api transmission error';
    const NUM_BYTES = 4096;
```

4. We then define a `send()` method that accepts as arguments an array of data, and enums that represent the HTTP method and the PHP extension to use. We return the results of a `match` expression that tests the enums and returns output from the appropriate method:

```
public static function send(array $data, EnumMethod $method,
EnumExt $ext) :
    mixed {
```

```
        return match ([$method, $ext]) {
            [EnumMethod::GET, EnumExt::STREAMS]  => static::streamsGet($data),
            [EnumMethod::GET, EnumExt::CURL]     => static::curlGet($data),
            [EnumMethod::POST, EnumExt::STREAMS] => static::streamsPost($data),
            [EnumMethod::POST, EnumExt::CURL]    => static::curlPost($data),
            default => static::streamsGet($data)
        };
    }
```

5. The `streamsGet()` method performs a REST API request using a simple `file_get_contents()` call. The handy `http_build_query()` function converts a PHP array into a valid HTTP query string. We then return a JSON string in response, with a boolean "success" response element:

```
    public static function streamsGet(array $data) : string {
        try {
            $text = file_get_contents(static::API_GET_URL . '?' .
    http_build_query($data));
            $response = ['success' => true, 'data' => $text];
        } catch (Throwable $t) {
            error_log(__METHOD__ . ':' . $t->getMessage());
            $response = ['success' => false, 'data' => static::API_ERROR];
        }
        return json_encode($response, JSON_PRETTY_PRINT);
    }
```

6. The `curlGet()` method illustrates how to make an `HTTP GET` request using the PHP cURL extension. The `CURLOPT_RETURNTRANSFER` option ensures that the response from the remote service is returned. The `CURLOPT_SSL_VERIFYPEER` and `CURLOPT_SSL_VERIFYHOST` options are set to `false` only for testing and development. *It's extremely important to set these two options to* `true` *in a production environment!* `curl_exec()` makes the actual external call and returns the response. We also use `curl_getinfo()` and `curl_error()` to check for potential transmission issues and throw an `Exception` if an issue is detected:

```
    public static function curlGet(array $data) : string {
        $ch = curl_init(static::API_GET_URL . '?' . http_build_query($data));
        curl_setopt($ch, CURLOPT_RETURNTRANSFER, true);
        // to make this work locally, set both CURLOPT_SSL* options to "false"
```

```
        curl_setopt($ch, CURLOPT_SSL_VERIFYPEER, true);
        curl_setopt($ch, CURLOPT_SSL_VERIFYHOST, 2);
        try {
            $response = curl_exec($ch);
            $error = curl_error($ch);
            if (!empty($error)) {
                error_log(__METHOD__ . ':' . curl_getinfo());
                throw new Exception(sprintf('ERROR %s',$error));
    }
            $response = ['success' => true, 'data' => $response];
        } catch (Throwable $t) {
            error_log(__METHOD__ . ':' . $t->getMessage());
            $response = ['success' => false, 'data' => static::API_ERROR];
        } finally {
            curl_close($ch);
        }
        return json_encode($response, JSON_PRETTY_PRINT);
    }
```

7. We can now develop two methods to generate `HTTP POST` requests, one using PHP Streams, and another using the cURL extension. Using Streams is somewhat complicated by the fact that when making an HTTP Streams request, the default method is `GET`. Accordingly, we bring in `stream_context_create()` to create a *context* in which we can adjust outgoing headers, data, and HTTP method:

```
    public static function streamsPost(array $data) : string {
        $send = http_build_query($data);
        $headers = [
            'Content-type: application/x-www-form-urlencoded',
            'Content-Length: ' . strlen($send)
        ];
        $options = [
            'http' => [
                'method' => 'POST',
                'header'=> implode("\r\n", $headers),
                'content' => $send
            ]
        ];
        $context = stream_context_create($options);
```

8. We can then apply the newly formed context as an argument for any of the standard Streams methods including `fopen()` and `file_get_contents()`. However, in this instance, we'll create an `SplFileObject` instance, which has the same constructor signature as `fopen()`, to serve as a basis for the outgoing POST request. You'll note that it seems illogical to set the mode to `r` (*read*) when making an outbound request. However, on further thought, you'll realize that although we're making an outbound request to an external service, we are *reading* the response. We then read the predefined number of bytes and continue reading in a loop until the entire response is captured:

```
        $fp = new SplFileObject(static::API_POST_URL, 'r', false, $context);
        $response = [];
        try {
            $text = $fp->fread(static::NUM_BYTES);
            while (!$fp->eof()) {
                $text .= $fp->fread(static::NUM_BYTES);
            }
            $response = ['success' => true, 'data' => $text];
        } catch (Throwable $t) {
            error_log(__METHOD__ . ':' . $t->getMessage());
            $response = ['success' => false, 'data' => static::API_ERROR];
        }
        return json_encode($response, JSON_PRETTY_PRINT);
    }
```

> **Tip**
>
> Even though using Streams-based functions and classes works for simple requests, most developers prefer to use cURL or components that leverage cURL (e.g. the Guzzle client, or the Symfony HttpClient). The reason for this preference is that cURL is based upon libcurl which is a highly performant and mature client library. The PHP cURL extension also has a much more extensive set of options for making REST requests compared to Streams.

9. By contrast, with the cURL extension, we can use the `CURLOPT_POST` option to indicate `POST` rather than `GET`. In this example, we show the use of `curl_setopt_array()`, which is a useful alternative to `curl_setopt()` in cases where you have a large number

of settings. In this example we also demonstrate placing the curl request in a `try / catch` block, and take advantage of `finally` to close the connection:

```
public static function curlPost(array $data) : string
{
    $send = http_build_query($data);
    $ch = curl_init(static::API_POST_URL);
    curl_setopt_array($ch, [
        CURLOPT_POST              => true,
        CURLOPT_HTTPHEADER        => [
            'Content-type: application/x-www-form-urlencoded',
            'Content-Length: ' . strlen($send),
        ],
        CURLOPT_POSTFIELDS        => $send,
        CURLOPT_RETURNTRANSFER    => true,
        CURLOPT_HEADER            => false,
        CURLOPT_TIMEOUT           => 60,
        // to make this work locally, set both CURLOPT_SSL* options to
"false"
        CURLOPT_SSL_VERIFYPEER => true,
        CURLOPT_SSL_VERIFYHOST => 2,
    ]);
    try {
        $text = curl_exec($ch);
        $response = ['success' => true, 'data' => $text];
    } catch (Throwable $t) {
        error_log(__METHOD__ . ':' . $t->getMessage());
        $response = ['success' => false, 'data' => static::API_ERROR];
    } finally {
        curl_close($ch);
    }
    return json_encode($response, JSON_PRETTY_PRINT);
}}
```

10. To test our four methods, in the `/path/to/php8cookbook/src/Chapter07` folder we create a file `ch07_rest_get_post.php`, set up some data to send, and make four calls to our new class. First, we execute the Composer autoloader and add a set of `use`

statements to identify needed components, and define a data array to transmit. In addition, we use an **arrow function** to create a callback to display the elapsed time:

```
<?php
include __DIR__ . '/../../vendor/autoload.php';
use Cookbook\REST\SimpleAPICall;
use Cookbook\REST\EnumMethod;
use Cookbook\REST\EnumExt;
$data = [
    'postcode' => strip_tags($argv[1] ?? $_GET['postcode'] ?? 13676),
    'country'  => strip_tags($argv[2] ?? $_GET['country'] ?? 'FR')
];
$display = fn (string $label, float $start) =>
    sprintf("\n%20s: Elapsed time: %.4f\n", $label, (microtime(true) -
$start));
```

11. We then make API calls to the four methods in our new class. We use the `microtime()` function to determine elapsed time:

```
// HTTP GET request using Streams
$start = microtime(true);
echo SimpleAPICall::send($data, EnumMethod::GET, EnumExt::STREAMS);
echo $display('Streams GET', $start);

// HTTP GET request using cURL
$start = microtime(true);
echo SimpleAPICall::send($data, EnumMethod::GET, EnumExt::CURL);
echo $display('cURL GET', $start);

// HTTP POST request using Streams
$start = microtime(true);
echo SimpleAPICall::send($data, EnumMethod::POST, EnumExt::STREAMS);
echo $display('Streams POST', $start);

// HTTP POST request using cURL
$start = microtime(true);
echo SimpleAPICall::send($data, EnumMethod::POST, EnumExt::CURL);
echo $display('cURL POST', $start);
```

How it works...

When we run our test script, we make identical GET requests to the postcode lookup API. As you can see from the elapsed time output, the request using cURL, although having more lines of code in its setup, delivers slightly better performance. In our example, a Streams-based GET request took 3.1154 seconds whereas the curl request took 3.0641 seconds. You'll also note that the Streams-based POST request only took 0.8744 seconds compared with the 0.9747 seconds taken by the curl equivalent. However, it's important to note that the cURL extension can support multiple simultaneous requests using the `curl_multi*` functions. Also, the larger the data payload, the greater will be the difference between cURL-based requests compared with Streams.

Here is the sample output:

```
php8:/repo# php src/Chapter07/ch07_rest_get_post.php
{
    "success": true,
    "data": "{\n    \"data\": [\n        {\n            \"id\":
223277,\n            \"country\": \"FR\",\n            \"postcode\": \"13676
CEDEX\",\n            \"city\": \"Aubagne\",\n            \"state_prov_name\":
\"Provence-Alpes-C\\u00c3\\u00b4te d'Azur\",\n            \"state_prov_code\":
\"93\",\n            \"locality_name\": \"Bouches-du-Rh\\u00c3\\u00b4ne\",
\n            \"locality_code\": \"13\",\n            \"region_name\":
\"Arrondissement de Marseille\",\n            \"region_code\": \"133\",
\n            \"latitude\": \"43.2928\",\n            \"longitude\": \"5.5707\",
\n            \"accuracy\": \"5\"\n        }\n    ]\n}"
}
        Streams GET: Elapsed time: 3.1154
{
    "success": true,
    "data": "{\n    \"data\": [\n        {\n            \"id\":
223277,\n            \"country\": \"FR\",\n            \"postcode\": \"13676
CEDEX\",\n            \"city\": \"Aubagne\",\n            \"state_prov_name\":
\"Provence-Alpes-C\\u00c3\\u00b4te d'Azur\",\n            \"state_prov_code\":
\"93\",\n            \"locality_name\": \"Bouches-du-Rh\\u00c3\\u00b4ne\",
\n            \"locality_code\": \"13\",\n            \"region_name\":
\"Arrondissement de Marseille\",\n            \"region_code\": \"133\",
\n            \"latitude\": \"43.2928\",\n            \"longitude\": \"5.5707\",
\n            \"accuracy\": \"5\"\n        }\n    ]\n}"
}
           cURL GET: Elapsed time: 3.0641
```

```
{
    "success": true,
    "data": "{\n    \"message\": \"This is what you sent\",\n    \"payload\":
{\n        \"postcode\": \"13676\",\n        \"country\": \"FR\"\n    }\n}"
}
        Streams POST: Elapsed time: 0.8744
{
    "success": true,
    "data": "HTTP\/2 200 \r\ncontent-type: application\/json\r\nx-ws-origin:
available\r\nx-ws-ratelimit-limit: 1000\r\nx-ws-ratelimit-remaining: 998\r\ndate:
Thu, 18 Jun 2026 04:04:42 GMT\r\nserver: Apache\r\n\r\n{\n    \"message\": \"This
is what you sent\",\n    \"payload\": {\n        \"postcode\": \"13676\",\n
\"country\": \"FR\"\n    }\n}"
}
          cURL POST: Elapsed time: 0.9747
```

Creating a middleware-based microservices REST service

Microservices is a frequently used term in IT. In brief, microservices is an architectural style in which an application is built as small, independent, loosely coupled services, each handling a specific business function. As part of a bigger picture, microservices form the basis of what is known as the **MACH architecture**. This is a modern software approach based on **Microservices, API-first, Cloud-native, and Headless** principles, enabling a flexible, scalable, and composable digital infrastructure.

Middleware is software that acts as a bridge between different applications, services, or system layers — handling communication, data translation, authentication, logging, or request/response processing between components. Many of the PHP-based micro frameworks, such as Slim or Mezzio (part of the Laminas project), use a middleware pipeline to direct the flow of logic.

In this recipe, we'll create microservices as middleware components, forming a GenAI-based REST service. We'll design a flexible structure where new GenAI microservices can be added by simply creating the appropriate middleware components. We'll also ensure compatibility by basing our components on the PSR-7 and PSR-15 standards.

Getting ready

To run the code in this recipe, you'll need API access for your preferred GenAI platform. In most cases, this will incur a nominal cost. However, it's been this author's experience that you can often purchase pay-as-you-go credits. As a general rule, most platforms allow small amounts, so the investment will be minimal. Bear in mind that the quality and style of code produced will vary depending on the platform and model. The better the model, the more credits it will use.

You'll also need to use Composer to install the `laminas/laminas-diactoros`, `laminas/laminas-stratigility`, and `psr/http-server-middleware` Composer packages. The latter package will also install `psr/http-message`, which we will use as well. The PSR packages give us the interfaces that we'll implement to produce PSR-15 compliant middleware. The Laminas Diactoros components provide ready-made HTTP message classes that implement the PSR-7 and PSR-17 interfaces. This allows us to create standards-based requests, server requests, responses, URIs, streams, and headers. The Laminas Stratigility library provides a ready-made basis to build and launch a middleware pipeline.

You can install these packages from inside the php8 container as follows:

```
ed@localhost:~/Repos/PHP-8-Programming-Cookbook
$ ./admin.sh shell php8
php8:/repo#
php composer.phar require laminas/laminas-diactoros
./composer.json has been updated
Running composer update laminas/laminas-diactoros
... some output omitted
Using version ^3.8 for laminas/laminas-diactoros
php8:/repo#
php composer.phar require psr/http-server-middleware
... some output has been omitted
Using version ^1.0 for psr/http-server-middleware
php8:/repo# php composer.phar require laminas/laminas-stratigility
... some output has been omitted
Using version ^4.3 for laminas/laminas-stratigility
php8:/repo#
```

In order to take advantage of the substantial decoupling advantage gained by using middleware, we'll make heavy use of the `Cookbook\Services\Container` service container described in *Chapter 4, Working with PHP Object-Oriented Programming*, in the *Creating a service container* recipe. We'll ensure that the fully loaded container is passed to each middleware component, giving them access to needed configuration and middleware pieces.

How to do it...

1. Our first step will be to create a `GenAiConnect` service that will be used for our GenAI-based middleware microservices. We define a file `GenAiConnect.php` in the `/path/to/php8cookbook/src/Services` folder. We add a number of `use` statements at the start to bring in the various PSR and Laminas Diactoros components that make the output of this class PSR-7 compliant. In the class constructor we accept our services container as an argument, and extract the AI configuration from it:

```
<?php
namespace Cookbook\Services;
use Exception;
use Psr\Container\ContainerInterface;
use Psr\Http\Message\ResponseInterface;
use Laminas\Diactoros\Response\JsonResponse;
class GenAiConnect {
    public const ERR_TRANS = 'Transmission error.';
    public const CALL_LOG  = __DIR__ . '/../Chapter07/api_call.log';
    public array $config = [];
    public function __construct(ContainerInterface $container) {
        $this->config = $container->get('ai_config');
    }
```

2. We then set up the PHP cURL extension arguments and execute the query in the `genAIcall()` method. The AI model, API endpoint, and other factors are drawn from the configuration:

```
public function genAIcall(string $prompt) : ResponseInterface {
    $httpCode = 500;
    $data = array_merge([
        'model'    => $this->config['ai_model'],
        'messages' => [
            ['role' => 'user', 'content' => $prompt]],
    ], $this->config['ai_opts'] ?? []);
    $json = json_encode($data);
    $ch = curl_init($this->config['ai_api_url']);
    curl_setopt_array($ch, [
        CURLOPT_RETURNTRANSFER => true,
        CURLOPT_POST   => true,
        CURLOPT_POSTFIELDS => $json,
```

```
            CURLOPT_HTTPHEADER => [
                'Content-Type: application/json',
                'Authorization: Bearer ' .  $this->config['ai_api_key'],
            ],
            // set both CURLOPT_SSL* options to false to test locally
            CURLOPT_SSL_VERIFYPEER => true,
            CURLOPT_SSL_VERIFYHOST => 2,
        ]);
```

3. We then wrap `curl_exec()` in a try/catch block, log the GenAI call in a call log, and check for errors. In terms of error handling, we check to see if the result from `curl_error()` is empty, followed by an HTTP status check. In the case of either success or failure, we return a PSR-7 compliant `JsonResponse`. You can also see that we close the cURL connection in the finally block:

```
        try {
            $result   = curl_exec($ch);
            $httpCode = curl_getinfo($ch, CURLINFO_HTTP_CODE);
            $error    = curl_error($ch);
            $message  = sprintf('%s|%d|%s' . PHP_EOL, __METHOD__, time(),
    $result);
            file_put_contents(static::CALL_LOG, $message, FILE_APPEND);
            if (!empty($error)) {
                error_log(__METHOD__ . ':' . $error);
                throw new Exception(sprintf('%s [%s]', static::ERR_TRANS,
    __LINE__));
            }
            if ((int) $httpCode >= 400) {
                throw new Exception(
                    sprintf('ERROR %s [HTTP:%s]', __LINE__, $httpCode));
            }
            $response = ['success' => true, 'data' => $result];
        } catch (\Throwable $t) {
            error_log(__METHOD__ . ':' . $t->getMessage());
            $response = ['success' => false, 'data' => static::ERR_TRANS];
        } finally {
            curl_close($ch);
        }
        return (new JsonResponse($response))->withStatus($httpCode);
```

4. In order to supply the middleware microservices with needed language and ISO2 country code information, in the `/path/to/php8cookbook/config` folder we defined two configuration files that return this information. `ch07_languages.php` returns an array with the language code as keys, and the language name (in English) as values. `ch07_iso2.php` returns an array with ISO2 country codes as keys, and country names (also in English) as values. We do not show these two files here, as they are too extensive. These two arrays will be added to our services container, making them available to the microservice that needs them.
5. Before we dive into the middleware components, it would be good to review the calling program. Once you see how the pieces fit together, examining the individual pieces of middleware will make more sense. In the `/path/to/php8cookbook/src/Chapter07` directory, we create a calling program `ch07_microservices_library.php`. This script sets up and runs our simple middleware pipe using the PHP built-in server. We start by setting up our autoloader and add a set of `use` statements that identify the classes we'll later use. As you can see, the list of classes is quite extensive, and draws heavily upon the Laminas project Diactoros and Stratigility components. In the list of `use` statements, you will also see the service classes already discussed. All of the custom middleware components are located in the `Cookbook\Middleware` namespace. Here's the starting portion of our calling program:

```
<?php
include __DIR__ . '/../../vendor/autoload.php';
use Cookbook\Middleware\Logger;
use Cookbook\Middleware\Translate;
use Cookbook\Middleware\Distance;
use Cookbook\Middleware\Capital;
use Cookbook\Services\Container;
use Cookbook\Services\GenAiConnect;
use Laminas\Diactoros\Response;
use Laminas\Diactoros\ResponseFactory;
use Laminas\Diactoros\ServerRequestFactory;
use Laminas\HttpHandlerRunner\Emitter\SapiEmitter;
use Laminas\HttpHandlerRunner\RequestHandlerRunner;
use Laminas\Stratigility\Handler\NotFoundHandler;
use Laminas\Stratigility\MiddlewarePipe;
use Laminas\Stratigility\Middleware\RequestHandlerMiddleware;
use function Laminas\Stratigility\middleware;
use function Laminas\Stratigility\path;
```

> **Note**
>
> The Laminas Stratigility component library is a barebones set of components that let you easily build a PSR-15 compliant middleware pipe. A **middleware pipe**, simply put, is an ordered chain of middleware components that process a request sequentially and pass control onward to produce a response.

6. We would also like to draw your attention to two `use` statements that import two useful `Laminas\Stratigility\*` functions: `middleware()` and `path()`. The former wraps a callable in a `CallableMiddlewareDecorator` so it can be piped as middleware. The latter decorates middleware with a path prefix via `PathMiddlewareDecorator`, causing it to run only for matching request paths:

```
use function Laminas\Stratigility\middleware;
use function Laminas\Stratigility\path;
```

7. Next, we define our GenAI configuration and load the services container with services that will be needed as the pipe is executed. You'll note that the services are all defined as callbacks using arrow functions. *None of the classes are actually instantiated at this point.* This lightens the load on the pipe, reducing startup overhead:

```
$config = [
    'ai_api_key' => trim(file_get_contents(
        __DIR__ . '/../../secure/monica_api_key.txt')),
    'ai_model'   => 'gpt-4.1-nano',
    'ai_api_url' => 'https://openapi.monica.im/v1/chat/completions',
];
$container = Container::getInstance();
$container->add('ai_config', fn () => $config);
$container->add('iso2', fn () =>
    include __DIR__ . '/../../config/ch07_iso2.php');
$container->add('languages', fn () =>
    include __DIR__ . '/../../config/ch07_languages.php');
$container->add('GenAiConnect', fn () => new GenAiConnect($container));
$container->add('translate', fn () => new Translate($container));
$container->add('distance', fn () => new Distance($container));
$container->add('capital', fn () => new Capital($container));
```

8. We then build the middleware using the additive `pipe()` method from `Laminas\Stratigility\MiddlewarePipe`. The middleware pieces run in the order they're added, meaning that our `Logger` runs first. The middleware components are added to the pipe using the `path()` method. This causes a three-way branch in the pipeline. If the path includes `/distance`, `/translate`, or `/capital`, the matching middleware will be invoked, and their direct response is returned. If not, the `NotFoundHandler` is invoked, returning an HTTP 404. You'll note that we obtain the `Capital`, `Translate`, and `Distance` middleware components from our services container and wrap them into a `RequestHandlerMiddleware` instance:

```
$app = new MiddlewarePipe();
$app->pipe(new Logger());
$app->pipe(path('/distance', middleware(
    function ($req, $handler) use ($container) {
        return $container->get('distance')->handle($req); }
)));
$app->pipe(path('/translate', middleware(
    function ($req, $handler) use ($container) {
        return $container->get('translate')->handle($req); }
)));
$app->pipe(path('/capital', middleware(
    function ($req, $handler) use ($container) {
        return $container->get('capital')->handle($req); }
)));
$app->pipe(middleware(function ($req, $handler) {
    return (new NotFoundHandler(new ResponseFactory()))->handle($req);
}));
```

9. The actual pipe execution is handled by `RequestHandlerRunner`, wrapped in a try/catch block to handle any serious errors. *Figure 7.1* in the *How it works...* section of this recipe gives you a visual idea of the flow:

```
$server = new RequestHandlerRunner(
    $app,
    new SapiEmitter(),
    static function () {
        return ServerRequestFactory::fromGlobals();
    },
    static function (\Throwable $e) {
```

```
        $response = (new ResponseFactory())->createResponse(500);
        $response->getBody()->write(sprintf(
            'An error occurred: %s',
            $e->getMessage()
        ));
        return $response;
    }
);
$server->run();
```

10. Let's now run through the middleware components, starting with `Cookbook\Middleware\Logger`. This relatively simple class extracts information from the request object and records that information to a log file. To meet the requirements of the PSR-15 `MiddlewareInterface`, the return value calls the `handle()` method of the `RequestHandlerInterface` which was passed as an argument to the Logger's `process()` method. This has the effect of handing control over to the next component in the pipe:

```
<?php
namespace Cookbook\Middleware;
use Psr\Http\Message\ResponseInterface;
use Psr\Http\Message\ServerRequestInterface;
use Psr\Http\Server\MiddlewareInterface;
use Psr\Http\Server\RequestHandlerInterface;
class Logger implements MiddlewareInterface  {
    const ERR_LOG = 'ERROR: unable to log entry';
    const OK_LOG  = 'SUCCESS: entry logged';
    const LOG_FILE = __DIR__ . '/../Chapter07/middleware.log';
    public function process(ServerRequestInterface $request,
        RequestHandlerInterface $handler) : ResponseInterface {
        $text = sprintf('%20s : %10s : %30s : %s' . PHP_EOL,
            date('Y-m-d H:i:s'),
            ($request->getParsedBody()['action'] ?? 'Unknown'),
            ($request->getParsedBody()['data'] ?? 'No Data'),
            ($request->getServerParams()['REMOTE_ADDR']) ?? 'Command
Line');
        file_put_contents(self::LOG_FILE, $text, FILE_APPEND);
        return $handler->handle($request);
    }
}
```

11. Moving now to our middleware microservices classes, we first define an abstract base class `BaseHandler`. In this class we define a `__construct()` method that allows us to inject the services container into the class. The reason why we need to declare this class as abstract is because it implements `Psr\Http\Server\RequestHandlerInterface` but does not define the mandated `handle()` method:

```
<?php
namespace Cookbook\Middleware;
use Psr\Container\ContainerInterface;
use Psr\Http\Server\RequestHandlerInterface;
abstract class BaseHandler implements RequestHandlerInterface
{
    public const ERR_UNKNOWN = 'Unknown error';
    public function __construct(public ContainerInterface $container)
    {}
}
```

12. What remains to show you in this recipe are the three microservices: `Translate`, `Distance`, and `Capital`. The first sends a prompt to our GenAI platform asking for a translation, the second produces a distance between two cities, and the third provides the name of the capital city given an ISO2 code or country name. For brevity, we'll only examine `Capital`. The other two microservices are identical, varying only in the GenAI prompt, input arguments, and validation process.

> **Tip**
>
> The `Translate`, `Distance`, and `Capital` microservices make calls to our GenAI platform, but you'll quickly see that these are trivial examples that don't make substantive use of the true power of GenAI. The main focus of this recipe is how to define microservices as middleware, and how to put them into a middleware pipe. Accordingly, we prefer to use simple middleware microservices examples.

The opening `use` statements are similar to the `Logger` class, adding imports for various `Exception` classes and the `Throwable` interface. We also import `JsonResponse` in exceptional cases where a valid custom PSR-7 response is needed:

```
<?php
namespace Cookbook\Middleware;
use Throwable;
```

```
use Exception;
use RuntimeException;
use InvalidArgumentException;
use Psr\Http\Server\RequestHandlerInterface;
use Psr\Http\Message\ResponseInterface;
use Psr\Http\Message\ServerRequestInterface;
use Laminas\Diactoros\Response\JsonResponse;
```

13. We then define constants that specify acceptable units, and also a usage string that gets returned in case incorrect parameters are given:

```
class Capital extends BaseHandler {
    public const USAGE = 'USAGE: iso2 : ISO2 code of the requested
country';
```

14. The `handle()` method is mandated by `RequestHandlerInterface`, and provides the core logic for our middleware microservice. Inside a try/catch block, we call the `getParsedBody()` method of the PSR-7 compliant request instance, which returns an array of `$_POST` values. We run `json_decode()` on the value for the `data` parameter, and from that extract the individual values needed for the GenAI prompt. In addition, we perform validation on any input arguments:

```
public function handle(ServerRequestInterface $request) :
ResponseInterface {
         try {
            $data = $request->getParsedBody()['data'] ?? '';
            $args = json_decode($data, associative: true,
                flags: JSON_THROW_ON_ERROR);
            $name = trim($args['iso2_or_name'] ?? 'Unknown');
            if (!$this->verify_iso2($name))
                throw new InvalidArgumentException("INVALID DESTINATION
ISO2 "
                    . "CODE OR COUNTRY NAME: $name: " . self::USAGE);
```

15. We then use the services container to get the `GenAiConnect` service, make the call to our GenAI platform, and return the results:

```
            $connect = $this->container->get('GenAiConnect');
            if (empty($connect)) {
                throw new RuntimeException(
```

```
                'Required service is offline. ' . self::USAGE);
        }
        $prompt = 'Give me the name of the capital of that country. '
                . 'Here is the country ' . ((strlen($name) === 2) ?
'ISO2 code ' : 'name ')
                . ':' . $name . '. Return only the name of the capital
city -- '
                . 'no additional explanation or text.';
        return $connect->genAIcall($prompt);
```

16. Finally, we wrap up with two catch blocks. The first catches any `Exception` derivation, returns a failure message, and sets the HTTP status to `400`. The second catches anything else, including `Error`-derived throwables, returning an unknown error with an HTTP status of `500`:

```
    } catch (Exception $e) {
        $response = ['success' => false, 'data' => $e->getMessage()];
        return new JsonResponse($response)->withStatus(400);
    } catch (Throwable $t) {
        $response = ['success' => false, 'data' => static::ERR_UNKNOWN];
        return new JsonResponse($response)->withStatus(500);
}}
```

17. The `verify_iso2()` method retrieves the `iso2` array from the service container and checks to see if the supplied ISO2 code or country name is valid:

```
public function verify_iso2(string $name) {
    $codes = $this->container->get('iso2');
    return (isset($codes[strtoupper($name)]) || in_array($name, $codes));
}
```

18. Our `Translate` and `Distance` middleware microservices (not shown) are identical in overall form to `Capital`. The main difference is that there is a different set of parameters, and the GenAI prompt differs. These classes are found in the `/path/to/php8cookbook/src/Middleware` folder.

How it works...

To test our microservices system, we open command shells into the PHP8 container using `admin.sh shell php8`. In the first command shell, we execute a command to run PHP using its built-in web server on port 8889. This avoids having to configure nginx for a new virtual host and allows us to generate curl requests to test our new microservices API. Here is how the output from the command shell and command might appear:

```
php8:/repo# php -S 0.0.0.0:8889 src/Chapter07/ch07_microservices_library.php
[Sat Jun 20 06:37:29 2026] PHP 8.4.16 Development Server (http://0.0.0.0:8889)
started
```

The nice thing about this approach is that any `error_log()` entries will appear on this console, facilitating troubleshooting. The second command shell can be either in our php8 container or simply a terminal window on your host system (assuming you have `curl` available from the command line).

In the second command shell, we can run `curl` commands to each of our services to test the system. The first `curl` POST tests the `capital` service. The output is in the form of a JSON string, leaving it to the client making the REST request to process the result. As you can see from the output, we request the capital of Cambodia (ISO2 code `"kh"`), receiving `Phnom Penh` as a response:

```
ed@localhost:~$
curl -X POST -F 'data={"iso2_or_name":"kh"}' http://localhost:8889/capital
{"success":true,"data":"{\u0022id\u0022:\u0022chatcmpl-llm-router-
openai\u0022,\u0022object\u0022:\u0022chat.completion\u0022,\u0022created\u0022:17
81942318,\u0022model\u0022:\u0022gpt-4.1-nano\u0022,\u0022choices\u0022:
[{\u0022index\u0022:0,\u0022message\u0022:
{\u0022role\u0022:\u0022assistant\u0022,\u0022content\u0022:\u0022Phnom
Penh\u0022},
\u0022finish_reason\u0022:\u0022stop\u0022,\u0022content_filter_results\u0022:
... output omitted ...
total_tokens\u0022:47,\u0022prompt_tokens_details\u0022:
{\u0022audio_tokens\u0022:0,\u0022cached_tokens\u0022:0},
\u0022completion_tokens_details\u0022:
{\u0022audio_tokens\u0022:0,\u0022reasoning_tokens\u0022:0}},
\u0022system_fingerprint\u0022:\u0022\u0022}"}
```

You'll also note that our error checking also works well. Invalid arguments return usage information along with a 400 HTTP status:

```
$ curl -v -X POST -F 'data={"iso2_or_name":"xx"}' http://localhost:8889/capital
* Host localhost:8889 was resolved.
```

```
... output omitted ...
* We are completely uploaded and fine
< HTTP/1.1 400 Bad Request
* Closing connection
{"success":false,"data":"INVALID DESTINATION ISO2 CODE OR COUNTRY NAME: xx: USAGE:
iso2 : ISO2 code of the requested country"}ed@localhost:~
```

Undefined services return a 404 error:

```
$ curl -v -X POST -F 'data={"iso2_or_name":"xx"}' http://localhost:8889/unknown
* Host localhost:8889 was resolved.
* We are completely uploaded and fine
< HTTP/1.1 404 Not Found
< Host: localhost:8889
< Date: Sat, 20 Jun 2026 08:04:42 GMT
< Connection: close
< X-Powered-By: PHP/8.4.16
< Content-type: text/html; charset=UTF-8
<
* Closing connection
Cannot POST http://localhost:8889/unknown
```

Each service in this small REST-style microservices application is formulated as a PSR-15 middleware/request handler, and requests are passed through a simple middleware pipeline. `Logger`, the first middleware service, records useful request information. Following that, the pipeline branches based on the request path.

Figure 7.1 summarizes the logic flow:

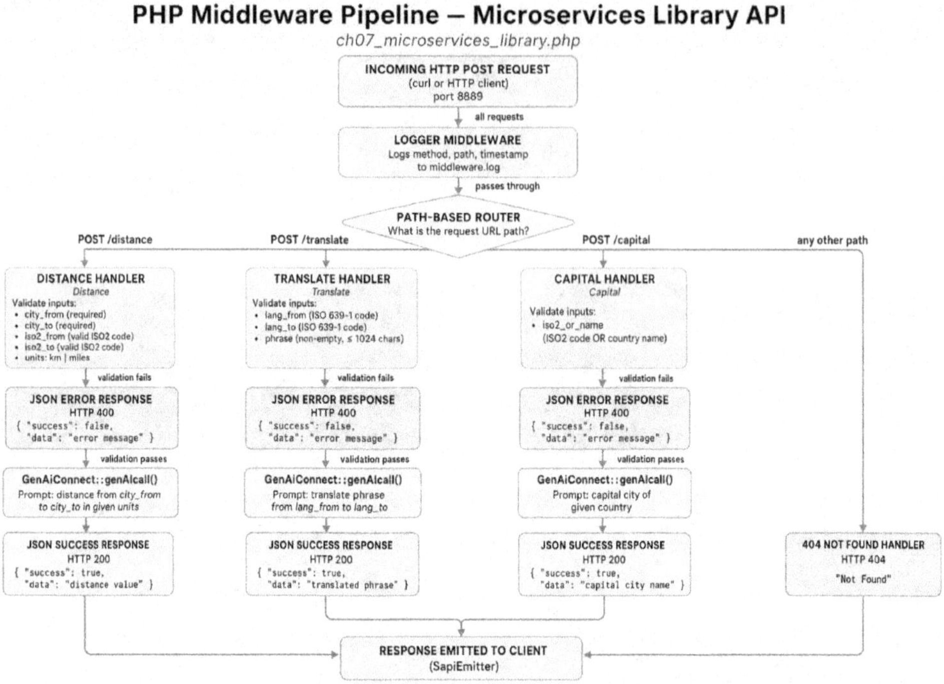

Figure 7.1 – Microservices middleware logic flow

This design makes the system easy to extend. Adding a new GenAI-powered microservice only requires creating a new handler class and registering it in the container under a new action name.

See also

You can find more information on the Laminas Diactoros components here: `https://docs.laminas.dev/laminas-diactoros/usage/`.

You can read up on the Laminas Stratigility middleware component library here: `https://docs.laminas.dev/laminas-stratigility/`.

Tracking GenAI token usage

Over and above the cost of a GenAI subscription is the hidden cost incurred by token usage. In this recipe, we show you how to create a simple GenAI token tracking application. Most of the GenAI platforms have model-specific pricing based on token usage. A single token roughly equates to 4 characters. Most platform pricing can be either a subscription or a pay-as-you-go plan. You are charged for both input tokens (including any file inputs) as well as output tokens. Pricing for images is more complicated and involves image dimensions and resolution.

Getting ready

In this recipe, we'll build a usage tracker based on the OpenAI GPT-4.1-nano model. Accordingly, to test the code in this recipe, you'll need access to the OpenAI models, either directly through openai.com or through a provider that gives you this access. For our example, we'll continue to access GPT via the `monica.im` platform. You'll also need to execute the code shown in the previous recipe, making several calls to the various microservices described, with the purpose of building up API call log data.

How to do it...

1. In the `/path/to/php8cookbook/src/Usage` folder, we create a file `GenAiUsageTracker.php`. In the opening lines of code, we add the appropriate `use` statements and initialize a set of important properties. Most notable is the `PlatformInterface` property. We create a series of classes that implement this interface in order to satisfy the requirements of different models:

```
<?php
namespace Cookbook\Usage;
use SplFileObject;
class GenAiUsageTracker {
    public const CSV_FN  = __DIR__ . '/../Chapter07/api_call_usage.csv';
    public const CALL_LOG  = __DIR__ . '/../Chapter07/api_call.log';
    public string $csv_fn     = '';
    public string $log_fn     = '';
    public string $separator = ',';
    public string $enclosure = '"';
    public string $escape    = '\\';
    public ?PlatformInterface $platform = null;
```

2. Next we define a class constructor that accepts a `PlatformInterface` instance and a configuration array as arguments. Aside from providing flexibility, the configuration arguments help formulate `fgetcsv()` and `fputcsv()` method calls. As of PHP 8.4, for example, failing to provide an `escape` argument generates a deprecation notice:

```
public function __construct(?PlatformInterface $platform = null,
    array $config = []) {
    $this->csv_fn    = $config['csv_fn']    ?? static::CSV_FN;
```

```
        $this->log_fn    = $config['call_log']  ?? static::CALL_LOG;
        $this->separator = $config['separator'] ?? $this->separator;
        $this->enclosure = $config['enclosure'] ?? $this->enclosure;
        $this->escape    = $config['escape']    ?? $this->escape;
        $this->platform  = $platform;
    }
```

3. To round out this class we define a method `updateCsv()` that uses the `PlatformInterface` instance to parse the API call log:

```
    public function updateCsv(bool $eraseLog = false) : int {
        $iter = $this->platform->parseLog($this->log_fn);
        $mode = ($eraseLog) ? 'w' : 'a';
        $csv = new SplFileObject($this->csv_fn, $mode);
        if ($eraseLog) {
            $csv->fputcsv($this->platform->headers, separator: $this-
    >separator,
                enclosure: $this->enclosure, escape: $this->escape);
        }
        foreach ($iter as $row) {
            $csv->fputcsv(array_values($row), separator: $this->separator,
                enclosure: $this->enclosure, escape: $this->escape);
        }
        return $iter->getReturn();
    }}
```

4. Next, in the same folder as above, we define `PlatformInterface`, mandating a method `parseLog()`. We also add useful constants needed by classes implementing this interface. Presuming that we'll execute an `explode()` command on each line in the log, using `FIELD_DELIM` as the split character, we also need to know which array element, following the `explode()` operation, represents the date or timestamp. Finally, and perhaps most importantly, we need to know which array element represents the position of the JSON data returned from the GenAI call:

```
    <?php
    namespace Cookbook\Usage;
    use Generator;
    interface PlatformInterface {
        public const FIELD_DELIM = '|';
```

```
    public const DATE_FIELD_LOC = 1;
    public const GENAI_RESULT_LOC = 2;
    public const ERR_LOG_FMT = 'ERROR: log file does not meet format [%s]';
    public function parseLog(string $log_fn) : Generator;
}
```

5. Finally, continuing in the same folder, `/path/to/php8cookbook/src/Usage`, we define our first `PlatformInterface` class instance, `OpenAiPlatform`. As the name implies, this class defines `parseLog()` with logic specific to OpenAI. To accommodate other platforms, simply create additional `PlatformInterface` class instances as suits your needs. At the start of the code file, as is our practice, we add a series of `use` statements that identify needed classes outside the current namespace:

```
<?php
namespace Cookbook\Usage;
use Generator;
use DateTime;
use SplFileObject;
use Throwable;
class OpenAiPlatform implements PlatformInterface {
```

6. Next we add a list of properties, and a class constructor that assigns values to those properties. We use the constants defined in `PlatformInterface` as defaults if the supplied argument values are null:

```
public array $headers = ['Timestamp','Y','M','D','H','Model',
    'Prompt Tokens','Completion Tokens','Total Tokens'];
public string $field_delim = '';
public int $date_field_loc = 1;
public int $genai_result_loc = 2;
public function __construct(?string $field_delim = null,
    ?int $date_field_loc = null, ?int $genai_result_loc = null) {
    $this->field_delim = $field_delim ?? PlatformInterface::FIELD_DELIM;
    $this->date_field_loc = $date_field_loc ??
PlatformInterface::DATE_FIELD_LOC;
    $this->genai_result_loc = $genai_result_loc
        ?? PlatformInterface::GENAI_RESULT_LOC;
}
```

7. We are now in a position to define the `parseLog()` method. It reads the API call log line by line and applies `explode()`. We use the `$date_field_loc` property to identify the timestamp, and the `$genai_result_loc` property to select the GenAI JSON response:

```
public function parseLog(string $log_fn) : Generator {
    $log = new SplFileObject($log_fn, 'r');
    $log->rewind();
    $lines = 0;
    $fmt_check = false;
    while (!$log->eof()) {
        $logInfo = [];
        $line = $log->fgets();
        $split = explode($this->field_delim, $line);
        $date_info = trim($split[$this->date_field_loc] ?? '');
        $genai_json = trim($split[$this->genai_result_loc] ?? '');
```

8. We then perform validation checks to ensure these two vital fields contain information. We also use a try/catch block to ensure that the GenAI result was properly parsed using `json_decode()`:

```
        $date_info = trim($split[$this->date_field_loc] ?? '');
        $genai_json = trim($split[$this->genai_result_loc] ?? '');
        if (empty($date_info) || empty($genai_json)) continue;
        try {
            $genai_result = json_decode($genai_json, true,
                flags: JSON_THROW_ON_ERROR);
        } catch (Throwable $t) {
            error_log(__METHOD__ . ':' . $t->getMessage());
            error_log(__METHOD__ . ':' . json_last_error_msg());
            continue;
        }
```

9. We then create a `DateTime` instance from the date information. If the value is an integer, we make a static call to `DateTime::createFromTimestamp()`. Otherwise, we create the `DateTime` instance as-is. We then use the `DateTime::format()` method with the appropriate flags to break down the timestamp into year, month, day and hour (24-hour format). You'll note that this breakdown is specific to OpenAI. For other GenAI

providers, the response format will differ, although almost universally the response will take the form of a JSON string:

```
        $date = (ctype_digit($date_info))
              ? DateTime::createFromTimestamp($date_info)
              : new DateTime($date_info);
        $y = $date->format('Y');
        $m = $date->format('m');
        $d = $date->format('d');
        $h = $date->format('H');
        $logInfo = [
            'timestamp' => $date_info,
            'y' => $y, 'm' => $m, 'd' => $d, 'h' => $h,
            'model' => $genai_result['model'],
            'prompt_tokens'       => $genai_result['usage']
['prompt_tokens'],
            'completion_tokens'  => $genai_result['usage']
['completion_tokens'],
            'total_tokens'       => $genai_result['usage']['total_tokens'],
        ];
        yield $logInfo;
        $lines++;
    }
    return $lines;
}}
```

10. In the /path/to/php8cookbook/src/Chapter07 directory, we create a calling program ch07_genai_usage_tracker.php that creates OpenAiPlatform and GenAiUsageTracker instances, using defaults. We then call the updateCsv() method, adding API call log entries to our usage CSV file. The file is then displayed as output along with the number of lines entered:

```
<?php
include __DIR__ . '/../../vendor/autoload.php';
use Cookbook\Usage\GenAiUsageTracker;
use Cookbook\Usage\OpenAiPlatform;
$tracker = new GenAiUsageTracker(new OpenAiPlatform('|',1,2));
$num = $tracker->updateCsv(eraseLog: true);
if (empty($num)) {
    echo 'No Updates' . PHP_EOL;
```

```
} else {
    echo 'Number of log entries added: ' . $num . PHP_EOL;
}
readfile(GenAiUsageTracker::CSV_FN);
```

How it works...

We first follow the instructions given in the previous recipe to set up our microservices API server and make a few calls to our microservices in order to add entries to the API call log. We then run the program. Here is how the output might appear:

```
php8:/repo# php src/Chapter07/ch07_genai_usage_tracker.php
Number of log entries added: 74
Timestamp,Y,M,D,H,Model,"Prompt Tokens","Completion Tokens","Total Tokens"
1774579337,2026,03,27,02,gpt-4.1-nano,33,5,38
1774579393,2026,03,27,02,gpt-4.1-nano,33,9,42
1774600605,2026,03,27,08,gpt-4.1-nano,33,20,53
1774600640,2026,03,27,08,gpt-4.1-nano,36,3,39
... rows omitted
php8:/repo#
```

We can then pull up the CSV file using our preferred spreadsheet program. At this point we're free to perform analysis on our GenAI usage as needed. For example, it might be of use to gather token usage totals to get cost estimate benchmarks. Further, you are now in a position to gather usage information based upon hours, days, weeks, or months.

Here is how the spreadsheet might appear (*note*: not all rows are shown):

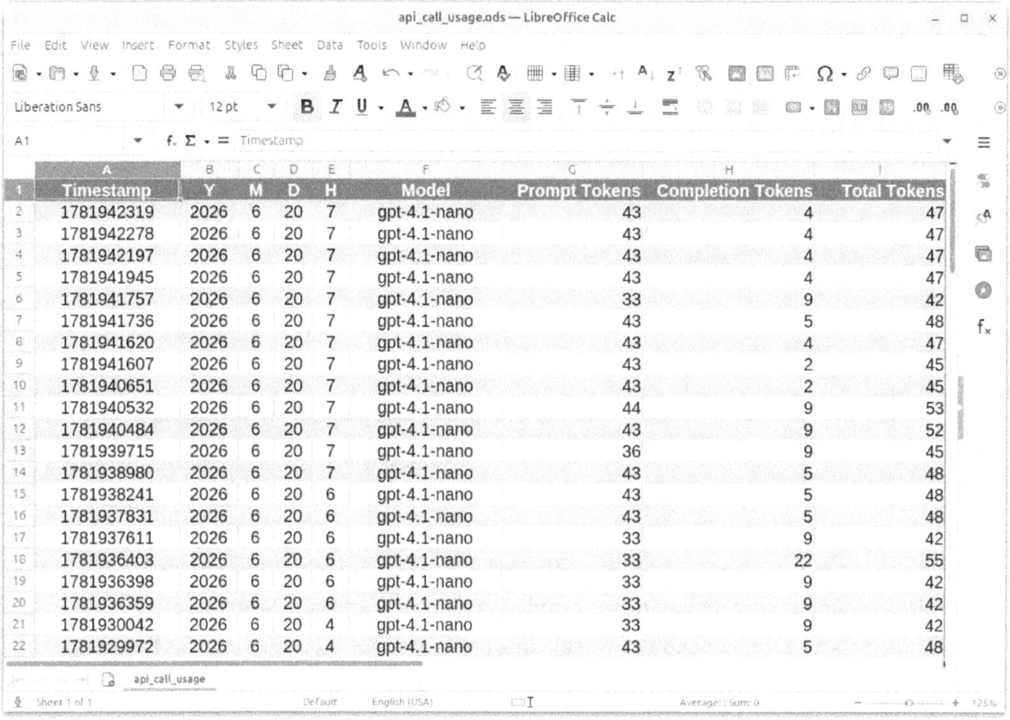

Timestamp	Y	M	D	H	Model	Prompt Tokens	Completion Tokens	Total Tokens
1781942319	2026	6	20	7	gpt-4.1-nano	43	4	47
1781942278	2026	6	20	7	gpt-4.1-nano	43	4	47
1781942197	2026	6	20	7	gpt-4.1-nano	43	4	47
1781941945	2026	6	20	7	gpt-4.1-nano	43	4	47
1781941757	2026	6	20	7	gpt-4.1-nano	33	9	42
1781941736	2026	6	20	7	gpt-4.1-nano	43	5	48
1781941620	2026	6	20	7	gpt-4.1-nano	43	4	47
1781941607	2026	6	20	7	gpt-4.1-nano	43	2	45
1781940651	2026	6	20	7	gpt-4.1-nano	43	2	45
1781940532	2026	6	20	7	gpt-4.1-nano	44	9	53
1781940484	2026	6	20	7	gpt-4.1-nano	43	9	52
1781939715	2026	6	20	7	gpt-4.1-nano	36	9	45
1781938980	2026	6	20	7	gpt-4.1-nano	43	5	48
1781938241	2026	6	20	6	gpt-4.1-nano	43	5	48
1781937831	2026	6	20	6	gpt-4.1-nano	43	5	48
1781937611	2026	6	20	6	gpt-4.1-nano	33	9	42
1781936403	2026	6	20	6	gpt-4.1-nano	33	22	55
1781936398	2026	6	20	6	gpt-4.1-nano	33	9	42
1781936359	2026	6	20	6	gpt-4.1-nano	33	9	42
1781930042	2026	6	20	4	gpt-4.1-nano	33	9	42
1781929972	2026	6	20	4	gpt-4.1-nano	43	5	48

Figure 7.2 – GenAI usage information

Each time a GenAI-powered microservice (described in the earlier recipe) calls the AI platform, the raw API response is written to an API call log. `GenAiUsageTracker` reads the log file and extracts its values. The main parsing work happens in `parseLog()`. This method reads the API call log one line at a time, and applies `explode()` to each line. The `$date_field_loc` property tells us which array element contains the date or timestamp information, and the `$genai_result_loc` property identifies the JSON result delivered by the GenAI call. The information derived from the log is then written to a spreadsheet where further analysis can be performed.

Building an AI-assisted real-time chat service using asynchronous PHP WebSockets

Over the past few years, there's been a proliferation of social media websites and apps, especially in the online dating arena. However, a big issue preventing meaningful connections between people is the language barrier. In this recipe, we show you how to build a real-time messaging platform using ReactPHP and Ratchet that leverages GenAI's ability to provide proper translations.

ReactPHP is a low-level library that forms the basis of an event-driven, non-blocking I/O application. It's notable in that it does not require a specialized asynchronous PHP extension such as OpenSwoole. ReactPHP enables **asynchronous** operations using an event loop, allowing your PHP code to efficiently handle multiple concurrent connections without multi-threading. Ratchet is a PHP **WebSocket** library built on ReactPHP that enables real-time, bidirectional communication between servers and clients.

> Note
>
> **What exactly is a WebSocket?**
>
> A WebSocket is a communication protocol that provides a persistent, full-duplex connection between a client and a backend server over a single TCP connection. Unlike traditional HTTP requests, WebSockets allow real-time, bidirectional data exchange without having to invoke a full request-response cycle. The traditional request-response approach is not only resource-intensive, but is relatively slow, and often results in your application having to completely redraw the screen. WebSocket technology is an excellent choice for real-time asynchronous scenarios such as live chat, gaming, financial tickers, and collaborative applications.

Getting ready

In order to leverage Ratchet and ReactPHP you'll need to open a command shell into the PHP 8 container and issue this command:

```
php8:/repo# php composer.phar require cboden/ratchet
```

You'll also need to obtain the following from your preferred GenAI platform:

- The API key, which you should store in the `/path/to/php8cookbook/secure` folder as `api_key.txt`
- The GenAI model you plan to use. Be sure to check the cost!
- The API endpoint for your preferred platform
- The exact location of the translated text in the JSON string returned by GenAI

For the purposes of this recipe, we installed Claude Code. Bear in mind that this choice is arbitrary. You can obtain similar results using other GenAI providers and interfaces (e.g. web interfaces, or other desktop interfaces similar to Claude Code).

How to do it...

1. To begin, we crafted a detailed prompt which we submitted to Anthropic Claude Code. We'll show you the prompt, but not the result because we ended up having to modify about 50% of the code produced. However, we feel that it gave us an excellent starting point and thus worth showing:

```
Create a website that comprises an  HTML/JavaScript/jQuery frontend and a
PHP 8.4 backend. The website needs to do the following:
0. When a User opens the main page, establish a WebSocket connection to the
backend.
1. Display an attractively styled main page to the User.
2. Provide a text input field to allow the User to enter a username which
is stored persistently.
3. Provide a set of radio buttons so the User can select his/her preferred
User Language. For this demonstration provide choices for English and
Khmer.
4. Display an HTML select element that provides a list of usernames or
other users who currently have WebSockets connections to this website.
* This list can be obtained by the frontend by making an AJAX call to the
backend.
* For the purposes of this demonstration assume that there will be two
browser tabs open, each with a different username.
* The name the User selects from this list, we'll call the Chosen User.
5. Once the User selects another user from the list of connected users,
open a textarea in which the User can send a message to the Chosen User.
* Have the backend make an API call to the preferred GenAI platform that
requests the message be translated from the User's preferred language into
the Chosen User's preferred language.
* Display both the original and the translated message in the message
textarea of both the User and the Chosen User.
6. When the Chosen User responds:
* Have the backend make an API call to the preferred GenAI platform that
requests the message be translated from the Chosen User's preferred
language into the User's preferred language.
* Display both the original and the translated message in the message
textarea of both the User and the Chosen User.
7. Allow messaging between User and Chosen User to continue until the User
presses the STOP button.
8. When the Stop button is pressed, go back to step 1.
```

2. For this recipe, we placed all files in the directory structure under `/path/to/php8cookbook/src/IndoChat`, as shown here. The `users.json` file is auto-generated and updated at intervals. It records users currently connected to the system:

```
IndoChat/
├── Platform
│   ├── OpenAi.php
│   └── PlatformInterface.php
├── Server
│   └── ChatServer.php
├── async
│   └── server.php
├── config
│   └── config.php
├── data
│   └── users.json     // (auto-generated)
├── prompt.txt
└── public
    ├── index.php
    └── users.php
```

3. Before getting into the main programming logic, let's have a look at the configuration file `config.php` located in the `/path/to/php8cookbook/src/IndoChat/config` folder. In this case, we demonstrate another technique for passing configuration information: using global constants. This approach is useful when you have a limited number of configuration settings. If you have more than half a dozen, consider using a configuration array instead. Of particular note is `API_CALLBACK`. This is a class that implements `Cookbook\IndoChat\Platform\PlatformInterface` (discussed later in this recipe), and is used to produce the final output from our chosen GenAI platform. In this file, we also define the *system* prompt that provides additional context and instructions to the AI:

```php
<?php
require __DIR__ . '/../../../vendor/autoload.php';
define('USERS_FILE', '/repo/src/IndoChat/data/users.json');
// switch API key files as needed:
define('AI_KEY_FN', __DIR__ . '/../../../secure/api_key.txt');
define('API_KEY', file_get_contents(AI_KEY_FN));
define('AI_MODEL', 'gpt-5.4-nano');
```

```
define('AI_INSTRUCT',  'You are a professional translator. Return only the
translated text: no explanations, no notes, no punctuation changes beyond
what translation requires.');
define('API_ENDPOINT',
    'https://api.openai.com/v1/responses');
define('WS_PORT', 8081);
define('WS_HOST', '0.0.0.0');
define('API_LOG_FN', __DIR__ . '/../../Chapter07/chat.log');
define('API_CALLBACK', new Cookbook\IndoChat\Platform\OpenAi());
```

4. The main workhorse in this recipe is `ChatServer`. We first add a set of `use` statements to bring in the necessary Ratchet library components. We also declare a constant defining the languages supported by the application, along with useful properties:

```
<?php
namespace Cookbook\IndoChat\Server;
use Ratchet\Server\IoServer;
use Ratchet\Http\HttpServer;
use Ratchet\WebSocket\WsServer;
use Ratchet\MessageComponentInterface;
use Ratchet\ConnectionInterface;
use Cookbook\IndoChat\Platform\PlatformInterface;
class ChatServer implements MessageComponentInterface{
    public const LANGS =
        ['en' => 'English', 'km' => 'Khmer'];
    public const DEF_LANG = 'en';
    public const MAX_NAME_LEN = 30;
    public array $clients = [];
    public string $usersFile;
    public PlatformInterface $platform;
```

5. The `__construct()` method creates the `users.json` file if it doesn't exist. We also check to ensure that the API key is found. You'll note that any output from ChatServer appears only on the async chat server console. We take advantage of this fact to display connection-related information:

```
public function __construct(string $usersFile, PlatformInterface
$platform) {
    $this->usersFile = $usersFile;
    if (file_exists($usersFile)) {
```

```
            $msg = "Users file found at: $usersFile";
        } else {
            $dir = dirname($usersFile);
            if (!file_exists($dir)) mkdir($dir, 0755, true);
            touch($usersFile);
            $msg = "Users file created at: $usersFile";
        }
        if (empty(API_KEY)) echo "[WARNING] API_KEY is not set.\n";
        $this->platform = $platform;
        echo 'IndoChat WebSocket server started on ' . 'port ' . WS_PORT .
    "\n";
        echo $msg . "\n";
        echo "Press Ctrl+C to stop.\n\n";
    }
```

6. What follows are a series of `on*()` methods required by `Ratchet\MessageComponentInterface`. They are invoked by Ratchet within ReactPHP's event loop, enabling asynchronous operation. The first we'll examine is `onOpen()`, called when a new WebSocket connection is established. Connection information is stored in the `$clients` property:

```
    public function onOpen(ConnectionInterface $conn) : void {
        $this->clients[$conn->resourceId] = [
            'conn'     => $conn,
            'username' => null,
            'language' => 'en',
        ];
        echo "[connect]   #{$conn->resourceId}\n";
    }
```

7. The `onMessage()` method responds to message events initiated by connected users. It routes the message to either `handleSetUser()` or `handleSendMessage()`, ensuring that the message is translated and then sent:

```
    public function onMessage(
        ConnectionInterface $from, $msg): void {
        $data = json_decode($msg, true);
        if (!is_array($data) || empty($data['type'])) return;
        match ($data['type']) {
            'set_user' => $this->handleSetUser($from, $data),
```

```
            'send_message' => $this->handleSendMessage($from, $data),
            default => null,
        };
    }
```

8. The `onClose()` method responds when a user disconnects. The user is removed and the `users.json` file is updated:

```
public function onClose(ConnectionInterface $conn) : void {
    $username = $this->clients[$conn->resourceId]['username'] ?? null;
    unset($this->clients[$conn->resourceId]);
    $this->writeUsersFile();
    $this->broadcastUsersList();
    echo "[disconnect] #{$conn->resourceId}"
        . ($username ? " ({$username})" : '') . "\n";
}
```

9. The last of the `on*()` methods handles errors:

```
public function onError(ConnectionInterface $conn, \Exception $e): void {
    echo "[error]     #{$conn->resourceId}: " . "{$e->getMessage()}\n";
    $conn->close();
}
```

10. The `handle*()` methods perform the actual mechanics of user setup and message transmission. We'll have a look at `handleSetUser()` first. This method sets the username and preferred language, and performs safety checks on the name and language information supplied by the new user:

```
public function handleSetUser(
    ConnectionInterface $conn, array $data): void {
    $username = trim(strip_tags($data['username'] ?? ''));
    $language = trim(strip_tags($data['language'] ?? self::DEF_LANG));
    if (!in_array($language, array_keys(self::LANGS))) $language =
self::DEF_LANG;
    if (empty($username)  || strlen($username) > self::MAX_NAME_LEN) {
        $this->send($conn, ['type' => 'error',
            'message' => sprintf('Username must be 1 '
            .'- %d characters.', self::MAX_NAME_LEN)]);
```

```
        return;
    }
```

11. Next, we check to make sure that the username is unique. Once assured that everything is OK, we save user information in the `$clients` array and send out notifications to all connections:

```
    foreach ($this->clients as $id => $client) {
        if ($id !== $conn->resourceId && $client['username'] ===
$username) {
            $this->send($conn, ['type' => 'error',
                'message' => 'Username "' . $username . '"  is already
taken.']);
            return;
        }
    }
    $this->clients[$conn->resourceId]['username'] = $username;
    $this->clients[$conn->resourceId]['language'] = $language;
    $this->send($conn, ['type' => 'user_set',
        'username' => $username, 'language' => $language]);
    $this->writeUsersFile();
    $this->broadcastUsersList();
    $langLabel = self::LANGS[$language];
    echo "[user_set]  #{$conn->resourceId} ->{$username} ({$langLabel})\n";
}
```

12. The `handleSendMessage()` method first safeguards the message to be sent and confirms that the recipient exists and is online:

```
public function handleSendMessage(
    ConnectionInterface $from, array $data): void {
    $toUsername = $data['to'] ?? '';
    $message    = trim(htmlspecialchars($data['message'] ?? ''));
    if (empty($message) || empty($toUsername)) return;
    $fromClient = $this->clients[$from->resourceId];
    if ($fromClient['username'] === null) {
        $this->send($from, ['type' => 'error',
             'message' => 'Set a username before ' . 'sending messages.']);
        return;
    }
```

```
        $toClient = $this->findClientByUsername($toUsername);
        if ($toClient === null) {
            $this->send($from, ['type' => 'error',
                'message' => "\"{$toUsername}\" is no longer connected."]);
            return;
        }
```

13. Once the message and its recipient are secured, the remaining method logic collects information into an array and invokes `send()`. Note that we need to *send* the message to both sender and recipient so that both chat screens reflect the same information. Also of note is a call to the `translate()` method. If the source and target languages are different, a GenAI call is made to obtain the translation:

```
        $fromLang   = $fromClient['language'];
        $toLang     = $toClient['language'];
        $translated = ($fromLang !== $toLang)
            ? $this->translate($message,$fromLang,$toLang)
            : $message;
        $payload = [
            'type'       => 'message',
            'from'       => $fromClient['username'],
            'to'         => $toUsername,
            'original'   => $message,
            'translated' => $translated,
            'fromLang'   => $fromLang,
            'toLang'     => $toLang,
            'timestamp'  => date('H:i'),
        ];
        $this->send($from, $payload);
        $this->send($toClient['conn'], $payload);
        echo "[message]   {$fromClient['username']} -> {$toUsername}\n";
    }
```

14. In the `translate()` method we write a console warning and return a translation-unavailable message if the `API_KEY` is unavailable. We then collect information to be sent to the GenAI and log what information gets sent. Note that the text is user-supplied. We sanitize it using `strip_tags()`; however, this does not protect against

prompt injection attacks. Accordingly, you may need to set a filter on your GenAI platform to add such extra protection:

```
public function translate(string $text,
    string $fromLang, string $toLang): string {
    if (empty(API_KEY)) {
        echo "[translate] API_KEY not set\n";
        return '[Translation unavailable]';
    }
    $data = [
        'model'        => AI_MODEL,
        'instructions' => AI_INSTRUCT,
        'input'        => 'Translate from '
            . self::LANGS[$fromLang] . ' to '
            . self::LANGS[$toLang] . ' this text: '
           . strip_tags($text) ];
    file_put_contents(API_LOG_FN,
        var_export($data, true) . PHP_EOL,
        FILE_APPEND);
```

15. We then use `file_get_contents()` along with a *context* created by `stream_context_create()` to make the actual GenAI call. In the *context*, by setting `ignore_errors`, we fetch a response body even on 4xx/5xx errors. We collect the GenAI response, log it, and use our `$platform` instance to extract the translated text according to the response format of the selected GenAI platform:

```
    $context = stream_context_create([
        'http' => [
            'method'        => 'POST',
            'header'        => [
                'Content-Type: application/json',
                'Authorization: Bearer ' . API_KEY,
            ],
            'content'       => json_encode($data),
            'ignore_errors' => true,
        ],
    ]);

    $raw = file_get_contents(API_ENDPOINT,
        false, $context);
```

```
        file_put_contents(API_LOG_FN, var_export(
            $raw, true) . PHP_EOL, FILE_APPEND);
        if ($raw === false) {
            echo "[translate] transmission error\n";
            return '[Translation error]';
        }
        $result = json_decode($raw, true);
        return $this->platform->get($result)
            ?? '[Translation failed]';
    }
```

> **Tip**
>
> The WebSocket server is event-driven, but the GenAI translation request is synchronous and blocks the event loop. This is acceptable for a small demo, but readers need to be aware that this design has limited scalability and should be replaced with non-blocking HTTP or a worker queue in production.

16. The `send()` method simply runs `ConnectionInterface::send()`, using `json_encode()` to package the data:

```
    public function send(ConnectionInterface $conn,
        array $data): void {
        $conn->send(json_encode($data));
    }
```

17. The remaining methods pertain to finding, notifying, and updating the list of online users:

```
    public function findClientByUsername(
        string $username): ?array {
        foreach ($this->clients as $client) {
            if ($client['username'] === $username)
                return $client;
        }
        return null;
    }

    public function connectedUsers(): array {
        return array_values(array_filter(array_map(
```

```
        fn(array $c): ?array => $c['username']
            ? ['username' => $c['username'],
               'language' => $c['language']]
            : null,
        $this->clients
    )));
}

public function writeUsersFile(): void {
    file_put_contents($this->usersFile,
        json_encode($this->connectedUsers()));
}

public function broadcastUsersList(): void {
    $payload = json_encode(['type' => 'users_list',
        'users' => $this->connectedUsers()]);
    foreach ($this->clients as $client)
        $client['conn']->send($payload);
}
```

18. Next, we define `PlatformInterface`, and a class `OpenAi` that implements the interface. This allows us to retain flexibility and to pop in other platforms or make adjustments as requirements and response formats change. Here's the code for `PlatformInterface`:

```
namespace Cookbook\IndoChat\Platform;
interface PlatformInterface {
    public function get(array $arr): string;
}
```

19. And here's the code for our `OpenAi` class:

```
<?php
namespace Cookbook\IndoChat\Platform;
class OpenAi implements PlatformInterface {
    public function get(array $arr) : string {
      return $arr['output'][0]['content'][0]['text'] ?? '';
    }
}
```

20. In the /path/to/php8cookbook/src/IndoChat/async folder, we define server.php. This script loads our configuration and runs the Ratchet\WebSocket\WsServer. This script is designed to run separately from the web server and is responsible for managing the WebSocket connections:

```
require __DIR__ . '/../config/config.php';
use Cookbook\IndoChat\Server\ChatServer;
use Ratchet\Server\IoServer;
use Ratchet\Http\HttpServer;
use Ratchet\WebSocket\WsServer;
$server = IoServer::factory(
    new HttpServer(new WsServer(
        new ChatServer(USERS_FILE, API_CALLBACK))),
    WS_PORT,
    WS_HOST
);
$server->run();
```

21. We treat the /path/to/php8cookbook/src/IndoChat/public folder as the web server's document root. In this folder, we create users.php and index.php. The former, shown here, is called at regular intervals and simply echoes the contents of the users.json file, if available:

```
require_once __DIR__ . '/../config/config.php';
header('Content-Type: application/json');
header('Cache-Control: no-cache');
echo (file_exists(USERS_FILE))
    ? file_get_contents(USERS_FILE)
    : '[]';
exit;
```

> Tip
>
> **Important**
>
> The code shown here should be expanded for production use by adding file locking, atomic writes, and a shared state if multiple WebSocket server instances are running.

22. Also in the `/path/to/php8cookbook/src/IndoChat/public` folder is our main `index.php` file. Of primary interest is the extensive JavaScript needed to work with WebSockets. We won't show the HTML code here; however, the complete source code can be found in the source repository associated with this course.
    Let's now walk through the main features. The initial PHP code loads configuration and writes initial information to the error log (or server console):

```
<?php
require_once __DIR__ . '/../config/config.php';
error_log(USERS_FILE);
?>
```

23. Avoiding the HTML, let's move our attention to the JavaScript / jQuery code. To begin, we initialize some variables:

```
<script>
const WS_PORT = <?= (int) WS_PORT ?>;
const WS_HOST = window.location.hostname || 'localhost';
let ws             = null;
let wsReady        = false;
let currentUser    = null;
let currentLang    = 'en';
let chosenUser     = null;
let chosenLang     = 'en';
let isSending      = false;
let reconnectTimer = null;
const LANG_LABEL = { en: 'GB English', km: 'ខ្មែរ (Khmer)'};
const LANG_FLAG  = { en: ' GB', km: ' KH' };
function langLabel(code) { return LANG_LABEL[code] || code; }
function langFlag(code)  { return LANG_FLAG[code] || '🌐'; }
```

24. Here are two functions that make the WebSocket connection to the backend Ratchet WebSocket server. We have it configured to run on port `8081`. You'll note that we needed to open this port on our Docker/Podman container so that the browser on your host computer is able to make this connection once you load up the demo page. You'll note that this JavaScript function is designed to reconnect if the WebSocket server goes

down and then comes back up. For the purposes of this recipe, we use the `ws` wrapper; however, for production purposes consider using `wss`:

```
function connectWS() {
  if (reconnectTimer) {
    clearTimeout(reconnectTimer);
    reconnectTimer = null;
  }
// NOTE: consider using "wss" for production:
  ws = new WebSocket(`ws://${WS_HOST}:${WS_PORT}`);
  ws.onopen = () => {
    wsReady = true;
    setStatus(true);
    $('#disconnected-notice').hide();
    if (currentUser) {
      wsSend({ type: 'set_user', username: currentUser, language:
currentLang });
    }
  };
  ws.onmessage = (evt) => {
    try { handleWSMessage(JSON.parse(evt.data)); }
    catch (e) { console.error('WS parse error', e); }
  };
  ws.onclose = () => {
    wsReady = false;
    setStatus(false);
    if (currentUser) {
        $('#disconnected-notice').show(); }
    reconnectTimer = setTimeout(connectWS, 3500);
  };
  ws.onerror = () => {
    wsReady = false;
  };
}
function wsSend(obj) {
  if (ws && ws.readyState === WebSocket.OPEN) {
    ws.send(JSON.stringify(obj));
  }
}
```

25. Next, we have a set of message-routing functions. `handleWSMessage()` is a sort of router that redirects to the appropriate helper function. `onUserSet()` manages new user connections. `onUsersList()` makes sure that the user dropdown `SELECT` element has an updated list. `onMessage()` kicks in when a message is sent. You'll note that it prevents users from sending messages to themselves:

```
function handleWSMessage(data) {
  switch (data.type) {
    case 'user_set':    onUserSet(data);    break;
    case 'users_list':  onUsersList(data);  break;
    case 'message':     onMessage(data);    break;
    case 'error':       showToast(data.message, 'error'); break;
  }
}
function onUserSet(data) {
  currentUser = data.username;
  currentLang = data.language;
  showMainPanel();
  loadUsersAjax();
}
function onUsersList(data) {
  populateSelect(data.users);
}
function onMessage(data) {
  const relevant = (data.from === currentUser || data.from === chosenUser)
&&
                   (data.to   === currentUser || data.to   === chosenUser);
  if (!relevant) return;
  if (data.from === currentUser) {
    isSending = false;
    $('#send-btn').prop('disabled', false).text('Send');
    $('#translating-bar').hide();
  }
  appendMessage(data);
}
```

26. The next block of JavaScript code makes an AJAX call to `users.php`, and populates the users dropdown list:

```
function loadUsersAjax() {
  $.ajax({
    url: '/users.php',
    type: 'GET',
    dataType: 'json',
    success: (users) => populateSelect(users),
    error: () => showToast(
        'Could not load user list.', 'error'),
  });
}
function populateSelect(users) {
  const $sel    = $('#users-select');
  const curVal = $sel.val();
  $sel.empty().append('<option value="">— Select a user —</option>');
  const others = users.filter(u => u.username !== currentUser);
  others.forEach(u => {
    $sel.append(
      $('<option>', {
        value: u.username,
        'data-lang': u.language,
        text: `${u.username}  (${langLabel(u.language)})`,
      })
    );
  });
  if (curVal) {
    $sel.val(curVal);
    const stillHere = others.some(
        u => u.username === curVal);
    if (!stillHere && chosenUser === curVal) {
      showToast(`${curVal} has disconnected.`,
          'error');
      closeConversation();
    }
  }
  const count = others.length;
  $('#user-count').text(count === 0 ? 'No other users online.' : `${count}
```

```
user${count > 1 ? 's' : ''} online`);
}
```

27. The `appendMessage()` function adds a *message bubble* to the user's chat screen:

```
function appendMessage(data) {
  const isSent     = data.from === currentUser;
  const samelang   = data.fromLang === data.toLang;
  const senderName = isSent ? 'You' : escHtml(data.from);
  const direction  = isSent ? 'sent' : 'recv';
  const targetLang = isSent ? data.toLang :
      ((data.fromLang === currentLang ) ? data.fromLang : data.fromLang);
  let translationHtml = '';
  if (!samelang) {
    if (isSent) {
      translationHtml = `
        <div class="msg-translation">
          <span class="flag">${langFlag(data.toLang)}</span>
          <span>${escHtml(data.translated)}</span>
        </div>`;
    } else {
      translationHtml = `
        <div class="msg-translation">
          <span class="flag">${langFlag(data.toLang)}</span>
          <span>${escHtml(data.translated)}</span>
        </div>`;
    }
  }
  const html = `
    <div class="message ${direction}">
      <div class="msg-meta">
        <span>${senderName}</span>
        <span>${langFlag(data.fromLang)}</span>
      </div>
      <div class="msg-bubble">${escHtml(data.original)}</div>
      ${translationHtml}
      <div class="msg-time">${escHtml(data.timestamp)}</div>
    </div>`;
  $('#message-history').append(html);
```

```
  scrollToBottom();
}
```

28. And finally, the main `jQuery` document-ready function that starts the ball rolling:

```
$(function () {

  connectWS();
  /* Setup form */
  $('#set-user-btn').on('click', setUser);
  $('#username').on('keydown', (e) => { if (e.key === 'Enter')
setUser(); });
  /* Language radio highlight */
  $('input[name="language"]').on('change', syncRadioHighlight);
  /* User selection */
  $('#users-select').on('change', onSelectUser);
  $('#refresh-btn').on('click', loadUsersAjax);
  /* Messaging */
  $('#send-btn').on('click', sendMessage);
  $('#message-input').on('keydown', (e) => {
    if (e.key === 'Enter' && !e.shiftKey) { e.preventDefault();
sendMessage(); }
  });
  $('#message-input').on('input', function () { autoGrow(this); });
  /* Stop */
  $('#stop-btn').on('click', () => {
    showSetupPanel();
    showToast('Conversation ended.', 'info');
  });
  /* Poll users every 8 s while in main panel */
  setInterval(() => {
    if(currentUser&&wsReady)loadUsersAjax();
  }, 8000);
});
</script>
</body>
</html>
```

29. To test our new system, we'll need to open two shells to our Docker/Podman PHP 8 container. You'll note that in the `/path/to/php8cookbook/docker-compose.yml` file,

for the php8 container, we expose two ports: `8889` and `8081`. In the first shell, we run the asynchronous WebSocket server on port `8081`, as shown here:

```
ed@localhost:~/Repos/PHP-8-Programming-Cookbook
$ ./admin.sh shell
php8:/repo# php /repo/src/IndoChat/async/server.php
IndoChat WebSocket server started on port 8081
Users file found at: /repo/src/IndoChat/data/users.json
Press Ctrl+C to stop.
[connect]   #64
[user_set]  #64 → Doug (English)
[connect]   #97
[user_set]  #97 → Nimol (Khmer)
[message]   Doug → Nimol
[message]   Nimol → Doug
```

30. We then open a second command shell into the PHP 8 container, and run the public-facing web server. In this case, we simply use the PHP built-in web server, and specify port 8889, also open to our host system. You'll note that the JavaScript starts making calls to `users.php` at intervals, continually refreshing the active user list:

```
ed@localhost:~/Repos/PHP-8-Programming-Cookbook
$ ./admin.sh shell
php8:/repo# php -S 0.0.0.0:8889 -t /repo/src/IndoChat/public
[Sun Apr  5 07:17:16 2026] PHP 8.4.16 Development Server (http://
0.0.0.0:8889) started
[Sun Apr  5 07:17:16 2026] 10.10.90.88:48536 Accepted
[Sun Apr  5 07:17:16 2026] 10.10.90.88:48536 [200]: GET /users.php
[Sun Apr  5 07:17:16 2026] 10.10.90.88:48536 Closing
[Sun Apr  5 07:17:21 2026] 10.10.90.88:35370 Accepted
[Sun Apr  5 07:17:21 2026] 10.10.90.88:35370 [200]: GET /users.php
[Sun Apr  5 07:17:21 2026] 10.10.90.88:35370 Closing
```

31. To complete the test, from your host computer, open two browser tabs, both set to `http://localhost:8889`. You can then supply a different username and language for each tab and start sending messages. You'll note that the message is translated on the opposite screen. It's also important to mention that each *user* first needs to select the other before sending and receiving translated messages. A possible future

improvement would be to give the sender the ability to notify the recipient automatically when a message is sent:

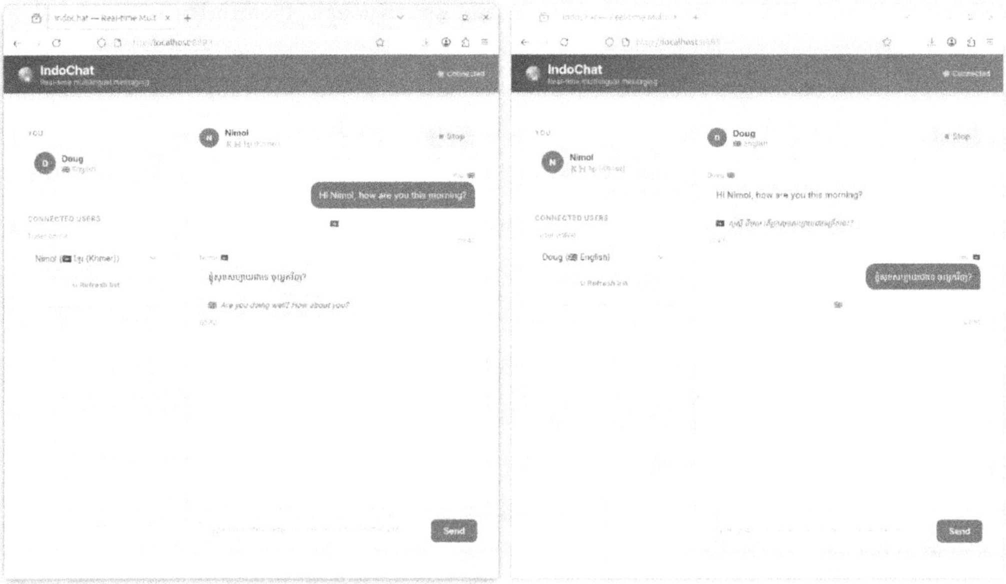

Figure 7.3 – Example translated chat session

The system is designed to log GenAI calls to `/path/to/php8cookbook/src/Chapter07/chat.log`, giving you a chance to analyze incoming responses from the GenAI platform.

How it works...

This recipe has two main runtime pieces:

- A public web server serving index.php and users.php
- A Ratchet/ReactPHP WebSocket server running separately on port `8081`

The web page is loaded from the public server, but once the page opens, JavaScript immediately creates a WebSocket connection to the backend chat server. The connection remains open, allowing messages to move between browser and server without repeatedly making new HTTP requests.

When a browser connects, Ratchet calls the server's `onOpen()` method. The server stores the connection in the `$clients` array using the connection's resource ID.

After the user enters a username and selects a language, the browser sends a WebSocket message. The server receives that message in `onMessage()`, routes it to `handleSetUser()`, validates the username and language, checks that the username is not already in use, and then stores the user information alongside the WebSocket connection.

The server also writes the current list of connected users to `users.json` and broadcasts an updated user list to all connected clients. The front end uses this information to populate the *available users* dropdown. In addition, the browser makes regular AJAX calls to `users.php`, which simply returns the contents of `users.json`. This keeps the displayed user list synchronized even if a browser misses a WebSocket update.

When one user selects another user and sends a message, the browser sends a WebSocket message that the server routes to `handleSendMessage()`. This method validates the message, confirms that the sender has registered a username, and looks up the recipient by username in the active `$clients` list.

If the sender and recipient use the same language, the original text is reused as the translated text. If their languages differ, the server calls `translate()`. This method sends a GenAI translation request to the configured GenAI API endpoint.

The raw GenAI response is decoded from JSON and passed to the configured platform adapter, in this case OpenAI.

The server sends that same payload to both the sender's WebSocket connection and the recipient's WebSocket connection. This keeps both chat windows in sync and ensures both users see the original and translated versions of the message.

On the browser side, incoming WebSocket messages are handled by JavaScript. A small router function checks the message type and calls the appropriate handler. User-list messages update the dropdown. Chat messages are checked to make sure they belong to the currently selected conversation, then rendered as message bubbles in the chat history. If the languages differ, the translated version is displayed beneath the original. The WebSocket server also handles disconnects and errors.

Figure 7.4 shows the overall logic flow:

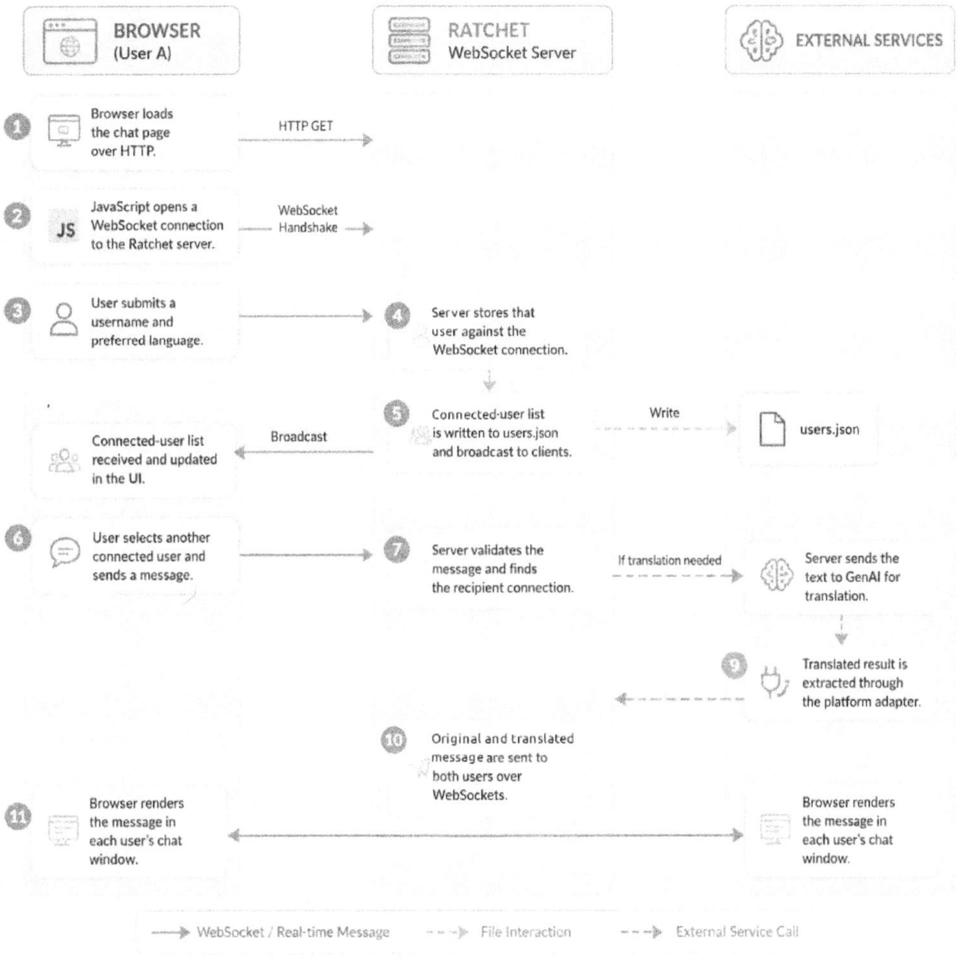

Figure 7.4 – Real-time WebSocket chat logic flow

See also

For more information on ReactPHP, have a look here: `https://reactphp.org/`.

The main Ratchet library website is found here: `http://socketo.me/`.

The living standard for WebSockets resides on this website: `https://websockets.spec.whatwg.org/`.

8

Working with Date/Time and International Aspects

In today's increasingly interconnected world, businesses face fierce global competition. This chapter equips you with the knowledge and strategies necessary to navigate the complexities of internationalization. We will explore key aspects such as handling diverse character sets (including complex scripts and emoticons), effective translation techniques, and the acquisition and management of regional information, including language settings, number and currency formats, and date/time preferences. Furthermore, this chapter will provide practical guidance on developing internationalized calendars that can effectively manage recurring events across different regions, enabling businesses to effectively engage with a global audience.

In this chapter, we're going to cover the following date/time and internationalization topics:

- Using emoticons or emojis
- Handling `DateTime` errors
- Getting the locale from the browser data
- Formatting numbers by locale
- Handling currency by locale
- Formatting date/time by locale
- Working with `` `str*` `` family differences on international websites
- Handling translations without `Gettext`

Technical requirements

In this chapter, it is essential to have the local environment properly set up using the instructions detailed in *Chapter 1, Building a Foundation*. It is also assumed that the reader has at least a basic understanding of Object-Oriented Programming concepts, which is an area also discussed in *Chapter 4, Working with PHP Object-Oriented Programming*.

Using emoticons or emojis

Emojis have become a common part of how we communicate online. They help us express ourselves better than just words alone, and they can be understood by people all over the world. Because emojis are so popular, websites need to be able to handle them. This means letting people use emojis when they type comments, messages, or search terms. It also means making sure those emojis look right on any device, whether it's a phone, tablet, or computer.

Getting ready

Unicode is the universal catalog that assigns every character, symbol, and emoji a unique number called a **code point**. UTF-8 is the encoding HTML5 uses to represent those code points as the bytes a browser actually receives over the network. The distinction matters: a code point like 128516 (the smiley 😄) exists in Unicode regardless of how a page is served, while UTF-8 is one of several ways to write that number down.

This means we don't need to store an image for a smiley — we can reference any character directly by its Unicode code point in our HTML. To do so, prefix the decimal code point with &# and suffix it with semicolon — so 😄 renders 😄, with no extra assets or special handling needed on the server side. Emojis and other non-English characters then *just work*, as long as your pages are served with <meta charset="utf-8"> so the browser knows how to decode the bytes back into code points.

You also need to ensure your HTML header includes a meta tag to handle UTF-8 encoding. In HTML5, you can do this with: <meta charset="UTF-8">:

```
<!DOCTYPE html>
<html>
<meta charset="UTF-8">
<body>

😄 <!-- Decimal smiley -->
😄 <!-- Hexadecimal smiley -->
```

```
</body>
</html>
```

If you run this in your browser, you'll get two identical smileys. To use hexadecimals for emojis, just prefix the hexadecimal value with &#x and suffix it with a semicolon ;.

In a dynamic web application, it's important to properly handle inputs containing emojis and special characters while ensuring security. This means sanitizing user input before storing it to prevent malicious scripts from being saved alongside valid content. To make this process reusable and maintainable, it's best to use object-oriented programming by creating a dedicated `InputCleaner` class to handle input sanitization.

How to do it...

1. Create a class to handle the work of cleaning the incoming data:
   `src/Chapter08/Cleaner/InputCleaner.php`

```
<?php

namespace Cookbook\Chapter08\Cleaner;

class InputCleaner
{
    public function clean($input): string
{
    $decoded = html_entity_decode($input, ENT_QUOTES, 'UTF-8');
    $stripped = strip_tags($decoded);
    return htmlspecialchars($stripped, ENT_QUOTES, 'UTF-8');
} }
```

2. Create a consumer PHP file to demonstrate the usage:
   `src/Chapter08/ch08_handling_emojis.php`

```
<?php

use Cookbook\Chapter08\Cleaner\InputCleaner;

include __DIR__ . '/../../vendor/autoload.php';

$inputCleaner = new InputCleaner();
$userInput = "😀 <script>alert('hi');</script>";
```

```
$sanitizedInput = $inputCleaner->clean($userInput);
echo $sanitizedInput;
```

You'll notice that we have inserted JavaScript that is not supposed to be executed at all in your output. This is important as we need to prevent cross-site scripting or XSS, but still be able to render other desired characters like emojis.

How it works...

Visit the following URL through your web browser, and you should see the following:

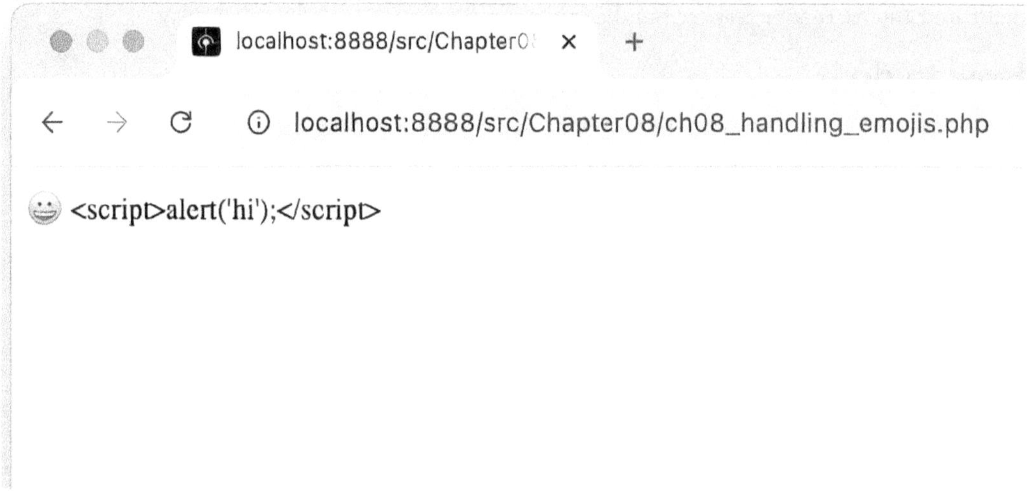

Figure 8.1 – Emoji with disabled script

As you can see from the preceding screenshot, we were able to display the emoji properly as well as render the JavaScript safely. If you modify the `ch08_handling_emojis.php` and `echo` of the `$userInput` directly, without cleaning the input, you'll get the following result instead:

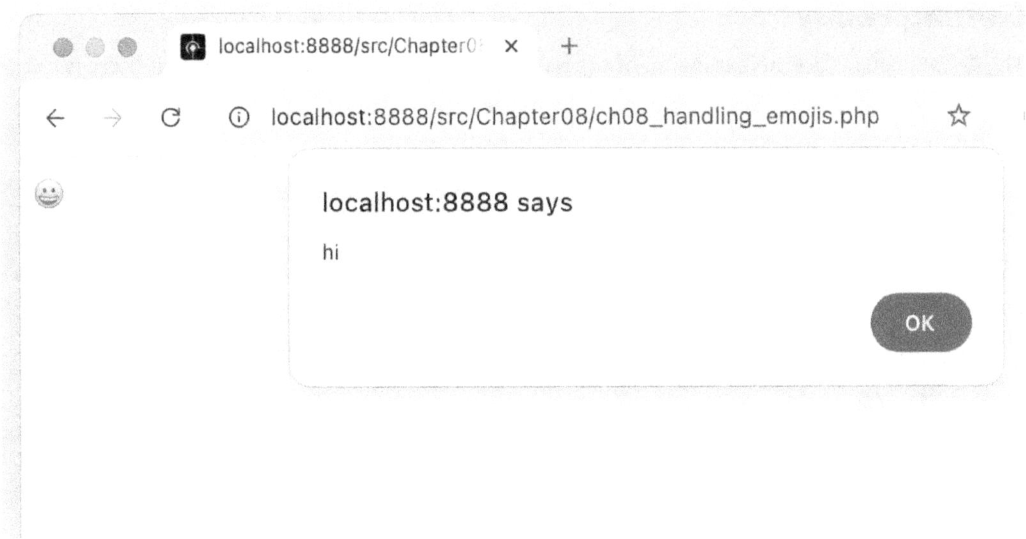

Figure 8.2 – No input cleaning

As you can see from the preceding screenshot, the JavaScript was executed by your browser, along with the smiley. As a developer, you can probably imagine the number of security problems you'll encounter if you simply accept all incoming data from your users.

`InputCleaner::clean()` runs a three-step pipeline. First, `html_entity_decode()` reverses any HTML entities already present in the input — without this step, an attacker could submit `<script>` and bypass the next stage. Second, `strip_tags()` removes any real HTML markup from the now-visible input. Third, `htmlspecialchars()` re-encodes the remaining text so any residual angle brackets render as literal characters when the output is displayed. The decode-strip-encode order matters: reversing any pair of steps would leave a path for tags to survive into the rendered page.

Handling DateTime errors

PHP 8.3 introduced `DateError` and `DateException` to improve how date/time-related issues are handled. Unlike earlier versions that threw generic exceptions, this new exception hierarchy allows developers to pinpoint specific problems—like invalid date strings or timezone errors—making debugging and error handling more precise and maintainable.

Getting ready

The DateError class is an extension of the base Error class. This class is thrown if there is an issue on the Date/Time extension itself or from the PHP runtime itself, meaning it should almost never occur unless the code you wrote is really wrong.

Since PHP 8.3, DateException is the primary exception used for handling errors related to invalid or malformed date/time values and operations. It acts as a base class for various specific date/time issues, such as invalid date strings, incorrect time zones, or unsupported operations on immutable objects. This structured exception system improves debugging and error clarity by allowing developers to catch and handle date-related problems more precisely.

How to do it...

As an example, create a new file called ch08_dateerror.php with the following content:

src/Chapter08/ch08_dateerror.php

```
<?php

try {
    // DateInvalidTimeZoneException
    $dateWithInvalidTimezone = new DateTime('now', new DateTimeZone('ABC123/
Timezone'));

    // DateMalformedStringException
    $malformedDateString = new DateTime('invalid_date_format');

    // DateMalformedIntervalStringException
    $interval = DateInterval::createFromDateString('invalid@invalid');

} catch (DateInvalidTimeZoneException $exception) {
    echo "DateInvalidTimeZoneException: " . $exception->getMessage();
} catch (DateMalformedStringException $exception) {
    echo "DateMalformedStringException: " . $exception->getMessage();
} catch (DateMalformedIntervalStringException $exception) {
    echo "DateMalformedIntervalStringException: " . $exception->getMessage();
}

?>
```

How it works...

If you comment each statement in the try block one at a time, you will encounter all three exceptions that are being caught in the catch blocks. Each of these exception classes extends the same `DateException` class. But catching specific exceptions like this can give you flexibility in handling each specific exception when encountered.

The following snippets will trigger the three different exceptions:

```
// DateInvalidTimeZoneException
new DateTime('now', new DateTimeZone('ABC123/Timezone'));

// DateMalformedStringException
new DateTime('invalid_date_format');

// DateMalformedIntervalStringException
DateInterval::createFromDateString('invalid@invalid');
```

Getting the locale from the browser data

ISO 639-1 defines around 184 two-letter language codes — the familiar *en*, *fr*, *ja*, and so on that browsers, lang attributes, and `setlocale()` calls all reference. Extended standards (ISO 639-2 and ISO 639-3) cover many more languages with three-letter codes, but for most web work the two-letter ISO 639-1 set is what you'll encounter. When working on a global project, you'll probably not support all of them in one go, but you might support some. Say, for example, you want to offer both an English and French language output to your web application; you can set this preferred language and locale in the browser, and with your PHP application you can retrieve the preferred locale and serve the preferred language pack to your consumers.

Getting ready

ISO 639 is a system that assigns unique codes to languages. Imagine it as a universal language identifier, much like how product codes help us distinguish between different items. These codes are crucial for computers to understand and process information related to different languages.

The most common part of ISO 639 uses two-letter codes. For example, *en* represents English, and *fr* represents French. These short and easy-to-remember codes are widely used in software, websites, and databases, making it easier to categorize and manage information in different languages.

How to do it...

1. Back to our example of a website that offers both English and French languages, we can let the consumers set their preferred language through the browser, then on the server side we retrieve this data, process it, then decide which language pack to show. Create a new file called `ch08_locale.php` with the following content:

   `src/Chapter08/ch08_locale.php`

```
<?php
session_start();

// On initial load, clear the session and use the language from
HTTP_ACCEPT_LANGUAGE
if (!isset($_SESSION['initialized'])) {
    session_unset();
    session_destroy();
    session_start();
    $_SESSION['initialized'] = true;

    // Detect browser language
    $acceptLanguageHeader = $_SERVER['HTTP_ACCEPT_LANGUAGE'] ?? '';
    $browserLocale = Locale::acceptFromHttp($acceptLanguageHeader);
    $supportedLanguages = [
        'en_US' => 'en',
        'en_GB' => 'en',
        'fr_FR' => 'fr',
    ];

    if ($browserLocale && array_key_exists($browserLocale,
$supportedLanguages)) {
        $_SESSION['current_language'] =
$supportedLanguages[$browserLocale];
    } else {
        $_SESSION['current_language'] = 'en'; // Default to English
    }
}

// Toggle language on each refresh
if ($_SESSION['current_language'] === 'en') {
    $_SESSION['current_language'] = 'fr';
```

```
} else {
    $_SESSION['current_language'] = 'en';
}

// Get the current language
$currentLanguage = $_SESSION['current_language'];

// Hardcoded language arrays
$translations = [
    'en' => [
        "hello" => "Hello",
    ],
    'fr' => [
        "hello" => "Bonjour",
    ]
];

// Set locale and headers based on the current language
if ($currentLanguage === 'fr') {
    setlocale(LC_ALL, 'fr_FR.UTF-8');
    header("Content-Language: fr");
    echo "Français.<br>";
} else {
    setlocale(LC_ALL, 'en_US.UTF-8');
    header("Content-Language: en");
    echo "English.<br>";
}

// Display the greeting message in the current language
if (isset($translations[$currentLanguage])) {
    echo $translations[$currentLanguage]["hello"];
} else {
    echo "Language not supported.";
}
?>
```

How it works...

In the code from the previous subsection, we retrieve the client's browser's available locales through `$_SERVER['HTTP_ACCEPT_LANGUAGE']`. (For this example, I added French to my Google Chrome browser's language settings so the recipe could demonstrate the toggle.) The session-management mechanism then flips the active language between English and French on each browser refresh, so the locale switch is observable when you reload.

> Note
>
> **A note on parsing HTTP_ACCEPT_LANGUAGE**
>
> The header is structured per RFC 7231 as a comma-separated list of locales with optional quality values — e.g. Accept-Language: `fr-CA`, `fr;q=0.9`, `en;q=0.8` means prefer Canadian French, then generic French, then English. A naive split misses the q-value ordering. The intl extension's `Locale::acceptFromHttp()` parses it correctly in a single call and is the right choice in production.

Once a language is chosen, two calls handle the rest: `setlocale(LC_ALL, 'fr_FR.UTF-8')` switches PHP's own locale-aware functions (date and number formatting, `strcoll`, `ctype_*`) into French/France conventions — comma decimals, day-month-year ordering, French collation. `header('Content-Language: fr')` does the opposite: it doesn't change PHP; it adds an HTTP header so clients (browsers, search engines, proxies) know what language the response is in. Both are needed — setting one without the other creates a mismatch where, for example, a French-formatted page is silently advertised as English.

Through your browser, visit the `http://localhost:8888/src/Chapter08/ch08_locale.php` URL and you should see the following result:

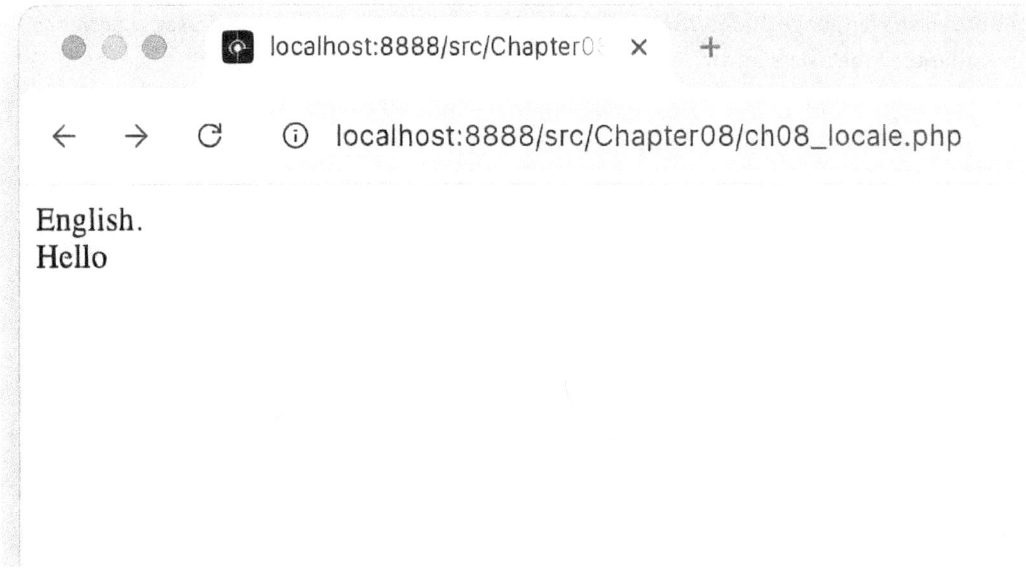

Figure 8.3 – English on first load

On your first load of the URL, you'll see an English translation of the word *Hello*. Since we added a mechanism in the PHP file to forcibly change the locale after each load, you should see a different result when you refresh the browser. Refresh the browser, with the same URL:

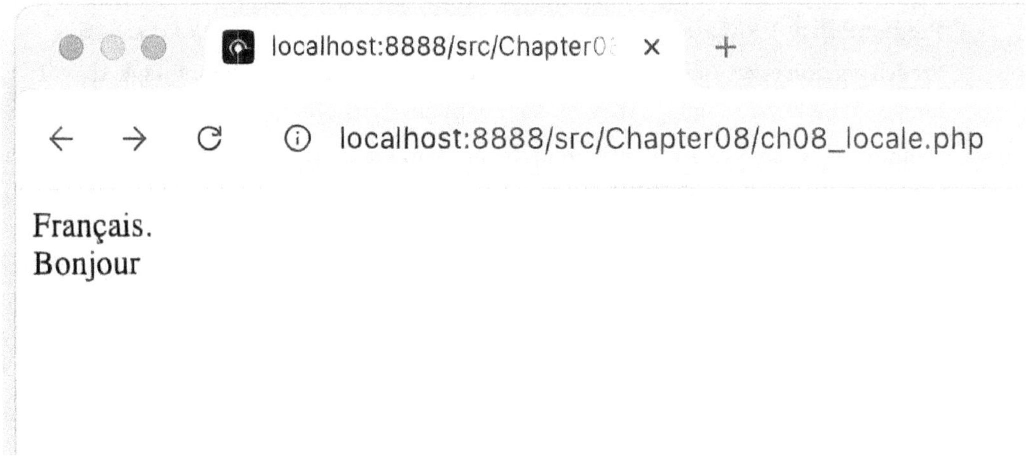

Figure 8.4 – French selected after the refresh

After refreshing the browser, you'll notice that the French translation of the word *Hello*, *Bonjour*, is now displayed. This demonstrates the dynamic language toggle functionality, which can seamlessly switch between supported languages on each page reload. By leveraging the browser's language preferences or session data, you can create a tailored user experience that adapts to the user's locale.

The possibilities with this setup are nearly limitless. Beyond simple arrays, you can expand your translations into dedicated PHP files, JSON files, or even integrate with external translation APIs. This approach provides a scalable and maintainable framework to support multilingual applications, making it easier to manage and update language resources as your application grows.

There's more...

The session-based toggle above is useful for demonstrating the mechanic — parsing Accept-Language, calling setlocale(), and swapping translation strings — in the smallest amount of code. In production, however, language almost never lives in the session. It lives in the URL, for three reasons:

- **SEO**: Search engines treat `/en/about` and `/fr/about` as separate, indexable pages and can apply `hreflang` links between them. Session-based language means the same URL serves different content per user, which crawlers can't reliably index.
- **Cacheability**: A URL is a cache key — a page at `/en/about` can be cached by CDNs, intermediate proxies, and the browser. Session-based language varies the response without varying the URL, which either breaks caching or forces a Vary: Cookie header that effectively defeats it.
- **Predictability**: URLs are shareable: a teammate who opens `/fr/checkout` sees the French version regardless of their own session. With session-based language, they'd land on whichever language their session happened to hold.

The two common URL shapes are a path prefix (`/en/`, `/fr/`) or a subdomain (`en.example.com`, `fr.example.com`). Both work; the path-prefix style is more common and easier to wire up in any routing framework. The `Accept-Language` parsing shown above still has a role — it's the right default on a user's first visit before they've picked a language explicitly — but the choice should then be reflected in the URL going forward.

Formatting numbers by locale

Some locales also have different number formatting conventions, reflecting their unique cultural and linguistic norms. For example, in Germany (Deutsch), numbers use periods to separate thousands, so one million would be written as *1.000.000*. Conversely, in the United States, commas are used for the same purpose, resulting in *1,000,000*. These differences extend beyond separators; the decimal symbol also varies. While the US uses a period as the decimal point (e.g., *1,234.56*), Germany and many other European countries use a comma (e.g., *1.234,56*). These conventions can influence how numbers are read, understood, and entered into systems.

Getting ready

Understanding and implementing these locale-specific conventions is critical when developing global applications. Users expect to see numbers formatted in a way that is familiar to them, especially in contexts like financial data, pricing, or reports. Failure to do so can lead to confusion or errors, such as interpreting *1.234* as one thousand two hundred thirty-four instead of one point two three four. By leveraging locale-aware functions in programming languages, such as `setlocale()` and `localeconv()` in PHP, developers can dynamically adapt number formatting to match the user's region, ensuring clarity and a seamless user experience. While PHP provides these older functions, modern applications should prefer the `NumberFormatter` class from the `intl` extension for consistent and locale-aware formatting.

How to do it...

1. The `NumberFormatter` class in PHP is a very handy tool that you can use to instantiate a specific formatter object you need for a specific locale. To demonstrate this, create a new file called `ch08_locale_numeric.php` with the following content:

   `src/Chapter08/ch08_locale_numeric.php`

```
<?php
$number = 1555231.36;

// NumberFormatter concrete instances
$formatter_us = new NumberFormatter('en_US', NumberFormatter::DECIMAL);
$formatter_de = new NumberFormatter('de_DE', NumberFormatter::DECIMAL);
$formatter_in = new NumberFormatter('en_IN', NumberFormatter::DECIMAL);
$formatter_ar = new NumberFormatter('ar_SA', NumberFormatter::DECIMAL);
$formatter_he = new NumberFormatter('he_IL', NumberFormatter::DECIMAL);

echo "<h3>Numeric Formats:</h3>";
echo "US: " . $formatter_us->format($number) . "<br>";
echo "German: " . $formatter_de->format($number) . "<br>";
echo "Indian: " . $formatter_in->format($number) . "<br>";
echo "Arabic: " . $formatter_ar->format($number) . "<br>";
echo "Hebrew: " . $formatter_he->format($number) . "<br>";
```

In this example, we've created individual instances of the `NumberFormatter` class by sending the specific locale we want as an argument, and sent the `NumberFormatter::DECIMAL` as a second argument. If you check your browser by visiting the `ch08_locale_numeric.php` file, you should see something like:

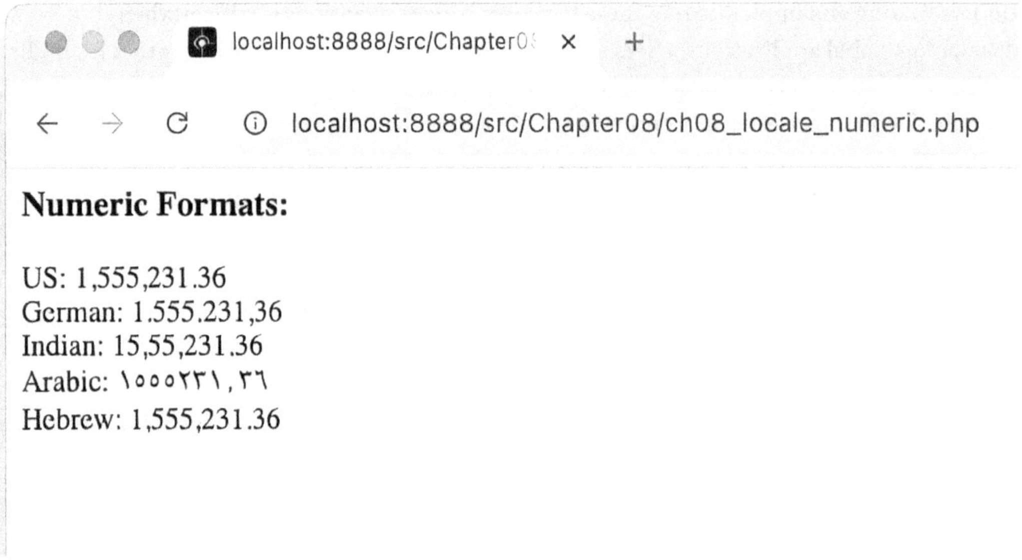

Figure 8.5 – Different numeric and currency formats

How it works...

As demonstrated in the preceding screenshot, we successfully formatted the base number `$number = 1555231.36` into multiple representations, each tailored to the conventions of the respective locales. This illustrates the flexibility of PHP's `NumberFormatter` class, which allows developers to dynamically adapt numeric and currency formats according to the cultural and linguistic preferences of their users.

For instance, the US locale (`` `en_US` ``) presents numbers with a comma as the thousands separator and a period as the decimal point (`` `1,555,231.36` ``). In contrast, the German locale (`` `de_DE` ``) adheres to its standard by using a period for the thousands separator and a comma for the decimal (`` `1.555.231,36` ``). Additionally, Arabic (`` `ar_SA` ``) showcases numerals in the Arabic-Indic script (`٢٣١,٣٦ ,٥٥٥ ,١'), while Hebrew (`` `he_IL` ``) formats numbers in a manner similar to Western conventions but adheres to **Right-to-Left** (**RTL**) alignment for proper contextual display.

This example highlights the significance of locale-aware formatting in building globalized applications that deliver seamless and intuitive user experiences by respecting regional norms.

Handling currency by locale

Currency formatting also varies by locale, reflecting regional cultural, and linguistic norms. For instance, in Germany, the euro symbol (€) typically appears after the amount with a comma as the decimal separator—such as *1.234,56 €*. In contrast, the United States places the dollar sign (*$*) before the amount and uses a period for the decimal—like *$1,234.56*. These differences are not just cosmetic; they affect how financial values are displayed, interpreted, and processed.

Getting ready

Very similar to number handling by locale, in PHP, you can handle locale-specific currency formatting using functions like `setlocale()` and `localeconv()`, which allow you to dynamically adapt the formatting based on the user's region, ensuring clarity and consistency across international applications.

One principle worth establishing first: always store numeric and monetary values as raw numbers — for currency, prefer integer minor units (cents, pence, paise) or a decimal/money type such as BCMath or moneyphp/money rather than floats, which accumulate rounding errors. Apply locale formatting only when displaying values to users. The recipe below covers the display side; storage is a separate concern.

How to do it...

1. Very similar to the approach we've taken in the previous section about numerics and locales, we can use the same approach to handle currencies as well. To demonstrate this, create a new file called `ch08_locale_currency.php` with the following content:

   `src/Chapter08/ch08_locale_currency.php`

```php
<?php
$number = 1555231.36;

// NumberFormatter concrete instances
$formatter_us = new NumberFormatter('en_US', NumberFormatter::DECIMAL);
$formatter_de = new NumberFormatter('de_DE', NumberFormatter::DECIMAL);
$formatter_in = new NumberFormatter('en_IN', NumberFormatter::DECIMAL);
$formatter_ar = new NumberFormatter('ar_SA', NumberFormatter::DECIMAL);
$formatter_he = new NumberFormatter('he_IL', NumberFormatter::DECIMAL);

// Currency formatters
$currency_us = new NumberFormatter('en_US', NumberFormatter::CURRENCY);
$currency_de = new NumberFormatter('de_DE', NumberFormatter::CURRENCY);
$currency_in = new NumberFormatter('en_IN', NumberFormatter::CURRENCY);
```

```
$currency_ar = new NumberFormatter('ar_SA', NumberFormatter::CURRENCY);
$currency_he = new NumberFormatter('he_IL', NumberFormatter::CURRENCY);

// Currency
echo "<h3>Currency Formats:</h3>";
echo "US: " . $currency_us->format($number) . "<br>";
echo "German: " . $currency_de->format($number) . "<br>";
echo "Indian: " . $currency_in->format($number) . "<br>";
echo "Arabic: " . $currency_ar->format($number) . "<br>";
echo "Hebrew: " . $currency_he->format($number) . "<br>";

// RTL Example
echo "<h3>RTL Styling:</h3>";
echo '<div style="float:left; width:300px; direction: rtl; text-align:
right; ">';

echo "מספרים: ". $formatter_he->format($number) . "<br>";
echo "מטבע: " . $currency_he->format($number);

echo '</div>';
?>
```

How it works...

Like in the previous section, we created multiple instances of the `NumberFormatter` class with different locales, and sent the `NumberFormatter::CURRENCY` constant as a second argument. Go to the `http://localhost:8888/src/Chapter08/ch08_locale_currency.php` URL in your browser and you should see the following currency formats:

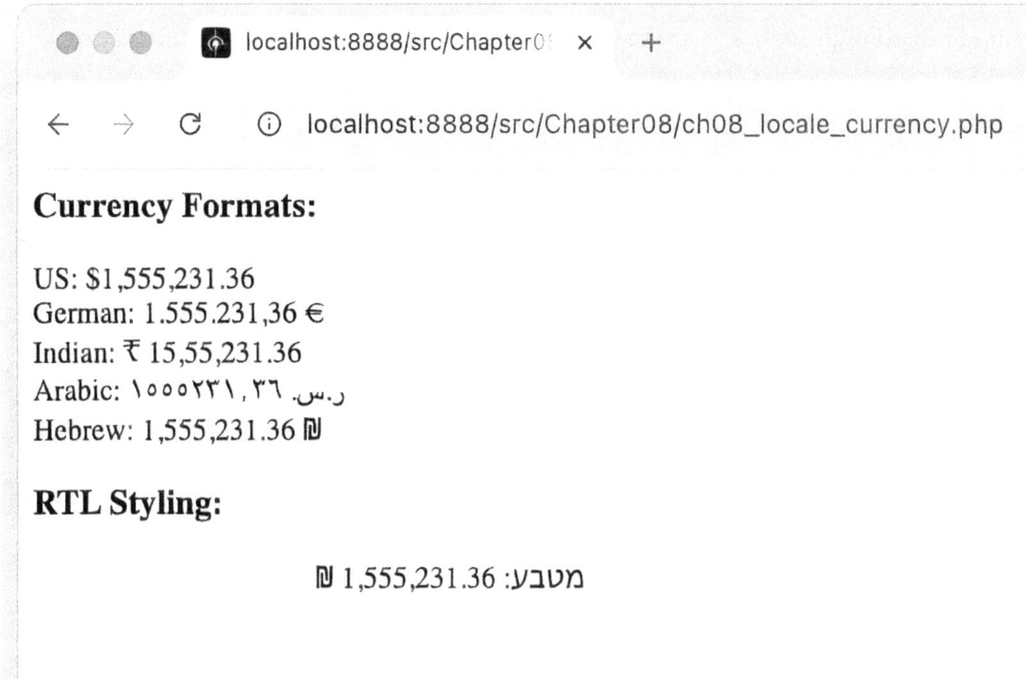

Figure 8.6 – Currency formats

As demonstrated in the preceding screenshot, the variable `$number = 1555231.36` has been seamlessly transformed into multiple currency formats, each tailored to the specific conventions of various locales. This showcases the power of PHP's `NumberFormatter` class, which intelligently adapts the display of numbers to align with regional standards, including currency symbols, grouping separators, and decimal points. For instance, the US locale (`en_US`) formats the number as `$1,555,231.36`, using a comma for the thousands separator and a period for the decimal. Meanwhile, the German locale (`de_DE`) presents it as `1.555.231,36 €`, swapping the separator conventions and appending the Euro symbol. Such locale-aware formatting is essential in creating applications that cater to global audiences, providing users with an intuitive and familiar experience regardless of their regional or linguistic preferences.

Formatting date/time by locale

Different locales often follow unique conventions for formatting dates and times, reflecting cultural and regional norms such as the order of day, month, and year, the use of 12-hour or 24-hour time formats, and specific separators. For example, the US locale (`en_US`) typically uses the format `MM/DD/YYYY` for dates, while the German locale (`de_DE`) prefers `DD.MM.YYYY`. Time formatting also varies, with the US commonly using a 12-hour format accompanied by AM/PM markers, whereas Germany and many other countries use the 24-hour clock. These differences are crucial to consider when developing applications for a global audience to ensure the display aligns with user expectations and regional practices.

Getting ready

In PHP, handling these locale-specific differences is made seamless with the `IntlDateFormatter` class. By specifying the desired locale and formatting style, developers can easily format and parse dates and times according to regional conventions without manually implementing complex logic. PHP applies the appropriate formatting rules based on the locale, ensuring that dates and times are displayed naturally and intuitively for users worldwide. This built-in functionality not only simplifies the process of creating internationalized applications but also significantly enhances the user experience by providing regionally accurate and culturally familiar outputs.

How to do it...

1. Create a new file called `ch08_locale_datetime.php` with the following content:

   `src/Chapter08/ch08_locale_datetime.php`

```php
<?php
// Date and time to format
// No timezone passed - DateTime falls back to the server's default
// (date_default_timezone_get()). Fine for this demo; in production,
// pass an explicit DateTimeZone so the same code yields the same
// instant on any server.
$date = new DateTime('2025-01-01 00:00:00');

// IntlDateFormatter per Locale instances:
$dateFormatter_us = new IntlDateFormatter('en_US',
IntlDateFormatter::LONG, IntlDateFormatter::SHORT);
$dateFormatter_de = new IntlDateFormatter('de_DE',
IntlDateFormatter::LONG, IntlDateFormatter::SHORT);
$dateFormatter_fr = new IntlDateFormatter('fr_FR',
IntlDateFormatter::LONG, IntlDateFormatter::SHORT);
$dateFormatter_in = new IntlDateFormatter('en_IN',
IntlDateFormatter::LONG, IntlDateFormatter::SHORT);
$dateFormatter_ar = new IntlDateFormatter('ar_SA',
IntlDateFormatter::FULL, IntlDateFormatter::SHORT);
$dateFormatter_he = new IntlDateFormatter('he_IL',
```

```
IntlDateFormatter::FULL, IntlDateFormatter::SHORT);

// Formatting
echo "<h3>Date and Time Formats:</h3>";
echo "US (en_US): " . $dateFormatter_us->format($date) . "<br>";
echo "German (de_DE): " . $dateFormatter_de->format($date) . "<br>";
echo "French (fr_FR): " . $dateFormatter_fr->format($date) . "<br>";
echo "Indian (en_IN): " . $dateFormatter_in->format($date) . "<br>";
echo "Arabic (ar_SA): " . $dateFormatter_ar->format($date) . "<br>";
echo "Hebrew (he_IL): " . $dateFormatter_he->format($date) . "<br>";

// RTL Example
echo "<h3>RTL Example:</h3>";
echo '<div style="float:left; width:400px; direction: rtl; text-align:
right;">';
echo "תאריך ושעה: ". $dateFormatter_he->format($date);
echo '</div>';
echo '</body></html>';
```

How it works...

In this PHP file, we've leveraged the power of the `IntlDateFormatter` class to handle locale-specific date and time formatting seamlessly. By creating multiple instances of this class, we have specified both the locale and the desired format (e.g., long date and short time). This allows us to dynamically adapt the display of dates and times based on cultural and regional norms. For instance, the US locale uses a *Month Day, Year* format, while the German locale follows a *Day. Month Year* convention. Similarly, Arabic and Hebrew locales provide full localization, including the use of RTL text direction for proper alignment and intuitive reading in those languages.

One subtle point about the input: the new `DateTime('2025-01-01 00:00:00')` constructor receives no explicit timezone, so PHP uses the server's default (`date_default_timezone_get()`). For this single-server demo that's fine, but production code that runs across regions — multi-region cloud deployments, containers, batch jobs that move between hosts — should pass a `DateTimeZone` so the same source line yields the same instant in time everywhere. UTC is the conventional default for storage; convert to the user's timezone only at display time, the same way you'd convert numbers to a display format.

As demonstrated in the numeric and currency examples, this file also includes an RTL example for languages such as Arabic and Hebrew. Here, we've not only formatted the date and time according to the respective locales but also applied RTL styling through HTML and CSS. This ensures that the output aligns correctly for RTL languages, providing an authentic and accessible user experience. The ability to customize and internationalize content with such precision highlights the robustness of PHP's `IntlDateFormatter` class in handling globalized applications effectively. Now, if you visit the URL `http://localhost:8888/src/Chapter08/ch08_locale_datetime.php`, you should see a list of date times in different formats:

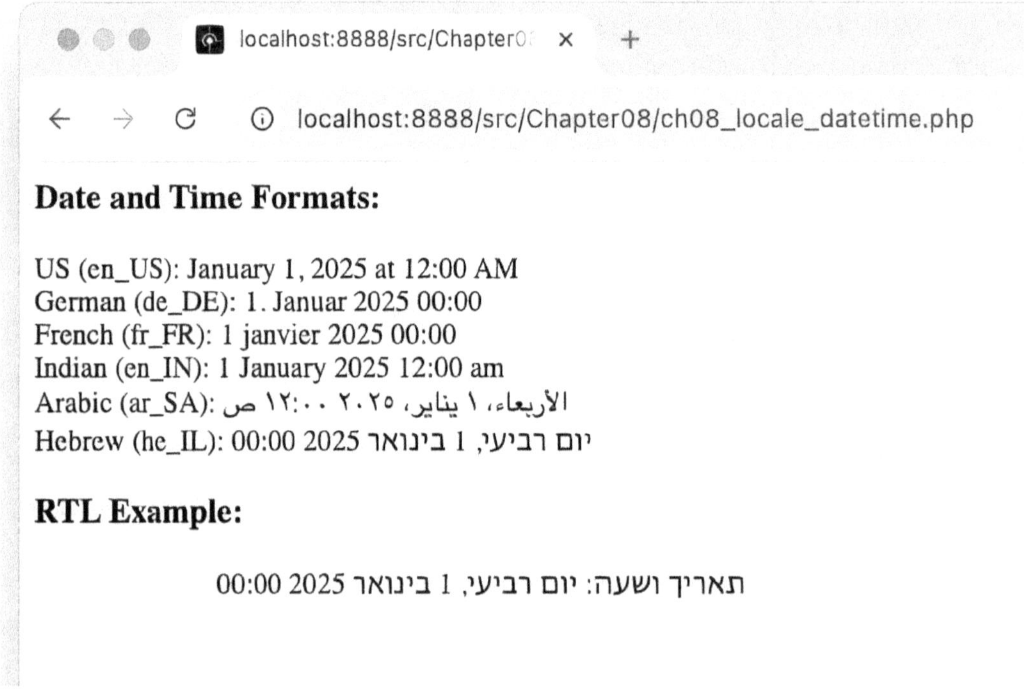

Figure 8.7 – Date time locale-based formats

As shown in the preceding screenshot, we have taken a single starting date, ``2025-01-01 00:00:00``, and dynamically converted it into various locale-based formats to demonstrate how date and time formatting can adapt to cultural and regional conventions. By utilizing PHP's `IntlDateFormatter` class, each locale's specific rules for date and time representation have been applied seamlessly. For instance, the US locale (`` en_US ``) displays the date in the **January 1, 2025** format with a 12-hour clock style, while the German locale (`` de_DE ``) adopts the **01. January 2025** format with a 24-hour clock. Similarly, the Arabic locale (`` ar_SA ``) not only uses a full textual representation of the day and month but also aligns the content RTL and includes Arabic-Indic numerals for time representation. This approach highlights the versatility of the `IntlDateFormatter` class in transforming a single date into formats that feel natural and familiar to users from diverse linguistic and cultural backgrounds, ensuring a localized and user-friendly experience.

Working with `str*` family differences on international websites

When handling non-ASCII characters and multilingual content in PHP, it's important to recognize the potential discrepancies between the expected results and the actual behavior of the `str*` family of functions. These functions, as their names suggest, are designed for basic string operations. However, their implementation is optimized for single-byte encodings, such as ASCII, and they often produce results that differ from expectations when applied to multibyte encodings like UTF-8, which is widely used for supporting international characters.

Getting ready

Take the `strlen` function as an example. From its name, one might reasonably assume that it returns the number of characters in the given string (string length). While this is true for single-byte encodings, such as ASCII, it does not hold for UTF-8 strings. Instead of counting the actual characters, `strlen` counts the number of bytes, which can result in misleading outputs for multibyte characters. For instance, a UTF-8 encoded string containing Arabic, Chinese, or emoji characters may have a visual length of 5 characters but could be represented internally as 10 or more bytes, leading strlen to report the latter.

This behavior arises because functions like `strlen` were originally designed for older, single-byte character encodings where the number of bytes and characters was always identical. With the advent of UTF-8 and its ability to represent characters using 1 to 4 bytes, such assumptions no longer hold. To accurately handle multibyte strings, PHP provides the `mb_*` family of functions, such as `mb_strlen`, which correctly calculates the character count by recognizing and respecting the encoding.

How to do it...

1. Create a new file called `ch08_str_functions.php` with the following content:

   `src/Chapter08/ch08_str_functions.php`

```
<?php
// UTF-8 strings
echo "=== Using strlen and mb_strlen ===\n";
$hebrewString = 'שָׁלוֹם';
echo "Source - Hebrew: $hebrewString\n";
echo "Single-byte strlen: " . strlen($hebrewString) . "\n";
```

```
echo "Multi-byte mb_strlen: " . mb_strlen($hebrewString, "UTF-8") . "\n";

echo "\n=== Using substr and mb_substr ===\n";
$germanString = "Ä Ö Ü ß";
echo "Source - German: $germanString\n";
echo "Single-byte substr: " . substr($germanString, 0, 3) . "\n";
echo "Multi-byte mb_substr: " . mb_substr($germanString, 0, 3, "UTF-8") .
"\n";

echo "\n=== Using strpos and mb_strpos ===\n";
$polishString = "Ą Ć Ł Ó Ś Ż";
$needle = "Ć";
echo "Source - Polish: $polishString\n";
echo "Single-byte strpos: " . strpos($polishString, $needle) . "\n";
echo "Multi-byte mb_strpos: " . mb_strpos($polishString, $needle, 0,
"UTF-8") . "\n";

echo "\n=== Using strtolower and mb_strtolower ===\n";
$spanishUpper = "Á É Í Ñ Ó Ú";
echo "Source - Spanish: $spanishUpper\n";
echo "Single-byte strtolower: " . strtolower($spanishUpper) . "\n";
echo "Multi-byte mb_strtolower: " . mb_strtolower($spanishUpper,
"UTF-8") . "\n";
```

How it works...

In the code we created, we have used `strlen`, `substr`, `strpos`, `strtolower` along with their `mb_*` counterparts. Each of the single and multibyte example pairs uses the same source string, yet will return different results. To see the results, using your terminal, run the following command:

```
$ php src/Chapter08/ch08_str_functions.php
=== Using strlen and mb_strlen ===
Source - Hebrew: שָׁלוֹם
Single-byte strlen: 14
Multi-byte mb_strlen: 7

=== Using substr and mb_substr ===
Source - German: Ä Ö Ü ß
Single-byte substr: Ä
Multi-byte mb_substr: Ä Ö
```

```
=== Using strpos and mb_strpos ===
Source - Polish: Ą Ć Ł Ó Ś Ż
Single-byte strpos: 3
Multi-byte mb_strpos: 2

=== Using strtolower and mb_strtolower ===
Source - Spanish: Á É Í Ñ Ó Ú
Single-byte strtolower: Á É Í Ñ Ó Ú
Multi-byte mb_strtolower: á é í ñ ó ú
```

The results of the provided PHP file clearly illustrate the differences between single-byte and multibyte string functions when working with UTF-8 encoded strings from various languages. For example, in the Hebrew string שָׁלוֹם (meaning *peace*), the `strlen` function counts the bytes and returns an unexpectedly high number because each Hebrew character occupies multiple bytes in UTF-8. In contrast, `mb_strlen` processes the string at the character level, accurately reporting the number of characters in the string. Similarly, in the German string Ä Ö Ü ß, extracting a substring using `substr` produces an incomplete result because the function operates at the byte level, potentially cutting through multibyte sequences. On the other hand, `mb_substr` correctly retrieves the first three characters, accounting for the multibyte nature of the string.

When locating a character in the Polish string Ą Ć Ł Ó Ś Ż, `strpos` fails to correctly find the position of Ć because it searches byte-by-byte, misinterpreting the multibyte structure. On the other hand, `mb_strpos` correctly identifies the character's position within the string. Finally, with the Spanish uppercase string Á É Í Ñ Ó Ú, `strtolower` has no effect on the accented characters since it isn't designed for multibyte encodings. Conversely, `mb_strtolower` successfully converts all the characters to their lowercase equivalents, such as á é í ñ ó ú. These examples underscore the importance of using the `mb_*` functions when working with UTF-8 encoded strings, as they ensure proper handling of multilingual content and preserve the integrity of the characters in internationalized applications.

Handling translations without Gettext

PHP Gettext offers significant advantages for managing translations in web applications, providing a structured, and efficient way to handle internationalization through `` `.po` `` and `` `.mo` `` files. It simplifies the process of separating application logic from translatable content, making it easier to support multiple languages. However, despite these benefits, PHP Gettext has notable drawbacks, particularly when it comes to deployment and server compatibility.

One of its major challenges is its reliance on the system's locale configuration. To function correctly, PHP Gettext requires the appropriate locales to be installed and properly configured on the server. This dependency introduces complexity, as every deployment environment (e.g., development, staging, production) must be configured to support the necessary locales for your application.

PHP Gettext can be difficult to use on some hosting providers—especially shared hosting—because it depends on system locales being installed and configured correctly. If a required locale is missing, translations may fail and show fallback text. This lack of portability makes Gettext harder to maintain across different environments, highlighting the need to consider more flexible alternatives like JSON files, PHP arrays, or database-driven translations.

Getting ready

A very simple and portable way of implementing a translation system in your PHP application would be the utilization of JSON files. Obviously, you can also do this with a PHP Array if you want, or even with a database. They all follow the same concept. If you can create a JSON-based translation system, it's going to be easy to replace this with a DB connection as well.

How to do it...

1. Let's first create some example translation files. Create the following JSON files with the following content:

   `src/Chapter08/Translations/en.json`

```
{
    "greeting": "Hello",
    "howAreYou": "How are you?"
}
```

   `src/Chapter08/Translations/he.json`

```
{
    "greeting": "שלום",
    "howAreYou": "מה שלומך?"
}
```

   `src/Chapter08/Translations/fr.json`

```
{
    "greeting": "Bonjour",
```

```
    "howAreYou": "Comment ça va?"
}
```

2. Next, create a new PHP file named `Translator.php` which will contain the PHP class code:
   `src/Chapter08/Translations/Translator.php`

```
<?php

namespace Cookbook\Chapter08\Translations;

class Translator
{
    public function loadTranslations(LanguageCode $language, $extension =
".json"): array
    {
        $file = "./translations/{$language->value}.json";
        if (!file_exists($file)) {
            $file = "./src/Chapter08/Translations/" .
LanguageCode::EN>value . $extension;
        }

        return json_decode(file_get_contents($file), true) ?: [];
    }

    public function translate(string $key, array $translations): string
    {
        return $translations[$key] ?? "[$key]";
    }
}
```

3. The preceding `Translator` class has two simple public functions: one to load the translation JSON file, and another function to do the actual translation. Also, create a new enum called `LanguageCode.php`:

```
<?php

namespace Cookbook\Chapter08\Translations;

enum LanguageCode: string
```

```
{
    case EN = 'en'; // English
    case DE = 'de'; // German
    case FR = 'fr'; // French
}
```

Enumerations were finally introduced in PHP, back when 8.1 was released. Using enums like `` `LanguageCode` `` in PHP provides type safety, ensuring only predefined values (e.g., `` `'en'` ``, `` `'de'` ``, `` `'fr'` ``) are used, reducing the risk of errors caused by invalid values. They improve readability and maintainability by clearly defining and grouping related constants in a single, self-documenting structure. Enums also enable code consistency and allow leveraging modern PHP features, such as methods and strict type enforcement, making it easier to extend or refactor the code.

4. Next, create the consumer PHP file named `ch08_translation.php` with the following content:
   `src/Chapter08/ch08_translation.php`

```
<?php

use Cookbook\Chapter08\Translations\Translator;
use Cookbook\Chapter08\Translations\LanguageCode;

include __DIR__ . '/../../vendor/autoload.php';

$languageParam = $_GET['lang'] ?? 'en';
$translator = new Translator();
try {
    $language = LanguageCode::from($languageParam);
} catch (ValueError $e) {
    $language = LanguageCode::EN;
} finally {
    $translations = $translator->loadTranslations($language);
}

echo "<!DOCTYPE html>
<html lang='{$language->value}'>
<head>
    <meta charset='UTF-8'>
    <meta name='viewport' content='width=device-width, initial-scale=1.0'>
```

```
        <title>Translations Example</title>
    </head>
    <body>
        <p>Language code: ". $language->value . "</p>
        <p>" . $translator->translate('greeting', $translations) . "</p>
        <p>" . $translator->translate('howAreYou', $translations) . "</p>
    </body>
    </html>";
```

How it works...

In the code above, the `$languageParam` variable is used to capture the `lang` query string from the URL, defaulting to `'en'` if no value is provided. This ensures that a language preference can be dynamically set by the user while also providing a fallback to English when no preference is specified. The query parameter value is then passed to the `LanguageCode` enum, where it is validated to match one of the predefined language codes.

If the provided `lang` value is invalid or not part of the enum, a `ValueError` is caught, and the language is safely set to the default English (`LanguageCode::EN`). After determining the correct language code, the `Translator` class is used to load the corresponding language's JSON file containing all translations. This step ensures the application has the appropriate translations ready for use.

Finally, the `translate` method of the `Translator` class is called to fetch language-specific translations for keys such as `greeting` and `howAreYou`. These translations are then dynamically displayed in the HTML output, alongside the language code being used. This setup allows the application to render content tailored to the user's language preferences seamlessly. If you visit the following URL from your browser, note the lang query string: `http://localhost:8888/src/Chapter08/ch08_translation.php?lang=fr`.

You should see the following result:

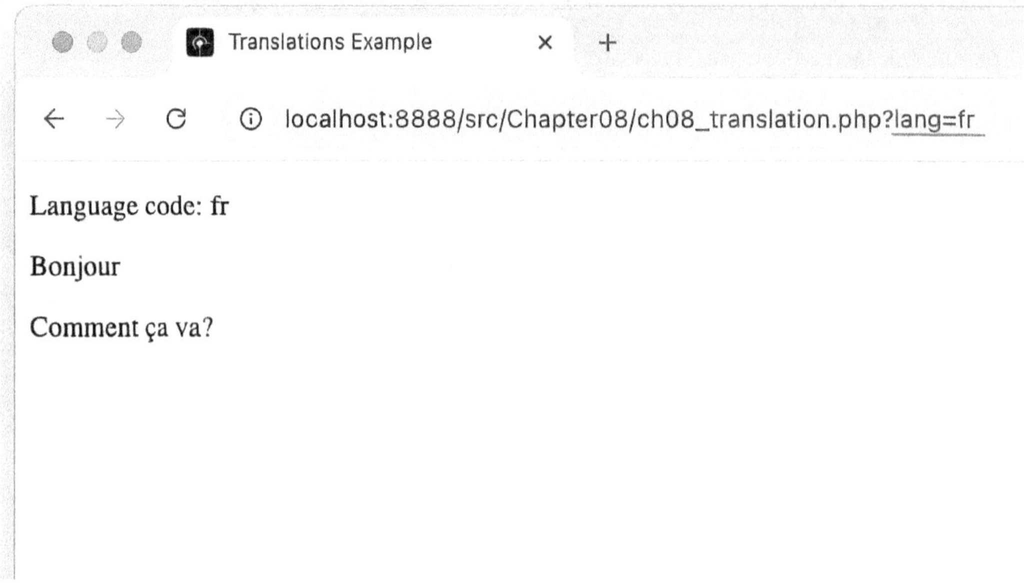

Figure 8.8 – JSON-based translation

As shown in the screenshot, the webpage displays French words such as *Bonjour* and *Comment ça va?* which were dynamically fetched from the `fr.json` translation file. This behavior occurred because the `?lang=fr` query string was included in the URL, prompting the program to load the corresponding French translations. The application detected the `fr` parameter, validated it against the predefined language codes in the `LanguageCode` enum, and successfully matched it to load the French JSON file.

This dynamic functionality highlights the flexibility of the system, as it allows users to switch between languages effortlessly by simply modifying the query string in the URL. Behind the scenes, the `Translator` class handled the process of reading the JSON file, and its `translate` method ensured that the appropriate translations were displayed on the webpage. By structuring the translations in this way, the program provides a robust and scalable solution for supporting multilingual content, offering a seamless experience for users interacting with the application in their preferred language.

The JSON files in this setup serve as a simple and efficient storage mechanism for managing translation data. They are lightweight, human-readable, and easily editable, making them a great choice for projects that don't require dynamic updates to translations. Each JSON file corresponds to a specific language and contains key-value pairs that map translatable terms to their localized equivalents. However, this approach is flexible, and the storage mechanism can be replaced with other options depending on the needs of your application.

For instance, instead of using JSON files, you could store the translations in a database. This would allow for dynamic management of translations, enabling you to update or add new translations without needing to redeploy the application. Alternatively, translations could be fetched from an API, which would centralize the management of translation data and allow seamless integration with other services or platforms. For simpler use cases or offline scenarios, you could even use plain text files or PHP arrays as the storage mechanism. The key takeaway is that the `` `Translator` `` class abstracts the retrieval of translation data, so the underlying storage format can be easily swapped out to suit your project's requirements without requiring changes to the rest of your code.

9

Implementing Test-Driven Development in a Feature

In this chapter, you will learn how to protect a feature by applying **test-driven development** (**TDD**) practices in PHP. The chapter is organized as a series of practical recipes that guide you through defining user acceptance criteria using the Gherkin language, generating intentionally failing automated tests with the assistance of AI, and incrementally building the solution code required to satisfy those tests. By following this workflow and validating the implementation by passing all tests, you ensure that the feature remains stable, verifiable, and aligned with the acceptance criteria throughout its lifecycle.

This chapter features the following recipes:

- User acceptance criteria definition through Gherkin
- Generating intentionally failing automated tests through AI
- Building solution code
- Scaling for complex behaviors
- Building on top of the solution without breaking existing code

User acceptance criteria definition through AI and Gherkin

Gherkin is a very easy to digest language used in **Behavior Driven Development** (**BDD**). It is widely used across different programming languages to help users develop software with clearly defined acceptance criteria. In this section, we will use AI to create a Gherkin feature.

Getting ready

In software development, the goal is to build solutions that address specific problems. Before writing any implementation code, it is therefore essential to clearly define what the solution is expected to accomplish and to describe the behavior the user anticipates. In BDD, this behavior is captured in a shared, structured format that serves as the foundation for both discussion and implementation.

How to do it...

1. We define the behavior we expect in plain English, something like: `"In a simple web page, I want to be able to enter two numbers, and when I select the + operator and clicked submit, I want to get the sum of both numbers"`
2. Next, you can just put this sentence into Claude and ask it to create a Gherkin syntax for you, and the result can be something like:

```
Feature: Simple calculator
As a user
I want to add two numbers So that I can see their sum
Scenario: Add two numbers using the plus operator Given I am on the
calculator page
And I have entered "5" into the first number field
And I have entered "3" into the second number field And I have selected the
"+" operator
When I submit the form
Then I should see "8" displayed as the result
```

Now you can save this plain English Gherkin feature in a file called `simple_calculator.feature`.

How it works...

In a PHP application, the Gherkin scenario serves as an executable specification that defines the expected behavior from the user's perspective. Each step in the scenario is mapped to PHP step definitions, commonly implemented using a BDD framework such as Behat.

The `Given` steps prepare the application state, the `When` step performs an action (submitting the form), and the `Then` step verifies the outcome (displaying the correct sum). Initially, these tests fail, guiding the incremental implementation of the feature.

The PHP application processes the form submission, performs the calculation through a dedicated handler or service, and renders the result back to the user. Once all steps pass, the behavior is verified and protected by automated tests.

By using Gherkin-driven development, the application remains aligned with user expectations while ensuring long-term stability and maintainability.

Generating intentionally failing automated tests through AI

At the core of TDD is the principle that tests are written before the implementation code. Each test is intentionally created in a failing state, as no solution code exists yet to satisfy its expectations. This deliberate failure establishes a clear development target. To streamline the creation of these initial tests, the Gherkin feature defined in the previous section can be used as input to generate corresponding failing PHP tests, providing a direct and traceable link between specified behavior and test coverage.

How to do it...

1. Depending on your IDE, you can easily generate PHP code based on the gherkin feature file we created earlier, or simply paste it into Claude (via the Claude desktop app, Claude.ai, or Claude Code in your terminal), and in the prompt ask it to do the following: `"Create a failing base PHPUnit test file using this simple_calculator.feature file"`
2. It should set up PHPUnit for you if it's not there already, but more importantly, to stay focused on this specific task, it should create a failing PHPUnit test for you: `src/Chapter09/test/SimpleCalculatorTest.php`

```
<?php
declare(strict_types=1);
use PHPUnit\Framework\TestCase;
/**
 * @see simple_calculator.feature
 */
final class SimpleCalculatorTest extends TestCase
{
/**
* Scenario: Add two numbers using the plus operator *
* @link simple_calculator.feature:8
*/
    public function test_add_two_numbers_using_plus_operator():
```

```
void
{
// Given I have entered "5" into the first number field // And I have
entered "3" into the second number field // And I have selected the "+"
operator
// When I submit the form
// Then I should see "8" displayed as the result
$this->fail("Test not implemented: implement calculator or business logic
to make this pass.");
}
}
```

3. Next, run the test either on your IDE environment or on your CLI by simply running the `PHPUnit` command:

```
$ ./vendor/bin/phpunit --testdox src/Chapter09/test
```

It should give you the following error:

```
There was 1 failure:

1) SimpleCalculatorTest::test_add_two_numbers_using_plus_operator
Test not implemented: implement calculator or business logic to make this
pass.

/path/to/tests/SimpleCalculatorTest.php:20

FAILURES!
Tests: 1, Assertions: 1, Failures: 1.
```

How it works...

As shown, we now have an intentionally failing PHPUnit test derived from the acceptance criteria defined earlier. The PHP test file references the previously created Gherkin feature file using a PHPDoc @see annotation, establishing a clear link between the executable test and its corresponding behavioral specification.

In the next section, we will implement an extensible solution code to pass the test and also to enable adding more features easily on top of it.

Building solution code

All software is written to satisfy specific criteria. In the previous section, these criteria were formalized in a Gherkin feature file and expressed as a failing PHPUnit test. This provides a clear and reliable foundation that guides the implementation of the feature.

With the failing test defining the expected behavior, development can now focus on writing only the solution code necessary to make the test pass. When the test passes, it confirms that the implementation meets the defined acceptance criteria and fulfills the original intent behind the feature.

How to do it...

1. Since we are using a simple calculator as an example, and from our first feature definition we only want to do an addition operation, we might as well create the foundation for the calculator solution to be able to support a few more operations in the future.
2. Create the Interface for the calculator called `SimpleCalculatorInterface`:
   `src/Chapter09/SimpleCalculatorInterface.php`

```php
<?php
declare(strict_types=1);
namespace Cookbook\Chapter09;
interface SimpleCalculatorInterface
{
    public function calculate(
        float $firstNumber,
        float $secondNumber,
        CalculatorOperation $operation
): float; }
```

3. Next, create a concrete implementation of the `SimpleCalculatorInterface`, along with other classes necessary:
   `CalculatorOperation.php`

```php
<?php
declare(strict_types=1);
namespace Cookbook\Chapter09;
enum CalculatorOperation: string
{
```

```
    case ADD = '+';
    case SUBTRACT = '-';
    case MULTIPLY = '*';
    case DIVIDE = '/';
}
```

`SimpleCalculator.php`

```
<?php
namespace Cookbook\Chapter09;
use InvalidArgumentException;

final class SimpleCalculator implements SimpleCalculatorInterface
{
    public function calculate(
        float $firstNumber,
        float $secondNumber,
        CalculatorOperation $operation
    ): float {
        return match ($operation) {
            CalculatorOperation::ADD => $firstNumber +
                $secondNumber,
            default => throw new InvalidArgumentException(
                sprintf(
                    'Operation "%s" is not yet supported.',
                    $operation->value
                )
            ),
        };
    }
}
```

How it works...

At this stage, the calculator feature is implemented by defining a clear contract and a minimal concrete implementation that satisfies the current acceptance criteria. The `SimpleCalculatorInterface` describes what the calculator must do without prescribing how it does it. The concrete `SimpleCalculator` class then provides the actual behavior, implementing only the addition operation required by the existing Gherkin scenario. This approach keeps the implementation focused and ensures that the code evolves strictly in response to validated requirements.

The interface plays a key role in test-driven and behavior-driven development. By programming against an interface, tests and consuming code depend on a stable abstraction rather than a specific implementation. This improves testability, encourages separation of concerns, and allows the implementation to change or expand without impacting the rest of the system. As new behaviors are introduced through additional Gherkin scenarios, the interface remains the guiding contract that ensures consistency across implementations.

Enums are used to represent calculator operations in a type-safe and explicit manner. Instead of relying on loosely defined strings, enums restrict input to a known set of valid operations, reducing runtime errors, and improving code clarity. They also make the supported behaviors self-documenting and easier to extend. As new operations are added, they can be introduced incrementally through new enum cases, with the compiler helping to identify any missing implementations.

Scaling for complex behaviors

To prepare our test suite and overall solution for larger-scale projects, we will utilize Behat in combination with Gherkin. Behat is a BDD framework for PHP that encourages collaboration between developers, testers, and non-technical stakeholders by expressing application behavior in a clear, human-readable format.

Using Gherkin syntax, requirements are written as executable specifications that describe how the system should behave from the user's perspective. These scenarios are then mapped to PHP step definitions, allowing tests to be automated while remaining easy to understand and maintain.

By adopting Behat with PHP 8, we ensure our testing approach is scalable, readable, and aligned with modern PHP standards. This approach improves test coverage, reduces ambiguity in requirements, and supports long-term maintainability as the codebase and team grow.

How to do it...

1. First thing to do is install Behat in the project; you can easily do this by using composer:

```
composer require --dev behat/behat
```

2. Next, follow the directory structure for `Chapter09`:

```
├── src
│   ├── CalculatorOperation.php
│   ├── SimpleCalculator.php
│   └── SimpleCalculatorInterface.php
└── test
```

```
    ├── Features
    │   ├── Bootstrap
    │   │   └── FeatureContext.php
    │   └── simple_calculator.feature
    └── SimpleCalculatorTest.php
```

3. In the root directory of the project, create a new file called `behat.yml` with the following content:

```
default:
  suites:
    default:
      paths:
        - src/Chapter09/test/Features
      contexts:
        - Cookbook\Chapter09\test\Features\Bootstrap\FeatureContext
```

4. Initialize behat. It will generate new files for you in the root directory, then move them to the `Chapter09` directory:

```
$ vendor/bin/behat --init
mv features/bootstrap/FeatureContext.php src/Chapter09/test/features/
bootstrap/
```

5. Behat will create a file called `FeatureContext.php` with the following code:

```
<?php

namespace Cookbook\Chapter09\test\Features\Bootstrap;

use Behat\Behat\Context\Context;

/**
 * Defines application features from the specific context.
 */
class FeatureContext implements Context
{
    /**
     * Initializes context.
     *
```

```
         * Every scenario gets its own context instance.
         * You can also pass arbitrary arguments to the
         * context constructor through behat.yml.
         */
        public function __construct()
        {
        }
    }
```

6. Now we can run behat and check the results:

```
$ vendor/bin/behat --config=behat.yml
Feature: Simple calculator
  As a user
  I want to add two numbers So that I can see their sum

  Scenario: Add two numbers using the plus operator Given I am on the
calculator page        # src/Chapter09/test/features/
simple_calculator.feature:4
    And I have entered "5" into the first number field
    And I have entered "3" into the second number field And I have selected
the "+" operator
    When I submit the form
    Then I should see "8" displayed as the result

1 scenario (1 undefined)
4 steps (4 undefined)
0m0.01s (10.47Mb)
```

7. Since we haven't created any functions or code inside the `FeatureContext.php` class, behat will suggest through the CLI to create those functions:

```
--- Cookbook\Chapter09\test\Features\Bootstrap\FeatureContext has missing
steps. Define them with these snippets:

    #[Given('I have entered :arg1 into the first number field')]
    public function iHaveEnteredIntoTheFirstNumberField($arg1): void
    {
        throw new PendingException();
    }
```

```
    #[Given('I have entered :arg1 into the second number field And I have
selected the :arg2 operator')]
    public function
iHaveEnteredIntoTheSecondNumberFieldAndIHaveSelectedTheOperator($arg1,
$arg2): void
    {
        throw new PendingException();
    }

    #[When('I submit the form')]
    public function iSubmitTheForm(): void
    {
        throw new PendingException();
    }

    #[Then('I should see :arg1 displayed as the result')]
    public function iShouldSeeDisplayedAsTheResult($arg1): void
    {
        throw new PendingException();
    }

--- Don't forget these 4 use statements:

    use Behat\Behat\Tester\Exception\PendingException;
    use Behat\Step\Given;
    use Behat\Step\When;
    use Behat\Step\Then;
```

8. You can literally just copy-paste this into the `FeatureContext.php` class, and then add the logic to instantiate the `SimpleCalculator` class we created earlier, and update the test methods. Update the `FeatureContext.php` class to the following:

```
<?php

namespace Cookbook\Chapter09\test\Features\Bootstrap;

use Behat\Behat\Context\Context;
use Cookbook\Chapter09\src\CalculatorOperation;
use Cookbook\Chapter09\src\SimpleCalculator;
use Behat\Step\Given;
```

```
use Behat\Step\When;
use Behat\Step\Then;
use Cookbook\Chapter09\src\SimpleCalculatorInterface;

/**
 * Defines application features from the specific context.
 */
class FeatureContext implements Context
{
    private int $firstNumber;
    private int $secondNumber;
    private string $operator;
    private ?int $result = null;
    private SimpleCalculatorInterface $calculator;

    /**
     * Initializes context.
     */
    public function __construct()
    {
        $this->calculator = new SimpleCalculator();
    }

    #[Given('I have entered :arg1 into the first number field')]
    public function iHaveEnteredIntoTheFirstNumberField($arg1): void
    {
        $this->firstNumber = (int) $arg1;
    }

    #[Given('I have entered :arg1 into the second number field And I have
selected the :arg2 operator')]
    public function
iHaveEnteredIntoTheSecondNumberFieldAndIHaveSelectedTheOperator($arg1,
$arg2): void
    {
        $this->secondNumber = (int) $arg1;
        $this->operator = $arg2;
    }

    #[When('I submit the form')]
    public function iSubmitTheForm(): void
```

```
    {
        if ($this->operator === '+') {
            $this->result = $this->calculator->calculate(
                $this->firstNumber,
                $this->secondNumber, CalculatorOperation::ADD
            );
        }
    }

    #[Then('I should see :arg1 displayed as the result')]
    public function iShouldSeeDisplayedAsTheResult($arg1): void
    {
        if ((int) $arg1 !== $this->result) {
            throw new \RuntimeException(
                sprintf('Expected result is %d, but got %d', $arg1, $this-
>result)
            );
        }
    }
}
```

9. Run the behat test again, and you should see the following result:

```
$ vendor/bin/behat --format=pretty
Feature: Simple calculator
  As a user
  I want to add two numbers So that I can see their sum

  Scenario: Add two numbers using the plus operator Given I am on the
calculator page        # src/Chapter09/test/features/
simple_calculator.feature:4
    And I have entered "5" into the first number
field                                        #
Cookbook\Chapter09\test\Features\Bootstrap\FeatureContext::iHaveEnteredInto
TheFirstNumberField()
    And I have entered "3" into the second number field And I have selected
the "+" operator #
Cookbook\Chapter09\test\Features\Bootstrap\FeatureContext::iHaveEnteredInto
TheSecondNumberFieldAndIHaveSelectedTheOperator()
    When I submit the
form                                                                      #
```

```
Cookbook\Chapter09\test\Features\Bootstrap\FeatureContext::iSubmitTheForm()
    Then I should see "8" displayed as the
result                                                  #
Cookbook\Chapter09\test\Features\Bootstrap\FeatureContext::iShouldSeeDispla
yedAsTheResult()

1 scenario (1 passed)
4 steps (4 passed)
0m0.01s (10.60Mb)
```

How it works...

As you can see, our test suite now successfully picks up the `simple_calculator.feature` file, runs it through Behat, and executes the scenario end to end. The feature describes the expected behavior in a clear, human-readable format:

```
Feature: Simple calculator
  As a user
  I want to add two numbers So that I can see their sum
  Scenario: Add two numbers using the plus operator Given I am on the calculator
page
    And I have entered "5" into the first number field
    And I have entered "3" into the second number field And I have selected the
"+" operator
    When I submit the form
    Then I should see "8" displayed as the result
```

Behat discovers this feature file, parses each step, and matches every `Given`, `When`, and `Then` statement to a corresponding PHP step definition. Any values defined directly in the feature file —such as `"5"`, `"3"`, `"+"`, and `"8"`—are extracted by Behat and passed as arguments into the PHP methods that implement those steps. This allows the feature file to remain expressive and declarative, while the PHP code focuses on execution and assertions.

A good example of this is how Behat captures values directly from the Gherkin step and injects them into the step definition. The following step definition matches both entering the second number and selecting the operator and receives those values as method arguments:

```
#[Given('I have entered :arg1 into the second number field And I have selected
the :arg2 operator')]
public function
iHaveEnteredIntoTheSecondNumberFieldAndIHaveSelectedTheOperator($arg1, $arg2):
```

```
void
{
    $this->secondNumber = (int) $arg1;
    $this->operator = $arg2;
}
```

Here, the placeholders defined in the step (`:arg1` and `:arg2`) are populated directly from the feature file. When Behat executes the scenario, the values `"3"` and `"+"` are passed into the method automatically, allowing the context to store them as state for later steps. This demonstrates how Behat bridges the gap between human-readable behavior definitions and executable PHP code.

That state is then used when the scenario reaches the *When I submit the form* step, which maps to the following PHP method:

```
#[When('I submit the form')]
public function iSubmitTheForm(): void
{
    if ($this->operator === '+') {
        $this->result = $this->calculator->calculate(
            $this->firstNumber,
            $this->secondNumber,
            CalculatorOperation::ADD
        );
    }
}
```

By the time this method is executed, all required inputs have already been provided by earlier steps and populated from the feature file. The step definition simply translates the high-level user action into a concrete operation on the calculator, delegating the actual calculation to the domain logic.

Because the calculator implementation is now complete, all steps execute successfully and the scenario passes. This confirms that the system behaves exactly as described by the feature, and that the PHP code correctly consumes the inputs defined in the Gherkin file to produce the expected result. Rather than testing internal implementation details, we are validating behavior from the user's perspective.

Although this may seem overcomplicated for a simple calculator example, the value of this approach becomes clear as projects grow in size and complexity. By capturing behaviors in Gherkin and enforcing them with Behat, we create a living specification that both documents and protects the system, giving us confidence to refactor, extend, and evolve the codebase without breaking existing behavior.

Building on top of the solution without breaking existing code

One of the most important aspects of building large-scale applications is ensuring long-term maintainability and extensibility. As a codebase grows, it must remain possible to introduce new features and evolve existing ones without unintentionally breaking what already works. This requires discipline, structure, and reliable feedback mechanisms throughout the development process.

One of the most effective mechanisms for achieving this is test automation. By protecting the codebase with automated tests, we gain continuous feedback on the impact of our changes and reduce the risk of regressions. Behavior-driven tests provide even more value, as they describe the system in terms of observable behavior rather than internal implementation details. This makes them easier to reason about, easier to maintain, and easier to align with real-world use cases as the system evolves.

In the previous section, we introduced a behavior-driven test that covers a simple addition operation. In this section, we will build on top of that foundation by completing the addition feature and extending the calculator with new capabilities such as multiplication and other operations. Throughout this process, the existing scenarios will remain unchanged and will continue to act as a safety net, ensuring that new functionality is added without unintentionally breaking existing behavior.

How to do it...

1. As with the core of test-driven development, if we want to add a new feature to the software, we will need to create the test first, which in turn will drive our development. Start with the feature test file, add the following scenario to our existing `simple_calculator.feature`:

```
Feature: Simple calculator
  As a user
  I want to add two numbers So that I can see their sum
  Scenario: Add two numbers using the plus operator Given I am on the
calculator page
    And I have entered "5" into the first number field
    And I have entered "3" into the second number field And I have selected
the "+" operator
```

```
    When I submit the form
    Then I should see "8" displayed as the result

  Scenario: Multiply two numbers using the multiplication operator
    Given I am on the calculator page
    And I have entered "6" into the first number field
    And I have entered "4" into the second number field
    And I have selected the "*" operator
    When I submit the form
    Then I should see "24" displayed as the result

  Scenario: Divide two numbers using the division operator
    Given I am on the calculator page
    And I have entered "15" into the first number field
    And I have entered "3" into the second number field
    And I have selected the "/" operator
    When I submit the form
    Then I should see "5" displayed as the result
```

2. Run the test. It will show you that you have two undefined scenarios:

```
vendor/bin/behat --format=pretty
// Redacted
3 scenarios (1 passed, 2 undefined)
16 steps (4 passed, 6 undefined, 6 skipped)
0m0.02s (10.63Mb)
```

3. We should fix those undefined scenarios for multiplication and division operations. Update the `FeatureContext.php` class:

```
<?php

namespace Cookbook\Chapter09\test\Features\Bootstrap;

use Behat\Behat\Context\Context;
use Cookbook\Chapter09\src\CalculatorOperation;
use Cookbook\Chapter09\src\SimpleCalculator;
use Cookbook\Chapter09\src\SimpleCalculatorInterface;
use RuntimeException;
use Behat\Step\Given;
use Behat\Step\When;
```

```
use Behat\Step\Then;

/**
 * Defines application features from the specific context.
 */
class FeatureContext implements Context
{
    private float $firstNumber = 0.0; // Initialize default value
    private float $secondNumber = 0.0; // Initialize default value
    private ?CalculatorOperation $operator = null; // Nullable
CalculatorOperation
    private ?float $result = null; // Result
    private SimpleCalculatorInterface $calculator;

    /**
     * Initializes context with a SimpleCalculator.
     */
    public function __construct()
    {
        $this->calculator = new SimpleCalculator();
    }

    #[Given('I am on the calculator page')]
    public function iAmOnTheCalculatorPage(): void
    {
        // This could be used for UI initialization, no operation needed
for now.
    }

    #[Given('I have entered :arg1 into the first number field')]
    public function iHaveEnteredIntoTheFirstNumberField($arg1): void
    {
        // Convert input to float and save to firstNumber
        $this->firstNumber = (float) $arg1;
    }

    #[Given('I have entered :arg1 into the second number field')]
    public function iHaveEnteredIntoTheSecondNumberField($arg1): void
    {
        // Convert input to float and save to secondNumber
        $this->secondNumber = (float) $arg1;
```

```
    }

    #[Given('I have selected the :arg1 operator')]
    public function iHaveSelectedTheOperator($arg1): void
    {
        // Map the operator to CalculatorOperation enum
        $this->operator = match ($arg1) {
            '+' => CalculatorOperation::ADD,
            '-' => CalculatorOperation::SUBTRACT,
            '*' => CalculatorOperation::MULTIPLY,
            '/' => CalculatorOperation::DIVIDE,
            default => throw new RuntimeException(sprintf('Unsupported
operator "%s".', $arg1)),
        };
    }

    #[Given('I have entered :arg1 into the second number field And I have
selected the :arg2 operator')]
    public function
iHaveEnteredIntoTheSecondNumberFieldAndIHaveSelectedTheOperator($arg1,
$arg2): void
    {
        // Set the second number
        $this->secondNumber = (float) $arg1;

        // Map the operator to CalculatorOperation enum
        $this->operator = match ($arg2) {
            '+' => CalculatorOperation::ADD,
            '-' => CalculatorOperation::SUBTRACT,
            '*' => CalculatorOperation::MULTIPLY,
            '/' => CalculatorOperation::DIVIDE,
            default => throw new RuntimeException(sprintf('Unsupported
operator "%s".', $arg2)),
        };
    }

    #[When('I submit the form')]
    public function iSubmitTheForm(): void
    {
        // Ensure operator is set
        if ($this->operator === null) {
```

```
            throw new RuntimeException('Operator is not set.');
        }

        // Perform the calculation using the SimpleCalculator
        $this->result = $this->calculator->calculate($this->firstNumber,
$this->secondNumber, $this->operator);
    }

    #[Then('I should see :arg1 displayed as the result')]
    public function iShouldSeeDisplayedAsTheResult($arg1): void
    {
        // Convert argument to float for comparison
        $expected = (float) $arg1;

        // Ensure the result is computed
        if ($this->result === null) {
            throw new RuntimeException('The result has not been calculated
yet.');
        }

        // Check if the calculated result matches the expected result
        if (abs($expected - $this->result) > 0.0001) { // Allow minor
floating-point differences
            throw new RuntimeException(
                sprintf('Expected result is %.2f, but got %.2f.',
$expected, $this->result)
            );
        }
    }
}
```

4. If you run the test now, you should see the failing tests (which is good):

```
3 scenarios (2 failed, 1 undefined)
16 steps (9 passed, 2 failed, 1 undefined, 4 skipped)
```

5. Now that we have failing tests, we can start to work on the solution code so we can pass those tests. Update the `SimpleCalculator` class so we can support both the multiplication and division scenarios:

```
<?php

namespace Cookbook\Chapter09\src;

use InvalidArgumentException;

final class SimpleCalculator implements SimpleCalculatorInterface
{
    public function calculate(
        float $firstNumber,
        float $secondNumber,
        CalculatorOperation $operation
    ): float {
        return match ($operation) {
            CalculatorOperation::ADD => $firstNumber + $secondNumber,
            CalculatorOperation::MULTIPLY => $firstNumber * $secondNumber,
            CalculatorOperation::DIVIDE => $this-
>handleDivision($firstNumber, $secondNumber),
            default => throw new InvalidArgumentException(
                sprintf(
                    'Operation "%s" is not yet supported.',
                    $operation->value
                )
            ),
        };
    }

    private function handleDivision(float $firstNumber, float
$secondNumber): float
    {
        if ($secondNumber === 0.0) {
            throw new InvalidArgumentException('Division by zero is not
allowed.');
        }

        return $firstNumber / $secondNumber;
```

```
    }
}
```

6. Run the test again, and we should now pass all the test scenarios:

```
vendor/bin/behat --format=pretty
Feature: Simple calculator
  As a user
  I want to add two numbers So that I can see their sum

  Scenario: Add two numbers using the plus operator Given I am on the
calculator page
    And I have entered "5" into the first number
field
    And I have entered "3" into the second number field And I have selected
the "+" operator
    When I submit the
form
    Then I should see "8" displayed as the result

  Scenario: Multiply two numbers using the multiplication operator
    Given I am on the calculator page
    And I have entered "6" into the first number field
    And I have entered "4" into the second number field
    And I have selected the "*" operator
    When I submit the form
    Then I should see "24" displayed as the result

  Scenario: Divide two numbers using the division operator
    Given I am on the calculator page
    And I have entered "15" into the first number field
    And I have entered "3" into the second number field
    And I have selected the "/" operator
    When I submit the form
    Then I should see "5" displayed as the result

3 scenarios (3 passed)
16 steps (16 passed)
0m0.01s (10.61Mb)
```

How it works...

When extending a system using BDD, the workflow closely mirrors the core principles of TDD: we describe the behavior first, then allow that behavior to drive the implementation. In Behat, this starts with the feature file. Instead of modifying existing, working behavior, we extend it by adding new scenarios that describe how the system should behave once new functionality is introduced.

In our case, the `simple_calculator.feature` file already contains a passing scenario for addition. We build on top of that by adding new scenarios for multiplication and division. Each scenario represents a distinct behavior, written from the user's perspective, and Behat treats them as independent executable specifications. The original addition scenario remains untouched and continues to act as a safety net while we extend the calculator.

Once the new scenarios are added, we run Behat. Behat scans the feature files, parses the Gherkin, and attempts to execute each step in order. At this stage, the original addition scenario still passes, but the multiplication and division scenarios are reported as undefined. This does not indicate a bug in the calculator; it simply means that Behat cannot yet find PHP step definitions that match the newly introduced Gherkin steps. The behavior has been described, but the glue code that connects those descriptions to PHP does not yet exist.

To resolve this, we update `FeatureContext.php`, which is responsible for mapping Gherkin steps to executable PHP methods. Each method annotated with `#[Given]`, `#[When]`, or `#[Then]` corresponds to a step that Behat can execute. This is also where Behat extracts values from the feature file and passes them into PHP as method arguments.

For example, the following step definition captures both the second number and the selected operator directly from the Gherkin step:

```
#[Given('I have entered :arg1 into the second number field And I have selected
the :arg2 operator')]
public function
iHaveEnteredIntoTheSecondNumberFieldAndIHaveSelectedTheOperator($arg1, $arg2):
void
{
    $this->secondNumber = (float) $arg1;

    $this->operator = match ($arg2) {
        '+' => CalculatorOperation::ADD,
        '-' => CalculatorOperation::SUBTRACT,
        '*' => CalculatorOperation::MULTIPLY,
        '/' => CalculatorOperation::DIVIDE,
```

```
        default => throw new RuntimeException(sprintf('Unsupported operator 
"%s".', $arg2)),
    };
}
```

Here, Behat extracts values such as "4" and "*" directly from the feature file and injects them into the method as arguments. These values are stored as state inside the context object, making them available to subsequent steps within the same scenario.

When the scenario reaches the action step, Behat executes the corresponding `When` definition:

```
#[When('I submit the form')]
public function iSubmitTheForm(): void
{
    if ($this->operator === null) {
        throw new RuntimeException('Operator is not set.');
    }

    $this->result = $this->calculator->calculate(
        $this->firstNumber,
        $this->secondNumber,
        $this->operator
    );
}
```

At this point, all inputs have already been populated from earlier steps, and the step definition simply translates the high-level user action into a concrete operation on the calculator. Behat does not care how the calculation is implemented internally; it only cares that the behavior defined in the feature file is satisfied.

Once all step definitions are in place, the scenarios are no longer undefined and begin to fail instead. This is an important transition: Behat is now able to execute the behavior end-to-end, but the underlying domain code does not yet fully support the new operations. These failures provide direct feedback on what the implementation is missing.

The final step is to update the `SimpleCalculator` itself to support multiplication and division:

```
return match ($operation) {
    CalculatorOperation::ADD => $firstNumber + $secondNumber,
    CalculatorOperation::MULTIPLY => $firstNumber * $secondNumber,
    CalculatorOperation::DIVIDE => $this->handleDivision($firstNumber, 
$secondNumber),
```

```
    default => throw new InvalidArgumentException(...),
};
```

Once this logic is implemented, running Behat again results in all scenarios passing. This confirms that the new behaviors have been added successfully and, just as importantly, that the original addition behavior continues to work unchanged.

This is where the real value of Behat and BDD becomes clear. Each feature file acts as both documentation and a regression safety net. As new behavior is added, existing scenarios protect what already works, giving us confidence to extend, refactor, and evolve the system without unintentionally breaking established behavior.

10

Looking at Advanced Algorithms

Mastering advanced algorithms is crucial for developers navigating an increasingly competitive field where numerous programmers and companies vie for the same opportunities. This chapter is designed to equip you with a robust understanding of key advanced algorithms using PHP 8, enabling you to distinguish yourself through technical excellence.

In this exploration, you will delve into both the theoretical foundations and practical applications of essential programming constructs, including getters and setters, linked lists, bubble sorts, stacks, binary trees, and binary search. Furthermore, the chapter illustrates the implementation of a search engine and provides strategies for effectively managing multi-dimensional arrays, thereby broadening your skill set and enhancing your competitive edge.

In this chapter, we'll cover the following topics:

- Using **getters** and **setters**
- Implementing a linked list
- Converting your application to a decoupled plugin architecture
- Implementing a stack
- Building a binary search class
- Implementing a search engine
- Displaying a multidimensional array and accumulating totals

Technical requirements

To fully benefit from the content presented in this chapter, it is imperative that your local development environment is correctly configured as outlined in *Chapter 1, Building a Foundation*. Additionally, this chapter presupposes a basic understanding of Object-Oriented

Programming concepts, for which further elaboration is provided in *Chapter 4, Working with PHP Object-Oriented Programming.*

You can download the example project and code for this book by following the instructions in the ***Download the example code files*** section in the *Preface* of this book.

This chapter's code files are included in the downloadable code bundle.

Using getters and setters

Getters and setters, often referred to as **accessors** and **mutators**, are fundamental mechanisms in object-oriented programming that provide controlled access to an object's properties. Getters allow external code to retrieve the value of a private or protected attribute, while setters enable the modification of these attributes. This dual approach ensures that any interaction with an object's state is mediated through clearly defined interfaces, promoting a cleaner and more maintainable code structure.

Encapsulation, one of the core principles of object-oriented programming, revolves around the idea of bundling data and the methods that operate on that data into a single, cohesive unit—a class. This concept emphasizes the importance of hiding an object's internal state and implementation details from the outside world, which is crucial for safeguarding against unintended modifications and misuse. By restricting direct access to an object's properties, encapsulation helps maintain data integrity and encourages the development of robust software systems.

To effectively implement encapsulation, an object's private properties should be accessed and modified solely through getters and setters. This practice not only enforces the boundaries of the object's internal state but also allows developers to incorporate additional logic—such as validation checks or logging—within these methods. As a result, any changes to the internal structure of the class can be made without affecting external code, ensuring that the system remains flexible, secure, and easier to maintain over time. Note that not every property needs a setter — read-only properties (PHP 8.1+), constructor injection, and constructor-only initialization are valid alternatives where immutability is preferred.

Getting ready

To demonstrate the proper usage of getters and setters in PHP 8, we will construct a class that encapsulates several properties along with their associated methods. In this example, properties are declared as private or protected to prevent direct external access, ensuring that internal data remains secure and well-managed.

Public getter and setter methods serve as controlled interfaces for reading and modifying these properties. This approach not only enables the inclusion of additional logic—such as validation or data transformation—within these methods but also reinforces encapsulation, a core principle of object-oriented programming that ultimately enhances the maintainability, security, and adaptability of modern software systems.

How to do it...

1. We'll divide this task into two files. First, the actual PHP class that demonstrates encapsulation. Second, the consumer class that demonstrates the usage of the getters and setters. We start with the Person class, which represents a person and composes an Address class for Australian-specific address validation:

   `src/Chapter10/GettersSetters/Person.php`

```
<?php

namespace Cookbook\Chapter10\GettersSetters;

use Cookbook\Chapter10\GettersSetters\Address;

class Person
{
    // Private Property Declarations
    private string $firstName;
    private string $lastName;
    private int $age;
    private Address $address;

    public function getFirstName(): string
    {
        return $this->firstName;
    }

    public function setFirstName(string $firstName): void
    {
        // Custom Logic in the mutator.
        if ($this->validateName($firstName)) {
            $this->firstName = $firstName;
        }
    }

    public function getLastName(): string
    {
```

```
        return $this->lastName;
    }

    public function setLastName(string $lastName): void
    {
        // Custom Logic in the mutator.
         $this->validateName($lastName); $this->lastName = $lastName;
    }

    public function getAge(): int
    {
        return $this->age;
    }

    public function setAge(int $age): void
    {
        // Custom Logic in the mutator.
        if ($this->validateAge($age)) {
            $this->age = $age;
        }
    }

    public function getAddress(): Address
    {
        return $this->address;
    }

    public function setAddress(Address $address): void
    {
        $this->address = $address;
    }

    private function validateName(string $name): bool
    {
        if (trim($name) === '') {
            throw new \ InvalidArgumentException ("Name string cannot be
empty.");
        }

        if (strlen($name) < 2) {
            throw new \ InvalidArgumentException ("Name should be at least
```

```
2 characters.");
        }

        return true;
    }

    private function validateAge(int $age): bool
    {
        if ($age < 0) {
            throw new \ InvalidArgumentException
("Age cannot be a negative value.");
        }

        return true;
    }
}
```

2. Next, we define the `Address` class, which enforces Australian-specific validation for state, postcode, and other address fields:
`src/Chapter10/GettersSetters/Address.php`

```
<?php

namespace Cookbook\Chapter10\GettersSetters;

class Address
{
    // Private properties to enforce encapsulation
    private string $street;
    private string $suburb;
    private string $state;
    private string $postcode;
    private string $country = "Australia";

    // Australian states and territories
    private static array $validStates =  ["ACT", "NSW", "NT", "QLD", "SA",
"TAS", "VIC", "WA"];

    public function getStreet(): string
    {
```

```
        return $this->street;
    }

    public function setStreet(string $street): void
    {
        if (trim($street) === '') {
            throw new \Exception("Street cannot be empty.");
        }
        $this->street = $street;
    }

    public function getSuburb(): string {
        return $this->suburb;
    }

    public function setSuburb(string $suburb): void
    {
        if (trim($suburb) === '') {
            throw new \Exception("Suburb cannot be empty.");
        }
        $this->suburb = $suburb;
    }

    public function getState(): string
    {
        return $this->state;
    }

    public function setState(string $state): void
    {
        $state = strtoupper(trim($state));
        if (!in_array($state, self::$validStates)) {
            throw new \Exception("Invalid Australian state or territory.
Allowed values: " . implode(', ', self::$validStates));
        }
        $this->state = $state;
    }

    public function getPostcode(): string
    {
        return $this->postcode;
```

```
    }

    // Setter for the postcode property with validation for a 4-digit
postcode
    public function setPostcode(string $postcode): void
    {
        $postcode = trim($postcode);
        if (!preg_match('/^\d{4}$/', $postcode)) {
            throw new \Exception("Postcode must be a 4-digit number.");
        }
        $this->postcode = $postcode;
    }

    // Getter for the country property
    public function getCountry(): string
    {
        return $this->country;
    }

    public function __get(string $name)
    {
        $method = 'get' . ucfirst($name);
        if (method_exists($this, $method)) {
            return $this->$method();
        }
        trigger_error("Property Does Not Exist: " . __CLASS__ . "::$name",
E_USER_NOTICE);
        return null;
    }
}
```

3. Next, we'll create two consumer PHP files that will both set and get values to and from the `Person` and `Address` classes.

   In this chapter, the first consumer file demonstrates using getters and setters with hard-coded property values:

   `src/Chapter10/ch10_getters_setters.php`

```
<?php

use Cookbook\Chapter10\GettersSetters\Person;
```

```
use Cookbook\Chapter10\GettersSetters\Address;

include __DIR__ . '/../../vendor/autoload.php';

// Create an instance of the Address class.
$address = new Address();
$address->setState('VIC');
$address->setPostcode('3006');
$address->setSuburb('Southbank');
$address->setStreet('Fawkner');

// Create an instance of the Person class, then also set the Address we
previously created.
$person = new Person();
$person->setFirstName('Alexis');
$person->setLastName('Gruet');
$person->setAge(31);
$person->setAddress($address); // Set an object to the property.

// Loop through the properties
function echoProperties(object $object, $indent = ''): void {
    // Get all public methods of the object.
    $methods = get_class_methods($object);

    // Filter methods that start with 'get'
    foreach ($methods as $method) {
        if (strpos($method, 'get') === 0) {
            // Determine property name from getter, e.g., getFirstName ->
firstName
            $property = lcfirst(substr($method, 3));
            $value = $object->$method();

            if (is_object($value)) {
                echo "{$indent}" . ucfirst($property) .  ": [Object]" .
PHP_EOL;
                // Recursively echo properties of the nested object.
                echoProperties($value, $indent . "  ");
            } else {
                echo "{$indent}" . ucfirst($property) . ": " . $value .
PHP_EOL;
            }
```

```
            }
        }
    }

    echo "Person Properties:\n" . PHP_EOL;
    echoProperties($person);
```

4. The dynamic version of the consumer file accepts user input from the CLI and demonstrates validation errors when invalid data is provided:
   `src/Chapter10/ch10_getters_setters_dynamic.php`

```
<?php

use Cookbook\Chapter10\GettersSetters\Person;
use Cookbook\Chapter10\GettersSetters\Address;

include __DIR__ . '/../../vendor/autoload.php';

// Handle exceptions if invalid inputs are set.
function safeSet(object $object, string $setter, $value): void {
    try {
        $object->$setter($value);
    } catch (Exception $e) {
        echo "Error: Invalid input provided. " . $e->getMessage() . "\n";
    }
}

function echoProperties(object $object, $indent = ''): void {
    $methods = get_class_methods($object);
    foreach ($methods as $method) {
        if (str_starts_with($method, 'get')) {
            $property = lcfirst(substr($method, 3));
            $value = $object->$method();
            if (is_object($value)) {
                echo "{$indent}" . ucfirst($property) . ": [Object]\n";
                echoProperties($value, $indent . "  ");
            } else {
                echo "{$indent}" . ucfirst($property) . ": " . $value .
"\n";
            }
        }
```

```
    }
}

// Prompt the user for address details from the CLI.
echo "Enter Address Details:\n";
$street   = readline("Street: ");
$suburb   = readline("Suburb: ");
$state    = readline("State (NSW, VIC, QLD, WA, SA, TAS, ACT, NT): ");
$postcode = readline("Postcode (4 digits): ");

$address = new Address();
safeSet($address, 'setStreet', $street);
safeSet($address, 'setSuburb', $suburb);
safeSet($address, 'setState', $state);
safeSet($address, 'setPostcode', $postcode);

// Prompt the user for person details from the CLI.
echo "\nEnter Person Details:\n";
$firstName = readline("First Name: ");
$lastName  = readline("Last Name: ");
$age       = readline("Age: ");

$person = new Person();
safeSet($person, 'setFirstName', $firstName);
safeSet($person, 'setLastName', $lastName);
safeSet($person, 'setAge', (int)$age);
safeSet($person, 'setAddress', $address);

echo "\nPerson Properties:\n";
echoProperties($person);
```

5. Now let's run both consumer files to verify the output. First, run the hard-coded example from your CLI. First, let's run the `ch10_getters_setters.php` file that contains hard-coded and valid property values, both for the `Person` and `Address`. From your CLI, run the following command, and you should see the following result:

```
$ php src/Chapter10/ch10_getters_setters.php
Person Properties:
FirstName: Alexis
LastName: Gruet
```

```
Age: 31
Address: [Object]
  Street: Fawkner
  Suburb: Southbank
  State: VIC
  Postcode: 3006
  Country: Australia
```

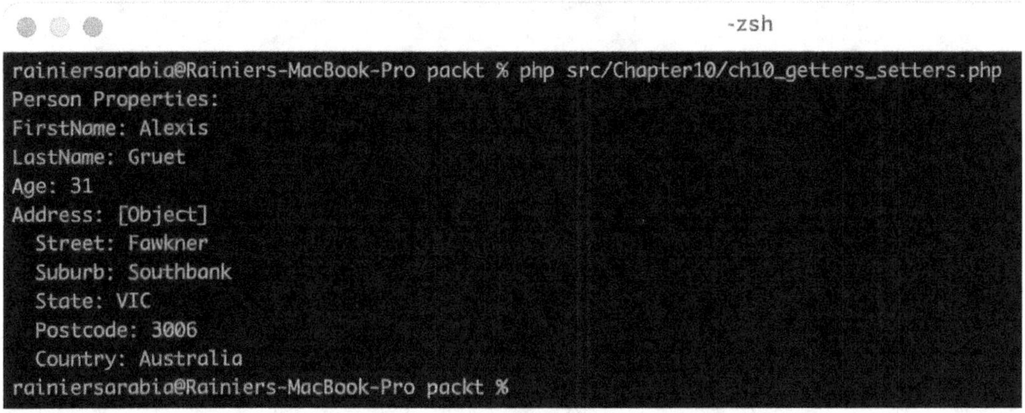

Figure 10.1 – Getters and setters usage

How it works...

This example is pretty straightforward. We've created an instance of the `Address` class, set its properties correctly, created an instance of the `Person` class, then set its properties correctly as well. We then looped through all of the properties using dynamically generated accessors. Normally, an accessor can be used like `$person -> getFirstName` → `$person- > getFirstName()`, but in some instances it's just easier to loop through the accessors or getters.

In this example, we've set a hard-coded, valid first name of *Alexis*. If you check the `Person` class, in the setter method `setFirstName(string $firstName)`, instead of just setting a string value to the `$firstName` property, we added additional custom logic that checks if the first and last names are not empty, and are greater than two characters long. This way, without giving access to the object's property directly, to set the name, we are forcing the consumer to enter a valid string for these properties, thus protecting the data integrity of the property.

Next, let's try running the dynamic version of the consumer. In your command line, run the following, and provide the following strings and integer to the command prompt, and you should get the following validation errors:

```
$ php src/Chapter10/ch10_getters_setters_dynamic.php
Enter Address Details:
Street: 42 Wallaby Way
Suburb: Oyster
State (NSW, VIC, QLD, WA, SA, TAS, ACT, NT): NSX
Postcode (4 digits): 20001
Error: Invalid input provided.Invalid Australian state or territory. Allowed
values: NSW, VIC, QLD, WA, SA, TAS, ACT, NT
Error: Invalid input provided.Postcode must be a 4-digit number.
```

Here, we were able to reject invalid input by adding custom validation logic to some of the properties by adding the validation logic into the setter or mutator function itself:

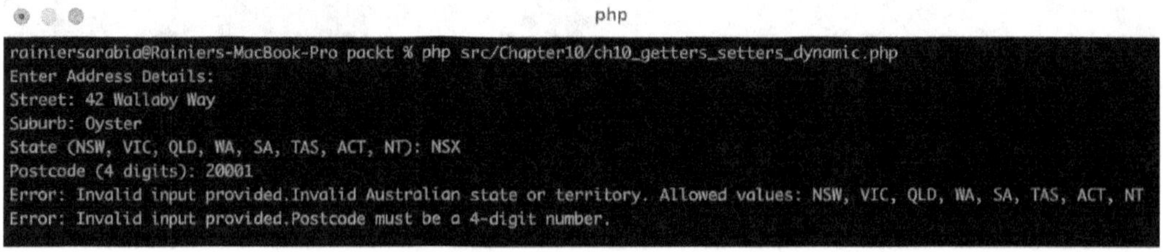

Figure 10.2 – Getters and setters – dynamic input example

There's more...

In PHP 8, there's also a way to dynamically get and set properties. You can read more about *Overloading* from the official PHP manual `https://www.php.net/manual/en/language.oop5.overloading.php`

In the `Address` class above, we have added a dynamic getter method `__get(string $name)` as an example. Dynamic property access via `__get/__set` can be useful for ORMs, DTO hydration, and dynamic models. That said, I'd recommend not using this method, though, as you'll have issues with type-hinting of the returned values and you might have issues with different IDEs. It's better to stick with defined getters and setters. That said, as an alternative, you can also refer to Property Hooks, which were introduced in PHP 8.4 to allow properties to be used directly without get and set methods: `https://www.php.net/manual/en/language.oop5.property-hooks.php`

Implementing a linked list

A **linked list** is a data structure in computer science that stores values in a sequence. To understand this, imagine you're driving from your house to the grocery store. You need to follow a specific route, making the correct turns on different streets in the correct order to reach your destination. The route will contain multiple waypoints.

If you wanted to store this route in a data structure, a linked list would be a great choice. In this linked list, each waypoint (such as a turn or street) would be stored in a node. Each node contains:

- Information about the current street or turn
- A link to the next node, which tells you what to do next
- (Optionally) a link to the previous node, allowing you to backtrack if needed

This way, as you move along your route, you can always check the next node for the next step in your journey, just like a computer program follows a sequence of tasks in a linked list.

In this example, using an array for a route is like having a fixed list of directions, which are quick to access but slow to modify. A linked list is like a chain of waypoints, where each step links to the next, making insertions and deletions easier but requiring step-by-step traversal. Arrays are faster for direct access, while linked lists are better for dynamic routes. In Big-O terms, array access is O(1) by index while linked-list traversal is O(n) — but insertion and deletion at a known position is O(1) for a linked list versus O(n) for an array.

Getting ready

To create a reusable solution where we can utilize the linked list data structure, we can create classes that are flexible enough to store a sequence of processes.

Linked lists have different parts, namely:

- Node – is the object that will hold the value and references to the previous and next node in the chain
- Next and Previous pointers – references to the next and previous nodes in the sequence
- Head – is the very first node in the list
- Tail – is the last node in the list

How to do it...

1. We will create two main classes and also create the abstract classes and interfaces we need to make this solution reusable for different purposes. Then we'll create one

consumer PHP file to demonstrate the usage. In this example, we implement a doubly linked list internally and expose it through a queue-like interface.
First, let's create the interfaces and classes. The `NodeInterface` defines the contract every node in our linked list must follow, including methods for the node's identifier, routine, and pointers to neighboring nodes:

`src/Chapter10/LinkedList/NodeInterface.php`

```
<?php

namespace Cookbook\Chapter10\LinkedList;

interface NodeInterface
{
    public function getNodeId(): string;
    public function getNext(): ?NodeInterface;
    public function getPrevious(): ?NodeInterface;
    public function setNodeId(string $nodeId): NodeInterface;
    public function  setRoutine(callable $routine): NodeInterface;
    public function getRoutine(): callable;
    public function setNext(?NodeInterface $next): NodeInterface;
    public function setPrevious(?NodeInterface $previous): NodeInterface;
}
```

2. The `QueueInterface` defines the contract that all queue implementations must follow, specifying how nodes are added and executed:
`src/Chapter10/LinkedList/QueueInterface.php`

```
<?php

namespace Cookbook\Chapter10\LinkedList;

interface QueueInterface
{
    public function addNode(NodeInterface $node): void;
    public function execute(): array;
}
```

3. The `AbstractNode` class provides a base implementation of `NodeInterface`, managing the node's ID, routine, and its references to neighboring nodes in the chain:

src/Chapter10/LinkedList/AbstractNode.php

```
<?php

namespace Cookbook\Chapter10\LinkedList;

abstract class AbstractNode implements NodeInterface
{
    private ?string $nodeId;
    private $routine = null;
    private ?NodeInterface $next = null;
    private ?NodeInterface $previous = null;
// Set by concrete subclasses to identify the node kind at runtime (e.g.
logging, routing).
    private string $nodeType;

    // Getter and setter methods for the node identifier.
    public function getNodeId(): string
    {
        return $this->nodeId;
    }

    public function setNodeId(string $nodeId): NodeInterface
    {
        $this->nodeId = $nodeId;
        return $this;
    }

// Getter and setter for the routine (the executable payload) attached to
the node.
    public function getRoutine(): object
    {
        return $this->routine;
    }

    public function setRoutine(callable $routine): NodeInterface
    {
        $this->routine = $routine;
        return $this;
    }
```

```
// Getter and setter for the pointer to the next node in the chain.
    public function getNext(): ?NodeInterface
    {
        return $this->next;
    }

    public function setNext(?NodeInterface $next): NodeInterface
    {
        $this->next = $next;
        return $this;
    }

// Getter and setter for the pointer to the previous node in the chain.
    public function getPrevious(): ?NodeInterface
    {
        return $this->previous;
    }

    public function setPrevious(?NodeInterface $previous): NodeInterface
    {
        $this->previous = $previous;
        return $this;
    }

    public function getNodeType(): string
    {
        return $this->nodeType;
    }

    public function setNodeType(string $nodeType): NodeInterface
    {
        $this->nodeType = $nodeType;
        return $this;
    }
}
```

4. With the abstract base in place, we can create a concrete node class for our hiring process use case. `HiringNode` extends `AbstractNode` and sets its node type in the constructor:

`src/Chapter10/LinkedList/HiringNode.php`

```
<?php

namespace Cookbook\Chapter10\LinkedList;

class HiringNode extends AbstractNode
{
    public function __construct()
    {
        $this->setNodeType("I'm a Hiring Step");
    }
}
```

5. `HiringProcessFlow` implements `QueueInterface` and manages the doubly linked list. It maintains head and tail references, and exposes methods to add nodes, execute them in order, and list pending processes:
   `src/Chapter10/LinkedList/HiringProcessFlow.php`

```
<?php

namespace Cookbook\Chapter10\LinkedList;

class HiringProcessFlow implements QueueInterface
{
    private ?NodeInterface $head;
    private ?NodeInterface $tail;

    public function __construct() {
        $this->head = null;
        $this->tail = null;
    }

    // Add a new process to the queue
    public function addNode(NodeInterface $node): void {
        if ($this->tail === null) {
            $this->head = $this->tail = $node;
        } else {
            $this->tail->setNext($node);
            $node->setPrevious($this->tail);
```

```
            $this->tail = $node;
        }
    }

    // Execute the processes in order
    public function execute(): array
    {
        $executedProcesses = [];

        if ($this->head === null) {
            return [];
        }

        $current = $this->head;
        while ($current !== null) {
// Invoke each node's routine (a callable) and capture its returned message
for the execution log.
            $executedProcesses[] = "Process #{$current->getNodeId()} | " .
$current->getRoutine()();
            $current = $current->getNext();
        }

        // Reset after execution
        $this->head = $this->tail = null;

        return $executedProcesses;
    }

    // Get list of pending processes
    // Return a preview of queued processes without executing or removing
them.
    public function getPendingProcesses(): array {
        $pendingProcesses = [];

        if ($this->head === null) {
            return ["No pending processes."];
        }

        $current = $this->head;
        while ($current !== null) {
            $pendingProcesses[] = "Process #{$current->getNodeId()} | " .
```

```
$current->getRoutine()();
                $current = $current->getNext();
            }

            return $pendingProcesses;
        }
    }
```

6. We now need to create the consumer PHP file, which is executable through the CLI:

   `src/Chapter10/ch10_linked_list.php`

```
<?php

use Cookbook\Chapter10\LinkedList\HiringNode;
use Cookbook\Chapter10\LinkedList\HiringProcessFlow;

include __DIR__ . '/../../vendor/autoload.php';

// Example Usage
$processQueue = new HiringProcessFlow();

// Process Item 1
$process1 = new HiringNode();
$process1->setNodeId( 'process-1');
$closure1 = fn() => ("Get budget approval from Yaron");
$process1->setRoutine($closure1);
$processQueue->addNode($process1);

// Process Item 2
$process2 = new HiringNode();
$process2->setNodeId( 'process-2');
$closure2 = fn() => ("Rain conducts interviews");
$process2->setRoutine($closure2);
$processQueue->addNode($process2);

// Process Item 3
$process3 = new HiringNode();
$process3->setNodeId( 'process-3');
$closure3 = fn() => ("Alexis submits for approval");
$process3->setRoutine($closure3);
$processQueue->addNode($process3);
```

```
// Process Item 4
$process4 = new HiringNode();
$process4->setNodeId( 'process-4');
$closure4 = fn() => ("Yaron approves");
$process4->setRoutine($closure4);
$processQueue->addNode($process4);

echo "\n\n***********************************\n";
echo "*        PENDING PROCESSES        *\n";
echo "***********************************\n";
foreach ($processQueue->getPendingProcesses() as $process) {
    echo "[PENDING] $process\n";
}
echo "***********************************\n";

echo "\n\n###################################\n";
echo "#         EXECUTING TASKS        #\n";
echo "###################################\n";
// Execute the queued processes in FIFO order and print each as it runs.
foreach ($processQueue->execute() as $executedProcess) {
    echo "[EXECUTING] $executedProcess\n";
}
echo "\n\n###################################\n";
echo "[COMPLETED] All processes executed.\n";
echo "###################################\n";

echo "\n\n***********************************\n";
echo "*        PENDING PROCESSES        *\n";
echo "***********************************\n";
// After execution, re-print the pending list to confirm the queue is now
empty.
foreach ($processQueue->getPendingProcesses() as $process) {
    echo "[PENDING] $process\n";
}
echo "***********************************\n";
```

How it works...

In this example, we added multiple processes to the queue in a certain sequence. You'll notice that the processor has executed the processes in a **FIFO** or **first-in, first-out** sequence as well.

The processor executes the first process, then moves to the next object by accessing the current node's next property.

In the consumer PHP file, we first create an instance of the `HiringProcessFlow` class. This class implements the `QueueInterface` we also created, which only has two main functions, `addNode` and `execute`. This means that we will need a node object as well, so we've also created multiple instances of the `HiringNode` class, which implements the `NodeInterface`. As previously mentioned, a node in a linked list contains the value, reference, and the next and previous objects next to it.

Execute the following command through your CLI:

```
$ php src/Chapter10/ch10_linked_list.php
**********************************
*        PENDING PROCESSES       *
**********************************
[PENDING] Process #948 | Get budget approval from Yaron
[PENDING] Process #751 | Rain conducts interviews
[PENDING] Process #329 | Alexis submits for approval
[PENDING] Process #230 | Yaron approves
**********************************


##################################
#         EXECUTING TASKS        #
##################################
[EXECUTING] Process #948 | Get budget approval from Yaron
[EXECUTING] Process #751 | Rain conducts interviews
[EXECUTING] Process #329 | Alexis submits for approval
[EXECUTING] Process #230 | Yaron approves

##################################
[COMPLETED] All processes executed.
##################################


**********************************
*        PENDING PROCESSES       *
**********************************
[PENDING] No pending processes.
**********************************
```

You should get the following result:

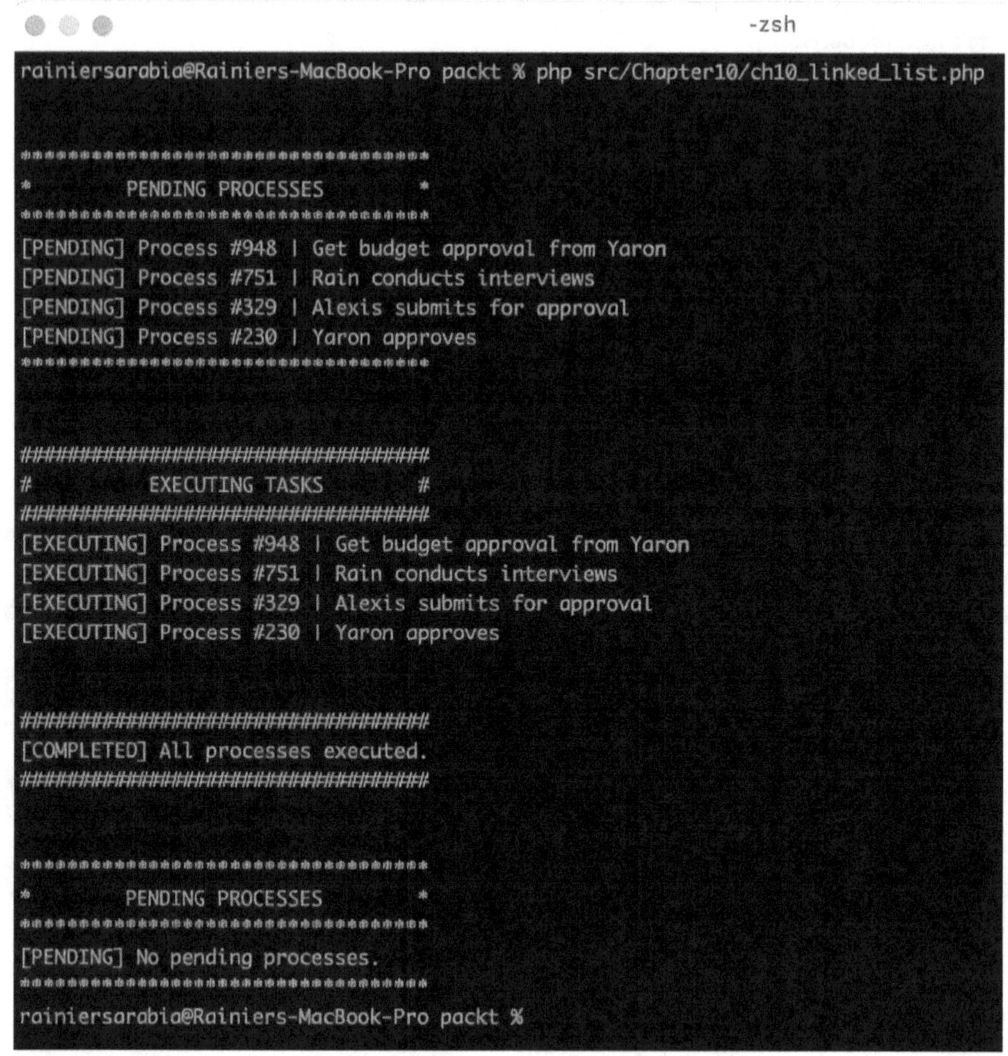

Figure 10.3 – Linked list processing result

There's more...

The `HiringProcessFlow` class is just a concrete implementation of the `QueueInterface`. You can use this recipe by creating new concrete queue and node classes, and inserting your own logic to handle your own complex processing needs.

Converting your application to a decoupled plugin architecture

In large-scale applications with numerous components and extensive functionality, maintaining a loosely coupled codebase is essential for flexibility and maintainability. Implementing a decoupled plugin architecture in your PHP project enables seamless extensibility, allowing you to integrate third-party software and leverage plugins developed by other teams efficiently. This approach enhances modularity, reduces dependencies, and facilitates easier long-term maintenance.

This recipe demonstrates a lightweight plugin-style pattern built around PHP's `__call()` magic method—a full plugin system would also include formal registration, discovery, and contract enforcement.

Getting ready

Imagine developing a program that facilitates money transfers through payment service providers such as PayPal and Wise. While you could write a program that directly supports both, numerous other providers exist, and a tightly coupled codebase would require extensive refactoring each time a new payment method is added. Alternatively, you can adopt a more flexible approach by designing a decoupled architecture that allows new payment methods to be registered dynamically, such as through a configuration file. This can be efficiently implemented using PHP's `__call()` magic method, enabling seamless integration of additional providers without modifying the core system. While `__call()` provides flexibility, it comes at the cost of type safety and IDE support — in production systems, explicit method calls or dependency injection are often preferred.

How to do it...

1. We'll create a core program that will handle the payment methods dynamically and handle exceptions if the method name that we send to it does not exist. Then, on the consumer program, we can demonstrate registering the example plugins that we need. First, create the main core program to handle the dynamic methods handler. The `PaymentMethodInterface` defines a single `send()` contract that every payment plugin must implement, ensuring consistency across different providers:

   `src/Chapter10/Plugin/PaymentMethodInterface.php`

   ```
   <?php

   namespace Cookbook\Chapter10\Plugin;
   ```

```
interface PaymentMethodInterface
{
    public function send(float $amount, string $sender, string
$recipient): array;
}
```

2. The `PaymentProcessor` class acts as the central hub. It stores registered payment methods and uses PHP's `__call()` magic method to dynamically dispatch calls to the correct registered handler:
`src/Chapter10/Plugin/PaymentProcessor.php`

```
<?php

namespace Cookbook\Chapter10\Plugin;

use Exception;

class PaymentProcessor
{
    private array $paymentMethods = [];

    public function registerPaymentMethod(string $name,
PaymentMethodInterface $paymentMethod): PaymentProcessor
    {
        $this->paymentMethods[$name] = $paymentMethod;
        return $this;
    }

    public function __call($name, $arguments)
    {
        if (isset($this->paymentMethods[$name])) {
            return $this->paymentMethods[$name]->send(...$arguments);
        }

        return [
            'success'   => 0,
            'error'     => "X Payment method {$name} does not exist."
        ];
```

```
    }
}
```

3. The `PayPalMethod` class is a concrete implementation of `PaymentMethodInterface` that simulates sending a payment through PayPal:
`src/Chapter10/Plugin/PayPalMethod.php`

```
<?php

namespace Cookbook\Chapter10\Plugin;

class PayPalMethod implements PaymentMethodInterface
{
    public function send(float $amount, string $sender, string
$recipient): array
    {
        // Some logic here

        return [
            'success' => true,
            'amount' => $amount,
            'sender' => $sender,
            'recipient' => $recipient,
            'method' => 'PAYPAL',
        ];
    }
}
```

4. Similarly, the `WiseMethod` class implements `PaymentMethodInterface` to simulate sending a payment through Wise:
`src/Chapter10/Plugin/WiseMethod.php`

```
<?php

namespace Cookbook\Chapter10\Plugin;

class WiseMethod implements PaymentMethodInterface
{
    public function send(float $amount, string $sender, string
$recipient): array
```

```
    {
        // Some logic here

        return [
            'success' => true,
            'amount' => $amount,
            'sender' => $sender,
            'recipient' => $recipient,
            'method' => 'WISE',
        ];
    }
}
```

5. Next, create the consumer PHP file.
   The consumer file registers both payment methods with the `PaymentProcessor` and demonstrates calling each of them, including an unregistered method to show the error handling:

   `src/Chapter10/ch10_decoupled_plugin.php`

```
<?php

use \Cookbook\Chapter10\Plugin\PaymentProcessor;
use \Cookbook\Chapter10\Plugin\PayPalMethod;
use \Cookbook\Chapter10\Plugin\WiseMethod;

include __DIR__ . '/../../vendor/autoload.php';

$paymentProcessor = new PaymentProcessor();
$paypalMethod = new PayPalMethod();
$wiseMethod = new WiseMethod();

// Can be refactored and placed into a configuration module:
$paymentProcessor
    ->registerPaymentMethod("sendToPayPal", $paypalMethod) // Register
PayPal class
    ->registerPaymentMethod("sendToWise", $wiseMethod); // Register Wise
class
// Can easily add more methods...

print_r($paymentProcessor->sendToPayPal(150, "john@doe.com",
```

```
"paypal@recipient.com"));
echo "\n";
print_r($paymentProcessor->sendToWise(64.23, "jane@doe.com",
"wise@recipient.com"));
echo "\n";
print_r($paymentProcessor->sendToMagicMoney(200, "jane@doe.com",
"magic@recipient.com"));
echo "\n";
```

How it works...

Payment ecosystems change frequently — new providers come and go. By using `__call()` to route by method name, the `PaymentProcessor` can pick up new providers via configuration alone, with no edits to the core class. This trades type safety for extension flexibility.

For clarity, the `PaymentProcessor` class combines registration, resolution, and error handling — in a production-grade plugin system you would typically split these responsibilities across separate collaborators. The `PaymentProcessor` class has a `registerPaymentMethod` function that only accepts instances of `PaymentMethodInterface`. This helps in providing strictness in what type of classes can be registered to your `PaymentProcessor` object. This makes it easier inside the magic method `__call()` to know that we do have to call the send method in this line `$this->paymentMethods[$name]->send(...$arguments)`.

Then, in the consumer file, we have created two instances of the `PaymentMethodInterface`, one for Wise and one for PayPal and have chained-set them using the `registerPaymentMethod` along with unique strings that we want to use as method names: `sendToPayPal` and `sendToWise`.

If you run the program through the CLI, you should see the following result:

```
$ php src/Chapter10/ch10_decoupled_plugin.php
Array
(
    [success] => 1
    [amount] => 150
    [sender] => john@doe.com
    [recipient] => paypal@recipient.com
    [method] => PAYPAL
)

Array
```

```
(
    [success] => 1
    [amount] => 64.23
    [sender] => jane@doe.com
    [recipient] => wise@recipient.com
    [method] => WISE
)

Array
(
    [success] => 0
    [error] => X Payment method sendToMagicMoney does not exist.
)
```

As you can see, both the `sendToPayPal` and `sendToWise` magic methods worked, but returned an error for the `sendToMagicMoney` as we have not registered that string at all.

Implementing a stack

A **stack** is a fundamental data structure in computer science that follows the **Last In, First Out** (**LIFO**) principle, meaning the most recently added element is the first to be removed. This structure is widely used in function call management, undo/redo operations, expression evaluation, and depth-first search algorithms, providing efficient data storage and retrieval when processing requires accessing the last inserted item first. Since operations occur at a single point (the *top*), both push and pop operations run in constant time, or O(1), because they operate only on the top of the stack regardless of its size — making stacks highly efficient for specific computational tasks. In contrast, a queue (often implemented using a linked list) follows a FIFO order, offering greater flexibility by allowing elements to be inserted or deleted from multiple positions.

For example, in a banking transaction system that handles money transfers between accounts by debiting and crediting the correct amounts, a failure during the process requires rolling back the transactions in reverse order. A stack is ideal for this scenario as it allows us to undo the last transaction first, ensuring consistency.

Getting ready

Building on the bank transaction scenario discussed in the previous section, we will implement a stack within a dedicated Stack class to manage and track transaction rollbacks. This class will encapsulate all stack-related operations, such as pushing successful transactions onto the stack and popping them off when a rollback is needed. Additionally, we will develop a separate `BankTransaction` class responsible for handling the entire transfer process, including debiting and crediting accounts, verifying balances, and utilizing the stack to ensure transactions can be safely reverted if an error occurs. By structuring the implementation this way, we promote modularity, improve code maintainability, and ensure that banking transactions remain reliable and consistent.

How to do it...

1. We'll create a standalone `Stack` class that will focus on stack-specific operations, and then create a `BankTransaction` class that will utilize this Stack class to handle the rollback process we want to demonstrate.
2. Let's first create the `Stack` and `BankTransaction` classes. The `Stack` class is a minimal wrapper around a PHP array that exposes only push, pop-equivalent, and empty-check operations, enforcing strict LIFO access:

   `src/Chapter10/Stack/BankTransaction.php`

```php
<?php

namespace Cookbook\Chapter10\Stack;

class Stack
{
    private array $stack = [];

    public function push(mixed $item): void
    {
        $this->stack[] = $item;
    }

    public function pop(): mixed
    {
        return empty($this->stack) ? null : array_pop($this->stack);
    }

    public function isEmpty(): bool
    {
        return empty($this->stack);
    }
}
```

3. Next, we create the `BankTransaction` class. It uses the `Stack` to record every debit and credit operation so that, if a transfer fails due to insufficient funds, it can pop operations off the stack and reverse them in LIFO order:

`rc/Chapter10/Stack/BankTransaction.php`

```
<?php

namespace Cookbook\Chapter10\Stack;

class BankTransaction
{
    private array $accounts;
    private Stack $rollbackStack;

    public function __construct(array $initialAccounts)
    {
        $this->accounts = $initialAccounts;
        $this->rollbackStack = new Stack();
    }

    public function transferFunds(string $fromAccount, string $toAccount,
float $amount): void
    {
        try {
            echo "+++ Processing Transfer: $amount +++ \n\n";

            $this->deductFromSender($fromAccount, $amount);
            $this->addToReceiver($toAccount, $amount);

            echo "=== Transaction completed ===\n\n";
        } catch (\Exception $e) {
            echo "\tError: " . $e->getMessage() . "\n";
            $this->rollbackTransaction();
            echo "=== Transaction Failed ===\n\n";
        }
    }

    private function deductFromSender(string $fromAccount, float $amount,
string $type = "DEBIT"): void
    {
```

```
        echo "\tDeducting \$$amount From sender: $fromAccount\n";
        $this->executeTransaction($type, $fromAccount, $amount * -1);
    }

    private function addToReceiver(string $toAccount, float $amount,
string $type = "CREDIT"): void
    {
        echo "\tCrediting \$$amount to recipient: $toAccount\n";
        $this->executeTransaction($type, $toAccount, $amount);
    }

    private function executeTransaction(string $type, string $accountName,
float $amount): void
    {
        if (!isset($this->accounts[$accountName])) {
            throw new \Exception("Account $accountName does not exist.");
        }

        if ($type === "DEBIT"&&$this->accounts[$accountName] + $amount <
0) {
            throw new \Exception("Declined $accountName.");
        }

        $this->accounts[$accountName] += $amount;
        $this->rollbackStack->push(["accountId" => $accountName, "amount"
=> -$amount]);

        $this->printAccounts();
    }

    private function rollbackTransaction(): void
    {
        echo "\t --- Rolling back transactions: ---\n";

        while (!$this->rollbackStack->isEmpty()) {
            $rollbackItem = $this->rollbackStack->pop();
            $this->accounts[$rollbackItem["accountId"]] +=
$rollbackItem["amount"];
            echo "\tRollback: " . $rollbackItem["accountId"] . " \$
{$rollbackItem["amount"]}\n";
        }
```

```
        echo "\tBalance after Rollback:\n";
        $this->printAccounts();
    }

    public function printAccounts(): void
    {
        foreach ($this->accounts as $key => $val) {
            echo "\t" . $key . ": " . $val . "\n";
        }
        echo "\n";
    }
}
```

src/Chapter10/ch10_stack.php

```
<?php

use Cookbook\Chapter10\Stack\BankTransaction;

include __DIR__ . '/../../vendor/autoload.php';

$initialAccounts = [
    "sender_account"    => 20000.00,
    "recipient_account" => 15000.00,
];
$bank = new BankTransaction($initialAccounts);

// Starting Balances:
echo "||| Starting Balances: |||\n";
$bank->printAccounts();
echo "\n";

$bank->transferFunds("sender_account", "recipient_account", 5555.00);
$bank->transferFunds("sender_account", "recipient_account", 253.00);
$bank->transferFunds("sender_account", "recipient_account", 30000.00); //
Will cause Rollback through Stack

// Closing Balances:
echo "||| Closing Balances: |||\n";
```

```
$bank->printAccounts();
echo "\n";
```

4. Then, we'll create a consumer PHP file that will use the classes:

```
<?php

use Cookbook\Chapter10\Stack\BankTransaction;

include __DIR__ . '/../../vendor/autoload.php';

$initialAccounts = [
    "sender_account"    => 20000.00,
    "recipient_account" => 15000.00,
];

// Starting Balances:
echo "Starting Balances: \n";
foreach ($initialAccounts as $k => $v) {
    echo $k . ": " . $v . "\n";
}
echo "\n";

$bank = new BankTransaction($initialAccounts);
$bank->transferFunds("sender_account", "recipient_account",
1000000.00); // Will cause Rollback through Stack
$bank->transferFunds("sender_account", "recipient_account", 5555.00);
```

How it works...

In this recipe, we've created a `Stack` class that will abstract an array so that we can only push new array items on top of the array, get the latest value from the array, and nothing else. We then created a `BankTransaction` class example that will utilize this `Stack` class to demonstrate the LIFO concept. Internally, PHP arrays already support stack operations via `array_push()` and `array_pop()`. The Stack class simply restricts access to enforce proper stack usage.

In the consumer file `ch10_stack.php`, we simply created an array of accounts with initial funds, and created a new instance of the `BankTransfer` class. We then executed two `transferFunds()` calls. The last call will fail because the amount requested to be transferred is more than the funds initialized for the sender, which in turn will cause a rollback of previous transactions based on the array stored in the `Stack` class. The rollback will happen in a LIFO order.

Each entry on the stack is an associative array recording the account name, the amount, and the operation type (debit/credit). When a transfer fails, the stack is popped and each entry is reversed in LIFO order, producing the following output.

Run the following command from your CLI, and you should get the following result:

```
$ php src/Chapter10/ch10_stack.php
||| Starting Balances: |||
     sender_account: 20000
     recipient_account: 15000


+++ Processing Transfer: 5555 +++

     Deducting $5555 From sender: sender_account
     sender_account: 14445
     recipient_account: 15000

    Crediting $5555 to recipient: recipient_account
    sender_account: 14445
    recipient_account: 20555

=== Transaction completed ===

+++ Processing Transfer: 253 +++

     Deducting $253 From sender: sender_account
     sender_account: 14192
     recipient_account: 20555

     Crediting $253 to recipient: recipient_account
     sender_account: 14192
     recipient_account: 20808

=== Transaction completed ===

+++ Processing Transfer: 30000 +++

     Deducting $30000 From sender: sender_account
```

```
    Error: Declined sender_account.
    --- Rolling back transactions: ---
    Rollback: recipient_account $-253
    Rollback: sender_account $253
    Rollback: recipient_account $-5555
    Rollback: sender_account $5555
    Balance after Rollback:
    sender_account: 20000
    recipient_account: 15000

=== Transaction Failed ===

||| Closing Balances: |||
    sender_account: 20000
    recipient_account: 15000
```

With the `Stack` class, the consumer is forced to adhere to the LIFO concept, as we have only exposed certain methods to manipulate the array inside it.

Building a binary search class

In computer science, binary search, also known as binary chop, is an efficient algorithm for locating a target value within a sorted array. It works by repeatedly dividing the search interval in half, starting at the middle of the array and determining whether the target value lies in the left or right half. This process continues until the target is found or the search space is exhausted, making it significantly faster than linear search for large datasets.

Getting ready

In a real-world application, there will be scenarios where optimizing performance is crucial. Instead of executing multiple queries against the database, which can be resource-intensive and impact efficiency, it may be more effective to search within the results of a previously executed database query. By leveraging in-memory search or filtering techniques, you can reduce the number of database or API calls to the data source, improve response times, and enhance overall system performance.

Binary search requires the dataset to be sorted on the search key. In this recipe we first sort the array by its keys, then perform a key-based binary lookup. For multi-field search, we delegate to a heap-based comparison so the data stays organized by the primary search field.

How to do it...

1. We will create a `BinarySearch` class that will contain the search algorithm, and create different methods for searching the source array by simulating method overloading using the `__call()` magic method. Then, we will also create a consumer PHP file to demonstrate its usage.
2. First, create the BinarySearch class. We will create two types of binary search implementations in this class: one for a single-dimensional array and one for a multi-dimensional array.
   The `BinarySearch` class implements two search variants—a simple single-dimension search and an associative-array search—and uses PHP's `__call()` magic method to dispatch to the correct one based on the argument type:

   `src/Chapter10/BinarySearch/BinarySearch.php`

```
<?php

namespace Cookbook\Chapter10\BinarySearch;

class BinarySearch
{
    public function __call(string $name, array $arguments)
    {
        // Manual method overloading:
        if ($name === 'search') {
            if (is_int($arguments[1])) {
                echo "\tRunning basic search: \n";
                return $this->searchSingleDimension($arguments[0],
$arguments[1]);
            } else {
                if (is_array($arguments[1])) {
                    echo "\tRunning associative array criteria search: \n";
                    return $this-
>executeAllAssociativeSearchMethods($arguments[0], $arguments[1]);
                } else {
                    throw new \Exception("Invalid search method");
                }
            }
        }
    }
```

```
    // Run both binary and heap-based associative searches and record how
long each takes.
    private function executeAllAssociativeSearchMethods(array $arg1, array
$arg2): array
    {
        $startTime1 = microtime(true);
        $result1 = $this->searchAssociative($arg1, $arg2);
        $endTime1 = microtime(true);
        $executionTime1 = $endTime1 - $startTime1;

        $startTime2 = microtime(true);
        $result2 = $this->searchAssociativeHeap($arg1, $arg2);
        $endTime2 = microtime(true);
        $executionTime2 = $endTime2 - $startTime2;

        return [
            "binary_search" => [
                "result" => $result1,
                "execution_time" => $executionTime1,
            ],
            "heap_search" => [
                "result" => $result2,
                "execution_time" => $executionTime2,
            ],
        ];
    }

    // Classic binary search on a flul sorted array. Returns the index or
null if not found.
    private function searchSingleDimension(array $arr, int $target): ?int
    {
        $left = 0;
        $right = count($arr) - 1;

        while ($left <= $right) {
            $mid = (int)floor(($left + $right) / 2);

            if ($arr[$mid] === $target) {
                return $mid;
            }
```

```
            if ($arr[$mid] < $target) {
                $left = $mid + 1;
            } else {
                $right = $mid - 1;
            }
        }

        return null;
    }

    // Binary search across an associative array, matching records against
multi-field criteria.
    function searchAssociative(array $dataArray, array $searchTerms): ?
array
    {
        $sortedKeys = array_keys($dataArray);
        sort($sortedKeys, SORT_NATURAL);

        $startIndex = 0;
        $endIndex = count($sortedKeys) - 1;

        while ($startIndex <= $endIndex) {
            $middleIndex = (int)floor(($startIndex + $endIndex) / 2);
            $middleKey = $sortedKeys[$middleIndex];
            $middleItem = $dataArray[$middleKey];

            $criteriaMatched = true;
            foreach ($searchTerms as $searchTermKey => $searchTermValue) {
                if (is_array($searchTermValue)) {
                    foreach ($searchTermValue as $subSearchTermKey =>
$subSearchTermValue) {
                        if (!isset($middleItem[$searchTermKey]
[$subSearchTermKey]) || $middleItem[$searchTermKey][$subSearchTermKey] !==
$subSearchTermValue) {
                            $criteriaMatched = false;
                            break 2;
                        }
                    }
                } else {
                    if (!isset($middleItem[$searchTermKey]) ||
```

```
$middleItem[$searchTermKey] !== $searchTermValue) {
                        $criteriaMatched = false;
                        break;
                    }
                }
            }

            if ($criteriaMatched) {
                return ['id' => $middleKey] + $middleItem;
            }

            $firstSearchTermKey = array_key_first($searchTerms);
            if (isset($middleItem[$firstSearchTermKey]) &&
isset($searchTerms[$firstSearchTermKey])) {
                if ($middleItem[$firstSearchTermKey] <
$searchTerms[$firstSearchTermKey]) {
                    $startIndex = $middleIndex + 1;
                } else {
                    $endIndex = $middleIndex - 1;
                }
            } else {
                return null;
            }
        }

        return null;
    }

    // Alternative search strategy using SplHeap to iterate entries in
priority order.
    private function searchAssociativeHeap(array $dataArray, array
$searchTerms): ?array
    {
        $heap = new HeapSearch($searchTerms);

        foreach ($dataArray as $key => $item) {
            $heap->insert(['key' => $key, 'item' => $item]);
        }

        $heap->top();
```

```
        while ($heap->valid()) {
            $current = $heap->current();
            $item = $current['item'];

            if ($heap->match($item)) {
                return ['id' => $current['key']] + $item;
            }

            $heap->next();
        }

        return null;
    }
}
```

3. The `HeapSearch` class extends PHP's built-in `SplHeap` to provide an alternative search strategy. It dynamically orders entries based on the search criteria, offering a different performance profile from the binary search:
`src/Chapter10/BinarySearch/HeapSearch.php`

```
<?php

namespace Cookbook\Chapter10\BinarySearch;use SplHeap;

class HeapSearch extends SplHeap
{
    private array $terms;

    public function __construct(array $terms)
    {
        $this->terms = $terms;
    }

    // Required SplHeap comparison callback - orders entries by the first
search-term key.
    public function compare(mixed $a, mixed $b): int
    {
        $key = array_key_first($this->terms);

        if (isset($a ['item'] [$key]) && isset($b ['item'] [$key])) {
```

```
                return $a['item'][$key] <=> $b['item'][$key];
            }

            if (isset($a[$key])) {
                return 1;
            }

            if (isset($b[$key])) {
                return -1;
            }

            return 0;
        }

        // Return true if the candidate item matches every field in the search
    criteria.
        public function match(array $item): bool
        {
            foreach ($this->terms as $k => $v) {
                if (is_array($v)) {
                    foreach ($v as $subK => $subV) {
                        if (($item[$k][$subK] ?? null) !== $subV) {
                            return false;
                        }
                    }
                } elseif (($item[$k] ?? null) !== $v) {
                    return false;
                }
            }
            return true;
        }
    }
```

4. Next, we'll create the consumer PHP file that will utilize the BinarySearch class. The consumer file demonstrates both search variants: first a basic integer search on a flat array, then a criteria-based search on a multi-dimensional user array:
   `src/Chapter10/ch10_binary_search.php`

```
<?php

use Cookbook\Chapter10\BinarySearch\BinarySearch;
```

```
include __DIR__ . '/../../vendor/autoload.php';

$binarySearch = new BinarySearch();

// Basic example:
$userIds = [1011, 2022, 3033, 4044, 5055];
$searchUserId = 3033;

echo "=== Binary Search on a single-dimensional array source: ===\n";
$result = $binarySearch->search($userIds, $searchUserId); // Run Search
echo "\tArray position: " . $result . "\n\n";

// Practical example:
$users = [
    "1011" => [
        "first_name" => "Anton",
        "last_name" => "Pavlov",
        "age" => 19,
        "address" => ["street" => "12 Ciambella", "city" => "Rome"],
    ],
    "2022" => [
        "first_name" => "Harel",
        "last_name" => "Kedem",
        "age" => 23,
        "address" => ["street" => "131 Flinders", "city" => "Sydney"],
    ],
    "3033" => [
        "first_name" => "Murali",
        "last_name" => "Ramakrishnan",
        "age" => 21,
        "address" => ["street" => "82 Hawthorn", "city" => "Melbourne"],
    ],
    "4044" => [
        "first_name" => "Kai",
        "last_name" => "Song",
        "age" => 24,
        "address" => ["street" => "782 Tottenham", "city" => "Paris"],
    ],
];
```

```
echo "=== Binary Search through an associative array criteria: ===\n";

$searchCriteria = ["first_name" => "Murali", "last_name" =>
"Ramakrishnan"];
$result = $binarySearch->search($users, $searchCriteria); // Run Search

echo "\tSearch Criteria: " . print_r($searchCriteria, true) . "\n";
echo "\nResult: \n";
echo print_r($result, true) . "\n";
```

How it works...

We created a `BinarySearch` class that has two main internal methods: a simple private `searchSingleDimension` function to just demonstrate the algorithm's way of starting at the middle of an array and dividing the array as the search goes on.

The next function is the `privatesearchAssociative` function that is more useful in programming, where we can send an associative array as a search criterion.

We then created a method overload mechanism using the `__call()` magic method, so that the program can serve two types of methods based on the method signature back to the consumer.

In the consumer PHP file, we executed both the simple and practical examples. If you run the following command through your CLI, you'll get the following result:

```
$ php src/Chapter10/ch10_binary_search.php
=== Binary Search on an single-dimensional array source: ===
     Running basic search:
     Array position: 2

=== Binary Search through a associative array criteria: ===
    Running associative array criteria search:

Result:
Array
(
    [binary_search] => Array
        (
            [result] => Array
                (
                    [id] => 3033
                    [first_name] => Murali
```

```
                [last_name] => Ramakrishnan
                [age] => 21
                [address] => Array
                    (
                        [street] => 82 Hawthorn
                        [city] => Melbourne
                    )

            )

        [execution_time] => 0.000017
    )

[heap_search] => Array
    (
        [result] => Array
            (
                [id] => 3033
                [first_name] => Murali
                [last_name] => Ramakrishnan
                [age] => 21
                [address] => Array
                    (
                        [street] => 82 Hawthorn
                        [city] => Melbourne
                    )

            )

        [execution_time] => 0.000111
    )

[execution_times] => Array
    (
        [binary_search] => 0.000017
        [heap_search] => 0.000111
    )

)
```

The introduction of the `SplHeap` implementation through the `HeapSearch` class offers an alternative search strategy that differs significantly from the traditional binary search approach used in `searchAssociative`. Instead of sorting keys and performing iterative comparisons, `SplHeap` constructs a priority queue that inherently orders elements based on the provided comparison logic. In this case, it prioritizes matches according to the search criteria. This heap-based approach dynamically organizes data, potentially improving performance for specific data distributions or when frequent insertions and removals are expected, as it maintains a sorted structure without requiring explicit sorting operations.

In our specific scenario, the `HeapSearch` class was considerably slower than the `BinarySearch` class:

1. `BinarySearch`: 0.000017 seconds
2. `HeapSearch`: 0.000111 seconds

There's more...

The following are optional extensions — feel free to skip if you're focused only on the binary search core.

PHP also has a built-in array search function called `array_search()`. You can learn more from the official PHP documentation: `https://www.php.net/manual/en/function.array-search.php`.

Implementing a search engine

When we build web applications that people use directly, like online stores or systems to keep track of inventory, it's super important to give them a good way to find what they're looking for. Imagine trying to find a specific product in a huge online shop, or a certain item in a massive warehouse list! That's why we need to create search tools that are easy to use. By letting users quickly search and filter, we make their lives easier and help them find exactly what they need, without having to dig through tons of information.

Getting ready

We'll use an inventory system as an example for this exercise. We will segregate the search engine solution into three parts, namely:

1. User interface – Can be PHP, JS, or CLI
2. Business logic – Server-side PHP
3. Persistence mechanism – Can be a database, an API, or a CSV file, etc.

In this recipe, we won't focus much on the user interface, which in a real project could be a micro-frontend app, a CLI output (as we'll work on), or a PHP-rendered front-end. Likewise, we won't dive deep into the persistence mechanism, which could be MySQL, PostgreSQL, or even a no-database setup. Instead, our main focus will be on building a reusable business logic solution—the core strength of PHP.

How to do it...

1. We will create four main areas for this example, we will build the business logic that will handle, route, the search routines, and we will also build a persistence-mechanism specific code reading from a MySQL database, and another one from a CSV file. We'll also create some sample datasource to read from. We will then create the consumer PHP CLI program to serve as our user interface.
   First, let's create the business logic handler. The `Search` class is the core business-logic handler. It accepts any `DataSourceHandler` implementation via dependency injection and exposes both a full-text search and a binary search across retrieved results:

   `src/Chapter10/SearchEngine/BusinessLogic/Search.php`

```
<?php

namespace Cookbook\Chapter10\SearchEngine\BusinessLogic;

use Cookbook\Chapter10\BinarySearch\BinarySearch;
use
Cookbook\Chapter10\SearchEngine\PersistenceHandler\DataSourceHandlerInterface;

class Search
{
    private array $result = [];

    private DataSourceHandlerInterface $dataSourceHandler;
    private BinarySearch $binarySearch;

// Cache of results from the underlying data source - populated by
executeSearch(), consumed by binarySearchThroughResults().
    private array $persistenceSearchResults = [];

    public function __construct(DataSourceHandlerInterface $dataSource,
BinarySearch $binarySearch)
    {
```

```
        $this->dataSourceHandler = $dataSource;
        $this->binarySearch = $binarySearch;
    }

    public function search(string $query, int $page = 1, int $pageSize =
10): array
    {
        // Can be customised depending on the persistence mechanism
available, and moved to a different class.
        $criteria = [
            'query' => $query,
            'page' => $page,
            'page_size' => $pageSize,
        ];

        $this->result = $this->dataSourceHandler->executeSearch($criteria);

        return $this->result;
    }

    public function binarySearchThroughResults(array $criteria): ?array
    {
        $dataSet = $this->result['results'];
        return $this->binarySearch->searchAssociative($dataSet, $criteria);
    }
}
```

2. The `DataSourceHandlerInterface` defines the contract for all persistence-layer implementations. Any data source—whether a database, CSV file, or external API—must implement this interface to be compatible with the Search class:
`src/Chapter10/SearchEngine/PersistenceHandler/DataSourceHandlerInterface.php`

```
<?php

namespace Cookbook\Chapter10\SearchEngine\PersistenceHandler;

interface DataSourceHandlerInterface
{
    public function prepare(array $options): void;
```

```
    public function executeSearch(array $criteria): array;
}
```

3. Next, we will create two concrete implementations of the `DataSourceHandlerInterface`.
   The `MysqlHandler` implements `DataSourceHandlerInterface` to query a MySQL database using PDO, with support for pagination and full-text LIKE matching:

   `src/Chapter10/SearchEngine/PersistenceHandler/MysqlHandler.php`

```
<?php

namespace Cookbook\Chapter10\SearchEngine\PersistenceHandler;

use PDO;

class MysqlHandler implements DataSourceHandlerInterface
{
    private PDO $databaseConnection;
    private string $dataTableName;

    public function prepare(array $options): void
    {
        $dataSourceName =
"mysql:host={$options['host']};dbname={$options['dbname']};charset=utf8mb4";
        $this->databaseConnection = new PDO(
            $dataSourceName,
            $options['username'],
            $options['password'],
            [
                PDO::ATTR_ERRMODE => PDO::ERRMODE_EXCEPTION,
                PDO::ATTR_DEFAULT_FETCH_MODE => PDO::FETCH_ASSOC,
            ]
        );

        $this->dataTableName = $options['table'];
    }

    public function executeSearch(array $searchParameters): array
    {
        $searchTerm = $searchParameters['query'];
```

```
        $currentPage = $searchParameters['page'];
        $resultsPerPage = $searchParameters['page_size'];
        $offset = ($currentPage - 1) * $resultsPerPage;

        // Search Query
// Note: this is a simple LIKE-based search for demonstration purposes
only. // In production systems, consider full-text indexing (FULLTEXT index
+ // MATCH ... AGAINST) or a dedicated search engine such as
Elasticsearch // for better performance and relevance scoring.
        $searchSql = "SELECT * FROM {$this->dataTableName}
                    WHERE CONCAT_WS(' ', Make, Model, Year, Price, Mileage,
`Condition`, Description)
                    LIKE :searchTerm
                    LIMIT :resultsLimit OFFSET :resultsOffset";

        $searchStatement = $this->databaseConnection->prepare($searchSql);
        $searchStatement->bindValue(':searchTerm', "%$searchTerm%",
PDO::PARAM_STR);
        $searchStatement->bindValue(':resultsLimit', (int)$resultsPerPage,
PDO::PARAM_INT);
        $searchStatement->bindValue(':resultsOffset', (int)$offset,
PDO::PARAM_INT);
        $searchStatement->execute();
        $searchResults = $searchStatement->fetchAll();

        // Get Total Count
        $countSql = "SELECT COUNT(*) FROM {$this->dataTableName}
                    WHERE CONCAT_WS(' ', Make, Model, Year, Price, Mileage,
`Condition`, Description)
                    LIKE :searchTerm";
        $countStatement = $this->databaseConnection->prepare($countSql);
        $countStatement->bindValue(':searchTerm', "%$searchTerm%",
PDO::PARAM_STR);
        $countStatement->execute();
        $totalResultsCount = $countStatement->fetchColumn();

        return [
            'total_results' => $totalResultsCount,
            'page' => $currentPage,
            'page_size' => $resultsPerPage,
            'results' => $searchResults,
```

```
        ];
    }
}
```

4. Next, we implement a CSV-based handler. This demonstrates how the persistence layer can be swapped without changing any core search logic—useful when the data source is a flat file rather than a relational database:

`src/Chapter10/SearchEngine/PersistenceHandler/CsvHandler.php`

```
<?php

namespace Cookbook\Chapter10\SearchEngine\PersistenceHandler;

use SplFileObject;

class CsvHandler implements DataSourceHandlerInterface
{
    private string $filePath;

    public function prepare(array $options): void
    {
        $this->filePath = $options['path'];
    }

    public function executeSearch(array $criteria): array
    {
        $query = $criteria['query'];
        $page = $criteria['page'];
        $pageSize = $criteria['page_size'];
        $data = $this->loadDataFromCsv();

        $filteredResults = array_filter($data, function ($row) use
($query) {
            return stripos(implode(' ', $row), $query) !== false;
        });

        $totalResults = count($filteredResults);
        $start = ($page - 1) * $pageSize;
        $paginatedResults = array_slice($filteredResults, $start,
$pageSize);
```

```
        return [
            'total_results' => $totalResults,
            'page' => $page,
            'page_size' => $pageSize,
            'results' => $paginatedResults
        ];
    }

    // Read the CSV file line by line and convert each row into an
associative array keyed by header.
    private function loadDataFromCsv(): array
    {
        $records = [];
        $csvFile = new SplFileObject($this->filePath, 'r');

        if (!$csvFile->eof()) {
            $columnHeaders = str_getcsv($csvFile->fgets(), ',', '"', '\\');
        }

        while (!$csvFile->eof()) {
            $rowData = str_getcsv($csvFile->fgets(), ',', '"', '\\');
            if ($rowData && count($rowData) === count($columnHeaders)) {
                $records[] = array_combine($columnHeaders, $rowData);
            }
        }

        return $records;
    }
}
```

5. Next, we will create some sample data sources. The seed SQL file creates the cars table and inserts a few sample vehicle records that the search examples will query against: `src/Chapter10/SearchEngine/Data/carseed.sql`

```
CREATE TABLE IF NOT EXISTS cars
(
    Make
    VARCHAR
(
    100
),Model VARCHAR
```

```
(
    100
), Year SMALLINT UNSIGNED,Price MEDIUMINT UNSIGNED,Mileage MEDIUMINT
UNSIGNED,`Condition` ENUM
(
    'New',
    'Used'
),Description TEXT);

INSERT INTO cars (Make, Model, Year, Price, Mileage, `Condition`,
Description)
VALUES ('Mercedes-Benz', 'CLA', 2025, 38000, 15000, 'Used', 'Compact luxury
car with modern design'),
       ('Toyota', 'Corolla', 2020, 20000, 30000, 'Used', 'Highly reliable
and fuel-efficient compact car'),
       ('Honda', 'Civic', 2025, 22000, 0, 'New', 'Reliable compact car'),
       ('BMW', '5 Series', 2025, 45000, 0, 'New', 'Luxury sedan with 5
seats'),
       ('Mercedes-Benz', 'S Class', 2010, 18000, 85000, 'Used', 'Full-sized
sedan with 5 seats');
```

6. We'll also create a simple standalone `Dockerfile` that you can run as part of the example. The `Dockerfile` builds a MySQL 8.0 container pre-seeded with the sample data, so you can run the examples without setting up a database locally: `src/Chapter10/SearchEngine/Data/Dockerfile`

```
FROM mysql:8.0
ENV MYSQL_ROOT_PASSWORD=password
ENV MYSQL_DATABASE=cookbook
ENV MYSQL_USER=chef
ENV MYSQL_PASSWORD=password

COPY carseed.sql /docker-entrypoint-initdb.d/
EXPOSE 3306
CMD ["mysqld"]
```

7. Finally, we'll also create a secondary data-source, which is a CSV file. The CSV file contains the same vehicle data as the MySQL seed, allowing us to demonstrate searching against a flat-file data source:

src/Chapter10/SearchEngine/Data/car_inventory.csv

```
Make,Model,Year,Price,Mileage,Condition,Description
Mercedes-Benz,CLA,2025,38000,15000,Used,Compact luxury car with modern
design
Toyota,Corolla,2020,20000,30000,Used,Highly reliable and fuel-efficient
compact car
Honda,Civic,2025,22000,0,New,Reliable compact car
BMW,5 Series,2025,45000,0,New,Luxury sedan with 5 seats
Mercedes-Benz,S Class,2010,45000,5000,Used,Full-sized sedan with 5 seats
```

How it works...

We created a Search class that allows the consumer program to execute searches against either a database or a CSV file, ensuring flexibility in handling various persistence mechanisms. Instead of the usual examples that demonstrate searches using SQL and PHP, we designed a more adaptable approach to accommodate real-world scenarios that developers frequently encounter in larger applications.

Run the following command to execute the Search program using a MySQL database, and you'll see the result:

```
$ php src/Chapter10/ch10_search_engine_mysql.php
Array
(
    [total_results] => 2
    [page] => 1
    [page_size] => 10
    [results] => Array
        (
            [0] => Array
                (
                    [Make] => Mercedes-Benz
                    [Model] => CLA
                    [Year] => 2025
                    [Price] => 38000
                    [Mileage] => 15000
                    [Condition] => New
                    [Description] => Compact luxury car with modern design
                )
```

```
            [1] => Array
                (
                    [Make] => Mercedes-Benz
                    [Model] => S Class
                    [Year] => 2010
                    [Price] => 45000
                    [Mileage] => 5000
                    [Condition] => Used
                    [Description] => Full-sized sedan with 5 seats
                )

        )

)
Array
(
    [id] => 0
    [Make] => Mercedes-Benz
    [Model] => CLA
    [Year] => 2025
    [Price] => 38000
    [Mileage] => 15000
    [Condition] => New
    [Description] => Compact luxury car with modern design
)
```

In many enterprise applications, data does not always reside in a MySQL database; sometimes, searches must be executed against NoSQL databases, local files, or even external APIs. To accommodate this diversity, we implemented an abstraction through the `DataSourceHandlerInterface`, allowing the data source to be an injectable dependency. This follows the principle of Inversion of Control, enabling greater flexibility and making the search functionality independent of a specific storage mechanism. By injecting the data source at runtime, developers can seamlessly switch between different persistence layers without modifying the core search logic.

Moreover, in addition to traditional searches, our implementation in some scenarios — particularly when working with sorted datasets — allows binary search to be used to quickly locate specific records in memory. The `Search` class includes a `binarySearchThroughResults` method that enables fast lookups within the retrieved dataset. This method utilizes a

`BinarySearch` instance to perform a search over the associative array of results, making it ideal for structured data retrieval scenarios where efficiency is critical.

Run the following command, and this time you will see the search result from a CSV file, just to demonstrate the flexibility of the solution:

```
$ php src/Chapter10/ch10_search_engine_csv.php
Array
(
    [total_results] => 2
    [page] => 1
    [page_size] => 10
    [results] => Array
        (
            [0] => Array
                (
                    [Make] => Mercedes-Benz
                    [Model] => CLA
                    [Year] => 2025
                    [Price ($)] => 38000
                    [Mileage] => 15000
                    [Condition] => Used
                    [Description] => Compact luxury car with modern design
                )

            [1] => Array
                (
                    [Make] => Mercedes-Benz
                    [Model] => S Class
                    [Year] => 2010
                    [Price ($)] => 45000
                    [Mileage] => 5000
                    [Condition] => Used
                    [Description] => Full-sized sedan with 5 seats
                )

        )

)
```

Additionally, we have completely decoupled the `Search` class from the user interface, allowing the consumer to integrate it seamlessly with any frontend technology. Whether using a micro-frontend architecture or any other UI framework, the search functionality remains independent and adaptable. This ensures that developers can display the search results in various ways without modifying the underlying search logic, fostering greater modularity and reusability.

By designing the `Search` class this way, we have ensured that it remains extensible and adaptable to various data retrieval needs. Developers can easily plug in new data sources—whether relational databases, NoSQL stores, or third-party APIs—without disrupting the overall architecture. Additionally, the separation of concerns between data retrieval, search processing, and presentation makes the class more maintainable and testable.

This approach aligns with modern software development practices, making the `Search` class a robust, scalable, and reusable solution for handling diverse search operations in large applications. Complexity at a glance: a database LIKE without an index is ≈ O(n); CSV filtering is ≈ O(n); binary search on sorted data is ≈ O(log n). Use database queries for large datasets, in-memory filtering for small datasets, and binary search only when the data is sorted and frequent lookups are required.

Displaying a multidimensional array and accumulating totals

From the previous section, we have implemented a simple search engine recipe where we can utilize different types of persistence solutions to search from. Now, we can also do the same thing for displaying the results. Search results themselves can and will most of the time return multidimensional arrays, either a PHP array or in JSON.

Getting ready

We'll create some PHP code to handle the outputting of the multidimensional array by building the DOM based on the multidimensional array result set.

How to do it...

1. We'll simply create consumer PHP programs for this example. We will use an example search result based on the previous section.
   Create the recipe PHP file. The recipe file takes a sample multi-dimensional result array and renders it as a collapsible HTML view, also accumulating the total price across all entries.

   For brevity this recipe combines data, rendering, and JS into one file. In a real project, separate these into a template, a controller, and an asset file:

src/Chapter10/ch10_multidimensional_display.php

```
<?php
$vehicleData = [
    "total_results" => 3,
    "page" => 1,
    "page_size" => 10,
    "results" => [
        [
            "Make" => "Mercedes-Benz",
            "Model" => "CLA",
            "Year" => 2025,
            "Price" => 38000,
            "Mileage" => 15000,
            "Condition" => "New",
            "Description" => "Compact luxury car with modern design",
            "Additional_Info" => [
                "Color" => "Red",
                "Tyres" => "Michelin",
            ],
        ],
        [
            "Make" => "Mercedes-Benz",
            "Model" => "S Class",
            "Year" => 2010,
            "Price" => 45000,
            "Mileage" => 5000,
            "Condition" => "Used",
            "Description" => "Full-sized sedan with 5 seats",
            "Additional_Info" => [
                "Color" => "White",
                "Tyres" => "Pirelli",
            ],
        ],
        [
            "Make" => "Honda",
            "Model" => "Civic",
            "Year" => 2025,
            "Price" => 45000,
            "Mileage" => 0,
            "Condition" => "New",
```

```
            "Description" => "Sedan with 5 seats",
            "Additional_Info" => [
                "Color" => "Black",
                "Tyres" => "Pirelli",
            ],
        ],
    ]
];

$totalPrice = array_sum(array_column($vehicleData["results"], "Price"));

// Recursively render nested array values as collapsible HTML sections.
function renderDetails(array $data, string $prefix, int $index)
{
    foreach ($data as $key => $value) {
        if (is_array($value)) {
            echo '<div class="additional-header"
onclick="toggleDetails(\'' . $prefix . '_' . $key . '_' . $index .
'\')">' . htmlspecialchars(
                    $key
                ) . '</div>';
            echo '<div class="additional-details" id="' . $prefix . '_' .
$key . '_' . $index . '" style="display:none">';
            renderDetails($value, $prefix . '_' . $key . '_' . $index .
'_', $index);
            echo '</div>';
        } else {
            echo '<p><strong>' . htmlspecialchars($key) . ':</strong> ' .
htmlspecialchars($value) . '</p>';
        }
    }
}

// Render a single car's details as a collapsible block, delegating nested
arrays to renderDetails().
function renderCarDetails(array $car, int $index)
{
    echo '<div class="car-details" id="car' . $index . '"
style="display:none">';
    foreach ($car as $key => $value) {
        if (is_array($value)) {
```

```
            echo '<div class="additional-header"
onclick="toggleDetails(\'additional' . $index . '\')">Additional Info</
div>';
            echo '<div class="additional-details" id="additional' .
$index . '" style="display:none">';
            renderDetails($value, 'additional' . $index . '_', $index);
            echo '</div>';
        } else {
            echo '<p><strong>' . htmlspecialchars($key) . ':</strong> ' .
htmlspecialchars($value) . '</p>';
        }
    }
    echo '</div>';
}

?>

<!DOCTYPE html>
<html lang="en">
<head>
    <meta charset="UTF-8">
    <meta name="viewport" content="width=device-width, initial-scale=1.0">
    <title>Collapsible Car Listings</title>
    <style>body{font-family:"Arial"}.container{width:300px;float:
left;}.car-header{background-color:black;color:white;padding:
5px;cursor:pointer;margin:0 0 3px 0}.car-details,.additional-
details{display:none;padding:5px;border:1px solid #000}.additional-
header{background-color:red;color:white;padding:5px;cursor:pointer}
p{margin:3px 0}</style>
    <script>
        (function () {
            function createToggleFunction(elementId) {
                return function () {
                    var detailsElement =
document.getElementById(elementId);
                    if (detailsElement.style.display === "none" ||
detailsElement.style.display === "") {
                        detailsElement.style.display = "block";
                    } else {
                        detailsElement.style.display = "none";
                    }
```

```
                };
            }

            window.toggleDetails = function (elementId) {
                var toggle = createToggleFunction(elementId);
                toggle();
            };
        })();
    </script>
</head>
<body>
<div class="container">
    <h2>Car Listings</h2>
    <h3>Total Price of All Vehicles: $<?= number_format($totalPrice) ?></
h3>
    <?php
    foreach ($vehicleData["results"] as $index => $car) : ?>
        <div class="car-header" onclick="toggleDetails('car<?= $index ?
>')">
            <?= htmlspecialchars($car["Make"] . " " . $car["Model"] .
" (" . $car["Year"] . ")") ?>
        </div>
        <?php
        renderCarDetails($car, $index); ?>
    <?php
    endforeach; ?>
</div>
</body>
</html>
```

How it works...

We specified a PHP multidimensional-array containing a list of cars and their respective details, then we created two PHP functions to render the array content into HTML.

The flow is: `renderCarDetails()` calls `renderDetails()`, which recurses on each nested array, rendering nested data as collapsible sections. The `renderDetails()` function contains a conditional check `if (is_array($value))` that will check if the value of the array value itself is an array as well. If it is true, then we will call the second PHP function `renderCarDetails()` to create a nested toggleable div.

If you access this URL `http://localhost:8888/src/Chapter10/ch10_multidimensional_display.php` from your browser, you should see the following result:

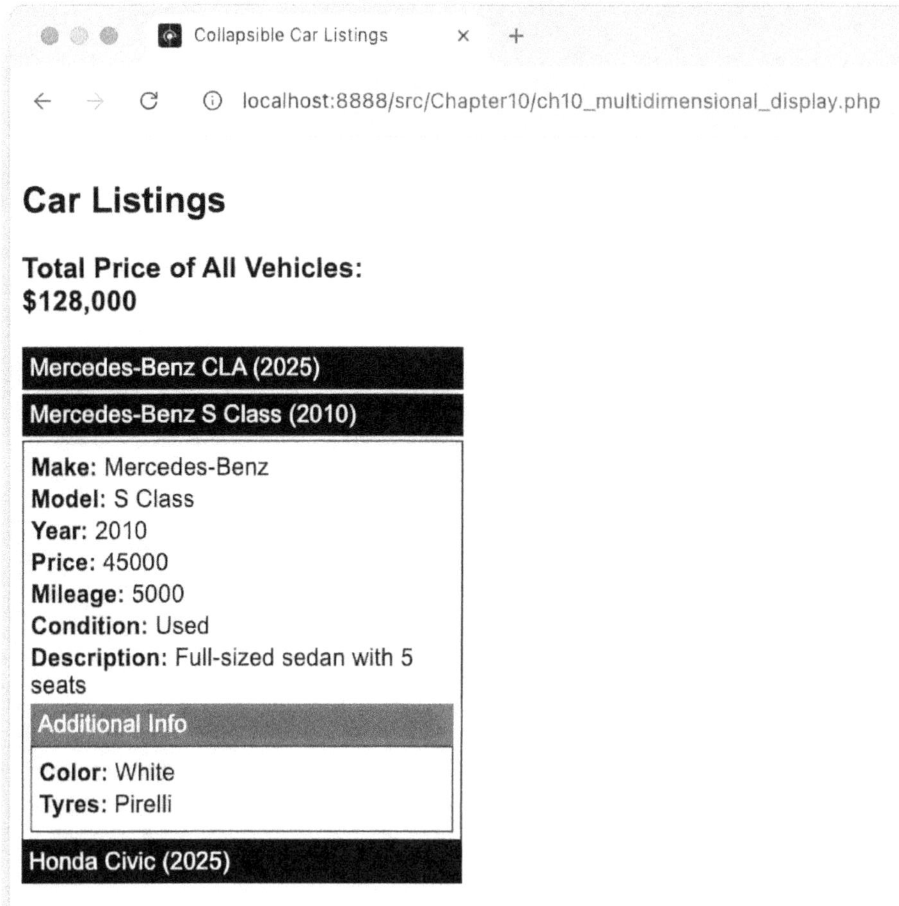

Figure 10.4 – Multidimensional array example HTML render

There's more...

Using generators for large datasets: when working with large datasets — thousands of records from a CSV file or database — PHP generators let you iterate one item at a time, significantly reducing memory usage. See `https://www.php.net/manual/en/language.generators.overview.php` for details. While PHP allows you to render multidimensional arrays directly, it's often more practical to convert them into a JSON object, especially in larger projects. If your frontend is handled by a separate team or application, transforming your PHP array into JSON enables seamless data exchange. This JSON object can then be consumed by a JavaScript or TypeScript frontend, a mobile app, or any other client-side application, ensuring a more flexible and scalable architecture.

11

Implementing Software Design Patterns

Design patterns are proven, reusable solutions to common software design challenges that engineers frequently encounter across projects. Rather than approaching every new problem from scratch, design patterns offer a structured way to address recurring requirements with clarity, efficiency, and consistency.

In practice, many engineering problems share similar traits—such as managing object creation, ensuring loose coupling between components, or enabling dynamic behavior. Design patterns provide a shared vocabulary and a set of best practices to solve these problems in a way that is both scalable and maintainable.

By leveraging these well-established patterns, engineers can avoid reinventing the wheel, reduce technical debt, and produce more robust and adaptable software. Additionally, because design patterns are widely recognized and documented, they improve collaboration among developers by making solutions easier to understand and communicate.

In short, software design patterns are not just techniques—they are strategic tools that help engineers build better software by applying lessons learned from decades of software development. In this chapter, we will cover the following:

- Creational design patterns
- Structural design patterns
- Behavioral design patterns

Technical requirements

A solid intermediate to advanced understanding of **Object-Oriented Programming (OOP)** is essential to fully grasp the concepts presented in this chapter. Many of the techniques and patterns discussed rely heavily on principles such as encapsulation, inheritance, polymorphism, and abstraction. Without a strong foundation in these areas, it may be difficult to appreciate how and why certain design decisions are made, or to understand the subtle differences between similar patterns. Familiarity with concepts like interfaces, dependency injection, and composition will also help in applying these patterns effectively in real-world scenarios.

Creational design patterns

Creational design patterns, as the name suggests, are design patterns specifically tailored to help you create or instantiate objects. An object is an instantiated manifestation of a class.

Getting ready

The **Factory design pattern** is one of the most practical and widely used creational design patterns in software development. It provides a powerful solution for scenarios where the application needs to determine which specific class or set of dependencies to instantiate at runtime. This situation is especially common in larger, modular applications where flexibility and scalability are critical.

As applications grow in complexity, hardcoding object creation can lead to tightly coupled code that is difficult to maintain and extend. The Factory pattern addresses this by encapsulating the instantiation logic within a dedicated factory class or method. This allows the system to delegate the responsibility of object creation, promoting loose coupling and adherence to two of the SOLID principles: the **Dependency Inversion Principle** (depend on abstractions rather than concrete implementations) and the **Open/Closed Principle** (code should be open for extension but closed for modification — new behavior added without changing existing code).

By using a factory, you ensure that object creation is centralized, configurable, and easily adaptable to changes. Whether you're working with different implementations of an interface, selecting components based on configuration, or injecting dependencies dynamically, the Factory design pattern offers a clean and scalable approach to managing object creation at runtime. Without a factory, an application typically relies on conditional logic—if/else or switch statements—scattered across the codebase, with every call site needing to know about every concrete type. A factory centralizes that decision in one place, so adding a new type means adjusting the factory and nothing else.

How to do it...

Consider an example of an application that sends notifications to users regarding their orders. Users are given the option to receive these notifications via SMS, email, or both. While the end goal remains the same—informing the user about their order—the mechanisms for sending an SMS versus sending an email differ significantly in terms of implementation, configuration, and external service dependencies.

Despite these differences, both methods serve a unified purpose and can be abstracted behind a common interface, such as `NotificationInterface`. Instead of manually instantiating the appropriate notification class based on the user's preference—cluttering the code with conditional logic—we can leverage the Factory Design Pattern to streamline this process:

1. First, create the `NotificationFactory` class:

   `src/Chapter11/NotificationFactory.php`

```php
<?php

namespace Cookbook\Chapter11;

use Cookbook\Chapter11\Medium\EmailNotification;
use Cookbook\Chapter11\Medium\SmsNotification;
use Cookbook\Chapter11\Models\Contact;

class NotificationFactory
{
    private array $config;

    public function __construct()
    {
        $this->setConfig();
    }

    public function create(NotificationType $type): NotificationInterface
    {
        $class = $type->value;
        $config = $this->getConfig()[$class];
        return new $class($config);
    }

    private function setConfig()
```

```
    {
        $emailSender = new Contact();
        $emailSender->setEmail('dummy@example.com');
        $emailSender->setName('John Doe');

        $this->config = [
            SmsNotification::class => [
                'api_key' => 'dummy_api_key',
                'sender_id' => 'dummy_sender_id',
            ],
            EmailNotification::class => [
                'sender' => $emailSender,
            ],
        ];
    }

    public function getConfig(): array
    {
        return $this->config;
    }
}
```

2. Next, create concrete implementations for the SMS and Email mechanisms, and the `NotificationInterface`:

   `src/Chapter11/NotificationInterface.php`

```
<?php

namespace Cookbook\Chapter11;

use Cookbook\Chapter11\Models\Contact;

interface NotificationInterface
{
    public function send(Contact $sender, Contact $receiver, string
$message, array $options): bool;
}
```

src/Chapter11/Medium/EmailNotification.php

```
<?php

namespace Cookbook\Chapter11\Medium;

use Cookbook\Chapter11\Models\Contact;
use Cookbook\Chapter11\NotificationInterface;

class EmailNotification implements NotificationInterface
{
    private string $headers;

    public function __construct(array $config)
    {
        $sender = $config['sender'];
        $fromName = $sender->getName();
        $fromEmail = $sender->getEmail();

        $fromHeader = $fromName
            ? "$fromName <$fromEmail>"
            : $fromEmail;

        $this->headers = "From: $fromHeader\r\n";
        $this->headers .= "Reply-To: $fromEmail\r\n";
        $this->headers .= "MIME-Version: 1.0\r\n";
        $this->headers .= "Content-Type: text/html; charset=UTF-8\r\n";
    }

    public function send(Contact $sender, Contact $receiver, string
$message, array $options): bool
    {
        return mail($receiver->getEmail(), $options['subject'], $message,
$this->headers);
    }
}
```

src/Chapter11/Medium/SmsNotification.php

```
<?php
```

```
namespace Cookbook\Chapter11\Medium;

use Cookbook\Chapter11\Models\Contact;
use Cookbook\Chapter11\NotificationInterface;

class SmsNotification implements NotificationInterface
{
    private string $apiUrl;
    private string $apiKey;
    private string $senderId;

    public function __construct(array $config)
    {
        // Dummy config:
        $this->apiUrl   = 'https://api.example.com/SMS';
        $this->apiKey   = $config['api_key'];
        $this->senderId = $config['sender_id'];
    }

    public function send(Contact $sender, Contact $receiver, string
$message, array $options): bool
    {
        $postData = http_build_query([
            'api_key'   => $this->apiKey,
            'to'        => $receiver->getPhone(),
            'sender'    => $this->senderId,
            'message'   => $message,
        ]);

        $context = stream_context_create([
            'http' => [
                'method'  => 'POST',
                'header'  => "Content-Type: application/x-www-form-
urlencoded\r\n",
                'content' => $postData,
                'timeout' => 10,
            ]
        ]);

        $result = file_get_contents($this->apiUrl, false, $context);
```

```
        return $result !== false;
    }
}
```

3. Create the models and enum:
   `src/Chapter11/Models/Contact.php`

```
<?php

namespace Cookbook\Chapter11\Models;

class Contact
{
    private string $name;
    private string $email;
    private string $phone;

    public function getName(): string
    {
        return $this->name;
    }

    public function setName(string $name): Contact
    {
        $this->name = $name;
        return $this;
    }

    public function getEmail(): string
    {
        return $this->email;
    }

    public function setEmail(string $email): Contact
    {
        $this->email = $email;
        return $this;
    }

    public function getPhone(): string
    {
```

```
        return $this->phone;
    }

    public function setPhone(string $phone): Contact
    {
        $this->phone = $phone;
        return $this;
    }
}
```

`src/Chapter11/NotificationType.php`

```
<?php

namespace Cookbook\Chapter11;

use Cookbook\Chapter11\Medium\EmailNotification;
use Cookbook\Chapter11\Medium\SmsNotification;

enum NotificationType: string
{
    case EMAIL = EmailNotification::class;
    case SMS = SmsNotification::class;
}
```

4. Finally, create a consumer file to demonstrate the usage:
   `src/Chapter11/ch11_factory.php`

```
<?php

use Cookbook\Chapter11\NotificationFactory;
use Cookbook\Chapter11\NotificationType;

include __DIR__ . '/../../vendor/autoload.php';

$notificationFactory = new NotificationFactory();

// Create an SMS Notification object
$sms = $notificationFactory->create(NotificationType::SMS);
```

```
// Create an Email Notification object
$email = $notificationFactory->create(NotificationType::EMAIL);
```

How it works...

A dedicated `NotificationFactory` can encapsulate the decision-making logic, dynamically creating the appropriate notification objects (e.g., `EmailNotification`, `SmsNotification`, or a composite of both) based on input criteria such as user settings or configuration. This approach not only simplifies the instantiation process but also enhances maintainability, promotes scalability, and adheres to SOLID design principles by decoupling object creation from business logic.

As you can see from `NotificationFactorycreate()` method, the body is just three lines: read the class name from the enum, look up its config, then instantiate. The enum stores fully qualified class names, which allows us to dynamically instantiate the correct class at runtime, and because both the class name and the config key come from the same enum, the user can't pass an unexpected notification type. Adding a new notification mechanism is then a matter of adding a case to the enum plus an entry in the config array.

There's more...

You may have noticed that we also applied the Factory design pattern in *Chapter 6, Building Scalable Forms*, specifically to manage the creation of various filters in a clean and consistent way. A critical aspect of this implementation is the explicit declaration of the return type in the create method. By specifying the interface of the object being returned, we ensure that the consumer of the factory receives a predictable and well-defined contract, making the resulting object easier to work with and integrate into the rest of the application.

`src/Chapter06/InputHandler/Filter/FilterFactory.php`

```
<?php

namespace Cookbook\Chapter06\InputHandler\Filter;

class FilterFactory
{
    public static function create(array $stack): FilterInterface
    {
        $filter = new BaseFilter();
        foreach ($stack as $className) {
            if (class_exists($className)) {
                $filter = new $className($filter);
```

```
            }
        }
        return $filter;
    }
}
```

You can find out more about Creational design patterns from `https://refactoring.guru/design-patterns/creational-pattern`. Patterns like Factory and Abstract Factory are some of the most useful and helpful creational patterns.

> Note
>
> **When to use this pattern**
>
> Reach for the Factory pattern when the same code needs to create objects of several concrete types that share a common interface, and the choice depends on runtime input (user setting, configuration, request data).
>
> You want to keep call sites unaware of the concrete class names so that adding a new type means changing one place—the factory—rather than every site that does new.
>
> Instantiation involves non-trivial wiring (config lookups, dependency resolution, decoration) that you don't want repeated at every call site.

Structural design patterns

Structural design patterns focus on addressing common challenges related to how classes and objects are composed to form larger structures. These patterns are concerned with the relationships between objects—how they are connected, organized, and interact with one another—while maintaining flexibility and efficiency in the codebase.

Getting ready

One of the most common challenges engineers face when joining an existing project is working with legacy code. In many cases, newly written code isn't immediately compatible with older implementations due to differences in structure, interfaces, or design approaches. Rather than allowing legacy code to influence or constrain the architecture of newer components, it's often better to isolate and adapt the old code so it can work seamlessly within the modern system.

This is where the **Adapter design pattern** becomes particularly useful. The adapter acts as a bridge between incompatible interfaces, allowing legacy components to be reused without modifying their internal logic. By introducing an adapter, we can ensure that the new codebase remains clean, consistent, and decoupled, while still benefiting from the functionality provided by existing systems. This approach not only preserves the integrity of the new design but also promotes better maintainability and long-term scalability.

How to do it...

Let's take the notification example from the previous section, *Creational design patterns*, and let's assume there's an existing mechanism to send notifications that doesn't conform with the `NotificationInterface` contract. We can solve this by utilizing an adapter.

1. First, create the incompatible notification mechanism example:
   `src/Chapter11/OldMedium/LegacyEmailSender.php`

```
<?php

namespace Cookbook\Chapter11\OldMedium;

class LegacyEmailSender
{
    public function SendEmail(array $options): bool
    {
        return true;
    }
}
```

2. Next, let's create an adapter. This adapter conforms with our `NotificationInterface` contract:
   `src/Chapter11/Medium/LegacyEmailSenderAdapter.php`

```
<?php

namespace Cookbook\Chapter11\Medium;

use Cookbook\Chapter11\Models\Contact;
use Cookbook\Chapter11\NotificationInterface;
use Cookbook\Chapter11\OldMedium\LegacyEmailSender;

class LegacyEmailSenderAdapter implements NotificationInterface
{
    private LegacyEmailSender $target;

    public function __construct(LegacyEmailSender $emailSender)
    {
```

```
        $this->target = $emailSender;
    }

    public function send(Contact $sender, Contact $receiver, string
$message, array $options): bool
    {
        // Adapt the data to the old format:
        $options = [
            'sender_email' => $sender->getEmail(),
            'receiver_email' => $receiver->getEmail(),
            'message' => $message,
            'subject' => $options['subject'],
        ];

        return $this->target->SendEmail($options);
    }

}
```

3. Update the `NotificationType` enum, and add this enum:

```
case LEGACY_EMAIL = LegacyEmailSenderAdapter::class;
```

4. Update the `NotificationFactory`'s config array, and add this key-value pair. Notice that this config entry looks different from the preceding SMS and Email ones: rather than an array of configuration values, it's a single `LegacyEmailSender` instance. That's because the adapter's constructor takes the legacy object itself as its only argument—so for an adapter, the `config` the factory passes in is literally the object being wrapped. When `create(NotificationType::LEGACY_EMAIL)` runs, `$class` resolves to `LegacyEmailSenderAdapter::class` and `$config` resolves to the `LegacyEmailSender` instance, so new `$class($config)` becomes new `LegacyEmailSenderAdapter(new`

`LegacyEmailSender())`—the factory wires the legacy object into the adapter automatically:

```
LegacyEmailSenderAdapter::class => new LegacyEmailSender()
```

5. And finally, update the `ch11_factory.php` consumer file to add the usage of the adapter:

```
$legacyEmail = $notificationFactory-
>create(NotificationType::LEGACY_EMAIL);
```

How it works...

The adapter allows us to integrate legacy code without modifying it, which is especially important when the original code is external, deprecated, or shared across systems.

We have created an example legacy class `LegacyEmailSender.php` that has a `SendEmail` method that does not comply with the `NotificationInterface` contract. Remember, our `NotificationFactory` returns an instance of the `NotificationInterface`. To be able to utilize the `LegacyEmailSender`'s functionality, we wrapped it inside a new class called `LegacyEmailSenderAdapter` that implements the correct `NotificationInterface` contract. Then, we assigned the legacy object to a private `$target` property using the factory. We then finally used the `$target` object, which contains an instance of the `LegacyEmailSender` class, in the send method of the adapter:

```
public function send(Contact $sender, Contact $receiver, string $message, array
$options): bool
    {
        // Adapt the data to the old format:
        $options = [
            'sender_email' => $sender->getEmail(),
            'receiver_email' => $receiver->getEmail(),
            'message' => $message,
            'subject' => $options['subject'],
        ];

        return $this->target->SendEmail($options);
    }
```

There's more...

There are a lot of other structural design patterns out there; you can check more of them from `https://refactoring.guru/design-patterns/structural-patterns`. Patterns such as Adapter and Facade are some of the most commonly used structural patterns.

> Note
>
> **When to use this pattern**
>
> Reach for the Adapter pattern when you need to integrate code that doesn't match your current contracts and you can't (or shouldn't) modify it—typically legacy, third-party, or shared code.
>
> You want to keep the rest of your codebase free of conditional special cases for the incompatible source; the adapter absorbs the impedance mismatch so callers stay uniform.
>
> The wrappee's surface is small and stable. If the legacy class is large or actively changing, an adapter postpones rather than resolves the integration problem.

Behavioral design patterns

Behavioral design patterns are concerned with how objects communicate and interact with one another to perform tasks, share responsibilities, and respond to changes. These patterns focus on defining clear protocols for communication, assigning duties appropriately across components, and enhancing the flexibility and scalability of the codebase.

Rather than dealing with object creation or structure, behavioral patterns emphasize the flow of control and exchange of information between different parts of a system. They help manage complex behavior by promoting loose coupling, making it easier to modify, extend, or reuse individual components without impacting others.

Getting ready

One of the most commonly used behavioral design patterns in everyday software development is the **State design pattern**. This pattern is especially useful when an object's behavior needs to change dynamically based on its internal state. Rather than using large conditional statements scattered throughout the code, the State pattern encapsulates state-specific logic into separate classes, promoting cleaner and more maintainable code.

We encounter situations suited to the State pattern frequently—whether it's managing the different stages of a workflow, handling user sessions, or building interfaces that respond differently depending on user interaction. By organizing each possible state and its corresponding behavior in a structured and extensible way, the State design pattern allows us to write code that is not only easier to understand but also more resilient to future changes.

How to do it...

Using a **Finite State Machine (FSM)** is one of the most common and effective ways to implement the State design pattern. An FSM models a system as a set of defined states, with strict rules governing the transitions between them based on specific inputs or events. This approach provides a clear and predictable structure for managing state-dependent behavior.

By mapping out possible states and transitions in advance, an FSM not only simplifies the implementation of the State pattern but also helps prevent invalid or unintended state changes. This makes it particularly useful in complex systems such as user workflows, UI components, game development, and communication protocols, where maintaining control over state transitions is critical to ensuring correct behavior.

1. First, create an FSM class, along with the state and event classes:
   `src/Chapter11/State/CoffeeMakerStateMachine.php`

```
<?php

namespace Cookbook\Chapter11\State;

class CoffeeMakerStateMachine
{
    private string $state;

    private array $transitions = [
        CoffeeMachineState::STANDBY => [
            CoffeeMachineEvent::START => CoffeeMachineState::HEATING,
        ],
        CoffeeMachineState::HEATING => [
            CoffeeMachineEvent::HEAT_COMPLETE =>
CoffeeMachineState::BREWING,
        ],
        CoffeeMachineState::BREWING => [
            CoffeeMachineEvent::BREW_COMPLETE => CoffeeMachineState::READY,
        ],
        CoffeeMachineState::READY => [
            CoffeeMachineEvent::SERVE => CoffeeMachineState::STANDBY,
        ],
    ];
```

```
    public function __construct()
    {
        $this->state = CoffeeMachineState::STANDBY;
    }

    public function getState(): string
    {
        return $this->state;
    }

    public function trigger(string $event): void
    {
        echo "=== Triggering Event: '{$event}' ===\n";
        echo "Current State: {$this->state}\n";

        if (isset($this->transitions[$this->state][$event])) {
            $newState = $this->transitions[$this->state][$event];
            echo "Transition allowed. Moving to state: {$newState}\n";
            $this->state = $newState;
        } else {
            echo "Error: Cannot trigger '{$event}' from state '{$this-
>state}'.\n";
        }

        echo "Updated State: {$this->state}\n\n";
    }
}
```

src/Chapter11/State/CoffeeMachineEvent.php

```
<?php

namespace Cookbook\Chapter11\State;

class CoffeeMachineEvent
{
    public const START = 'start';
    public const HEAT_COMPLETE = 'heat_complete';
    public const BREW_COMPLETE = 'brew_complete';
```

```
    public const SERVE = 'serve';
}
```

src/Chapter11/State/CoffeeMachineState.php

```
<?php

namespace Cookbook\Chapter11\State;

class CoffeeMachineState
{
    public const STANDBY = 'standby';
    public const HEATING = 'heating';
    public const BREWING = 'brewing';
    public const READY = 'ready';
}
```

2. Next, create the example usage:
   src/Chapter11/ch11_state.php

```
<?php

use Cookbook\Chapter11\State\CoffeeMakerStateMachine;
use Cookbook\Chapter11\State\CoffeeMachineEvent;

include __DIR__ . '/../../vendor/autoload.php';

$machine = new CoffeeMakerStateMachine();

$machine->trigger(CoffeeMachineEvent::START);
$machine->trigger(CoffeeMachineEvent::HEAT_COMPLETE);
$machine->trigger(CoffeeMachineEvent::BREW_COMPLETE);
$machine->trigger(CoffeeMachineEvent::SERVE);
```

How it works...

FSMs explicitly define all the possible states that an object or system can be in during a specific flow or process. This clear declaration of states allows developers to model behavior in a predictable, organized manner. Each state is known and finite—meaning the system can only be in one of a limited set of defined states at any given time.

FSMs also provide a structured way to define transitions between states. These transitions are triggered by events or conditions, which can be either positive (such as a successful operation or user action) or negative (such as an error, timeout, or failed validation). By including both types of events, FSMs allow us to account for alternate paths, error recovery, and fallback strategies, making the system more robust and fault-tolerant.

In the consumer file `ch11_state.php`, we progress the transition of the events using the `$machine->trigger(CoffeeMachineEvent::<event_name>)` line. Depending on the event we trigger, it transitions the machine's state. Running the command through the CLI will show how it works.

A note on modernization: the state and event types here are modeled as classes with public const values, which keeps the FSM example focused on the State pattern itself. In a current PHP 8.1+ codebase you would typically use backed enums instead—`enum CoffeeMachineState: string { case STANDBY = 'standby'; ... }`—which gives you exhaustiveness checks, IDE autocompletion, and a proper type for the `$state` property. We use a backed enum in the Factory recipe earlier in this chapter (`NotificationType`); the same shape applies here, but converting the FSM would cascade through the transitions-array keys and the `trigger()` method's signature, so we've kept the class form for clarity in the recipe:

```
$ php src/Chapter11/ch11_state.php
=== Triggering Event: 'start' ===
Current State: standby
Transition allowed. Moving to state: heating
Updated State: heating

=== Triggering Event: 'heat_complete' ===
Current State: heating
Transition allowed. Moving to state: brewing
Updated State: brewing

=== Triggering Event: 'brew_complete' ===
Current State: brewing
Transition allowed. Moving to state: ready
Updated State: ready

=== Triggering Event: 'serve' ===
Current State: ready
Transition allowed. Moving to state: standby
Updated State: standby
```

There's more...

Behavioral patterns are very diverse, as there are so many different ways to handle software behavior. To find out more about other behavioral design patterns, you can check `https://refactoring.guru/design-patterns/behavioral-patterns`. Patterns such as Strategy and Observer patterns are widely used among PHP Frameworks.

> Note
>
> **When to use this pattern**
>
> Reach for the State pattern when an object's behavior depends on its internal state, and you find yourself writing if/switch blocks on a state field across multiple methods.
>
> The set of states is finite and known up-front, and the legal transitions between them are bounded—typical of workflows, UI components, communication protocols, and game state.
>
> Adding a new state or transition is something you expect to do over time; isolating each state's logic in its own class (or, for an FSM, its own row in the transitions table) makes that change local.

12

Improving Web Security

In this chapter, we will focus on implementing practical yet robust techniques to protect your web application without adding unnecessary complexity. Security is not a feature to be considered later—it is a core requirement from the very start. Every user interaction, no matter how benign it may appear, should be treated as potentially harmful, as even small oversights can be exploited. We will examine ways to strengthen the integrity of user sessions, ensure that forms are resilient against automated abuse and cross-site attacks, and apply strong authentication practices that make it harder for attackers to compromise accounts. You will also learn how to protect sensitive data through secure encryption methods and how to keep critical application logs safe from prying eyes. By adopting these strategies, you will be better equipped to guard your application against both common and sophisticated threats.

In this chapter, we'll cover the following topics:

- Safeguarding the PHP session
- Securing forms with a token
- Building a secure password generator
- Safeguarding forms with CAPTCHA
- Using AI to develop an encryption and decryption solution

Technical requirements

As with the previous chapters, you will only need a functional PHP development environment to follow along. The concepts covered here are straightforward and do not require an advanced understanding of object-oriented programming or design patterns, making them accessible even if you are still building your expertise in these areas.

You can download the example project and code for this book by following the instructions in the ***Download the example code files*** section in the *Preface* of this book.

This chapter's code files are included in the downloadable code bundle.

Safeguarding the PHP session

A PHP session begins when the `session_start()` function is called. If no active session exists, PHP will create a new one and assign a unique session identifier (**Session ID**). By default, this identifier is stored in the client's browser as a cookie, allowing the server to associate subsequent requests with the correct session data. However, if a Session ID is intercepted or stolen, an attacker could potentially hijack the user's session. This risk highlights the importance of securing session handling, especially when dealing with sensitive operations.

Getting ready

First, we need to understand the most common attack vectors against PHP Session IDs. These are:

- **Session hijacking**: The unauthorized takeover of a user's session by stealing the session ID, typically through methods such as **cross-site scripting** (**XSS**), network sniffing, or malware that gains access to browser cookies
- **Session replay**: The reuse of a stolen session ID after logout when the session has not been properly invalidated
- **Cross-Site Request Forgery** (**CSRF**): When a third-party website tricks your browser into sending a request to a site where you are already authenticated

How to do it...

1. Now, we can implement mechanisms to help protect your application against the attack vectors identified in the previous section.
2. On your PHP file where you call the `session_start()` method, you can send a set of arguments to secure your PHP session better:

```
session_start([
     // Send the session cookie only over HTTPS. Note: if the app is NOT
served
    // over HTTPS, the browser will not transmit this cookie at all - so
this
    // assumes TLS is in place (as it should be in production).
    'cookie_secure'        => true,
    'cookie_httponly'      => true,

       // Strict CSRF prevention: blocks the cookie on cross-site requests.
    // This mitigates CSRF but does not replace per-request CSRF tokens -
```

```
    // always combine the two (see the next recipe, "Securing forms with a
token").
    'cookie_samesite'      => 'Strict',

    // Prevent session ids in the url
    'use_only_cookies'     => true,
    'use_strict_mode'      => true,
    'sid_length'           => 64,
    'sid_bits_per_character' => 6,
    'cookie_lifetime'      => 0,
]);
// Regenerate the session ID after any change in privilege level – most
importantly,
// right after a successful login – to prevent session fixation attacks.
Passing
// `true` deletes the old session file so the previous ID can no longer be
used.
session_regenerate_id(true);
// Idle timeout: destroy the session after 30 minutes of inactivity to
limit
// the window for session replay. Run this on every request after
session_start().
$timeout = 1800; // 30 minutes
if (isset($_SESSION['last_activity']) && (time() -
$_SESSION['last_activity']) > $timeout) {
    session_unset();
    session_destroy();
}
$_SESSION['last_activity'] = time();
```

3. One of the easiest things to forget as well is destroying the session after a period of time or after logging out; simply calling `session_destroy();` after a period of time or on logout is mandatory to prevent session replay.
4. You can also use the `ini_set()` to configure your PHP application before running the `session_start()` function:

```
// Before session starts:
ini_set('session.cookie_httponly', '1');
ini_set('session.use_only_cookies', '1');
ini_set('session.cookie_secure', '1');
```

```
ini_set('session.use_strict_mode', '1');
ini_set('session.cookie_samesite', 'Strict');

session_start();
```

5. Now, for the CSRF you can generate a `csrf_token` that you can check against:

```
if (empty($_SESSION['csrf_token'])) {
    $_SESSION['csrf_token'] = bin2hex(random_bytes(32));
}
```

6. On the POST handler, you can then check against the token:

```
session_start();
$token  = $_SESSION['csrf_token'] ?? '';
$posted = $_POST['csrf_token'] ?? '';

if ($token === '' || !hash_equals($token, $posted)) {
    http_response_code(403);
    exit('Forbidden');
}
```

How it works...

On the arguments sent through the `session_start()` function, and the `ini_set()` function configures PHP to do the following:

- Use **Transport Layer Security** (**TLS**) when sending the cookie
- Prevent JavaScript from reading the cookie
- Prevent session IDs from being exposed through the URL or query strings
- Reject uninitialized session IDs
- Stops the browser from sending the cookie if the request comes from another site (cross-site/cross-origin)

On the CSRF PHP code token generation, we simply generate a secure string, store it in the session, and compare it against the same string sent through the `$_POST` variable to see if they are the same.

Securing forms with a token

Forms are particularly vulnerable to attacks such as CSRF. When an authenticated user visits a malicious website, that site can generate a forged request to the application where the user is already logged in. Because the browser automatically includes the user's credentials—commonly stored as cookies—the target application cannot easily distinguish the forged request from a legitimate one. As a result, the attacker can trick the application into performing actions on the user's behalf, such as changing account details or initiating transactions, without the user's knowledge or consent.

Getting ready

One effective way to protect against CSRF attacks is by securing forms with a token using the **Synchronizer Token Pattern**. In this approach, the server generates a random, unpredictable token, and embeds it directly into the form when it is rendered. Because the token is tied to the user's session and not known to external websites, an attacker cannot replicate it. When the form is submitted, the server verifies that the token included in the request matches the one it originally issued. If the tokens do not match, the request is rejected, preventing forged requests from being treated as legitimate.

How to do it...

1. Create a `CsrfToken` class that will handle all the CSRF token operations, then create a form that will utilize the token generator. We will also create a simple form handler that will do the logic of comparing if the tokens from both the form and the server match.
2. First, create the `CsrfToken` class, which handles token generation, session setup, validation, and single-use invalidation:
   `src/Chapter12/CsrfToken.php`

```php
<?php

namespace Cookbook\Chapter12;

class CsrfToken
{
    private ?string $token = null;

    public function __construct()
    {
        session_set_cookie_params([
```

```
            'lifetime' => 0,
            'path'     => '/',
            'domain'   => '',
            'secure'   => true,
            'httponly' => true,
            'samesite' => 'Lax',
        ]);

        if (session_status() === PHP_SESSION_NONE) {
            session_start();
        }

        // Initialize token if not already set
        if (!isset($_SESSION['csrf_token'])) {
            $this->generate();
        } else {
            $this->token = $_SESSION['csrf_token'];
        }
    }


//Generate a new CSRF token and store it (with a timestamp) in the
session
    public function generate(): string
    {
        $this->token = bin2hex(random_bytes(32));
        $_SESSION['csrf_token'] = $this->token;
        $_SESSION['csrf_token_time'] = time();
        return $this->token;
    }

    // Confirm the posted token matches the session token, then invalidate
it for one-time use.
 public function validate(?string $submittedToken): bool
{
    // Tokens are time-limited as well as single-use: reject anything older
than 5 minutes.
    $maxAge = 300; // 5 minutes
    if (
        !isset($_SESSION['csrf_token_time'])
        || (time() - $_SESSION['csrf_token_time']) > $maxAge
```

```
        ) {
            return false;
        }

        if (empty($submittedToken) || empty($this->token)) {
            return false;
        }
        $isValid = hash_equals($this->token, $submittedToken);
        if ($isValid) {
            unset($_SESSION['csrf_token'], $_SESSION['csrf_token_time']);
            $this->token = null;
            session_regenerate_id(true);
        }
        return $isValid;
    }

        // Accessors for the current token value.
        public function getToken(): ?string
        {
            return $this->token;
        }

        public function setToken(string $token): CsrfToken
        {
            $this->token = $token;
            $_SESSION['csrf_token'] = $token;
            return $this;
        }
    }
```

3. Next, create the form submission handler, which validates the posted CSRF token against the one stored in the session:
   `src/Chapter12/Submit.php`

```
<?php

use Cookbook\Chapter12\CsrfToken;

include __DIR__ . '/../../vendor/autoload.php';

$csrf = new CsrfToken();
```

```
if ($_SERVER['REQUEST_METHOD'] === 'POST') {
    $submitted = $_POST['csrf_token'] ?? null;
    if ($csrf->validate($submitted)) {
        echo "CSRF token is valid.";
    } else {
        echo "Invalid CSRF token.";
    }
}
```

4. And finally, create the HTML form generator, which instantiates the `CsrfToken` class and embeds the token as a hidden field so it travels back with the submission: `src/Chapter12/ch12_csrf_form.php`

```
<?php

use Cookbook\Chapter12\CsrfToken;

include __DIR__ . '/../../vendor/autoload.php';

$csrf = new CsrfToken();
$token = $csrf->getToken();
?>
<form method="post" action="Submit.php">
    <input type="hidden" name="csrf_token" value="<?php echo
htmlspecialchars($token, ENT_QUOTES, 'UTF-8'); ?>">
    <input type="text" name="message" required>
    <button type="submit">Submit</button>
</form>
```

How it works...

When the user loads the form page, the `CsrfToken` class is instantiated, and a secure session is established using `session_set_cookie_params()` in the constructor. This ensures that the session cookie has the proper security flags, such as `Secure`, `HttpOnly`, and `SameSite`, which help reduce common attack vectors. The class then generates a cryptographically secure token and stores it in the server-side session. That same token is then retrieved and embedded into the HTML form as a hidden field so that it travels back with the user's submission. For clarity, `CsrfToken` bundles session configuration, token generation, and validation in one place. In a production codebase, session configuration is normally centralized in a bootstrap or middleware layer rather than repeated inside each class that uses the session — but keeping it together here makes the CSRF pattern easier to follow in a single file.

When the user submits the form, the form handler (`submit.php`) pulls the stored token from the session and compares it against the token received from the hidden field. If the values match, the server can confirm that the request originated from the legitimate form and the action is processed. If the tokens do not match, the request is rejected as a potential CSRF attempt. This mechanism protects the application because an attacker cannot guess or reproduce the secret token, which means they cannot forge a valid request on behalf of the user.

Building a secure password generator

The risks of weak or predictable passwords are significant. Attackers can exploit common patterns such as names, dates, or dictionary words, and use automated tools to run brute-force attacks that try billions of combinations in a short time. Reusing the same password across multiple services makes the problem even worse, since a breach in one system can give criminals access to many others. Phishing attempts add another layer of danger, as users may unknowingly hand over credentials that are easy to reuse elsewhere.

A secure password generator helps address these risks by creating long, random, and highly complex passwords that are far harder to guess or crack. Because each generated password is unique, a stolen password from one account cannot be used to access another. This combination of unpredictability, strength, and uniqueness provides a level of protection that is extremely difficult for attackers to overcome and difficult to achieve consistently through manual password creation.

Getting ready

To simplify the process of creating strong passwords, we can build a `PasswordGenerator` class that handles the complexity of random number generation, character selection, and security rules behind the scenes. This class can then be used on a web page to produce new secure passwords whenever needed, ensuring they meet modern standards without requiring the user or developer to understand the technical details. It provides a simple, reliable, and consistent way to generate unique credentials that enhance security across applications.

How to do it...

1. Create the `PasswordGenerator` class, which defines the character sets, length bounds, and ambiguous-character filters, and uses `random_int()` for cryptographically secure character selection:

src/Chapter12/Password/PasswordGenerator.php

```
<?php

declare(strict_types=1);

namespace Cookbook\Chapter12\Password;

use InvalidArgumentException;

final class PasswordGenerator
{
    private const MIN_LEN = 8;
    private const MAX_LEN = 128;
    private const MAX_COUNT = 100;

    private const LOWER = 'abcdefghijklmnopqrstuvwxyz';
    private const UPPER = 'ABCDEFGHIJKLMNOPQRSTUVWXYZ';
    private const DIGITS = '0123456789';
    private const SYMBOLS = '!@#$%^&*()-_=+[]{};:,.?';

    /** @var array<int, string> */
    private const AMBIGUOUS = [
        '0', 'O', 'o', '1', 'l', 'I', '|', '`', "'", '"', '~', ';', '.',
',',
    ];

    private int $length = 20;
    private bool $useLower = true;
    private bool $useUpper = true;
    private bool $useDigits = true;
    private bool $useSymbols = false;
    private bool $noAmbiguous = false;

    public function __construct()
    {
        // Configure via setters or applyOptions().
    }

    /** Configure from options model (no arrays). */
    // Bulk-configure the generator from a PasswordOptions value object.
```

```
    public function applyOptions(PasswordOptions $options): self
    {
        $this->setLength($options->getLength());
        $this->setUseLower($options->isUseLower());
        $this->setUseUpper($options->isUseUpper());
        $this->setUseDigits($options->isUseDigits());
        $this->setUseSymbols($options->isUseSymbols());
        $this->setNoAmbiguous($options->isNoAmbiguous());

        return $this;
    }

    // Setters for each individual generation rule, all returning $this for
fluent chaining.
    public function setLength(int $length): self
    {
        if ($length < self::MIN_LEN || $length > self::MAX_LEN) {
            throw new InvalidArgumentException(
                sprintf('Length must be between %d and %d.',
self::MIN_LEN, self::MAX_LEN)
            );
        }
        $this->length = $length;

        return $this;
    }

    public function setUseLower(bool $useLower): self
    {
        $this->useLower = $useLower;
        return $this;
    }

    public function setUseUpper(bool $useUpper): self
    {
        $this->useUpper = $useUpper;
        return $this;
    }

    public function setUseDigits(bool $useDigits): self
    {
```

```
        $this->useDigits = $useDigits;
        return $this;
    }

    public function setUseSymbols(bool $useSymbols): self
    {
        $this->useSymbols = $useSymbols;
        return $this;
    }

    public function setNoAmbiguous(bool $noAmbiguous): self
    {
        $this->noAmbiguous = $noAmbiguous;
        return $this;
    }

    public function generate(): string
    {
        $sets = [];
        if ($this->useLower) {
            $sets[] = self::LOWER;
        }
        if ($this->useUpper) {
            $sets[] = self::UPPER;
        }
        if ($this->useDigits) {
            $sets[] = self::DIGITS;
        }
        if ($this->useSymbols) {
            $sets[] = self::SYMBOLS;
        }

        if ($sets === []) {
            throw new InvalidArgumentException('At least one character
class must be enabled.');
        }

        $pool = $this->uniqueChars(implode('', $sets));

        if ($this->noAmbiguous) {
            $pool = $this->removeChars($pool, self::AMBIGUOUS);
```

```
            foreach ($sets as $i => $set) {
                $clean = $this->removeChars($this->uniqueChars($set),
self::AMBIGUOUS);
                if ($clean === '') {
                    unset($sets[$i]);
                } else {
                    $sets[$i] = $clean;
                }
            }

            $sets = array_values($sets);

            if ($pool === '') {
                throw new InvalidArgumentException(
                    'Character pool became empty after removing ambiguous
characters.'
                );
            }
        }

        $passwordChars = [];

        foreach ($sets as $set) {
            $passwordChars[] = $this->randomCharFrom($set);
        }

        while (count($passwordChars) < $this->length) {
            $passwordChars[] = $this->randomCharFrom($pool);
        }

        $this->secureShuffle($passwordChars);

        return implode('', $passwordChars);
    }

    /**
     * @return array<int, string>
     */
    // Generate several passwords at once, capped by MAX_COUNT to avoid
runaway requests.
```

```
public function generateMany(int $count): array
{
    if ($count < 1 || $count > self::MAX_COUNT) {
        throw new InvalidArgumentException(
            sprintf('Count must be between 1 and %d.', self::MAX_COUNT)
        );
    }

    $out = [];
    for ($i = 0; $i < $count; $i++) {
        $out[] = $this->generate();
    }

    return $out;
}

// Cryptographically secure random character pick from a string.
private function randomCharFrom(string $chars): string
{
    $idx = random_int(0, mb_strlen($chars, '8bit') - 1);
    return $chars[$idx];
}

// Fisher-Yates shuffle backed by random_int() for unbiased ordering.
private function secureShuffle(array &$arr): void
{
    for ($i = count($arr) - 1; $i > 0; $i--) {
        $j = random_int(0, $i);
        [$arr[$i], $arr[$j]] = [$arr[$j], $arr[$i]];
    }
}

// Strip duplicate characters while preserving original order.
private function uniqueChars(string $s): string
{
    $seen = [];
    $out = '';
    $len = strlen($s);

    for ($i = 0; $i < $len; $i++) {
        $ch = $s[$i];
```

```
            if (!isset($seen[$ch])) {
                $seen[$ch] = true;
                $out .= $ch;
            }
        }

        return $out;
    }

    /**
     * Filter out any characters listed in $charsToRemove.
     * @param array<int, string> $charsToRemove
     */

    private function removeChars(string $base, array $charsToRemove):
string
    {
        $map = array_fill_keys($charsToRemove, true);
        $out = '';
        $len = strlen($base);

        for ($i = 0; $i < $len; $i++) {
            $ch = $base[$i];
            if (!isset($map[$ch])) {
                $out .= $ch;
            }
        }

        return $out;
    }
}
```

2. Next, create the `PasswordOptions.php` model class, which is to help prevent setting incorrect options in the class:
   `src/Chapter12/Password/PasswordOptions.php`

```
<?php

declare(strict_types=1);

namespace Cookbook\Chapter12\Password;
```

```
final class PasswordOptions
{
    private int $length = 20;
    private bool $useLower = true;
    private bool $useUpper = true;
    private bool $useDigits = true;
    private bool $useSymbols = false;
    private bool $noAmbiguous = false;

    public function getLength(): int
    {
        return $this->length;
    }

    public function isUseLower(): bool
    {
        return $this->useLower;
    }

    public function isUseUpper(): bool
    {
        return $this->useUpper;
    }

    public function isUseDigits(): bool
    {
        return $this->useDigits;
    }

    public function isUseSymbols(): bool
    {
        return $this->useSymbols;
    }

    public function isNoAmbiguous(): bool
    {
        return $this->noAmbiguous;
    }

    public function setLength(int $length): self
```

```
{
    $this->length = $length;

    return $this;
}

public function setUseLower(bool $useLower): self
{
    $this->useLower = $useLower;

    return $this;
}

public function setUseUpper(bool $useUpper): self
{
    $this->useUpper = $useUpper;

    return $this;
}

public function setUseDigits(bool $useDigits): self
{
    $this->useDigits = $useDigits;

    return $this;
}

public function setUseSymbols(bool $useSymbols): self
{
    $this->useSymbols = $useSymbols;

    return $this;
}

public function setNoAmbiguous(bool $noAmbiguous): self
{
    $this->noAmbiguous = $noAmbiguous;

    return $this;
```

```
    }
}
```

3. Finally, create the consumer PHP file, which reads generation options from the query string, produces a password, and renders a simple HTML form so the user can regenerate with different settings:
`src/Chapter12/ch12_password_gen.php`

```
<?php
declare(strict_types=1);

use Cookbook\Chapter12\Password\PasswordOptions;
use Cookbook\Chapter12\Password\PasswordGenerator;

include __DIR__ . '/../../vendor/autoload.php';

// Minimal options from query string (plain & simple)
$length      = isset($_GET['len']) ? (int) $_GET['len'] : 20;
$useSymbols  = isset($_GET['symbols']);
$noAmbiguous = isset($_GET['no_ambiguous']);

try {
    $options = (new PasswordOptions())
        ->setLength($length)
        ->setUseSymbols($useSymbols)
        ->setNoAmbiguous($noAmbiguous);

    $generator = (new PasswordGenerator())->applyOptions($options);
    $password  = $generator->generate();
    $error     = null;
} catch (Throwable $e) {
    $password = '';
    $error    = $e->getMessage();
}
?>
<!doctype html>
<html lang="en">
<head>
    <meta charset="utf-8">
    <title>Random Password</title>
</head>
```

```
<body>
<h1>Random Password</h1>

<?php if ($error !== null): ?>
    <p><?php echo htmlspecialchars($error, ENT_QUOTES, 'UTF-8'); ?></p>
<?php else: ?>
    <p><strong><?php echo htmlspecialchars($password, ENT_QUOTES,
'UTF-8'); ?></strong></p>
<?php endif; ?>

<form method="get">
    <label>
        Length:
        <input type="number" name="len" min="8" max="128"
value="<?php echo (int) $length; ?>">
    </label>
    <br>
    <label>
        <input type="checkbox" name="symbols" <?php echo $useSymbols ?
'checked' : ''; ?>>
        Include symbols
    </label>
    <br>
    <label>
        <input type="checkbox" name="no_ambiguous" <?php echo
$noAmbiguous ? 'checked' : ''; ?>>
        No ambiguous characters
    </label>
    <br>
    <button type="submit">Generate</button>
</form>

<p>Reload or press "Generate" to get a new password.</p>
</body>
</html>
```

How it works...

The `PasswordGenerator` class is responsible for the actual creation of secure passwords. It defines which character sets can be used (lowercase letters, uppercase letters, digits, and optional symbols) and ensures that passwords meet certain rules, such as minimum and maximum length and the removal of ambiguous characters if requested. When generating a password, the class randomly selects characters from the allowed pool using PHP's cryptographically secure `random_int` function. It also guarantees that at least one character from each enabled category is included, then shuffles the final characters so the order is unpredictable. This makes the generated password both strong and random, protecting against predictable patterns or weak randomness.

Safeguarding forms with CAPTCHA

A **CAPTCHA**, which stands for **Completely Automated Public Turing test to tell Computers and Humans Apart**, is a security measure used online to verify whether a user is human or an automated bot. It typically presents tasks that are easy for people but difficult for machines, such as identifying objects in images, typing distorted text, or checking a box. CAPTCHA helps protect websites from spam, fake registrations, brute force attacks, and automated data scraping. Modern versions, like Google's **reCAPTCHA**, often use advanced behavioral analysis to confirm human activity with minimal user effort, making them both more secure and user-friendly.

Getting ready

Rather than implementing a CAPTCHA system from scratch, it's usually better to rely on mature, battle-tested providers such as Google reCAPTCHA.

How to do it...

1. To keep your application flexible and extensible, we will define a `CaptchaInterface` that serves as a contract, making it possible to inject different CAPTCHA implementations into the core business logic without disrupting the overall design.
2. Create the `CaptchaInterface`, which defines a single `verify()` contract so any CAPTCHA provider can be injected into the application: `src/Chapter12/Captcha/CaptchaInterface.php`

```
<?php

namespace Cookbook\Chapter12\Captcha;

interface CaptchaInterface
{
    /**
     * @param string $token
     * @param string|null $remoteIp
```

```
     * @return array
     */
    public function verify(string $token, ?string $remoteIp = null): array;
}
```

3. Next, create the `ReCaptcha` concrete implementation, which posts the token to Google's siteverify endpoint and normalizes the response into a structured ok/error array. **Siteverify** is Google's server-to-server verification endpoint: your backend POSTs the client's CAPTCHA token together with your secret key, and Google replies with a JSON object indicating whether the challenge passed, plus metadata such as the hostname the token was issued for, the time it was solved (`challenge_ts`), and—for reCAPTCHA v3—a confidence score. Doing this server-side keeps the secret out of the browser and stops attackers replaying tokens harvested from the page: `src/Chapter12/Captcha/ReCaptcha.php`

```
<?php

namespace Cookbook\Chapter12\Captcha;

final class ReCaptcha implements CaptchaInterface
{
    private ?string $secret = null;
    private ?string $expectedHost = null;
    private int $timeoutSeconds = 5;
    private bool $initialised = false;

    private string $endpoint = 'https://www.google.com/recaptcha/api/
siteverify';

    public function __construct()
    {
        // No arguments; properties must be set via setters
    }

    public function initialise(): void
    {
        if ($this->secret === null) {
            throw new \RuntimeException('ReCaptcha secret must be set
before initialisation.');
        }
```

```
        $this->initialised = true;
    }

    // Verify a token by POSTing it to Google's siteverify endpoint and
parse the JSON response.
    public function verify(string $token, ?string $remoteIp = null): array
    {
        if (!$this->initialised) {
            return ['ok' => false, 'error' => 'recaptcha not initialised'];
        }

        if ($token === '') {
            return ['ok' => false, 'error' => 'missing token'];
        }

        $post = [
            'secret'   => $this->secret,
            'response' => $token,
        ];
        if ($remoteIp !== null && $remoteIp !== '') {
            $post['remoteip'] = $remoteIp;
        }

        $raw = $this->post($this->endpoint, $post);
        if ($raw['error'] !== null) {
            return ['ok' => false, 'error' => 'recaptcha request failed:
' . $raw['error']];
        }

        try {
            /** @var array<string,mixed> $data */
            $data = json_decode($raw['body'] ?? 'null', true, flags:
JSON_THROW_ON_ERROR);
        } catch (\Throwable) {
            return ['ok' => false, 'error' => 'invalid response from
recaptcha'];
        }

        if (!(bool)($data['success'] ?? false)) {
            $codes = $data['error-codes'] ?? [];
```

```
                $msg = 'recaptcha failed' . (!empty($codes) ? ': ' .
implode(', ', (array)$codes) : '');
                return ['ok' => false, 'error' => $msg, 'raw' => $data];
            }

            if ($this->expectedHost !== null && ($data['hostname'] ?? '') !==
$this->expectedHost) {
                return ['ok' => false, 'error' => 'invalid hostname', 'raw' =>
$data];
            }

            return ['ok' => true, 'raw' => $data];
        }

        // Wrapper around curl that returns a normalized [body, error] result.
        private function post(string $url, array $fields): array
        {
            $ch = curl_init($url);
            if ($ch === false) {
                return ['body' => null, 'error' => 'curl init failed'];
            }

            curl_setopt_array($ch, [
                CURLOPT_POST           => true,
                CURLOPT_POSTFIELDS     => http_build_query($fields),
                CURLOPT_RETURNTRANSFER => true,
                CURLOPT_TIMEOUT        => $this->timeoutSeconds,
                CURLOPT_SSL_VERIFYPEER => true,  // verify the server's TLS
certificate chain
               CURLOPT_SSL_VERIFYHOST => 2,      // verify the cert hostname
matches the endpoint
            ]);

            $body = curl_exec($ch);
            $err  = curl_error($ch);
            curl_close($ch);

            if ($body === false) {
                return ['body' => null, 'error' => $err ?: 'unknown error'];
            }
```

```
        return ['body' => $body, 'error' => null];
    }

    public function getSecret(): ?string
    {
        return $this->secret;
    }

    public function getExpectedHost(): ?string
    {
        return $this->expectedHost;
    }

    public function getTimeoutSeconds(): int
    {
        return $this->timeoutSeconds;
    }

    public function setSecret(string $secret): void
    {
        $this->secret = $secret;
    }

    public function setExpectedHost(?string $expectedHost): void
    {
        $this->expectedHost = $expectedHost;
    }

    public function setTimeoutSeconds(int $timeoutSeconds): void
    {
        $this->timeoutSeconds = $timeoutSeconds;
    }
}
```

4. Lastly, create the consumer file that wires up a `ReCaptcha` instance, reads the token from the `POST`ed form, and verifies it before accepting the submission: `src/Chapter12/ch12_recaptcha.php`

```
<?php
```

```
use Cookbook\Chapter12\Captcha\ReCaptcha;

include __DIR__ . '/../../vendor/autoload.php';

$captcha = new ReCaptcha();

// configure via setters
$captcha->setSecret('YOUR_SECRET_KEY');
$captcha->setExpectedHost('your-domain.example'); // optional
$captcha->setTimeoutSeconds(5);

// must call initialise() after setting
$captcha->initialise();

if ($_SERVER['REQUEST_METHOD'] !== 'POST') {
    http_response_code(405);
    exit('method not allowed');
}

$email = trim($_POST['email'] ?? '');
$token = $_POST['g-recaptcha-response'] ?? '';

if ($email === '' || $token === '') {
    http_response_code(400);
    exit('missing fields');
}

// REMOTE_ADDR is the IP of whatever connected directly to PHP. Behind a
proxy,
// load balancer, or CDN this is the proxy's IP — derive the real client IP
from a
// trusted forwarded header (e.g. X-Forwarded-For), and only trust that
header when
// the request actually came through your known proxy, since it is easily
spoofed.
$result = $captcha->verify($token, $_SERVER['REMOTE_ADDR'] ?? null);

if (!$result['ok']) {
    http_response_code(400);
    exit('verification failed: ' . ($result['error'] ?? 'unknown error'));
}
```

```
echo 'form submitted successfully';
```

How it works...

The interface-and-class design applies dependency inversion so the rest of your code depends on the `CaptchaInterface` contract rather than a concrete vendor. In practice, controllers or services accept a `CaptchaInterface`, which lets you swap `ReCaptcha` for another provider without touching call sites. This also improves testability: in unit tests, you inject a fake that implements `CaptchaInterface` and deterministically returns pass/fail without making network calls. The `ReCaptcha` class exposes setters for secret, `expectedHost`, and `timeoutSeconds`, and an `initialise()` method that validates required state before use. This empty-constructor-plus-setters shape is used consistently across the classes in this chapter. If you prefer fewer lines, PHP 8 named arguments let you configure everything in a single call—new `ReCaptcha(secret: '...', expectedHost: '...', timeoutSeconds: 5)`—by moving the assignments into a constructor. Both approaches are valid; the setter style is used here for uniformity across the recipes. Verification posts to Google's siteverify endpoint using curl with explicit options for POST, return-transfer, and a finite timeout to avoid hanging requests. The response body is decoded with `JSON_THROW_ON_ERROR` for strict parsing; the method then enforces success and optionally checks the returned hostname against `expectedHost`. Every successful verification response includes the hostname of the page that originally rendered the CAPTCHA widget; setting `expectedHost` to your own domain ensures that a token issued on your site can't be replayed from an attacker's clone of your form on another origin. If you leave `expectedHost` unset, the hostname check is skipped—useful in local development, but you should set it in production. Failures return a normalized structure with `ok/error/raw` so callers can log raw details while showing safe messages upstream. For the recipe we use a plain associative array (`ok/error/raw`) to keep things simple. In larger applications, consider returning a dedicated value object—for example, a `VerificationResult` class exposing `isOk()`, `getError()`, and `getRaw()`—so the result's shape is enforced by the type system and discoverable through your IDE rather than relying on string keys.

From an integration and security perspective, the pattern separates configuration from behavior: you load secrets from the environment or a vault, set them through setters, call `initialise()` once during bootstrap, and reuse the instance. The verify method accepts an optional remote IP, which Google may use in its risk analysis; pass it when available. You should still apply server-side validation on the form payload since CAPTCHA is only one signal. Consider rate limiting and CSRF protections alongside CAPTCHA to reduce credential stuffing and automated submissions. For reCAPTCHA v3 or invisible variants, you can extend

ReCaptcha to read score and action fields from raw and enforce a minimum score or action match before returning ok. For example, after decoding the response you would reject low-confidence submissions before returning ok:

```
// reCAPTCHA v3 only: enforce a minimum score (0.0-1.0; higher means more likely
human).
if (($data['score'] ?? 0) < 0.5) {
    return ['ok' => false, 'error' => 'low score'];
}
```

In production, prefer dependency injection containers for wiring, add retries or circuit breakers around siteverify if your error budget demands it, and emit structured logs including error codes and challenge_ts (the ISO 8601 timestamp of when the user solved the CAPTCHA, returned by Google with every verification—useful for correlating events in logs and for spotting unusually large gaps between solve-time and verification, which can indicate a replayed token) for observability. Finally, ensure TLS verification is enabled by default in your PHP build, restrict outbound egress if possible, and monitor for elevated failure rates that might indicate a key or DNS misconfiguration.

Using AI to develop an encryption and decryption solution

Encrypting sensitive data—such as personally identifiable information, payment details, or session secrets—is a non-negotiable requirement in any production application. PHP ships with the OpenSSL extension, which provides battle-tested primitives for symmetric encryption, but the small details (algorithm choice, IV handling, authentication tag management, and key derivation) are easy to get wrong. A subtle mistake in any of these can render the encryption ineffective even when the code appears to work.

In this recipe, we will use **Claude Code**, Anthropic's command-line coding assistant, to scaffold a small, well-structured PHP 8 encryption helper that uses AES-256-GCM. **AES-256-GCM** is an authenticated encryption mode, which means it both encrypts the data and produces a tag that lets the receiver detect any tampering. We will direct Claude with a clear, requirement-based prompt and then review the generated code line by line to ensure it meets our security expectations.

Getting ready

Before starting, install Claude Code by following the instructions at https://docs.claude.com/en/docs/claude-code. You will need a working PHP 8 environment as in the previous recipes, and the OpenSSL extension enabled (it ships with most PHP distributions by default). You should also create a dedicated working directory so Claude Code can read and write files in a contained location:

```
$ mkdir -p src/Chapter12/Encryption
$ cd src/Chapter12/Encryption
$ claude
```

Once Claude Code launches in your terminal, you can issue prompts directly. The model has access to read, write, and edit files in the current directory, run shell commands, and iterate based on your feedback.

We will guide Claude Code through three steps:

1. Scaffold the encryption class.
2. Create a small consumer that demonstrates round-tripping a payload.
3. Review the generated code and ask Claude to refine anything that does not meet our standards.

How to do it...

1. First, send Claude a precise prompt describing the class you want. The more specific the requirements, the closer the first output will be to production-ready:

```
> Create a PHP 8 class called SecureCipher in the namespace
> Cookbook\Chapter12\Encryption that uses AES-256-GCM via the OpenSSL
> extension. It should expose two methods: encrypt(string $plaintext,
> string $key): string and decrypt(string $ciphertext, string $key):
> string. The key must be 32 bytes; reject anything else with an
> InvalidArgumentException. Generate a fresh 12-byte IV per call using
> random_bytes(). Pack the IV, the auth tag, and the ciphertext into a
> single base64-encoded string for transport. On decrypt, validate the
> tag and raise a RuntimeException on any failure. Save it as
> SecureCipher.php.
```

2. Claude Code will create the file and show you the result. The generated `SecureCipher.php` should look similar to the following—a single, focused class with strict typing and clear validation:

src/Chapter12/Encryption/SecureCipher.php

```
<?php
declare(strict_types=1);

namespace Cookbook\Chapter12\Encryption;

use InvalidArgumentException;
use RuntimeException;

final class SecureCipher
{
    private const CIPHER = 'aes-256-gcm';
    private const KEY_BYTES = 32;
    private const IV_BYTES = 12;
    private const TAG_BYTES = 16;

    public function encrypt(string $plaintext, string $key): string
    {
        $this->assertKey($key);
        $iv = random_bytes(self::IV_BYTES);
        $tag = '';
        $ciphertext = openssl_encrypt(
            $plaintext,
            self::CIPHER,
            $key,
            OPENSSL_RAW_DATA,
            $iv,
            $tag,
            '',
            self::TAG_BYTES
        );
        if ($ciphertext === false) {
            throw new RuntimeException('Encryption failed.');
        }
        return base64_encode($iv . $tag . $ciphertext);
    }

    public function decrypt(string $ciphertext, string $key): string
    {
        $this->assertKey($key);
```

```
        $raw = base64_decode($ciphertext, true);
        if ($raw === false || strlen($raw) < self::IV_BYTES +
self::TAG_BYTES) {
            throw new RuntimeException('Malformed ciphertext.');
        }
        $iv = substr($raw, 0, self::IV_BYTES);
        $tag = substr($raw, self::IV_BYTES, self::TAG_BYTES);
        $payload = substr($raw, self::IV_BYTES + self::TAG_BYTES);
        $plaintext = openssl_decrypt(
            $payload,
            self::CIPHER,
            $key,
            OPENSSL_RAW_DATA,
            $iv,
            $tag
        );
        if ($plaintext === false) {
            throw new RuntimeException('Decryption failed or data tampered
with.');
        }
        return $plaintext;
    }

    private function assertKey(string $key): void
    {
        if (strlen($key) !== self::KEY_BYTES) {
            throw new InvalidArgumentException(
                sprintf('Key must be exactly %d bytes.', self::KEY_BYTES)
            );
        }
    }
}
```

3. Next, ask Claude to create a small consumer file that demonstrates round-tripping a payload. The consumer should generate a key, encrypt a message, then decrypt it and confirm the result matches the original:

```
> Now create a consumer file ch12_secure_cipher.php in the parent
> directory that generates a 32-byte key with random_bytes(), encrypts
```

```
> the string 'Hello, secure world!', prints the base64 ciphertext, then
> decrypts it and prints the recovered plaintext.
```

`src/Chapter12/ch12_secure_cipher.php`

```php
<?php
declare(strict_types=1);

use Cookbook\Chapter12\Encryption\SecureCipher;

include __DIR__ . '/../../vendor/autoload.php';

$cipher = new SecureCipher();
// For this demo we generate the key at runtime. In production, the key
must come
// from a secure secret-management system (a KMS, vault, or injected
environment
// secret) and be persisted securely – a key generated at runtime is lost
on the
// next request, so you could never decrypt previously stored data.
$key    = random_bytes(32);

$secret    = 'Hello, secure world!';
$encrypted = $cipher->encrypt($secret, $key);
$decrypted = $cipher->decrypt($encrypted, $key);

echo 'Ciphertext: ' . $encrypted . PHP_EOL;
echo 'Recovered : ' . $decrypted . PHP_EOL;
echo 'Match     : ' . ($secret === $decrypted ? 'yes' : 'no') . PHP_EOL;
```

4. Run the consumer file from your CLI to verify the round-trip works end-to-end:

```
$ php src/Chapter12/ch12_secure_cipher.php
Ciphertext: kPq3l3kF2v6Y...rZeVfQ==
Recovered : Hello, secure world!
Match     : yes
```

5. Finally, review the generated code with Claude before committing it. AI-generated code is a starting point, not a final answer—always inspect security-sensitive code yourself.

Never deploy cryptographic code generated by AI without human review, testing, and validation against established security guidance. Useful follow-up prompts include:

- `"Add unit tests with PHPUnit covering successful encryption, key length validation, and tampered-ciphertext rejection"`
- `"Refactor the class to accept an optional associated authenticated data (AAD) parameter in both methods"`
- `"Explain why a fresh random IV is required for every call rather than a fixed value"`

How it works...

The `SecureCipher` class uses AES in Galois/Counter Mode, an authenticated encryption mode that produces both the ciphertext and a 16-byte authentication tag in a single pass. The 32-byte key gives 256 bits of strength, which is the level recommended by **NIST** (the **US National Institute of Standards and Technology**), whose Special Publication 800-series sets the cryptographic standards widely adopted across industry and government and most modern security guidelines. Each call to `encrypt()` generates a fresh 12-byte **initialization vector** (**IV**) via `random_bytes()`, PHP's cryptographically secure random source. Reusing an IV with the same key in GCM mode is catastrophic—it leaks information about the plaintext—so the class never lets the caller supply one.

On the wire, the IV, the authentication tag, and the ciphertext are concatenated and base64-encoded into a single string. This packaging keeps the API simple: callers store and transmit one opaque blob, and the `decrypt()` method takes it apart again in a single step. The `openssl_decrypt()` call verifies the tag before returning—if the ciphertext, tag, or IV has been altered, decryption returns false, and the class raises a `RuntimeException`. This is what makes GCM appropriate for storing user data: any tampering is detected, not silently ignored.

Using Claude Code for this kind of task offers two clear benefits. First, it removes friction for the parts of cryptographic code that are mechanical—namespacing, type hints, parameter validation, and packaging—letting you focus your attention on the security-critical decisions. Second, it makes follow-up changes fast and consistent—for example, adding **Additional Authenticated Data** (**AAD**) support (data that is bound into the authentication tag but left unencrypted, useful for tying a ciphertext to its context—a record ID, message header, or recipient—so an attacker can't move a valid ciphertext into a different row without breaking decryption), swapping cipher modes, or generating tests. The trade-off is that you must still understand the cryptography you are asking it to write—which is genuinely difficult without a background in cryptography or the underlying mathematics. The practical answer is to lean on what already exists: use authenticated modes from PHP's OpenSSL extension (as in this recipe), follow standards published by bodies like NIST, and put cryptographic code through review by someone who has done it before. Treat AI-generated security code the way you would treat a pull request from a junior engineer: helpful, time-saving, and worth careful review before it ships.

13

Unlock the Code Bundle and the PDF Version

Your copy of this book includes the following exclusive benefits:

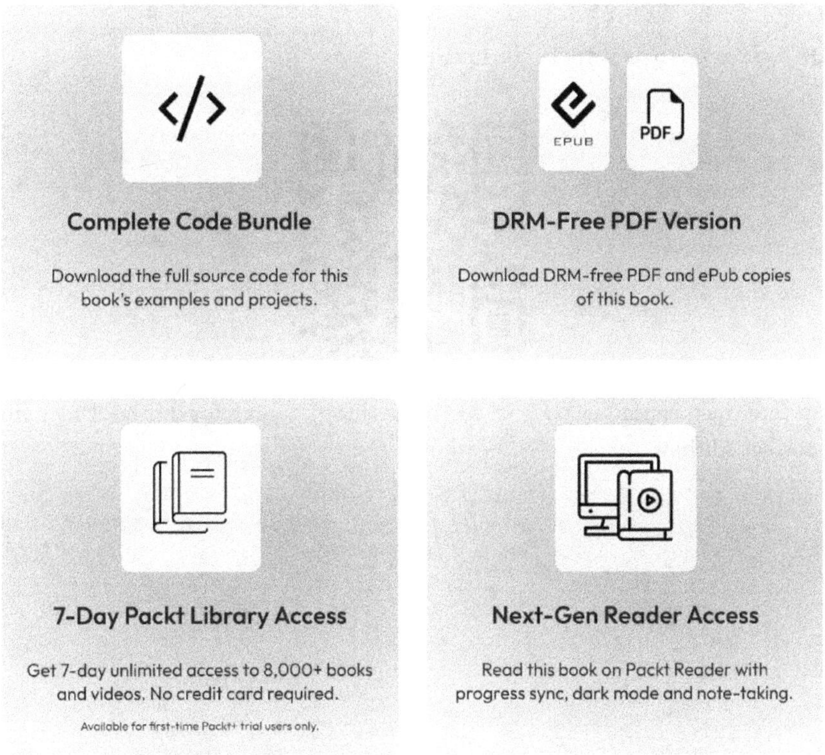

Follow this guide to unlock them. The process takes only a few minutes and only needs to be completed once.

Unlock this book's free benefits in three easy steps

Step 1

Have your purchase invoice ready for *step 3*. If you have a physical copy, scan it using your phone and save it as a PDF, JPG, or PNG.

For more help on finding your invoice, visit `https://www.packtpub.com/unlock-benefits/help`.

> Note
>
> **Note**: If you bought this book directly from the Packt website, no invoice is required. After *step 2*, you can access your exclusive content right away.

Step 2

Scan the QR code or go to `packtpub.com/unlock`.

On the page that opens (similar to *Figure 13.1* on desktop), search for this book by name and select the correct edition.

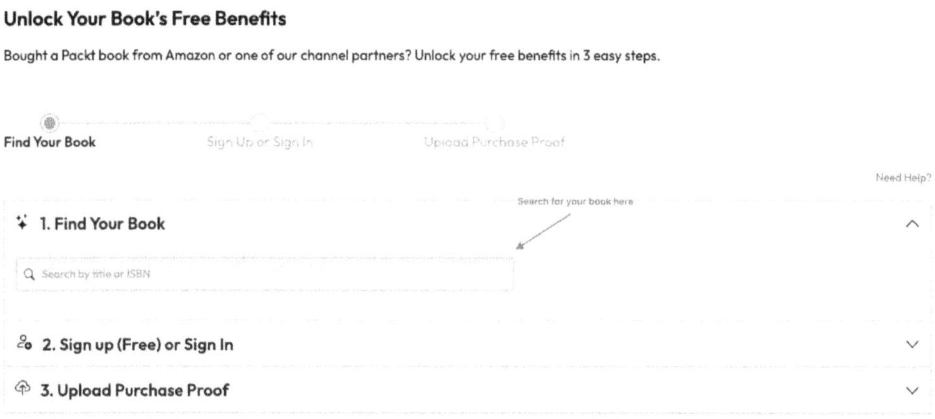

Figure 13.1: Packt unlock landing page on desktop

Step 3

After selecting the book, sign in to your Packt account or create one for free. Then, upload your invoice (PDF, PNG, or JPG, up to 10 MB). Follow the on-screen instructions to finish the process.

Need help?

If you get stuck and need help, visit `https://www.packtpub.com/unlock-benefits/help` for a detailed FAQ on how to find your invoice and more. This QR code will take you to the help page.

> Note
>
> **Note**: If you are still facing issues, reach out to `customercare@packt.com`.

Other Books You May Enjoy

If you enjoyed this book, you may be interested in these other books by Packt:

Agentic Coding with Claude Code

Eden Marco

ISBN: 978-1-80602-259-5

- Design agentic coding workflows in the terminal and IDE using Claude Code
- Build custom automations with reusable slash commands and hooks
- Use Claude Code with a Next.js project to implement AI-driven workflows
- Create persistent AI memory using Claude Code memory files
- Apply MCP for structured context sharing across tools and agents
- Design multi-agent systems using subagents and orchestration patterns
- Enforce coding standards using project documentation and context control

Web Dev with an AI Sidekick

Mark J. Price

ISBN: 978-1-80611-125-1

- Optimize your chatbot to act as your web development learning mentor
- Structure, style, add images, and animate content with HTML, SVG, and CSS
- Add web page interactivity with JavaScript and TypeScript
- Store and query data using practical SQL exercises
- Build backend features in Python and Django step by step
- Collaborate with an AI coding expert: Codex, Claude Code, or Copilot

Packt is searching for authors like you

If you're interested in becoming an author for Packt, please visit `authors.packt.com` and apply today. We have worked with thousands of developers and tech professionals, just like you, to help them share their insight with the global tech community. You can make a general application, apply for a specific hot topic that we are recruiting an author for, or submit your own idea.

Index

I

J

L

M

N

O

P

T

U

V

W

Z

www.ingramcontent.com/pod-product-compliance
Lightning Source LLC
LaVergne TN
LVHW060017210926
848481LV00013B/3731